CALIFORNIA REAL ESTATE FINANCE

EIGHTH EDITION

Robert J. Bond, Ph.D.
Certified Financial Planner

Dennis J. McKenzie, REALTOR®
College of the Redwoods

Alfred Gavello

Technical Editor:
John Fesler
Consultants West Financial Service, Inc.

THOMSON
SOUTH-WESTERN

Australia • Canada • Mexico • Singapore • Spain • United Kingdom • United States

THOMSON

SOUTH-WESTERN

California Real Estate Finance,

Eighth Edition

Robert J. Bond, Dennis J. McKenzie,
and Alfred Gavello
Technical Editor: John Fesler

VP/Editorial Director
Jack W. Calhoun

VP/Editor-in-Chief
Dave Shaut

Executive Editor
Scott Person

Associate Acquisitions Editor
Sara Glassmeyer

Developmental Editor
Arlin Kauffman/LEAP

Sr. Manufacturing Coordinator
Charlene Taylor

Sr. Marketing Manager
Mark Linton

Sr. Content Project Manager
Cliff Kallemeyn

Art Director
Linda Helcher

Cover Designer
Grannan Graphic Design Ltd.

Production House
Cadmus Communications Inc.

Printer
Westgroup Eagan, MN

Library of Congress Control
Number: 2006926044

For more information about
our products, contact us at:

Thomson Learning Academic
Resource Center
1-800-423-0563

Thomson Higher Education
5191 Natorp Boulevard
Mason, OH 45040
USA

CONTENTS

CHAPTER 4
Adjustable Rate and Other Alternative Mortgage Instruments   79

CHAPTER 11
Foreclosures and Other Lending Problems   267

PREFACE

The eighth edition continues to expand treatment of significant topics and graphics to improve comprehension. Further details are discussed on institutional and noninstitutional lenders, amplified Alternative Mortgage Instruments (AMIs) and other loan variations, hard money loans, new buyer qualification requirements, buyer and seller closing costs, and other topics designed to enhance understanding of an increasingly complicated specialty, the financing of real estate. The Home Mortgage Disclosure Act (HMDA) is treated for the first time. This edition is one of the most current and practical textbooks on real estate financing principles and practices in California.

With so much of our lives influenced by the Internet, readers will appreciate numerous references to helpful websites sprinkled throughout the text. Internet-related "Additional Resources" appear in some chapters and are included in the new Appendix. After all, more and more transactions are being done over the Internet, according to the Federal National Mortgage Association, one of the primary players in the mortgage market. Over time, some are likely to become outdated and irrelevant, and many sites may well have as their mission to "sell" products or services to the public. But, to the extent that they prove useful, they are included throughout the text. It should be noted that the inclusion of firms promoting their lending policies and products on the Web is not to construe endorsement of the firms or their offerings. Some sites may be of little interest to the reader, for example, those found on the last pages of Chapter 11 that deal with refinancing. Finally, most sites are unable to really analyze a borrower's specific financial status, resulting in either borrowers becoming overly enthusiastic or disappointed.

As with previous editions, readers should find the section on the use and application of the financial calculator to solve real estate math problems to be especially useful, augmenting what is available with personal computer programs without having to be in front of a PC when calculating solutions to a variety of loan choices. Some have said that they found this extremely valuable and challenging and that they plan to use the financial calculator to solve a whole array of real estate and even business-related problems. Thus, the TI Business

Analyst and the HP 12-C detailed in Chapter 13 contain a wide array of problems and exercises to challenge even the most savvy math enthusiast.

Because the financing field is full of terms that are not used in one's everyday speech (indeed, many agree that real estate vocabulary is itself a foreign language) readers are encouraged to turn to the Glossary whenever the meaning of a word or term is unknown or forgotten. So go ahead and check the expression, "hard money loan," that was cited previously, found on page 460. At first reading, terms may appear complicated, but they become simpler as you progress through the text.

Upon completion of the book, the reader should be able to put into practice the information and concepts that have been presented. Each chapter in the book is self-contained, allowing instructors to adapt the book to various course formats. Instructors and students alike will appreciate the Multiple-Choice Questions, together with Questions for Discussion, all designed for testing, learning, and reviewing of the material covered in each chapter. The text may be integrated with the Instructor Guide and Student Study Guide published by the California Community College Real Estate Education Center.

It is not possible to acknowledge all the assistance received from students, colleagues, and friends. We hope we've successfully communicated the insights that they have generously given us. Particular thanks go to the many real estate instructors who have participated with us at instructor and coordinator workshops sponsored by the California Community College Real Estate Education Center and the California Real Estate Education Association.

Here's to a successful journey into the exciting world of real estate finance! May you blossom as you travel over each successive page. You've already come this far, so you may well be on your way to some satisfying, gratifying challenges. Best wishes from each of the undersigned.

Robert J. Bond
Dennis J. McKenzie
John Fesler

CHAPTER 1
INTRODUCTION TO REAL ESTATE FINANCE

PREVIEW

This chapter provides a short overview of real estate finance.

After completing this chapter, you should be able to:

1. Describe current financing trends in the real estate market.

2. Trace the flow of money and credit into the mortgage market.

3. Discuss the role of the Federal Reserve System.

4. List five characteristics of the California mortgage market.

5. Explain and illustrate two basic types of promissory notes.

6. Describe the differences among a deed of trust, a mortgage, and an installment sales contract.

1.1 Welcome to the Real World of Real Estate Finance

Real estate is expensive, and few people ever accumulate enough savings to pay for it with all cash. Most real estate transactions hinge, therefore, on the buyer's ability to obtain financing. Even people who have sufficient funds rarely pay cash for real estate because (as noted in a later chapter) income tax deductions and investment yields favor purchasing real estate with borrowed funds, called "leverage." Thus, whether by necessity or by choice, financing is essential for most real estate transactions.

Old Rules Are Changing

Historically, real estate finance had been a rather static field governed by a basic set of rules and guidelines laid down by conservative lenders and government agencies. Borrowers were expected to bow to certain cash-down payment, credit, income, and work experience requirements. The borrower had to fit the lender's mold, and the lender was not expected to modify loan guidelines to fit the unique needs of a specific borrower.

Not so today! You can qualify for a loan online on the Internet with no money down or with interest-only payments. Today, lenders are vigorously competing for the real estate borrower's business, resulting in the introduction of new loan products as a way for buyers to afford the increasing cost of real estate.

However, this does not mean that so-called flaky borrowers will obtain real estate loans or that lenders do not have guidelines. What it does mean is that lenders and government agencies are recognizing the changing lifestyles of the 21st century and are creating real estate loan programs that fit these lifestyles. In addition, there are many new loan programs for targeted groups, such as first-time home buyers, economically disadvantaged people who have historically been shut out of the housing market, and homeowners with equities who may wish to refinance or create a home equity line of credit.

Throughout this book you will learn the basic principles of real estate finance and read about the most updated real estate home loan programs in the California real estate market. Although the main emphasis will be on financing the residential real estate market, Chapter 15 will discuss the financing of residential income properties.

Roller-Coaster Ride

Real estate in the form of land and improvements comprises a substantial amount of the total net worth of the United States. In recent years (2000–2006), skyrocketing appreciation, accompanied by historically low interest rates, has encouraged homeowners to tap their equity and use these funds for consumer spending. This in turn, helped fuel the economic growth of the United States from 2003 to 2006. In addition, the real estate industry is a major employer, providing billions of dollars in income for millions of American workers and

Figure 1.1 The roller-coaster ride of the housing market.

investors. When mortgage funds are scarce, real estate activity and employment decline, and a general hardship is felt throughout the economy. Unfortunately, the housing cycle is irregular and wild, with great booms followed by disastrous busts, as shown in Figure 1.1.

Several "boom times" in real estate occurred in the early 1960s, 1971–1973, 1975–1979, 1982–89, and the late 1990s to mid-2000s. However, between these periods were some bad years—1966, 1969, 1974, 1980–1981—and a severe housing crash from 1990 to 1996 in many parts of California.

What causes a bust in the real estate market? Things such as high interest rates, government deficits, and better investment opportunities can cause what is known as ***disintermediation***, which is the sudden flow of funds out of thrift institutions (which grant real estate loans) into the general money market (where real estate loans are not common). This drying up of real estate funds raises havoc in the housing market. In short, real estate activity is directly tied to the availability and cost of mortgage funds and to the general state of the economy. As these two items shift up and down, so goes the real estate market.

Therefore, an agent's or an investor's success in real estate partially depends on a thorough understanding of trends in the mortgage market. The remainder of this book is devoted to an explanation of real estate finance, including the wide range of creative and alternative financing techniques used in buying and selling real estate.

1.2 Short Overview of the Mortgage Market

Real estate financing usually requires the buyer to find a new loan at a lending institution, or occasionally the seller is asked to carry paper, or a combination of both. In all cases the interest rate and terms of real estate loans are dictated by the operations of the money and mortgage market. This section is a short primer on the operations of the mortgage market, stressing the functions of money and the role of the *Federal Reserve System*.

1.3 The Meaning of Money

Money has been defined in a variety of ways: a medium of exchange, a standard of value, a storehouse of value. In general, money is anything that people will accept in exchange for goods and services. Its value lies primarily in our confidence that other people will accept the money in exchange for their goods and services. Contrary to popular belief, money does not have to be a precious metal. Anything that is universally accepted by society can be used as money. Figure 1.2 outlines the many forms of money.

How Is Money Created?

Our money supply is usually thought to consist only of coins and paper currency issued by the government. But money is comprised of more than the "cash" that people have in their wallets and purses. Indeed, the bulk of what is called the money supply is in the form of checking accounts—that is, money that individuals and businesses have deposited into checking accounts, plus the money "created" by the banking system under what is called *fractional reserve banking*. This will be explained and illustrated shortly.

How Is Money Accumulated?

Money accumulates in many ways. The principal method is through savings—that is, spending less than one earns. Money is earned in one of four ways:

1. Wages, fees, and commissions in exchange for labor and services.

2. Interest and dividends in exchange for the use of capital.

Money is commonly considered to be:

1. Coins.

2. Paper currency.

3. Checking accounts, technically called demand deposits.

4. Negotiable orders of withdrawal accounts, or NOW for short.

5. Money market accounts issued by financial institutions.

Near money consists of assets that can be quickly converted to cash, such as:

1. Savings accounts, technically called time deposits.

2. U.S. government bonds.

3. Cash value of life insurance.

4. Preferred and common stocks on organized exchanges.

5. Money market mutual funds.

The following items operate like money but are forms of **credit**:

1. Personal credit cards ("electronic IOUs"). Not debit cards which are merely a way to access funds in a checking account.

2. Bank-allowed overdrafts (ODs).

3. Credit reserves.

4. Home equity lines of credit.

Money and credit are frequently used interchangeably—but they are not the same. *Money* means currency and checking accounts, while *credit* consists of loan funds or savings that a saver or lender makes available to a borrower. Both money and credit can be used to purchase real property; that is why both terms are frequently used in the real estate business.

Figure 1.2 Money is . . .

3. Profits in exchange for management and entrepreneurship.

4. Rents in exchange for real and personal property usage.

To repeat, savings are accumulated funds not needed at the time that they are earned. Savings represent surplus money put aside for future use. There are many ways to save money, and where those savings will ultimately accumulate depends upon the needs, degrees of risk, and personal preferences of individuals. Although it is not necessary to explain the various methods of saving, it is important to recognize that *the ultimate source of funds for borrowing is savings*. In other words, one person's savings becomes another person's source for borrowing. If people spent all of their income, there would not be any funds for borrowing! The greater the rate of savings inflows, the greater the reservoir for borrowing.

It should be noted that, in today's global economy, the borrower may be from one country and the saver or lender from another.

1.4 The Flow of Money and Credit into the Mortgage Market

If the source of all loans, including mortgage loans, is ultimately savings, how do savings via money and credit flow into the mortgage market? Stated differently, how does capital for real estate financing accumulate? This occurs through a process called the *circular flow of the economy*. Do not be troubled by this section, which appears to be heavy stuff! We have tried to simplify, but if you are not comfortable with the basic economics, just read lightly and go on to the next section dealing with the Federal Reserve, which gets into the nitty-gritty of how money is created to finance real estate transactions.

As noted in Figure 1.3, the production of goods and services requires that money be paid for the use of labor, raw materials, entrepreneurship, and capital. This money is called personal income, and all or some of it may be taxed, spent on goods and services, or saved. That which is saved is usually deposited in financial intermediaries, which, in turn, pump funds back into production. Figure 1.3 is a simplified model of how U.S. savings accumulate to become the reservoir for future loans. Carefully trace this circular flow until you understand that individuals "own" land, labor, capital, and entrepreneurship (the supply components), and businesses need these supply components to produce. Thus, businesses "buy" land, labor, and capital from individuals, thereby

Figure 1.3 Simplified circular flow of the economy, excluding the impact of foreign trade and savings entering the U.S. economy.

giving individuals income in the form of wages, rents, interest, and profits. This personal income is then taxed, spent, or saved. That which is saved becomes capital for borrowing.

Intermediation of Savings

According to the circular flow of the economy, income that is not taxed away or consumed in the marketplace represents savings. Where these savings go depends largely on the kinds of returns desired by the saver. Many dollars flow into savings or commercial bank accounts, CDs, credit unions, life insurance premiums, and so on.

Savings or commercial banks, credit unions, life insurance companies, and other financial institutions are referred to as "intermediaries," since they are wedged between the saver and the ultimate investment outlet into which the money will be placed. Pooling the savings of many people is called *intermediation*, or acting as a "go-between" for saver–depositors and borrowers on home loans.

Many of the dollars saved through intermediaries are loaned to real estate buyers, builders, developers, and investors. This in turn stimulates the real estate market and generates income and profits for sellers, real estate agents, loan brokers, and lending institutions. At the same time, this process makes it possible for people to buy homes and investors to acquire income property.

Disintermediation of Savings

Where savers place their funds depends on convenience and on how much depositories or investment outlets are willing to pay in interest. It can be said that a bidding process takes place, with savings going to the highest bidder, commensurate with safety and other criteria laid out by the saver. Money may be deposited with virtually absolute safety, up to designated dollar amounts, in an insured savings account in a bank or other thrift institution. However, when opportunities for greater returns present themselves, people withdraw part or all of their deposits and seek higher returns elsewhere. Since banks and thrift institutions frequently place their funds into real estate loans, the withdrawal of deposits is referred to as disintermediation—that is, deposits are removed from the institutions that act as intermediaries. When such withdrawals occur on a massive scale, the impact on the real estate market can be drastic. If people suddenly withdraw their savings and buy government notes and money market funds, the supply of mortgage money declines and the real estate market can enter into a slump.

Reintermediation of Savings

When the flow of savings again returns to the thrift institutions that act as intermediaries for the placement of mortgage loans, this process is referred to as **reintermediation**. If yields on government bonds plunge or the stock market crashes, money may reenter banks and thrift institutions in search of safety. As money returns to thrift institutions, the funds available for real estate loans increase, interest rates soften, more buyers can qualify for loans, and the housing market begins to pick up.

Thus the processes of intermediation, disintermediation, and reintermediation all have a dramatic impact on the real estate market. To understand this process fully, we must examine the role of the Federal Reserve System and the U.S. Treasury.

1.5 Federal Control of the Money Supply

Although some economists disagree, most believe that manipulating the supply and cost of money and credit helps to achieve economic balance. To this end, the Federal Reserve System and the U.S. Treasury are each involved in efforts to balance the national economy. Though not always successful, these agencies have a profound effect on the financing of real estate. In this section the Federal Reserve System and the U.S. Treasury are discussed in detail.

The Federal Reserve System (Monetary Policy)

The Federal Reserve System (often called the "Fed") is sometimes viewed as the "fourth branch" of the U.S. government. It is charged with maintaining sound credit conditions to help counteract inflation and deflation, to encourage high employment, and to safeguard the purchasing power of the dollar.

The Federal Reserve System contains 12 districts located throughout the United States. Each district is served by a regional Federal Reserve Bank that is coordinated and directed by a seven-member board of governors appointed by the president. The Fed has control over all banks and thrift institutions.

The Fed performs numerous functions, including the issuance of currency. However, this section is concerned only with its ability to influence the money supply. After all, money is the key to real estate transactions, without which real estate activities would come to a grinding halt. This ability to control the supply and cost of money and credit is referred to as **monetary policy**. The principal ways in which the Fed exerts its influence on the money supply are through **reserve requirements**, **open-market operations**, and **discount rates**.

Reserve Requirements

All banks and thrift institutions must set aside reserve funds in order to protect depositors. Even more important than the security, the Fed is able to manipulate the amount of money in circulation by adjusting the reserve rate up or down. For example, if the reserve requirement is 20 percent, banks would need $200 in reserves for every $1,000 of deposits. (In reality, reserve requirements vary with the size of the institution and form of account—the 20 percent used here is illustrative only.) Any money beyond the required reserves may be lent out at a ratio, in this case, of 5 to 1. In other words, the banks may then create $5 of credit for every excess reserve dollar.

To see how banks actually create money, let us return to our example of a $1,000 deposit. Assume that bank policy requires that 20 percent of each deposit in checking accounts must be kept as a reserve against withdrawals. The remaining 80 percent can be used to create a loan.

Now let us assume that $1,000 is deposited into Bank A. Bank A will put $200 in reserve and loan out $800 to Mr. X. Mr. X will take the $800 and spend it. The receiver of this money will probably deposit

Table 1.1 How banks create money.

Banks	Deposits	Reserves (@20%)	Loans ("Debt Fiat")
Bank A	$1,000.00	$ 200.00	$ 800.00
Bank B	800.00	160.00	640.00
Bank C	640.00	128.00	512.00
Bank D	512.00	102.40	409.60
Bank E	409.60	81.92	327.68
Plus all others	1,638.40	327.68	1,310.72
Totals	$5,000.00	$1,000.00	$4,000.00

the funds into Bank B. Bank B now has an $800 deposit, of which $160—20 percent—is kept in reserve, and $640 is lent to Ms. Y. She spends the $640 and the receiver deposits the money into Bank C. Bank C now has a $640 deposit, of which $128 is kept in reserve and $512 is lent to others. In theory, this process continues until all funds are exhausted. Table 1.1 illustrates this process.

A single $1,000 deposit under a 20 percent reserve requirement can expand to become a $5,000 deposit, $4,000 of which is loaned out. In essence, the banking system has created additional purchasing power through demand deposits. This has the same effect on spending as increasing the amount of coin and paper money.

In the real world, does this creation of bank money always occur at a constant, smooth rate? Not usually. Some banks differ in their reserve policy, and the amount of loans available from each deposit varies between banks. In addition, "leakage" occurs when people fail to deposit money in banks. Referring to Table 1.1, what would happen if the borrower of the $640 from Bank B buys merchandise and the store owners put the $640 under their mattress instead of depositing the money in Bank C?

Change in the Reserve Requirements

All banks that are members of the Federal Reserve System are required to keep a certain percentage of each deposit as reserves. These reserves are kept at the regional Federal Reserve Bank. If the Fed feels that *easy money* and credit are feeding inflation, it can raise the reserve requirements, which will force banks to restrict their lending, as money must be diverted from loans to cover the shortage in reserves. This action is designed to decrease the amount of money in circulation, drive up interest rates, and eventually lessen inflation by slowing down spending.

What will happen if the Fed decreases the reserve requirements? Will this increase or decrease the money supply? Will this raise or lower interest rates? Trace the steps that were outlined above to check your understanding.

Open-Market Operations

As part of its money-management tools, the Fed is allowed to buy and sell government securities, called *open-market* operations. Banks must buy them, but the public, consisting of private citizens and *financial institutions*, also may buy and sell government securities as a form of investment. When the Fed buys government securities from the public, the seller of these securities (the public) receives the Fed's check, which the seller then deposits in a local bank. The local bank forwards the check to the Fed for payment. When the Fed receives its own check, it increases the reserves of the local bank by the amount of that check. The local bank now has more reserves than are required and therefore can grant more loans. *Thus, when the Fed buys government securities from the public, it increases the money supply by increasing bank reserves, which, in turn, will support more loans.*

What happens to the money supply when the Fed sells government securities to the public? The money supply tightens up, which increases interest rates and discourages borrowing.

To review, let us trace what happens when the Fed sells government securities. When government securities are sold, the public purchases them by writing checks on their local bank. The Fed receives the buyer's check and subtracts it from the reserve account of the local bank. The local bank now has less in reserve and therefore must constrict its lending. *So when the Fed sells government securities, it decreases bank reserves, which, in turn, decreases the bank's ability to grant loans.*

Once again we notice that the ultimate effect is a change in the money supply by manipulating bank reserves. But the Fed still has another important tool—changes in the discount rate.

Discount Rates

To avoid having their reserves dip below the required minimum and for various other reasons, banks and thrifts may borrow from the Fed. Hence the term "banker's bank" is used to describe the relationship of the Federal Reserve Bank to a member bank. The interest rate charged by the Fed is called the *discount rate*. This is not to be confused with the so-called **prime rate** (rate given to a bank's most favored corporate borrowers) that is charged by commercial banks. The two are compared in Figure 1.4.

The higher the Fed's discount rate charged to the bank, the higher the rate of interest charged by the bank to the real estate borrower. A high interest rate has a dampening effect on potential buyers of real estate. Many

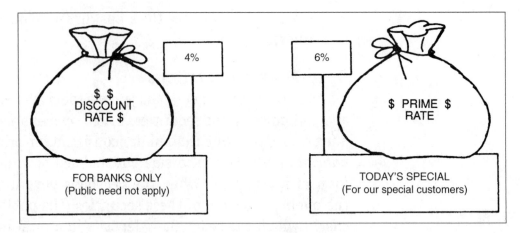

Figure 1.4 Discount rate versus prime rate.

prospective home buyers will simply postpone the purchase of a home, for example, in the hope that interest rates will soon come down.

The reverse is also true. The lower the discount rate, the lower the rate of interest charged by the bank to borrowers. A greater demand for loans is expected to follow, and the number of real estate loans actually placed will increase.

Federal Funds Rate

Although not technically listed as a major tool of the Fed, the *federal funds rate* is one of the most closely watched indicators as to the current thinking of the Federal Reserve managers. What is the federal funds rate? When one bank is at a maximum loan-to-reserve requirement, it cannot grant additional loans to expand business until its reserves are increased. Or if the bank has granted too many loans relative to its existing reserves, it must by law either call in some loans or increase its reserves. One way to solve these problems is to borrow excess reserves from another bank that currently is not granting additional loans. The federal funds rate, then, is the rate of interest one bank charges another for the overnight use of excess reserves.

The federal funds rate should not be confused with the *prime rate*. The prime rate is the rate of interest a bank charges its larger, most favored customers, such as major corporations. The federal funds rate is what one bank charges another bank for overnight use of excess reserves.

The Federal Reserve, in its efforts to fight inflation or recession, increases or decreases the money supply to keep the federal funds rate in a certain trading range. This will encourage one bank to borrow the excess reserves of another and use the reserves to grant more loans, which should expand the economy. If the Fed wishes to slow the economy, it may tighten up the money supply and force the federal funds rate to rise. This discourages one bank from borrowing excess reserves from another bank, thereby discouraging the granting of additional loans. This will tend to keep the economy from expanding.

Summary of the Major Federal Reserve Tools*

Changes in the reserve requirements, open-market operations, and changes in the discount rate all help the Fed to control the supply of bank money. Of these tools, the most commonly used is open-market operations. To increase the money supply, the Fed will either decrease the reserve requirement, buy government securities, decrease the discount rate, or use some combination of all three.

To decrease the money supply, the Fed will either increase the reserve requirement, sell government securities, increase the discount rate, or use some combination of all three. In addition, the Fed will keep a close eye on the federal funds rate and attempt to raise or lower this rate, depending on its economic goals.

The U.S. Treasury (Fiscal Policy)

Whereas the Federal Reserve Board determines monetary policy, the U.S. Treasury, under the direction of Congress and the president, acts as the nation's fiscal agent, managing the federal government's enormous debt. The government's spending and taxing policy is referred to as *fiscal policy*, in contrast to the monetary policy of the Fed. How much the federal government spends, and how much it takes in through taxation, will decidedly affect real estate financing. For example, if the U.S. Treasury decides to issue long-term debt instruments called treasury certificates, consisting of notes and bonds, to help finance government spending, more money is therefore siphoned off from mortgage investments. The impact is similar to the Fed's increasing the reserve requirement. Fewer homes would be constructed and purchased because of the reduction in available capital. This is called the "crowding out" effect. The opposite is, of course, also true. If the government decides to curtail or reduce its spending, more money is made available for the capital markets, including the financing of real estate.

In recent years, the "crowding out" effect has been minimal because of the massive amount of U.S. government notes, bonds,

---

* *The Essentials of Real Estate Economics*, 5th ed., Dennis J. McKenzie and Richard Betts, Thomson South-Western, 2006, Mason, OH.

mortgages, and other securities purchased by foreign countries and their citizens.

The Treasury is more than just the supplier of funds for federal spending. It has long been involved in the initial funding of new programs designed to bolster the economy. For example, it helped establish the Federal National Mortgage Association, the Government National Mortgage Association, the Federal Land Bank system, and other agencies that have played such important roles in real estate financing activities.

Much more could be said about taxing policy, deficit spending, and other interrelated topics. However, these are better left to a course in economics. Suffice it to say that when government spending exceeds revenue from taxation, deficit spending occurs, which leads the U.S. government to borrow more, driving up interest rates which in turn tends to fan the flames of inflation. Inflation occurs when prices for goods and services increase, usually from too much money chasing too few goods. The net result of inflation can be a mixed blessing to real estate owners and licensees. Real estate values usually keep up with—and very often exceed—the rate of inflation. However, inflation drives up the cost of housing and interest rates, which can prevent some people from acquiring homes.

1.6 Cost Characteristics of the Mortgage Market

From a lender's point of view, cost, interest rates, and profits are the economic factors that drive the mortgage market. This section describes the underlying cost issues that influence the California loan market.

Cost of Mortgage Money

Many economic variables affect the price of money available for California real estate loans. International factors, such as an unfavorable trade balance, can have an impact on local lending. National factors, such as actions taken by the Federal Reserve Board and the U.S. Treasury, inflation, and business cycles, are even more important. Local factors that affect the cost of mortgage money include the level of employment, population trends, and the level of development in the community. Discussions of these larger issues are better left to economists. Closer to home, the institutional factors that affect the local cost of mortgage money include the following:

1. *Deposit cost.* This is the raw cost a lender must pay to attract depositors. The higher the interest rate paid on savings accounts, the higher the rate of interest the institution must charge for lending out mortgage money.

2. *Borrowing costs.* Many lenders need to tap the bond and other markets to obtain working capital. The costs of underwriting and floating a stock or bond offering will be passed on to the real estate borrower.

3. *Sales cost.* Promotional costs to attract borrowers, including advertising, loan solicitors, and so on, will be passed on in the form of higher interest rates.

4. *Administration.* Needless to say, there are overhead and administrative expenses in any business. Rent, utilities, management, maintenance, and other operating costs must be recouped and will affect the cost of borrowing.

5. *Reserves.* As pointed out earlier, reserves are required to be set aside by commercial banks and other institutional lenders. This presents an opportunity cost, the price of money that must sit idle and unproductive.

6. *Liquidity.* With the many past problems that have plagued institutional lenders, capital requirements and the need to liquidate assets are more critical than ever. This has to be factored into the cost of money for institutional lenders.

7. *Profit.* Again, as with any enterprise, lenders are in the business of making a profit for their stockholders and for themselves.

The cost of a loan to a borrower is essentially the sum of these seven factors. An old rule of thumb that has been followed by real estate lending institutions is that it takes a spread of approximately 2 to 4 percent over the deposit interest rate paid to savers to break even before profit.

In the highly competitive California mortgage market, this spread has sometimes been squeezed down to only 2 percent or even less. Hence, if a bank is paying 4 percent interest to attract deposits, it must receive 6 percent on its loans just to break even. Of course, there are some exceptions and variations in this rule, including the type of loan, term, points, and so on. However, it should be clear that, as in other types of businesses, the most efficient institution is likely to be the one that can make the most profit while lending at the lowest rate. Those that cannot compete because their costs exceed their income will fail.

In short, it can be said that lending institutions, like retailers, try to buy money at wholesale (interest rate paid to depositors) and mark it up and sell it at retail (interest rate charged borrowers).

What Causes Mortgage Interest Rates to Change?

Underlying all interest rate changes for real estate loans are the market forces of supply and demand. After all, credit is a product that is bought and sold. Borrowers compete in the credit markets, just as buyers do for other goods and services. Specific forces influencing changes in mortgage interest rates include:

1. *Excessive government spending.* Government deficit spending tends to cause higher inflation and/or interest rates as the government drains away funds from the private sector or inks up the printing presses for more money.

2. *Large government borrowing amounts.* As the federal government increases its spending faster than its collection of tax revenues, it will out of necessity (barring congressional approval of a raise in its debt ceiling) need to compete in the capital markets for money. Such competition invariably raises interest rates (this is the so-called crowding out effect).

3. *Inflation.* As a companion to excessive government spending and borrowing, inflation is an inevitable consequence that tends to cause increases in interest rates even with increases in the money supply. Monetarists hold that a rise in the supply of money may help lower interest rates, but only for a brief period. As the money supply swells, so do expectations of rapid inflation. Thus, over the long run, lenders increase interest rates to protect or maintain their real profit margins against the expected increase in inflation.

4. *Supply.* As income increases, the money stock also increases, fueling economic expansion. If demand for loans does not keep pace, interest rates trend downward.

5. *Demand.* A strong demand for credit pushes interest rates upward. Even as the money supply continues to grow, the economy becomes overheated and competing borrowers (buyers of credit) bid up prices. As prices begin to climb, lenders naturally want higher interest rates to hedge against inflation.

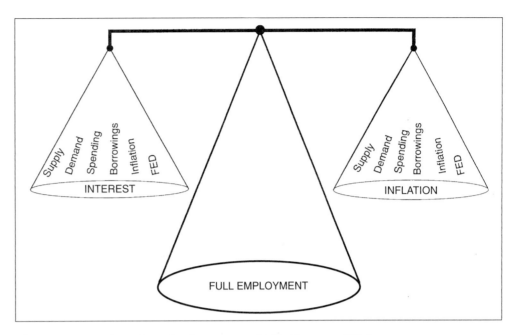

Figure 1.5 Balancing the interest–inflation conflict.

6. *Federal Reserve actions.* (Review the discussion of the Federal Reserve in the previous section.) Figure 1.5 illustrates how the Fed attempts to balance the problem of high interest rates against excessive inflation rates.

"Tight" versus "Easy" Money

Tight money, a frequent expression among real estate practitioners, refers to restrictive money policies of the Federal Reserve System as it attempts to combat inflation by reducing the money supply. Any action to reduce the money supply will ordinarily cause interest rates to rise, unless of course the demand for funds is correspondingly reduced. On the other hand, when demand remains the same or actually increases, competition for the restricted supply of money climbs. Money invariably is taken out of thrift institutions for "greener pastures," those places where higher returns are paid for funds. This condition was referred to earlier as disintermediation.

Easy money, by contrast, is a relatively loose money policy of the Fed, which attempts to combat recession by increasing the supply of money in circulation. As money supplies increase, employment will normally increase, leading to increased income and, in theory, savings. As savings build up in the coffers of thrift institutions, interest rates move downward. With the return of funds to the thrift institutions—the major dispensers of mortgage funds—reintermediation is said to occur. Real estate activities usually pick up steam under easy money and low interest rate conditions.

The California Mortgage Market

California is unique in terms of the national mortgage market because of characteristics peculiar to this state.

1. *Large population and high demand*. California is the most populous state, continues to attract new residents, and has a high birth rate. State officials expect California's population to rise from approximately 36 million in the year 2005 to 60 million by 2050!

2. *Financial institutions*. California contains the largest number of banks and thrift institutions. Obviously, thrift institutions want to be where the greatest demand for real estate loans can be found. Californians have a greater choice of lenders than do residents of other states.

3. *Mortgage loan correspondents*. California has attracted many experienced and diversified mortgage loan correspondents (brokers) who represent out-of-state life insurance companies and other institutional and noninstitutional lenders. This brings additional mortgage money to California.

4. *Title companies*. Title insurance originated in California and it continues to increase in volume. Escrow companies, too, are peculiar to this state, though the use of both title and escrow firms is spreading to other states. This easy, low-cost closing process attracts lenders and borrowers.

5. *Security*. The **deed of trust** is used almost exclusively, rather than the mortgage instrument, as the legal basis for securing real estate loans. This gives greater protection to lenders, because it allows a quick foreclosure process.

6. *Active secondary market*. This is where existing real estate loans are sold to U.S. and foreign purchasers. These secondary market sales bring fresh capital to the California real estate market.

7. *Diversification*. California's economy is one of the most diversified worldwide and is growing with a mix of ethnic and social diversity that is creating new opportunities for housing and financing.

1.7 Instruments of Real Estate Finance

The economic environment of the mortgage market establishes the trends for interest rates and financing terms, but the actual loan is created using a variety of financing instruments. This section introduces instruments of real estate finance, leaving specific details to later chapters.

Promissory Notes

When money is borrowed to purchase real estate, the borrower agrees to repay the loan by signing a *promissory note*, which outlines the terms of repayment and sets the due date. The promissory note is legal evidence that a debt is owed. The two most common types of promissory notes in general use are the **straight note** and the **installment note.**

The *straight note* is an *interest-only note*. Under a straight note, the borrower agrees to pay the interest periodically (or all at one time, when the note matures) and to pay the entire principal in a lump sum on the due date. For example, if you borrow $100,000 for five years at 8 percent interest rate, the monthly payments are $666.67 per month ($100,000 × 8% by 12 months). The $666.67 payments cover just the monthly interest. Thus, five years hence, on the due date, you must pay back the entire $100,000 principal. In other words, your payments were only large enough to cover the monthly interest and did not reduce the $100,000 principal.

The second type of real estate promissory note, and by far the most common, is the *installment note*. An installment note requires periodic payments that include both principal and interest. This reduction in principal is referred to as *amortization*. Suppose you borrowed $100,000 for 30 years at 8 percent interest, payable at $733.76 per month, including both principal and interest. At the end of 30 years you would find that the entire principal had been paid back. Each monthly payment of $733.76 not only included the monthly interest due but also reduced the $100,000 principal. An installment loan that includes both principal and interest in equal installment payments that self-liquidate the debt is called a **fully amortized loan.** Under such an amortized loan there is no **balloon payment** on the due date of the loan. The Civil Code defines a balloon payment as any payment on an amortized loan that is more than double the amount of a regular installment.

One variation of the installment note is to have monthly payments that are large enough to pay the monthly interest and reduce some of the principal, but the monthly principal portion is not sufficient to entirely liquidate the debt by the due date. Thus, on the due date the remaining unpaid principal must be paid in a balloon payment. For example, a $100,000, 30-year loan at 8 percent interest payable at $700 instead of $733.76 per month would require a balloon payment of $50,321.35 on the due date. Why? Because the $700 per month was enough to cover the monthly interest ($666.67), but it was not enough to cover the monthly interest plus all of the monthly principal, which would have taken $733.76 per month. Thus the unpaid balance over the 30-year life of the loan, $50,321.35, must be paid on the due date in the form of a balloon payment.

Finally, some borrowers sign negative amortized promissory notes. Negative amortized means that the loan payment does not even cover the monthly interest. Each month this shortage is added to the principal owed, resulting in an increased loan balance, which in turn incurs additional interest. As mentioned previously, a $100,000 loan at 8 percent payable interest only would result in a $666.67 monthly payment ($100,000 × 8% ÷ 12 months). If a borrower only paid $600 per month, the difference between an interest only payment of $666.67 and the $600 payment = $66.67. Each month, this $66.67 shortfall would be added to the $100,000 loan and begin to accrue interest. If this shortfall continued for 30 years, the borrower would still owe a balloon payment of $199,357.30 on top of paying $600 per month for 30 years! Total paid would be $600 × 360 payments (30 years × 12) = $216,000 + $199,357.30 balloon payment, for a grand total of $415,357.30 to pay off a $100,000 negative amortized during a 30-year period.

Variations on Fixed Interest Rate Notes

In recent years, lenders have introduced many variations of the standard promissory notes, with alphabet-soup-sounding names such as ARM, GPM, and so on. These are collectively called Alternative Mortgage Instruments, or AMIs for short. Chapter 4 is devoted to these loans.

Deed of Trust (Trust Deed)

To give added assurance that the promissory note will be paid when due, real estate lenders require security for the obligation. The most logical security is real estate currently owned or about to be acquired by the borrower. To secure an interest in the borrower's property, most lenders in California use a deed of trust (or trust deed).

A deed of trust is a three-party instrument between a borrower, called the *trustor*; a third party, called the trustee; and a lender, called the *beneficiary*. Under a deed of trust, the trustor deeds bare legal title to the trustee, who keeps the title as security until the promissory note is repaid. Once the debt is repaid, the beneficiary (lender) orders the trustee to reconvey the title to the trustor (borrower) using a deed of reconveyance. If the trustor should default on the loan, the beneficiary can order the trustee to hold a trustee's sale and sell the property to obtain the cash needed to pay the loan. Figure 1.6 illustrates how title is passed between a trustor and trustee in a deed of trust.

In other states, frequently a mortgage is used instead of a deed of trust to secure a real estate loan. But in California mortgages are rare—most lenders insist on deeds of trust instead. Why? Because in most cases deeds of trust favor the lender over the borrower. If the borrower should default under a deed of trust, the lender can order the trustee to sell the property without a court proceeding, and it can be accomplished in approximately four months. Once the sale takes place, the borrower loses all rights to redeem the property.

Foreclosure under a mortgage usually requires a court proceeding and can take up to one year. After this foreclosure takes place, the borrower could have a one-year right of redemption. Most California real estate lenders therefore prefer to use deeds of trust rather than mortgages as security instruments because foreclosure is quicker, cheaper, and has no right of redemption after the sale.

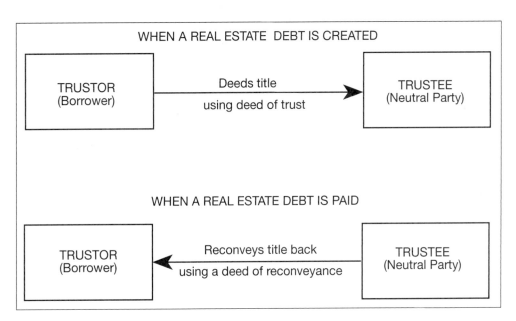

Figure 1.6 The creation of a real estate debt and its payment, using a deed of trust.

Installment Sales Contracts

Another real estate financing instrument is an **installment sales contract** (agreement of sale). An installment sales contract is an agreement between the buyer and seller, where the buyer is given possession and use of the property and in exchange agrees to make regular payments to the seller. Legal title to the property remains with the seller until the terms of the contract are met, at which time the seller formally deeds the property to the buyer. In essence, under an installment sales contract, the seller becomes the lender. Outside lending institutions such as banks or thrift institutions are not needed in such a transaction.

The lack of a legal title poses some risks for the buyer. It is often several years between the time the buyer signs the installment sales contract and the time the seller delivers the deed. If the seller should die, become bankrupt, become incompetent, or encumber the title during this interim, the buyer could become involved in legal entanglements. In addition, if the seller under a contact of sale has an existing loan on the property, the use of this contract violates the lender's "due on sale" clause if one is present. In light of these possibilities, except for the special area of large land developments, the advantages that an installment sales contract may have had in the past seem to fade away in favor of the use of a deed of trust.

Special Clauses

In addition to repayment terms, many real estate financing instruments contain special clauses or loan conditions that the borrower and lender agree to honor. These clauses are known by such names as acceleration clause, alienation clause, escalation clause, prepayment penalty clause, interest change clause, and so on. These clauses will be examined in detail as we progress through the textbook and they are defined in the Glossary.

The Language of Real Estate Finance

By now you have discovered that the field of real estate finance has developed a language consisting of specific terms and concepts. As you read this textbook, try to learn the language and then use it in your real estate discussions. Refer to the Glossary from time to time to reacquaint yourself with words and terms that tend to lose their meaning when we don't use them on a regular basis. Learning the terms and concepts will help you communicate with inexperienced clients and friends who do not understand financial terms, as well as enable you to converse with real estate professionals. Once again, welcome to the real world of real estate finance.

1.8 The Five-Step Financing Process

Borrowing money to purchase, exchange, refinance, construct, or make capital improvements to an existing home can be viewed as a *five-step financing process*:

1. *Application*. The loan process begins with the application filled in by the borrower, as detailed in Chapter 10. The form includes information on the applicant's financial condition, including the amount and consistency of income, along with outstanding debts and expenses. The application also requests information concerning the property, including location, age, size of lot, and improvements. If the application is for a construction loan, details concerning the proposed improvements are required by lenders.

2. *Analysis/Processing*. After the completed application form is received, the lender reviews it to determine if the borrower and the property appear to meet the lender's standards. If the application was taken by an intermediary, such as mortgage broker, it is forwarded to the ultimate lender for analysis. If the applicant is acceptable, the lender presents the proposed financing terms to the borrower. The applicant may accept, reject, or attempt to negotiate with the lender to obtain more favorable terms. This topic is detailed in Chapters 8 and 9.

3. *Qualifying/Underwriting*. After an agreement is reached, loan documents are drawn, disclosure forms are prepared, and instructions for the escrow and title insurance companies are issued. Lenders establish processing patterns in accordance with their own policies and procedures. Much more is said about this step in Chapters 7 through 10.

4. *Funding/Closing*. After processing, the loan closing phase begins. This involves signing all loan papers and transferring the title. Practices vary within the state in the handling of the escrow. Closing is detailed in Chapter 10.

5. *Servicing*. This refers to loan collections and recordkeeping. It includes necessary follow-up to ensure that the property is maintained; that insurance, taxes, and other obligations are paid; and that delinquency is prevented in order to reduce the possibility of foreclosure. Some lenders do their own servicing, while others pay independent servicing companies fees for handling the paperwork. Chapters 10 and 11 deal with servicing and other postclosing issues.

SUMMARY

Real estate finance is the key factor in most real estate transactions. When mortgage funds are available, real estate sales take place. When mortgage money is scarce, activity in the real estate market declines.

Money is created by the banking system using fractional reserve banking, and this money is added to the supply of money issued by the U.S. government.

Money is earned through wages, interest, profits, and rents. Some of these earnings ultimately find their way into savings in banks and thrift institutions, which account for a sizable amount of the credit extended for real estate purchases and construction. When savings are withdrawn from these banks and thrift institutions and used elsewhere for higher returns, disintermediation occurs, which can result in a decline in the real estate market.

The Federal Reserve System (the Fed) is able to increase the supply of money by decreasing reserve requirements of member banks, buying government securities in the open market, decreasing its discount rate to borrowing banks, and other means. The Fed is able to decrease the availability of mortgage funds by increasing reserve requirements, selling government securities, increasing the discount rates, and other means.

The U.S. Treasury, as the fiscal agent of the federal government, also greatly affects the availability of real estate funds through its spending and taxing policies. When the government reduces its spending and borrowing, more money is available for real estate lending. And, conversely, when the government increases its spending and borrowing, less credit is pumped into real estate transactions.

The cost of mortgage money is affected by the price paid to attract deposits, lenders' borrowing costs, sales costs, administration, reserves, and profit goals. Interest rate fluctuations are largely influenced by government spending, government borrowing, inflation, and supply and demand.

The California market is unique in terms of the national mortgage market because of characteristics peculiar to this state. Among these are its large population, high demand, large amount of big institutional lenders, existence of many diversified mortgage loan correspondents, title insurance and escrow companies, and a very active secondary market.

Just like many other professionals, real estate lenders use tools or instruments to complete a task. In California, the major instruments of real estate finance are the promissory note, the deed of trust, and, to a lesser extent, the installment sales contract.

IMPORTANT TERMS AND CONCEPTS

Amortized loan

Balloon payment

Beneficiary

Deed of trust (trust deed)

Discount rate

Disintermediation

Easy money

Federal funds rate

Federal Reserve System

Fiscal policy

Five-step financing process

Fractional reserve banking

Installment note

Installment sales contract

Intermediation

Monetary policy

Negative amortized loans

Open-market operations

Prime rate

Reintermediation

Reserve requirement

Straight note

Tight money

Trustor

REVIEWING YOUR UNDERSTANDING

Questions for Discussion

1. In addition to coins, what are two other types of money? Do the terms *credit* and *money* mean the same?

2. "The source of all mortgage funds is ultimately savings." In your own words, explain this statement.

3. Explain how the Federal Reserve Board can increase or decrease the money supply using each of the following tools: reserve requirements, open-market activities, and discount rates.

4. How does an interest-only promissory note differ from an installment note?

5. Why are trust deeds used in California instead of mortgages?

6. How does an installment sales contract differ from a deed of trust as a security device for real estate financing?

7. Explain this statement: "Finance is the fuel that makes a real estate transaction run."

Multiple-Choice Questions

1. The real estate housing market can best be characterized as having
   a. a steady growth.
   b. a cyclical up-and-down movement.
   c. no influence in the general economy.
   d. none of the above.

2. According to the circular flow of the economy, when people supply the land, labor, and capital to business, the people receive in return
   a. goods and services.
   b. savings.
   c. income.
   d. taxes.

3. The ultimate source for borrowing comes from
   a. savings.
   b. stock options.
   c. bonds.
   d. financing instruments.

4. An example of disintermediation is the flow of funds from
   a. money markets to thrift institutions.
   b. bond markets to mortgage markets.
   c. thrift institutions to money market funds.
   d. money markets to mortgage markets.

5. If the Federal Reserve Board wished to expand the money supply using open-market operations, it would
   a. cut federal taxes.
   b. increase government spending.
   c. sell government securities.
   d. buy government securities.

6. Which of the following statements is true?
   a. The prime rate is the same as the discount rate.
   b. A decrease in reserve requirements will tend to decrease the money supply.
   c. The California mortgage market usually has an oversupply of loanable funds.
   d. The federal funds rate is the interest one bank charges another for the use of overnight funds.

7. A $100,000 real estate loan at 8 percent, payable at $733.76 per month for 30 years, illustrates
   a. an interest-only note.
   b. an amortized installment note, including principal and interest.
   c. a straight note.
   d. a negatively amortized note.

8. On a deed of trust, the borrower is called the
   a. trustor.
   b. trustee.
   c. beneficiary.
   d. mortgagee.

9. When a borrower pays off a real estate loan, the trustee issues a
   a. deed of trust.
   b. trustee's deed.
   c. deed of repayment.
   d. deed of reconveyance.

10. A $100,000 loan at 8 percent interest, amortized for 30 years, all due and payable in 5 years, secured by a deed of trust, will involve
    a. periodic payments.
    b. a balloon payment.
    c. a lien on the borrower's title.
    d. all of the above.

11. If savers withdraw their funds from savings banks to buy corporate bonds, this is an example of
    a. mediation.
    b. intermediation.
    c. disintermediation.
    d. reintermediation.

12. The fiscal agent of the federal government is the
    a. U.S. Treasury.
    b. Federal Reserve System.
    c. commercial banking system.
    d. Federal Housing Finance Board.

13. Amortization is best defined as
    a. periodic payments of interest.
    b. periodic reduction of principal.
    c. payments on a contract of sale.
    d. income tax write-off on account of interest deductions.

14. Qualifying a borrower takes place at what step in the financing process?
    a. analysis.
    b. application.
    c. servicing.
    d. closing.

15. All of the following can cause mortgage interest rates to rise except
    a. rapid inflation.
    b. excessive government borrowing.
    c. a large increase in the money supply.
    d. a large increase in the demand for loan funds.

16. What is sometimes called the "fourth branch" of government?
    a. U.S. Treasury.
    b. Federal Reserve System.
    c. Resolution Trust Corporation.
    d. U.S. Congress.

17. Promissory notes with interest-only payments and a balloon payment of the entire principal on the due date also are known as:
    a. self-amortizing notes.
    b. straight notes.
    c. fully amortized notes.
    d. variable notes.

18. Loan collection and recordkeeping is referred to as loan
    a. processing.
    b. servicing.
    c. analysis.
    d. closing.

19. The lender in a deed of trust is called the
    a. trustor.
    b. vendor.
    c. trustee.
    d. beneficiary.

20. The party holding bare legal title under a trust deed is the
    a. beneficiary.
    b. trustor.
    c. title company.
    d. trustee.

CASE & POINT
Homebuying Base Gets Bigger & Bigger

According to the Harvard University Joint Center for Housing Studies, the number of American households will likely increase by an average of 1,150,000 each year from now until 2010. The biggest rise? Immigrants, to the tune of at least 25 percent of the growth. Two-thirds of the increase will come from demographic shifts toward older and single individuals. The fastest population growth is taking place in the 85+ age category, 70 percent of whom are women, many widowed and living alone.

"Baby boomers"—those born between 1946 and 1965—are driving up homeownership rates and values. Their offspring, dubbed "echo boomers," are expected to account for at least 10 percent of households. Many "echoes" will be immigrants, minorities, and second-generation Americans. They will be better educated, better paid, and therefore better able to afford housing, as opposed to renting. Though surging housing prices restrict many buyers in high-priced areas, especially in California, the increasing trend toward low down payments and other practices that are detailed in Chapter 5 help offset this problem.

All of these demographic shifts are presenting some very interesting challenges to home buyers, sellers, agents, lenders, builders, and others connected with the housing industry. Financing needs of singles and other nontraditional households will be different from those of married households, with the lending industry providing many options for financing homes based on the unique needs of home buyers, as we'll see throughout the text.

It can be reasonably concluded from the study that real estate agents will need to address the issue of changing consumer profiles and expectations. The NAR, for example, reported that its "At Home with Diversity: One America" program was originally set up to educate agents in dealing with buyers of different minority groups, cultures, and ethnic backgrounds as part of their real estate training.

Since the inception of this program, the NAR (National Association of REALTORS®) and other trade associations have continued to expand training of their members in this growing segment of the real estate market.

CHAPTER 2
INSTITUTIONAL LENDERS

PREVIEW

An institutional lender, also known as a financial intermediary, is any depository that pools funds of clients and depositors and invests them in real estate loans. The lending policies of these institutions have a profound impact on the real estate market. In California, institutional lenders include savings banks (former savings and loan associations), commercial banks, and life insurance companies. They are differentiated from noninstitutional lenders, such as individual or private lenders, in the following important ways:

- Institutional lenders are highly regulated and closely supervised by federal and state agencies, whereas private lenders are relatively free of regulations.

- Private lenders invest their own funds directly, or through mortgage brokers, into real estate loans, rather than through a financial intermediary.

- Regulated institutional lenders are not subject to usury laws and may charge any rate of interest. In contrast, many private lenders make "personal" loans that are subject to usury laws, which place legal limits on rates of interest. (See Chapter 3 for details.)

- Many institutional lenders qualify to make Department of Veterans Affairs (DVA) and Federal Housing Administration (FHA) loans.

- There is an active secondary market for institutional loans, as described in Chapter 7.

- Institutional lenders and federal regulations in some cases set private mortgage insurance (PMI) requirements, discussed in Chapter 5.

- Most conforming lenders offer rate lock-in periods, guaranteeing an agreed-upon interest rate in advance of closing, typically for 14, 30, 45, or 60 days. Generally, the shorter the lock-in period, the lower the rate.

Figure 2.1 distinguishes three broad classifications of lenders: institutional, noninstitutional, and private lenders. How these lenders fit into the mortgage market will be explained in this and upcoming chapters. Then, in Figure 2.2, we show how savings become real estate loans.

After completing this chapter, you should be able to:

1. **Demonstrate how savings deposits become real estate loans.**

2. **Differentiate institutional from noninstitutional lenders.**

3. **List three types of institutional lenders and briefly explain the differences between them.**

4. **Discuss several of the trends facing institutional lenders.**

5. **Decide when to use one institutional lender over another.**

6. **List five regulatory agencies that supervise the operations of institutional lenders.**

Figure 2.1 Sources of money in the mortgage market.

Figure 2.2 How savings become real estate loans.

2.1 Savings Banks

What Is a Savings Bank?

In simple terms, a savings bank is a ***financial intermediary*** that accepts savings from the public and invests these savings principally in real estate trust deeds and mortgages. Previously called savings and loan associations, most changed their name after the S&L crisis of the 1980s. Today they are frequently referred to as "thrift" institutions.

Savings banks may be either mutual or capital stock institutions. As a mutual institution, depositors and borrowers are given share certificates or receipts in return for deposits of money. This is why a deposit in a mutual thrift is often referred to as a *share liability* rather than a savings deposit. A capital stock institution, on the other hand, issues shares of stock to its investors, representing fractional shares of ownership of the institution.

A savings bank is also classified as either a state-chartered or a federally chartered institution. A *state-chartered* thrift institution is licensed by the State of California and operates under the supervision of a state commissioner and, if insured, also under the ***Federal Housing***

Finance Board. By contrast, a *federally chartered* savings bank is licensed by the Federal Housing Finance Board and is readily identified by the word *federal* in its corporate title, such as Fidelity Federal Savings. To the saver or borrower, however, there is little difference between state and federal institutions, so similar are the laws and regulations under which they operate. They have substantially "parallel authority," which means that home buyers can shop for loans almost anywhere.

Lending Characteristics of Savings Banks (Thrifts)

The chief lending characteristics of savings banks include the following:

- Government regulations require that a majority of their assets must be in real estate loans. Business and consumer loans are permitted to a limited extent but pale when compared with loans secured by real property.

- As a general rule, most home loans do not exceed 95 percent of the appraised value or sales price of the home, whichever is lower. Exceptions include government-backed loans, such as FHA and DVA. With the new millenium, loans in excess of 100 percent have become very popular. Most thrifts limit the maximum amount on a single loan to 1 percent of their total assets. Hence, larger thrifts are able to accommodate large loan requests more readily than smaller savings banks.

- Most thrifts limit their loans to 30 years, although 40-year loans are permitted in some cases. Fifteen-year loans are also widely promoted, especially in the home refinancing market. Sometimes, during periods of rising interest rates, many of these loans include provisions for due dates (balloons) in as few as three to five years, or for rollovers thereafter at the prevailing market rate. These have monthly payments amortized for 30 years, but the unpaid balance is due in three, five, or seven years.

- Interest rates in the past were highest among the institutional real estate lenders. This was due to the large demand for loans and to the higher risks associated with higher ***loan-to-value ratios*** (LTV). (High loan-to-value means that the amount of the loan is high in relation to the appraised value or sales price of the property.) Currently, rates charged by commercial banks and savings banks are basically the same.

- Their basic real estate lending is on single-family, owner-occupied dwellings, but in a favorable market thrifts will also finance mobile home loans, nonowner-occupied dwellings, apartments, and commercial and industrial properties.

- Combination loans are often available. Such loans combine construction (short-term financing) and **take-out loans** (long-term or permanent financing) into one loan.

- Savings banks are permitted to make collateral loans secured by the borrower's savings accounts, savings certificates, bonds, existing secured notes, and certain other forms of readily liquid assets.

Trends in the Savings Bank Industry

Increased competition from commercial banks and mortgage companies, combined with imbalances between money-scarce and money-surplus areas that create demands for multiregional lending programs, have contributed to the loss of stature of savings banks (thrifts) as the principal source of home loans.

2.2 Commercial Banks

What Is a Commercial Bank?

A **commercial bank** is, as the name implies, a commercial institution that functions as a depository for funds and a place from which to borrow money. They are not to be confused with "industrial banks" or so-called finance companies. Commercial banks have two different forms of deposits, demand deposits and time deposits. The bulk of their funds are in demand deposits, which are deposits in business and personal checking accounts. Rarely are such funds used for long-term mortgage lending, due to the highly volatile nature of such funds—that is, they may be withdrawn on demand by the depositor and therefore cannot be depended on to remain in the account for very long. For this reason they are also referred to as transaction money or transaction accounts.

Time deposits, or interest-bearing savings accounts, provide the bank with long-term funds that are invested into a variety of outlets, including real estate financing.

Commercial banks may make almost any type of loan on virtually any type of reasonable collateral. Although their primary function is to make short-term business loans, California banks are aggressive players in the home loan market.

Commercial banks are always stock corporations that operate under a license or charter from either the state or the federal government. A state-chartered bank is licensed to do business by the California Department of Financial Institutions. A nationally chartered bank is given its license by the Comptroller of the Currency and is readily identifiable by the word *national* in its title, such as South Coast National Bank.

Lending Characteristics of Commercial Banks

Commercial banks are a primary source for short-term construction financing, when the builder or developer has a "take-out" commitment from some other lender—most often a savings bank—for the permanent mortgage loan following completion of improvements. Large commercial banks play a major role in financing business and commercial properties, while some smaller ones deal largely with home loans.

Banks may make home loans up to 95 percent loan-to-value ratio, for as long as 30 years on single-family dwellings. Many banks require private mortgage insurance on loans whose ratio of loan-to-value is in excess of 80 percent.

The chief characteristics of bank real estate loans are the following:

- Active in the regular home loan market, commercial banks can make FHA and DVA loans with more liberal loan-to-value ratios and fewer limitations than imposed on nongovernmental or conventional loans.

- Construction loans are favored and have maturity dates generally of 24 months or less, though they may extend to 60 months. Many banks require a firm take-out agreement whereby a responsible, permanent investor—such as a savings bank or life insurance company—will extend long-term financing upon completion of construction.

- The property offered as collateral is usually in close proximity to the bank or one of its branches.

- Commercial banks are active seekers of home improvement and home equity loans, even though they constitute a junior lien against the property.

- Banks make **swing loans**, sometimes referred to as **bridge loans**, which are short-term **interim loans** used to bridge the time during which a property remains unsold. For example, if you as homeowner purchase a replacement house before selling the first house, a swing loan would provide the funds to fill the gap until the sale proceeds provide the funds to pay off the loan. In short, you found the right house at the right price, but haven't sold your existing home, so you secure a loan to purchase the replacement dwelling, with the loan to be repaid as soon as the existing house sells. The lien may exist on both the "old" and the "new" homes. Swing/bridge loans may have monthly payments or may be set up to be paid in a single lump sum upon sale of the old home.

Trends in the Commercial Banking Industry

Recent developments in commercial banking that have or will have an impact on lending activities include:

1. *Larger banks.* With acquisitions and mergers, along with stiffened competition, big banks will absorb smaller ones or force them out of business.

2. *Interstate banking.* Banks are going nationwide. Geographical restraints are largely ineffective because of interstate deposit-taking, automatic teller machines, and electronic banking that knows no state borders. Acquisitions of failing banks by out-of-state banks continue throughout the nation.

3. *Longer maturities.* Despite reliance on demand deposits as their principal sources of capital, banks are allowing longer payoff terms. This is especially true when a bank is located in an area where there are few savings banks. In such situations, commercial banks are the only source of real estate loans and can exercise considerable control over loan rates, terms, and, in effect, even local building activity. Banks have become a powerful force in the housing market in recent years.

4. *Diversification.* The trend is to permit banks to underwrite commercial paper, mortgage-backed securities, municipal revenue bonds, and other financial undertakings. In addition, there is a movement to allow banks in the future to directly sell insurance and securities, and perhaps even broker real estate transactions. These possibilities are being fought by insurance, securities, and real estate **trade associations** that feel threatened by the competition.

5. *Electronic banking.* Many banks without walls have sprung up in recent times, under such names as Bank of Internet USA, Ing Direct, Virtual Bank, etc., that effectively operate without walls, functioning instead via electronic media. Virtual banks require no rent for brick and mortar, no tellers or even paper, and never close. Depositors, borrowers, and investors can do virtually all their

transactions on the Internet. Nonetheless, traditional banks can retain their customer base by moving their existing customers to lower-cost web-based banking.

Battle for Depositors

Commercial banks and savings banks have traditionally been rivals for depositors. It used to be that savings banks, when they were S&Ls under old laws, were allowed to pay regular passbook savers a slightly higher interest rate than commercial banks were allowed to pay. On the other hand, only commercial banks were allowed to handle checking accounts.

Not so today! Current legislation (1) allows savings banks to handle checking (Negotiable Order of Withdrawal, NOW for short) accounts and make a variety of personal consumer loans; (2) permits both commercial banks and savings banks to pay interest on checking accounts; and (3) eliminates the interest-rate differential between regular passbook accounts in thrifts and in banks. As a result, the war for depositors continues to escalate. The impact of this legislation on the real estate market continues to be debated by housing experts, consumer groups, and the two industries (thrifts and commercial banks) themselves. There are pros and cons on both sides of the issue.

Community Reinvestment Act (CRA)

To guarantee fair lending practices, Congress passed the CRA, which requires all federally supervised financial institutions (thrifts, commercial banks, credit unions, etc.) to disclose lending data in their lobbies and elsewhere. Lenders are required to report data regarding the race, gender, income, and census tract of people to whom they make loans. Its stated purpose is "to assist in identifying discriminatory practices and enforcing antidiscrimination statutes." The CRA encourages lenders to offer mortgages for low- and moderately priced housing and meet other credit needs for low- and moderate-income families. The basic idea is that if an institution accepts deposits from a certain area, it should also offer loans in that area.

CRA ratings are made public for all banks and **thrift institutions**. The government grades each institution on how well it

- Knows the credit needs of its community

- Informs the community about its credit services

- Involves its directors in setting up and monitoring CRA programs

- Participates in government-insured, guaranteed, or subsidized loans

- Distributes credit applications, approvals, and rejections across geographic areas
- Offers a range of residential mortgages, housing rehabilitation loans, and small business loans

All of these criteria are designed to protect consumers against unlawful discrimination. A positive CRA rating is a prerequisite for institutions to open new branches and to engage in expansions, acquisitions, and mergers, since outside third parties can petition agencies to deny these activities to institutions with poor CRA grades.

Home Mortgage Disclosure Act (HMDA)

The CRA requirements include having lenders retain borrower information from which any discriminatory acts can be determined. The primary source of information for this enforcement is the information gathered via the Fannie Mae/Freddie Mac loan application (known as the 1003). The Information for Government Monitoring Purposes section of the 1003 seeks information regarding a borrower's ethnicity, race, and sex. This section is considered so important that if the borrower refuses or fails to provide the information, the lender is required to "note the information on the basis of visual observation or surname."

2.3 Life Insurance Companies

Life insurance companies are another important source of real estate financing, particularly for commercial properties, such as shopping centers and office buildings. They are also a major source of credit for large apartment house projects, hotels and motels, industrial buildings, and regional shopping malls.

What Is a Life Insurance Company?

A **life insurance company** is a firm that specializes in the insuring of lives for specified amounts in exchange for specified premium payments. The premiums are invested until such time as funds are needed to pay claims or to establish reserves for losses. These premiums are invested in many outlets, including trust deeds and mortgage loans.

Life insurance companies are organized either as mutual companies owned by the policyholders (insureds) who share in the earnings through premium rebates, or as stock companies owned by the stockholders who, as with any other corporation, are entitled to dividends on earnings. Regardless of whether stock or mutual, insurance companies are licensed by the state in which they are incorporated and/or where they have their principal offices. Each insurance company is governed by the state where it conducts business, and each state regulates the permitted types of loans, maximum loan-to-value ratios, and other conditions.

Lending Characteristics of Life Insurance Companies

In general, life insurance companies have the broadest lending powers of the *institutional lenders*. Their investment policies are flexible and cover a wide range of financing activities. The laws governing life insurance companies' activities vary from state to state. Under California laws and regulations, any company not incorporated within this state, but doing business here, is subject to the same restrictions that are placed upon California-based companies.

The chief lending characteristics of life insurance companies include the following:

- Loan-to-value ratios are apt to be on the cautious side, frequently less than 80 percent.

- Payback terms are long, usually 30-year amortizations, with occasional *lock-in clauses* that prevent a loan from being paid off before a specified date. For example, there might be a 10- or 15-year lock-in clause on a 30-year loan.

- Interest rates and other fees on conventional loans have traditionally been the lowest among the institutionals, though in recent times they have been steadily climbing.

- Insurance companies prefer to grant large real estate loans (in the millions) as opposed to smaller residential home loans. Many major commercial and industrial developments have insurance company take-out loans.

- Construction loans generally are not desired. Instead, life insurance companies will make the take-out, or permanent, loan after the structure has been completed according to plans and specifications.

- Loan *correspondents*, such as mortgage companies, are widely used as agents of insurance companies. Many life insurance companies will contract for such representation whenever they deem it profitable. In this way the insurance company is relieved of the burden of originating and processing loans, as well as some administrative and service functions. Correspondents are especially used in California, where there is a high demand for loans, but where few insurance companies are actually headquartered. Detailed information concerning lending authority for insurance companies is found in the California Insurance Code, especially in Section 1150.

Trends in the Life Insurance Industry

Trends that affect life insurance lending practices include the following:

1. *Equity conversion positions during inflationary periods.* Here the lender has the option to convert part of the mortgage into an equity position in the property—a shared investment. In short, the lender has the right to convert a portion of the mortgage owed into a part of the ownership of the property at a later date.

2. *Upfront participations (piece of the action).* As a condition of granting a loan, an insurance company may require an upfront share of the income produced by the property to help increase the yield on the loan. Such sharing is called **equity participation**. Participation may also take the form of an "equity kicker" such that, instead of income, the lender takes a percentage ownership in the property. Increasingly, however, insurance companies are buying whole projects as sole owners. In periods of rapid inflation, when fixed interest rates become discouraging as investment funds become scarce, participations become an attractive supplement.

3. *Variable and fixed annuities.* As more people purchase insurance company annuity contracts, larger supplies of funds become available for reinvestment. Real estate loans are one way insurance companies reinvest annuity contributions.

4. *Holding companies and joint ventures.* Where state law does not prohibit the practice, a number of life insurance companies are purchased or reorganized under the umbrella of holding companies. In such instances, interrelated lending activities are made possible because other firms that may be joined together under the parent holding company include such entities as commercial banks, savings banks, and even development companies that furnish construction financing, permanent financing, and so forth.

A variation of this concept of pooling resources is through the media of joint ventures. Under such a venture, a life insurance company may provide the needed financing while a well-established developer will furnish the requisite know-how and codevelop a project.

2.4 Mutual Savings Banks

Mutual savings banks operate much like former savings and loan associations, but they exist chiefly in the northeastern United States. None exist in California, but it is important to consider them because of the large contribution they make in furnishing capital for residential loans via the secondary marketplace.

Mutual savings banks, also called mutual thrifts, are not commercial banks. They are organized in substantially the same way regardless of the state in which they are chartered. They are banks for savings deposits that have no stockholders and are organized to pool the interests of those of moderate means. Managed by a board of trustees, directors, or managers, mutual savings banks distribute their earnings, after payment of necessary business expenses and taxes, to the depositors in the form of dividends, or the earnings are added to the bank's surplus or reserve funds.

Depending on state law, the maximum loan-to-value ratio varies from 50 to 90 percent, exclusive of government-backed loans. When money becomes tight and the yields on other investment outlets increase, mutual savings banks pull back on their real estate lending activities and expand their lending in non-real-estate areas. *Special note:* When California-based American Savings was sold to Washington Mutual, all offices changed their name to Washington Mutual. But Washington Mutual in California is a savings bank, not a northeastern-style mutual savings bank outlined above.

2.5 Depository Institutions and Monetary Control Act

The Monetary Control Act completely phased out restrictions on interest rates that lenders can pay depositors. As a result, new systems for raising, mobilizing, and investing money have arisen. All of this is intended to increase the yields offered to savers and depositors based upon the terms of their checking and savings accounts.

In deregulating financial institutions, we are seeing the homogenization of these institutions. It is becoming difficult to distinguish between savings banks (thrifts) and commercial banks, so close are their respective functions. Reserves are more or less uniform, consumer lending powers of every variety will ultimately be granted, territorial lending restrictions are to be phased out, and restrictions against junior financing have been lifted; a wave of new types of deposits and classes of savings accounts continues to emerge out of the deregulation process.

Additionally, the act expands the lending authority of federal thrift institutions to invest in consumer loans, commercial paper, corporate debt securities, and junior trust deeds. It authorizes these institutions to make acquisitions, development, and construction loans, and removes the geographical lending restrictions along with certain dollar limitations on residential real estate loans.

2.6 Pension and Retirement Funds

Potentially the largest sources of real estate financing are public and private **pension funds**. There are hundreds of thousands of private pension funds and state, local, and federal pension funds nationwide, representing more than $1 trillion in assets. The Mortgage Bankers Association of America projects the growth of these funds will create an enormous amount of potential mortgage funds that could become available to prop up housing and other real estate markets.

Administration and Lending Policies of Pension and Trust Funds

Administrators of pension funds include trust departments of commercial banks and life insurance companies; trustees of unions; boards of trustees appointed by a governor or mayor, in the case of state and local government employees; and employers. Lending policies vary considerably from fund to fund, with no uniform administrative practices followed. Prudence, market conditions, size of the fund, philosophy of the administrators, and other factors dictate how the funds might best be invested at any given time. In California, the massive PERS (Public Employees Retirement System) has a very large home loan program as does the STRS (State Teachers Retirement System).

Individual Retirement Accounts (IRAs) and Keogh Plans

As private pension programs became more popular with liberalized tax-deferred contributions for Individual Retirement Accounts for employees, and allowances under the Keogh Plan for self-employed persons, substantially more of these dollars are entering the capital markets. These funds are an important source of real estate financing on all levels. New money is being brought into the capital market from employers, employees, and the self-employed in what might be viewed as a captive market, since the steady inflow of such funds is often more stable and dependable than savings inflow into thrift institutions. (Pension funds accumulate until each member reaches retirement age, whereas savings strictly as time deposits are more volatile.)

Until recently, most pension funds had been invested in government securities and in corporate stocks and bonds. However, the rapid increase in the assets of pension funds and the desire to diversify these investments are causing some fund managers to look at real estate loans as an additional source for investment.

2.7 Government Regulatory Agencies

A variety of federal and state agencies govern activities and practices of institutional lenders. For real estate financing purposes, the most significant are briefly outlined below and discussed in greater depth in other chapters.

Massive changes in the regulatory structure at the federal level were instituted as a result of widespread failures of thrift institutions in the 1980s and early 1990s. A whole new alphabet soup of acronyms has replaced many of the old, beginning with the law itself, the ***Financial Institutions Reform, Recovery, and Enforcement Act (FIRREA)***, leading to the creation of many new federal agencies:

1. *Office of Thrift Supervision (OTS).* This is a branch of the U.S. Treasury. It was created by FIRREA to replace the Federal Home Loan Bank Board as the chief regulator of all savings banks whose deposits are federally insured.

2. *Savings Association Insurance Fund (SAIF).* This agency was created by FIRREA to replace the Federal Savings and Loan Insurance Corporation (FSLIC), which became insolvent. SAIF collects insurance premiums on checking and savings deposits from all federally insured savings associations. It is managed by the FDIC (Federal Deposit Insurance Corporation), but SAIF insurance premiums are kept separate from premiums paid by commercial and savings banks.

3. *Federal Deposit Insurance Corporation (FDIC).* This familiar federal agency insures deposits of up to designated amounts per account

for commercial and savings banks, and manages the Savings Association Insurance Fund as well as the Bank Insurance Fund.

4. *Federal Housing Finance Board (FHFB)*. This agency oversees mortgage lending by the 12 regional Federal Home Loan Banks. This regulatory function was previously performed by the Federal Home Loan Bank Board. Savings institutions that fail to meet so-called qualified thrift lender (QTL) requirements are not able to borrow or access funds from any of the Federal Home Loan Banks.

5. *Federal Reserve Bank Board (FRBB)*. This agency oversees the Federal Reserve System, regulates activities of commercial banks, and regulates the flow of money and credit, as discussed in Chapter 1.

6. *Federal Home Loan Mortgage Corporation (FHLMC)*. Popularly called Freddie Mac, this organization was created by Congress but it is effectively owned and operated by thrift institutions as they go about their business of buying and selling existing real estate loans—the "secondary mortgage market," detailed in Chapter 7.

7. *Office of Comptroller of the Currency (OCC)*. The OCC is the federal agency responsible for chartering and overseeing the operations of national banks and bank holding companies.

8. *California Department of Financial Institutions*. Under the jurisdiction of the California Business, Transportation and Housing Agency and a cabinet-level post, the Financial Commissioner supervises all state-chartered banks. If insured, state institutions also operate under supervision of the FHFB.

2.8 Trade Associations

In addition to statutory regulatory agencies, a variety of trade associations help foster and promote the interests of member firms. Membership is strictly voluntary but the benefits are great enough to provide broad appeal to lenders to join. It is axiomatic that where a community of interests exists, firms will band together in order to protect and enhance those interests.

Several important trade associations are the following:

1. *California League of Savings Institutions*. Headquartered in Los Angeles, this organization consists of both state and federally chartered California-based savings institutions.

2. *Mortgage Bankers Association of America (MBA)*. This trade association comprises the principal investors and lending interests in

the mortgage banking field. The organization and its members have as their chief interest the urban mortgage field. Membership combines into one group all of the leading lenders in the mortgage industry. For over a half century the MBA has devoted extensive research and study to providing better and more readily available mortgage financing so that large numbers of people in various income groups can acquire homes.

3. *American Bankers Association (ABA).* Commercial banks throughout the nation, both federally and state chartered, may join this association. This voluntary organization provides valuable financial data to member banks, government agencies, economists and researchers, and the public at large. The ABA also offers a broad educational program through the American Institute of Banking.

4. *National Association of Independent Mortgage Bankers (NAIMB).* This association consists of many members whose banks are not part of a large bank chain. Many independent bankers hold membership in the ABA as well.

5. *Institute of Life Insurance.* This institute, located in New York, comprises the voluntary membership of most of the 1,800 life insurance companies operating throughout the United States. Its *Life Insurance Fact Book* is published annually and is highly informative not only as to life insurance facts but also for those interested in real estate portfolios of member firms.

6. *National Association of Mortgage Brokers.* This is the lobbying group for the 75,000 loan brokers nationwide.

SUMMARY

Savings banks (thrifts), commercial banks, and life insurance companies are major providers of real estate mortgage funds. Each operates according to statutory provisions of federal and state laws, by-laws of the individual institutional lender, and self-imposed policies, which vary according to market conditions. In general, savings banks offer the highest loan-to-value ratios in the area of conventional loans, and they specialize in the financing of residential properties.

Commercial banks historically favored commercial and industrial properties but recently have been very active in residential properties. Another major bank role is in construction financing, since banks are more prone to quick turnover of deposits held in the form of checking (or demand) accounts. Life insurance companies have the broadest lending powers of the institutional lenders but favor only prime properties and large loan packages. They deal through loan correspondents in areas where loan demand is high but where they have no offices.

Besides policing themselves through individual efforts, institutional lenders (institutionals) are subjected to rules and regulations by various government agencies and trade associations. Federally chartered savings banks are regulated by the Federal Housing Finance Board and the Savings Association Insurance Fund, while state-chartered savings banks are supervised by the California Banking Commissioner. Federally chartered commercial banks are governed by the Federal Reserve Board of Governors, the Comptroller of the Currency, and the Federal Deposit Insurance Corporation, while the California Department of Banking oversees state-chartered commercial banks.

IMPORTANT TERMS AND CONCEPTS

Bridge loan

Commercial bank

Correspondents

Equity participation

Federal Deposit Insurance Corporation (FDIC)

Federal Home Loan Mortgage Corporation (FHLMC)

Federal Housing Finance Board

Federal Reserve Bank Board (FRBB)

Financial Institutions Reform, Recovery, and Enforcement Act (FIRREA)

Financial intermediary

Home Mortgage Disclosure Act

Institutional lenders

Interim loans

Life insurance company

Loan-to-value ratios

Lock-in clause

Mutual savings bank

Office of Thrift Supervision (OTS)

Pension funds

Private lenders

Rate lock-in

Savings Association Insurance Fund (SAIF)

Savings banks

Swing loan

Take-out loans

Thrift institutions

Time deposits

Trade associations

Usury

REVIEWING YOUR UNDERSTANDING

Questions for Discussion

1. Briefly explain the difference between a commercial bank and a savings bank (thrift).

2. List three lending characteristics for each of the following:
   a. savings bank
   b. commercial bank
   c. life insurance company

3. Identify one trend affecting the lending policies for each one of the principal lending institutions operating in California.

4. What is the difference between a regulatory agency and a trade association?

Multiple-Choice Questions

1. Which of the following is *not* an institutional lender?
   a. mortgage company.
   b. commercial bank.
   c. savings bank.
   d. life insurance company.

2. Which lender typically specializes in construction loans?
   a. life insurance company.
   b. mortgage company.
   c. savings bank.
   d. commercial bank.

3. A checking account is also known as a
   a. time deposit.
   b. demand deposit.
   c. certificate of deposit.
   d. personal account.

4. Variable annuities are most typically associated with
   a. commercial banks.
   b. mutual savings banks.
   c. life insurance companies.
   d. savings banks (thrifts).

5. The relatively sudden flow of funds out of thrift institutions into the stock market is called
   a. reverse annuity.
   b. disintermediation.
   c. reintermediation.
   d. variable annuity.

6. Which class of lenders experienced the greatest "crisis" in the 1980s?
   a. commercial banks.
   b. mutual savings banks.
   c. life insurance companies.
   d. savings and loan associations.

7. Loans combining construction and permanent financing are commonly referred to as
   a. dual.
   b. take-out.
   c. all-inclusive.
   d. combination.

8. Which institutional lender favors very large commercial property loans?
   a. savings banks.
   b. credit unions.
   c. life insurance companies.
   d. savings and loan associations.

9. Passbook savings accounts are technically
   a. time deposits.
   b. demand deposits.
   c. commercial deposits.
   d. industrial deposits.

10. Which law deregulated portions of the lending industry?
    a. Equal Credit Opportunity Act.
    b. Truth-in-Lending Act.
    c. Depository Institutions and Monetary Control Act.
    d. none of the above.

11. In their efforts to raise money for mortgage lending, savings banks have turned to such devices as
    a. mortgage-backed bonds.
    b. disintermediation.
    c. unsecured personal loans.
    d. all of the above.

12. The bulk of funds held by commercial banks is in the form of
    a. certificates of deposit (CDs).
    b. cash.
    c. demand deposits.
    d. securities.

13. Some institutional lenders have a threshold that requires private mortgage insurance for loan-to-value ratios that exceed:
    a. 50%
    b. 80%
    c. 70%
    d. 60%

14. A loan provision that prevents an early payoff of a loan prior to a set date is called
    a. a prepayment clause.
    b. a lock-in clause.
    c. a subordination clause.
    d. an acceleration clause.

15. Freddie Mac was established to
    a. provide insurance for savings accounts.
    b. govern the operations of savings banks.
    c. create a secondary market for savings banks.
    d. regulate checking accounts for savings banks.

16. The federal agency that replaced the Federal Home Loan Bank Board as the chief regulator of savings institutions is the
    a. Office of Thrift Supervision.
    b. Savings Association Fund.
    c. Resolution Trust Corporation.
    d. Federal Home Loan Mortgage Corporation.

17. Insuring the deposits of commercial banks and savings banks is the
    a. Office of Thrift Supervision.
    b. Savings Association Fund.
    c. Federal Home Loan Mortgage Corporation.
    d. Federal Deposit Insurance Corporation.

18. When a lender takes an upfront share of the income produced by a property it is called
    a. equity participation.
    b. a roll-over provision.
    c. a shared investment.
    d. intermediary subordination.

19. Which federal law tracks the lending practices of banks and thrift institutions to ensure fair borrower treatment?
    a. Borrower's Right's Act.
    b. Home Fairness Act.
    c. Resolution Trust Act.
    d. Community Reinvestment Act.

20. California-chartered banks are regulated through the
    a. Department of Thrift Supervision.
    b. Office of Comptroller.
    c. Department of Real Estate.
    d. Department of Financial Institutions.

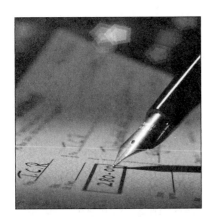

CHAPTER 3
NONINSTITUTIONAL LENDERS AND THE CALIFORNIA REAL PROPERTY LOAN LAW

PREVIEW

In Chapter 2, institutional lenders were described as real estate lenders whose activities are highly regulated by various state and federal agencies.

In this chapter you will study noninstitutional lenders—real estate lenders whose activities are not as strictly regulated as institutional lenders. Noninstitutional lenders include private parties, mortgage companies, syndicates, real estate investment trusts, pension and trust funds, endowment funds, and credit unions.

After completing this chapter, you should be able to:

1. List five major noninstitutional lenders.

2. Describe major provisions of the California Real Property Loan Law.

3. Discuss the role that mortgage correspondents, mortgage bankers, mortgage companies, and mortgage brokers play in real estate finance.

4. Discuss why pensions, trust funds, and credit unions are increasing in importance in the financing process.

5. Describe how and why the role of the real estate broker as a financial advisor is becoming increasingly challenging.

3.1 Private Party Lenders

Although the term ***private party lenders*** in its broadest sense refers to virtually all nongovernment lenders, for our purpose a private lender means a person who lends directly to another person. This narrow definition will help to distinguish a private lender from the other forms of noninstitutional lenders discussed in this chapter.

Lack of Structure

There is no formal structure to the private lender industry. Individuals ordinarily do not operate in concert with one another. Private lenders have no association such as those found with other forms of lenders and are, at best, highly fragmented and scattered throughout California. An individual may, of course, form a partnership or a corporation, but these are mere business organizations designed to facilitate the operation of the individual's investments into real estate trust deeds or mortgage loans.

Unlike institutional lenders, private individuals have fewer laws and regulations that restrict their lending activities. There are no uniform policies; practices, procedures, and policies vary considerably from one private lender to another. However, individuals can be subject to the usury statutes that dictate the maximum interest rate that may be legally charged. Exemptions from the usury law are discussed later in this chapter.

Types of Private Lenders

Direct Private Lenders

People invest in real estate loans for a variety of reasons, primarily because they are not satisfied with the returns paid on other forms of investments. For example, a long-term bank or thrift institution savings account might pay a depositor 5 percent interest. Despite the fact that the account is insured by the government up to a designated amount, the depositor may be dissatisfied with this low interest rate. After all, the bank or thrift institution will turn around and reloan the deposit money at a much higher rate of interest. In an effort to get a higher return, the potential depositor may seek to eliminate the intermediary and make direct loans on real estate. Of course, by eliminating the go-between, the private lender also eliminates the appraisal, loan screening, and other services provided by the intermediary. Thus, private lenders must perform these loan services themselves. On the plus side, however, where the risks are greater, the rewards for the private lender may also be greater in the form of higher interest rate yields.

Indirect Private Lenders

In order to obtain a higher interest rate or to overcome the loan screening burdens of direct lending, many private individuals place money through ***mortgage brokers***. People who have money to invest in real estate loans but do not know the market often turn to mortgage brokers to do their bidding for them in locating suitable transactions. Figure 3.1 shows how mortgage brokers bring a lender and a borrower together for real estate loans. The use of mortgage brokers helps to overcome the lack of knowledge and sophistication that characterizes the typical private lender. In addition, the commission for the mortgage broker's services is usually paid by the borrower, not the private lender.

Sellers as Private Lenders

In the process of selling their properties, sellers sometimes become lenders. Buyers either do not have enough money to pay cash down to the existing loan or a new loan, or choose not to tie up their capital in equity. Hence the seller is placed in the position of either having to turn down the offer, renegotiate more favorable terms, or "carry back paper" for the difference between the down payment plus a new loan and the sales price. The vast majority of these seller carryback loans are in the form of junior encumbrances, typically second trust deeds. On some occasions they may be first loans, where sellers are willing to finance the entire transaction themselves, such as on a free and clear property (property free of any loans). In effect, sellers become lenders by financing part or all of their equities.

It should also be mentioned that seller carryback loans are exempt from usury laws; that is, sellers can charge any interest rate they wish, as noted later in this chapter.

Figure 3.1 The role of the mortgage broker.

Characteristics of Private Lenders

Private lenders generally have some common characteristics, regardless of whether the loan is made directly by the individual or indirectly through a loan broker:

- Private lenders are for the most part less formal and therefore make highly subjective loan decisions, especially when making a loan directly to a borrower. On the other hand, mortgage brokers who represent some private lenders are usually very sophisticated.

- High interest rates are normally charged, due to the high risks involved. However, exceptions exist in seller carryback transactions where a relatively low rate may be acceptable due to offsetting benefits. To compensate for, say, a 6 percent rate, a seller might either increase the price of the property or be willing to settle for the lower rate when the rates quoted on new first loans are so high that buyers are unwilling to pay higher than market high rates on the junior loan.

- Most private lenders operate in the second trust deed market. As pointed out previously, this is often created by the dictates of the marketplace, when a seller carries back a second deed of trust in order to close the transaction. Frequently these second loans are thereafter sold to investors, usually at a discount, when the seller needs cash.

- Private lenders rarely make prime loans and almost never get involved in construction financing. (Prime loans are those that involve the least risk to lenders and are usually first liens.)

- Most loans are on single-family dwellings because this type of property is most familiar to the typical private investor, and also because the size of the loan is relatively modest.

- The vast majority of loans by private individuals are made within the local geographic areas.

- The term of a private loan is usually short—most commonly between two and five years—and often calls for a **balloon payment**.

- Monthly collections may be performed through a mortgage company or financial institution, though individual lenders may in some cases collect themselves. The setup and collection fees charged by commercial and savings banks are relatively small, since these institutions are interested in obtaining the customer's account. Some offer free collection service when the customer maintains a minimum balance in a savings or checking account.

- A large number of private party loans are seller carrybacks.

3.2 Usury Law

Many states have passed laws establishing the maximum rate of interest that can be charged on various types of loans. Interest rates that exceed the maximum rate are considered usurious and therefore illegal. In some instances if a lender is found guilty of usury, the borrower would not have to pay any interest!

In California the maximum rate for loans secured by real property is the greater of 10 percent or 5 percent above the Federal Reserve Bank discount rate, unless the lender is exempt from the law. California regulations exempt from the usury law institutional lenders such as banks and their loan *correspondents*, thrift institutions, and life insurance companies. Also exempt from usury laws are noninstitutional lenders including *mortgage companies*, industrial loan companies, *credit unions*, personal property brokers, owners who carry back paper when they sell, and any transaction that uses a real estate broker. However, direct private lenders are not exempt. For example, real estate loans from regulated institutional lenders can be at any rate, whereas an actual direct hard money real estate loan (not a seller carryback loan) from a private lender is not exempt, unless a real estate licensee is handling the transaction.

The pros and cons of usury laws are currently being debated. Proponents believe that usury laws protect consumers against certain greedy lenders, while opponents believe usury laws restrict the supply of loan funds and drive some borrowers to do business with illegal loan sharks. See Figure 3.2.

Figure 3.2 A loan shark.

3.3 Mortgage Companies

The terms **mortgage bankers**, **mortgage brokers**, and **mortgage companies** frequently are used interchangeably, but they are not the same. These entities are not thrift institutions, nor are they depository institutions, but they do assist by bringing the borrower together with a lender and charge a fee for this service.

Structure and Types of Mortgage Agencies

Mortgage bankers are generally incorporated businesses that can make loans with their own funds or through a line of credit. The mortgage banker originates, finances ("funds"), and closes loans secured by real estate and then resells them to various investors.

When a mortgage banking company represents a life insurance company, bank, thrift association, pension fund, or other lender, it is called a **mortgage correspondent**. It "corresponds" on behalf of its principals in dealing with prospective borrowers. The mortgage correspondent is paid a fee in exchange for originating, processing, closing, and frequently servicing loans. The mortgage company may be given exclusive territories, in which case the correspondent will be entitled to a fee, even if it had not actively solicited the loan; or it may be nonexclusive, in which case the correspondent is in effect in competition with the lenders that it represents. Whatever the type of arrangement, mortgage loan correspondents serve a very valuable function in real estate financing for lenders whose headquarters or principal offices are located great distances from the properties on which they make loans. Correspondents have been especially successful in the Far West, particularly in California.

Although most mortgage companies act as correspondents in investing others' funds, there are many firms that invest their own funds exclusively. Another category of mortgage lender is a hybrid, both investing money into real estate trust deeds and mortgages for others in an agency or fiduciary capacity and investing its own funds in the role of a principal.

Mortgage loan brokers are in the business of locating borrowers and lenders and arranging loans between them, and in the process they earn a commission or fee. As such the loan broker takes no risk of loss. Another distinction between a *mortgage banker* and a *mortgage (or loan) broker* is that mortgage bankers frequently service the loans of the lenders that they represent, whereas loan brokers usually do not.

Lending Characteristics of Mortgage Companies

Mortgage companies that do not loan their own funds are restricted in their lending activities to the same restrictions that govern their principal(s). Thus, if a California mortgage correspondent or banker represents an eastern life insurance company, the correspondent would have the same loan-to-value limitations placed on its loans as the insurance company has. This is easy to understand in that the mortgage broker is a mere agent and stands, therefore, in the shoes of its principal, the lender. Aside from the legal strictures, the correspondent reflects the lending philosophy, policies, and practices of those lenders—whether giant institutionals or individuals—that it represents. This applies to both construction and permanent loans.

In California, mortgage companies are licensed by either the Department of Corporations or the Department of Real Estate and they are subject to lending and other general business regulations.

Mortgage companies may also engage in a number of related real estate activities. These include brokerage, development, construction, and property management. This is especially true when activity in the mortgage market slows down.

3.4 Real Property Loan Law

Subprime Borrowers and Predatory Lending

Subprime loans usually are granted to homeowners with low credit scores who wish to refinance their property. Occasionally, subprime loans also are granted to credit-damaged or lower-income people who wish to buy a home. These loans are granted at higher interest rates and fees to reflect the additional risk incurred by the lender.

Consumer advocates and various government agencies are becoming increasing concerned that some lenders may be taking advantage of the situation by changing excessive interest and fees beyond a reasonable markup for the additional risk of granting loans to subprime borrowers. This is frequently called predatory lending.

Of special concern is the practice of enticing subprime homeowners into to a series of refinances in which their equity is stripped away by high fees and balloon payments that lead to still-another larger refinance, and the process is repeated until the homeowner's equity is depleted, often resulting in foreclosure.

As pointed out earlier, individuals may become **indirect lenders** by investing through an intermediary, called a mortgage broker. In California, this intermediary must be a licensed real estate broker, and is hence called a loan broker, who is governed by Sections 10240 through 10248 of the California Business and Professions Code (B&P) (Article 7: Real Property Loans). This segment of the real estate law is popularly referred to as the "Mortgage Loan Broker Law" by real estate practitioners.

Purpose of the Mortgage Loan Broker Law

The purpose of the **Real Property Mortgage Loan Law** is to protect certain borrowers who take out small loans secured by real estate. The law requires that prospective borrowers be supplied with complete loan information. In other words, the broker must give the applicant a filled-in **Mortgage Loan Disclosure Statement** before the loan is agreed upon. This disclosure statement will give the borrower a reasonably close picture of the final amount of the loan.

Figure 3.3 is a reproduction of the Mortgage Loan Disclosure Statement produced by the California Department of Real Estate. It contains information about estimated costs, expenses, and commissions to be paid by the applicant for a loan. It also informs the borrower of the approximate net amount that will be received from the loan after paying commissions, costs and expenses, payoffs on liens against the property, and other incidental charges.

Exceptions to the Mortgage Loan Broker Law

It is easier to state which lenders and what transactions are not covered by the law than to list those that are covered. *Exempt from the Real Property Loan Law are:*

- Regulated institutional lenders.

- Purchase money transactions in which a seller carries back the loan as part of the sale price. However, if a seller is in the business of carrying back loans in eight or more transactions per year, the Mortgage Loan Broker Law does apply.

- Loans secured by first trust deeds when the principal amount is $30,000 or more.

- Loans secured by junior trust deeds when the principal amount is $20,000 or more.

STATE OF CALIFORNIA   DEPARTMENT OF REAL ESTATE
                                                                                           MORTGAGE LENDING
MORTGAGE LOAN DISCLOSURE STATEMENT (Borrower)

RE 882 (Rev. 10/05)

Name of Broker	Business Address

I.   SUMMARY OF LOAN TERMS
    A. PRINCIPAL AMOUNT $ _____
    B. ESTIMATED DEDUCTIONS FROM PRINCIPAL AMOUNT
        1. Costs and Expenses (See Paragraph III-A) $ _____
      *2. Broker Commission/Origination Fee (See Paragraph III-B) $ _____
        3. Lender Origination Fee/Discounts (See Paragraph III-B) $ _____
        4. Additional compensation will/may be received from lender not deducted from loan
            proceeds.   ☐ YES $_____ *(if known)*   ☐ NO
        5. Amount to be Paid on Authorization of Borrower (See Paragraph III-C) $ _____
    C. ESTIMATED CASH PAYABLE TO BORROWER (A LESS B) $ _____

II. GENERAL INFORMATION ABOUT LOAN
    A. If this loan is made, borrower will be required to pay the principal and interest at _____% per year, payable as follows:
        _____ *(number of payments)*   _____ *(monthly, quarterly, annual)*   payments of
        $_____ and a FINAL/BALLOON payment of $_____ to pay off the loan in full.

        NOTICE TO BORROWER: IF YOU DO NOT HAVE THE FUNDS TO PAY THE BALLOON PAYMENT WHEN IT COMES DUE, YOU MAY HAVE TO OBTAIN A NEW LOAN AGAINST YOUR PROPERTY TO MAKE THE BALLOON PAYMENT. IN THAT CASE, YOU MAY AGAIN HAVE TO PAY COMMISSIONS, FEES AND EXPENSES FOR THE ARRANGING OF THE NEW LOAN. IN ADDITION, IF YOU ARE UNABLE TO MAKE THE MONTHLY PAYMENTS OR THE BALLOON PAYMENT, YOU MAY LOSE THE PROPERTY AND ALL OF YOUR EQUITY THROUGH FORECLOSURE. KEEP THIS IN MIND IN DECIDING UPON THE AMOUNT AND TERMS OF THIS LOAN.

    B. This loan will be evidenced by a promissory note and secured by a deed of trust on property identified as (street address or legal description):
        _____
        _____

    C. 1. Liens presently against this property (do not include loan being applied for):

Nature of Lien	Priority	Lienholder's Name	Amount Owing

        2. Liens that will remain against this property after the loan being applied for is made or arranged (include loan being applied for):

Nature of Lien	Priority	Lienholder's Name	Amount Owing

        NOTICE TO BORROWER: Be sure that you state the amount of all liens as accurately as possible. If you contract with the broker to arrange this loan, but it cannot be arranged because you did not state these liens correctly, you may be liable to pay commissions, fees and expenses even though you do not obtain the loan.

    D. If borrower pays all or part of the loan principal before it is due, a PREPAYMENT PENALTY computed as follows may be charged:
        _____
        _____

    E. Late Charges: ☐ YES, see loan documents   ☐ NO

    F. The purchase of credit life and/or credit disability insurance by a borrower is not required as a condition of making this loan.

Figure 3.3 Sample mortgage loan disclosure statement.

RE 882 — Reverse

III. DEDUCTIONS FROM LOAN PROCEEDS

   A. Estimated Maximum Costs and Expenses of Arranging the Loan to be Paid Out of Loan Principal

PAYABLE TO: Broker   Others

   1. Appraisal fee
   2. Escrow fee
   3. Title insurance policy
   4. Notary fees
   5. Recording fees
   6. Credit investigation fees
   7. Other costs and expenses:

   Total Costs and Expenses $ _____

* B. Compensation
   1. Broker Commission/Origination Fee $ _____
   2. Lender Origination Fee/Discounts $ _____

   C. Estimated Payment to be Made Out of Loan Principal on Authorization of Borrower

PAYABLE TO: Broker   Others

   1. Fire or other hazard insurance premiums
   2. Credit life or disability insurance premiums
       (See Paragraph II-F)
   3. Beneficiary statement fees
   4. Reconveyance and similar fees
   5. Discharge of existing liens against property

   6. Other:

   Total to be Paid on Authorization of Borrower $ _____

If this loan is secured by a first deed of trust on dwellings in a principal amount of less than $30,000 or secured by a junior lien on dwellings in a principal amount of less than $20,000, the undersigned licensee certifies that the loan will be made in compliance with Article 7 of Chapter 3 of the Real Estate Law.

* This loan may/will/will not *(delete two)* be made wholly or in part from broker-controlled funds as defined in Section 10241(j) of the Business and Professions Code.

* **NOTICE TO BORROWER:** This disclosure statement may be used if the broker is acting as an agent in arranging the loan by a third person or if the loan will be made with funds owned or controlled by the broker. If the broker indicates in the above statement that the loan "may" be made out of broker-controlled funds, the broker must notify the borrower prior to the close of escrow if the funds to be received by the borrower are in fact broker-controlled funds.

Name of Broker   *License Number*   *Broker Representative*   *License Number*

_____OR_____

Signature of Broker   *Signature*

NOTICE TO BORROWER

DO NOT SIGN THIS STATEMENT UNTIL YOU HAVE READ AND UNDERSTAND ALL OF THE INFORMATION IN IT. ALL PARTS OF THE FORM MUST BE COMPLETED BEFORE YOU SIGN.

Borrower hereby acknowledges the receipt of a copy of this statement. *Dated* _____

Borrower   *Borrower*

BROKER REVIEW

Signature of real estate broker after review of this statement as required by Section 2725 of the Real Estate Commissioner's Regulations.

Dated   *Real Estate Broker or Designated Representative*

Department of Real Estate license information telephone number: (916) 227-0931, or check license status at www.dre.ca.gov

Figure 3.3 Sample mortgage loan disclosure statement *(continued).*

Maximum Commissions

The maximum commission rates mortgage loan brokers can charge are regulated by law as shown in Table 3.1.

As the table shows, the shorter the term of the loan, the less commission the broker may charge as a percentage of the face amount of the loan. On loans of $30,000 and over for first liens, and $20,000 for junior liens, the broker may charge as much as the borrower agrees to

Table 3.1 Maximum commissions.

	PERCENTAGE COMMISSION			
Type of Loan	Less Than Two Years	Two Years but Less Than Three	Three Years and Over	Exempt Transactions
First trust deeds	5%	5%	10%	Loans of $30,000 and over
Junior trust deeds	5%	10%	15%	Loans of $20,000 and over

Table 3.2 Maximum charges for other costs and expenses.

LOAN AMOUNT	Under $7,801	$7,801 to $13,999	$14,000 to $29,999	First Loans of $30,000 and over and Junior Loans of $20,000 and over
MAXIMUM CHARGES	$390	5% of loan	$700	No legal limitations
	—But not to exceed actual costs and expenses—			

pay. Even for loans covered by the law, however, competition frequently keeps the rates below the maximum allowed.

Other Costs and Expenses

Mortgage brokers are also limited as to the amount of costs and expenses, other than commissions, that they may charge a borrower under the Real Property Loan Law. As shown in paragraph III A of the form in Figure 3.3, these costs include fees for appraisal, escrow, title insurance, notary, recording, and credit investigation. Such costs and expenses may not exceed 5 percent of the amount of the loan. However, if 5 percent of the loan is less than $390, the broker may charge up to that amount, provided that the charges do not exceed actual costs and expenses paid, incurred, or reasonably earned by the broker. Regardless of the size of the loan, as long as it comes under the Real Property Loan Law, the borrower cannot be charged more than $700 for miscellaneous costs and expenses.

To simplify, the foregoing costs and expenses can be translated into chart form, as shown in Table 3.2.

As the table shows, the broker may charge as much as the borrower is willing to pay on first loans of $30,000 and above, or on junior loans of $20,000 and over. Thus it is possible for a borrower to net less cash from a loan that exceeds the limits imposed by law than one would have received had the principal amount of the loan been lower than the limits. Again, however, competition plays a significant role in keeping down the costs and expenses.

Balloon Payments

As mentioned earlier, the term balloon payment describes the final payment owing when an amortized loan becomes due if this amount is more than twice the amount of the smallest installment. Under the Real Property Loan Law, a balloon payment is prohibited if (1) the term of the loan is for six years or less, and (2) the loan is secured by the dwelling place of the borrower. Again, this provision does not apply to loans carried by sellers. These particular balloon payment rules apply only if the loan is covered by the Real Property Loan Law.

Insurance

A borrower is not required to purchase credit life or disability insurance as a condition of obtaining the loan. However, the lender can insist for self-protection and by the terms of the trust deed that fire and hazard insurance be obtained on improved property until the loan has been repaid. If licensed to sell such insurance, the loan broker may also act as the insurance agent for the borrower, but borrowers are not obligated to purchase the coverage through the mortgage loan broker. They may purchase insurance from their own insurance agent.

Miscellaneous Provisions of the Mortgage Loan Broker Law

Mortgage brokers are prohibited from charging loan servicing or collection fees to be paid by the borrower. Late charges, if any, may not exceed $5 or 10 percent of the principal and interest part of an installment payment, whichever is greater. If the installment payment is made within 10 days of its due date, however, no late charge can be assessed.

3.5 Syndications

Loosely defined, a **syndication** is an association of two or more people who combine their financial resources for the purpose of achieving specific investment objectives. Investment capital can be pooled or combined for the purpose of financing real estate transactions or for the purchase of real property. Syndicates may take the legal form of a limited partnership, which is the most favored in California; a general partnership; corporation; real estate investment trust; or a joint venture.

Syndicates are formed for a variety of reasons, including these:

1. *Improved purchasing power* obtained by combining the resources of many who could not afford to purchase individually, but through the principle of leverage could acquire a relatively high-priced property.

2. *Better bargaining power*, again due to the application of the principle of leverage, wherein a larger capital base can command lower prices, and in which larger properties can be acquired, where lower operating expense ratios are usually present.

3. *Diversification*, which enables investors to spread their capital and thereby limit their loss exposure in any one investment.

4. *Professional management and administration* of the real estate portfolio in order to minimize costs and maximize the benefits. Professional services may be too costly for the average investor and disproportionate to capital investment. By pooling resources with others, however, specialists such as attorneys, appraisers, real estate brokers, accountants, and investment analysts are affordable.

Individuals may participate in a syndication and collectively invest in a wide variety of real estate ventures. There are basically three types of syndication: (1) equity syndicates, which purchase real estate; (2) mortgage (or debt) syndicates, which grant loans to others for the purchase of real property, creating creditor–debtor relationships; and (3) a hybrid of these two, combining both equity and debt.

3.6 Real Estate Investment Trusts and Endowment Funds

The **Real Estate Investment Trust (REIT)** is a creature of the federal tax law. It was created in 1960 with the goal of encouraging small investors to pool their resources with others in order to raise venture capital for real estate transactions. It has been called the "mutual fund" of the real estate business. Just as mutual funds invest in a diversified portfolio of corporate stocks and bonds, REITs invest in a diversified portfolio of real estate and mortgage investments, using a large number of investors who combine or pool their funds.

Types of REITs

As with syndications, there are three types of REITs:

1. *Equity trusts*—investors buy income-producing property and obtain their income from current income and capital gains upon the disposition of appreciated properties.

2. *Mortgage trusts*—investors loan money secured by real estate and obtain their income from interest and loan fees.

3. *Hybrid trusts*, which are a combination of these two types.

To qualify as a trust, there are many tests that must be met, such as the requirement that at least 95 percent of its ordinary income be distributed to the investors each year to avoid the double taxation aspect of some corporations. The legal ramifications of REITs are beyond the scope of this book; anyone interested in forming or participating in REITs should seek legal counsel.

REITs as a Source of Financing

The favorable income tax incentives of REITs attract funds from thousands of small investors, which, in turn, become an important source of real estate financing. REITs concentrate on income-producing properties. REITs generally do not limit themselves to one area or type of loan, but diversify their holdings both as to type of property and geographical location.

Lending activities of REITs center primarily around land development and take-out loans for such projects as condominiums, office buildings, shopping centers, garden and high-rise apartment complexes, hotels and motels, industrial properties, warehouses, and major single-family subdivision developments.

The Ups and Downs of REITs

During the economic crisis of the 1970s, many REITs folded under the pressures of poor management, excessive speculation, withdrawal and cancellation of take-out commitments, termination of bank lines of credit, poor credit analysis, excess building in many parts of the country (particularly in the condominium market and in recreational projects), and sagging demand.

In the 1980s, to restore confidence in the REIT, concessions worked out between REITs and the banking and securities industries slowly revived REITs. This slow revival continued until the late 1990s, when a hot stock market put a damper on REITs. By 2001, the stock market declined and some money began to flow back into REITs. Within a few years, REITs were once again booming.

Pension Funds

Pension funds collect monthly contributions from workers, and occasionally from the employer, and then invest the proceeds in an attempt to create a lump sum of money upon which the worker may draw upon at retirement age. Examples include the California State Teachers Retirement Fund and various union funds, such as the United Auto Workers. The bulk of pension funds are invested in traditional securities, such as stocks, bonds, and various government instruments and are normally not used to make a direct loan in the real estate market.

However, with the advent of mortgage-backed securities, pension funds indirectly are becoming a significant player in the real estate market though the purchase of existing real estate loans in the secondary market. When a pension fund buys an existing loan from a traditional real estate lender, it gives said lender the funds to make another direct real estate loan to a new borrower. Although there have been cases in which pension funds were used directly to fund certain real estate projects, for the most part, pension funds enter into the real estate market via the purchase of already-existing loans.

However, a trend is developing in which pension funds are being used to help the contributor to the fund purchase a home under favorable loan terms. The best examples are the teacher and state employee pension programs, which help their contributors acquire a home in California's high-priced housing market.

Endowment Funds

Endowment funds of colleges and universities, hospitals, cemeteries, charitable foundations, and other endowed institutions operate like pension funds. They receive their funds in the form of gifts and attempt to invest in "safe" mortgages that will offer high returns. Accordingly, they offer a good source of financing for commercial and industrial properties, and in sale-leaseback arrangements. Many commercial banks and mortgage companies handle investments for endowment funds.

3.7 Credit Unions and Finance Companies

A credit union is a mutual, voluntary, cooperative organization of people who agree to save their money together and to make loan to each other. Originally, credit unions were formed by members of a particular group, commonly by occupational or professional affiliation. Today, credit unions are formed without any occupational or professional affiliation. There are credit unions throughout the United States, representing many millions of members. Figure 3.4 discusses some impact of their growing role.

For the most part, credit union lending in real estate has been short term. Some attempts at long-term loans have been tried in some areas of California and are working. Savings in credit unions are expected to grow significantly, since there is no longer any restriction on the rate of interest they can pay to their depositor-members.

Finance Companies

Although involved chiefly in personal and consumer loans, **finance companies** (also known as credit companies or industrial banks), are increasing their participation in real estate lending. These are normally high-risk loans with high rates and short-term duration, typically less than seven years, secured by a combination of real and personal property. Most are junior trust deeds. The typical borrower is one who does not qualify for a prime loan from a thrift institution or bank. Some finance companies continue to make interim loans for construction projects, with interest rates that are usually much greater than the prime rate.

Figure 3.4 The growing role of credit unions.

3.8 Financial Advisory Role of the Real Estate Broker

With many real estate agents increasing their knowledge and their access to high-speed computers, it is only logical that they broaden the scope of their real estate activities, including helping their clients—those to whom the agent has just sold a home—obtain financing, and collect additional compensation for their efforts. Real estate agents are in a prime position to fulfill the mortgage needs of their clients.

Computerized Loan Origination

With advances in automated lending services by institutional lenders, some real estate brokers and salespersons assist buyers with loans through their computers, dubbed **computerized loan origination**, or CLO for short. This does not make you a loan officer. But your California license does permit you as agent to access lenders via a terminal tied into a lender's computer containing that lender's underwriting requirements and other essential data so that agents can help clients obtain the best financing. Agents are able to offer loan comparisons that allow borrowers to quickly see the amount of finance charges and closing costs, and to compare fixed vs. ARM rates and other loan programs and features before making a decision. With full disclosure, real estate agents may collect a fee for this service. However, regulations mandate that the agent must perform actual services to legally collect a fee. Recent court cases have emphasized that collecting referral fees carries with it personal liability for providing accurate loan information that is compatible to the needs of the client. In light of these events, many real estate agents refer loan questions to mortgage brokers and/or lenders to avoid getting into areas beyond their level of expertise.

Buyer-Borrower Going Directly On-Line to Obtain a Real Estate Loan

Although this will be covered in more detail later in the book, it should be noted here that with the surge of Internet use, coupled with heavy website advertising by lenders and mortgage brokers, many consumers are obtaining real estate loans on-line. If this trend continues to expand, it could diminish the financial advisory role of real estate sales agents, and also reduce the need for face-to-face interaction between borrower and lender. Welcome to the world of cyberspace underwriting!

SUMMARY

Noninstitutional lenders include private parties, mortgage companies, syndicates, a variety of funds, and credit unions. Compared with institutional lenders, there are fewer restrictions placed upon their lending activities.

Private lenders include direct private lenders, indirect private lenders, and sellers who carry back purchase money trust deeds. They deal primarily in junior loans of comparatively small amounts.

Mortgage bankers and mortgage companies are usually incorporated businesses that act as agents, or loan correspondents, for institutional lenders. As such they are generally subject to the same laws and regulations as their principals. Many mortgage bankers also lend out their own funds, while mortgage brokers do not.

Under the Real Property Loan Law, mortgage loan brokers are limited as to the amount of costs, expenses, and commissions they may charge borrowers. These restrictions apply only to first loans of less than $30,000 and junior loans of less than $20,000.

Syndicates and real estate investment trusts each pool the funds of many people to invest in real estate and mortgages. In theory, they should be able to offer improved purchasing power, stronger bargaining positions, diversification, and professional management of their portfolios. But, to date, their success has been mixed.

Pension funds, trust funds, endowment funds, and credit unions are playing ever-expanding roles in financing real estate transactions, particularly where the traditional sources of financing are unwilling or unable to lend.

Computerization and rapidly expanding Internet use are expected to continue to change the way real estate loans are analyzed and granted.

IMPORTANT TERMS AND CONCEPTS

Balloon payment

Credit unions

Direct private lender

Endowment funds

Finance company

Indirect private lender

Mortgage banker

Mortgage broker

Mortgage loan correspondent

Mortgage Loan Disclosure Statement

On-line loans

Real estate investment trust (REIT)

Real Property (Mortgage) Loan Law

Syndication

Usury law

REVIEWING YOUR UNDERSTANDING

Questions for Discussion

1. Differentiate between institutional and noninstitutional lenders.

2. What is the chief difference between direct private lenders and indirect private lenders?

3. How do sellers of real estate help finance the sale? To what extent are they governed by the usury law?

4. Who is exempt from the California Usury Law?

5. Distinguish among the following:
   a. mortgage banker
   b. mortgage company
   c. mortgage broker
   d. mortgage loan correspondent

6. What is a syndicate? How does it differ from a real estate investment trust?

Multiple-Choice Questions

1. The law specifically governing the amount of commissions of loan brokers is called the
   a. Real Estate Law.
   b. Real Property Loan Law.
   c. Mortgage Loan Disclosure Law.
   d. Real Property Securities Act.

2. The Real Property Loan Law is embodied in the
   a. Civil Code.
   b. Code of Civil Procedures.
   c. Real Estate Code.
   d. Business and Professions Code.

3. Exempt under the Real Property Loan Law are
   a. first trust deeds of under $30,000.
   b. second trust deeds of under $20,000.
   c. purchase money loans carried back by sellers.
   d. loans maturing in more than six years.

4. As a mortgage broker, you have arranged a loan for $17,000 secured by a second trust deed on an owner-occupied home valued at $400,000. The first loan has a balance of $344,000 and carries an interest rate of 6%. The new $17,000 second loan is payable at $141.67 per month with an interest rate of 10%, all due and payable in four years. The expenses charged the borrower are $700 for actual cost, plus a $1,700 commission. This transaction constitutes a violation of the Real Property Loan Law because the:
   a. combined loans exceed the allowable maximum of 90% of the property's value.
   b. balloon payment is due in less than six years.
   c. monthly payment, when annualized, amounts to more than 10% and is therefore usurious.
   d. charges for actual costs and commission exceed the allowable limits.

5. Above in Question #4, what is the maximum commission that could be charged? (Hint: Review Table 3.1)
   a. $850
   b. $1,700
   c. $2,100
   d. none of the above

6. An owner of a small condominium lists the property for $400,000. After two months a broker submits an offer for $370,000 and the seller counters for $385,000, which the buyer accepts. The buyer's acceptance included a $2,000 deposit and the following terms: 10% down, a new first of $300,000 and the seller to carry back the difference. This seller carry back is an example of a/an:
   a. hard money loan.
   b. purchase money loan.
   c. installment sales contract.
   d. secondary market loan.

7. In Question #6, ignoring financing fees and other cost, the amount of the seller carry back second trust deed will be:
   a. $46,500
   b. $38,500
   c. $34,650
   d. $31,500

8. The most popular organizational form of real estate syndication in California is the
   a. general partnership.
   b. living trust.
   c. limited partnership.
   d. real estate investment trust.

9. An organized group of people who agree to save their money and to make loans to one another is called a
   a. syndication.
   b. credit union.
   c. pension fund.
   d. trust fund.

10. As a rule, credit unions most often deal with which of the following types of loans?
    a. apartment property loans.
    b. short-term consumer loans.
    c. industrial property loans.
    d. commercial property loans.

11. What is popularly called the "mutual fund" of the real estate business?
    a. pension fund.
    b. credit union.
    c. syndication.
    d. real estate investment trust.

12. Under the Real Property Loan Law, before a loan can be made, a loan broker must provide the applicant with
    a. an escrow closing statement.
    b. a Mortgage Loan Disclosure Statement.
    c. a RESPA Disclosure Statement.
    d. a deposit receipt.

13. A balloon payment is
    a. the same as a lump sum payment due on a straight note at maturity.
    b. a term used to describe a prepayment penalty.
    c. any payment made on a loan when the sales price has been inflated.
    d. any payment on a loan that is more than double the amount of the regular payment.

14. A mortgage loan broker who is licensed to sell insurance
    a. may legally require the borrower to obtain hazard insurance as a condition of making a loan on improved property.
    b. cannot, by law, act as the insurance agent of the borrower.
    c. may legally require credit life and disability insurance as a condition of making a loan.
    d. need not disclose this fact to a borrower-applicant, as long as his or her insurance company operates under another name.

15. California law sets the usury maximum for certain limited types of loans secured by real property at
    a. 10 percent.
    b. the discount rate charged by the Fed.
    c. 10 percent, or 5 points above the current Fed discount rate, whichever is higher.
    d. 5 points above the prime rate.

16. Who is *not* exempt from California's usury law?
    a. private hard money lenders who make direct loans.
    b. commercial banks.
    c. transactions involving a real estate broker.
    d. seller who carries back a loan on behalf of the buyer of an owner-occupied home.

17. The chief characteristic of private lenders is that they invest
    a. their own funds.
    b. in prime real estate loans.
    c. large sums of money in any one loan.
    d. primarily in commercial real estate properties.

18. The trend toward on-line loan services is
    a. making the real estate loan market less competitive.
    b. reducing the choice of financing packages for borrowers.
    c. not subject to government regulations.
    d. expected to increase in the future.

19. To prevent from being taxed on its income, an REIT must distribute annually at least what percent of its ordinary income to its shareholders?
    a. 100%
    b. 95%
    c. 90%
    d. 85%

20. Which of the following, using a line of credit, lends its "own" money?
    a. mortgage broker.
    b. mortgage banker.
    c. loan agent.
    d. real estate agent.

CASE & POINT
Fair or Foul? The Use of Yield-Spread Premiums

Subprime borrowers are consumers with lower credit scores as the result of less-than-wonderful handling of financial responsibilities or have personal problems, such as major health costs, loss of job, and so on. If they own a home, frequently they turn to the equity in their home for additional funds. These homeowners are called subprime borrowers.

Many mortgage companies specialize in the refinancing of homes owned by subprime borrowers. They use promotional slogans such as "Call us even if your credit is less than perfect," " We understand and will listen," "Call us even it you have been turned down by other lenders," "Pay no loan fees or closing costs," and so on. They saturate the airways via radio, television, and pop-up ads on the Internet.

According the Center for Responsible Lending (www.responsible lending.org), "In a high percentage of these subprime loans ... as many as 90% ... brokers receive a fee known as a 'yield spread premium' (YSP). A YSP is a cash bonus that a broker receives from a lender for placing borrowers in a loan with a higher interest than what the lender would otherwise accept. The higher the interest rate, the higher the premium received by the broker." That website mentions a case in which a single mother took out a loan for $43,750 and thought she was paying 10%, but the actual rate was 13.74%. For this, the grateful lender paid the broker a yield spread premium of $2,680 above and beyond the regular mortgage broker commission.

Questions

1. Does this YSP motivate mortgage brokers to talk borrowers into paying a higher rate than what a lender would be willing to accept just to increase their take on the loan? In other words, the lender might lend at a lower rate if asked, but the mortgage broker does not tell the borrower that information. In the lending industry, this is called "interest rate steering."

2. Although in many cases the payment of a YSP is legal, is it ethical?

3. Mortgage brokers frequently defend the payment of YSP on the grounds that they helped a person get a loan who otherwise might not have the skills to obtain the loan or who might not be able to pay the closing costs associated with getting a loan. They point out that frequently the mortgage broker uses the YSP to help the borrower pay for some of the closing costs. Discuss.

4. According to the Center for Responsible Lending noted above, "Not all loans with YSPs are abusive, but because they are permitted and easy to hide, unscrupulous brokers can make excessive profits without adding value to borrowers." What are your thoughts on the use of YSPs in the real estate lending industry?

CHAPTER 4
ADJUSTABLE RATE AND OTHER ALTERNATIVE MORTGAGE INSTRUMENTS

PREVIEW

Adjustable rate mortgages (ARMs) and other alternative mortgage instruments (AMIs) are financing instruments that compete against the standard fixed rate, fully amortized loan program. This competition has been evolving for over 30 years.

There is a dizzying choice of mortgages, both traditional and nontraditional, particularly with adjustable rate mortgages (ARMs), each with enormous number of variations, combinations, and permutations. For example, suppose you're considering a five-year ARM loan. This begs answers to the question, what type of five-year ARM: interest only? Option ARM interest only with 20 percent down? Option ARM minimum payment? The variation that finally is selected will determine the initial interest rate, initial monthly payment, rate adjustment after five years, mortgage balance at the end of five years, and so on. With hundreds of different home loan products in the marketplace, buyers are afforded opportunities to get mortgages that better fit their specific requirements.

After completing this chapter, you should be able to:

1. **Discuss why, under certain market conditions, the fixed rate mortgage may not be popular with some lenders.**

Note: You'll encounter some math in this chapter, but all problems have been completed for you and you can jump ahead to Chapter 13 to see how they are solved using two different calculators, the TI BA Real Estate Calculator and the HP 12C.

2. **List and briefly describe five types of alternative mortgage instruments.**

3. **Explain how negative amortization works.**

4. **Give reasons why balloon mortgages are not favored by consumers.**

5. **Demonstrate how a reverse annuity mortgage may be helpful for some older homeowners.**

6. **Compare the differences between 15-year loans and biweekly loan payments, and the payments on a standard 30-year loan.**

4.1 Objectives and Rationale

The principal objective of ARMs and AMIs is to transfer some of the risk of continually rising inflation from the lender to the borrower, while at the same time tailoring loans more closely to the borrower's financial circumstances. There is a money revolution in this country. Americans are becoming better informed about money and altering the ways in which they think about and handle money, and the revolt is challenging the nation's financial institutions.

To remain competitive, many lenders who traditionally granted only standard fixed interest rate loans need to make changes to meet market needs. What is the driving force behind this change? There is no single cause, but the most notable are low, but steady, inflation; fluctuating interest rates; the advent of mortgage-backed securities; economic uncertainties; and rapid changes in information technology (I.T.).

Purpose of Adjustable Rate and Other Alternative Loans

Alternative real estate loans have been recommended by some financial experts and real estate economists for many years. Here are some of the reasons.

Historically, lenders have a problem with cycles of tight and loose money. This unsteady flow of funds is disruptive to their operations and to the housing industry. When money is tight, it flows out of thrift institutions because depositors can obtain higher yields elsewhere—the phenomenon described in Chapter 1 as disintermediation.

Advocates of alternative loans say that this problem can be reduced by using **adjustable rate mortgages**. If money gets tight and interest rates rise, the thrift institutions should be allowed to increase the rate they pay their depositors in order to prevent an outflow of savings.

However, in order to pay higher interest on savings accounts, lenders must receive a higher interest rate on their existing loans. With an adjustable rate mortgage, lenders could increase interest rates on their existing loans when they need to increase the interest rate to attract or keep savings accounts. This overcomes the problem referred to as "borrowing short and lending long": savings and checking deposits constitute loans from depositors to the financial institutions, for which they pay a modest return to the depositor, who usually keeps funds for very short periods; but a home loan to that same depositor would commit the financial institution to a long term, typically 30 years.

Another problem facing lending institutions deals with old, low, fixed interest rate loans currently on the lenders' books. If the current cost of money exceeds the interest rates on these older loans, the institutions are losing money on these loans. If the lender attempts to sell these low interest rate loans to investors, the lender will need to sell at a low discount price. That means that the interest rate on new loans must be increased to compensate for the loss on these old loans. In effect, new borrowers are subsidizing the old borrowers. If all the borrowers were on an adjustable rate, this subsidizing process would not be as severe.

Those who are opposed to ARM-type loans argue that lenders are merely shifting part of the risk of rising interest rates to the borrower. They point out that many of today's lenders no longer keep a large portfolio of loans. Instead, the lenders merely originate the loans, keep the loan fees, then resell the loans in the secondary mortgage market. Therefore, there is no risk of a portfolio of low interest rate loans. Of course, this omits the point that the low fixed interest rate loans would be in the hands of investors, who are now suffering losses, and in the future would be less willing to buy existing low interest rate loans from the originating lender!

Adjustable rate mortgages are not new. They have been used for many years in Canada and in many European countries. In California, the Cal-Vet loan program has been using adjustable rates since the program was started over 80 years ago.

4.2 Adjustable Rate Mortgages (ARMs)

What Is an Adjustable Rate Loan?

If you were buying a home today and were applying for a conventional loan, you could choose either a fixed interest rate or an adjustable rate loan. The *fixed interest rate* is the traditional loan on which the interest rate and term do not change over the life of the loan. Under an *adjustable interest rate* loan, the rate may move up or down. Therefore, your principal and interest payment may increase or decrease over the life of the loan.

Adjustable rate mortgages are usually made by mortgage companies, thrift institutions, and banks. The earliest adjustables were labeled variable rate mortgages (VRMs), variable interest rate loans (VIRs), and adjustable mortgage loans (AMLs). Although there may be some minor differences between these and today's ARMs, they basically work the same way. For our purposes, ARM means any loan without a fixed interest rate during its term.

General Characteristics of ARM Loans

An adjustable rate mortgage loan has the following major characteristics:

1. *Lower initial interest rates.* ARMs are usually offered at a lower initial interest rate than traditional fixed rate loans. In highly competitive markets, lenders offer so-called *teaser* rates. Teaser rates are abnormally low rates designed to attract borrowers. Once the loans are granted, the low teaser rate soon disappears and the usually higher ARM rates take effect. The low teaser rate allows some buyers to qualify for a loan that they would not otherwise be able to obtain. Some lenders are now offering teaser rates but insist that the borrower be able to qualify at the normal or "fully indexed" ARM rate.

2. *Index and margin.* Once the initial interest rate is established, the rate is tied to some *neutral index*, which is one that is beyond the control of the lender or the borrower. A government **index**, such as the "cost of funds index" of the 11th District of the Federal Home Loan Bank of San Francisco, is an example. Some ARMs are tied to certain U.S. Treasury notes. Others are tied to international indexes, such as the London Interbank Offered Rate (LIBOR). The **margin**, often referred to as the lender's profit, refers to the amount which is added to the index rate at each adjustment period. The margin remains the same for the life of the loan whereas the index typically changes, up or down, regularly. Although a typical margin ranges from 2 to 3 percent, it can be higher or lower depending upon the borrower's credit score, the prepayment terms, and other

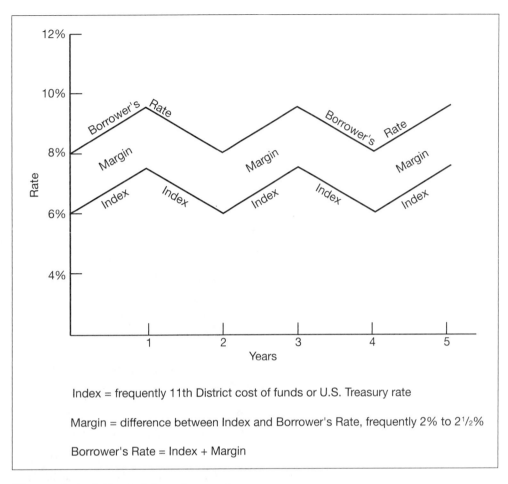

Figure 4.1 Adjustable rate mortgage.

risk features of the loan. Figure 4.1 demonstrates the concept.

3. *Interest and mortgage payment adjustment periods.* How frequently the lender can change the borrower's interest rate depends on changes in the index and the legal language in the loan contract. The frequency of the rate adjustment generally will determine whether the loan is negatively amortized or whether the monthly loan payments adjust at the same time as the interest rate adjustment (commonly called a no-neg loan). Loans in which the interest rate adjusts monthly (the index rate plus the margin) but the mortgage payment remains the same for a stated period of time most often will result in negative amortization. In those instances in which the interest rate changes only every six months or one year, the monthly payment typically adjusts as well, resulting in the loan remaining fully amortizing. In the latter situation, the borrower is usually notified in advance of the anticipated

change and may be given the right to pay off the loan without penalty prior to the adjustment taking place. In the case of a negatively amortized loan, the borrower is notified when the monthly payment is scheduled to change, normally once a year. These loans typically cap the amount of increase for the monthly payment at 7.5 percent a year, resulting in the possibility that if interest rates increase rapidly, the amount of deferred interest could grow substantially. Although not necessarily required, the monthly loan payment change is usually tied to the interest rate change; that is, if interest can be changed once per year, so can the loan payment. Borrowers must be notified at least 30 days prior to a change. After notification, the borrower usually has a 90-day right to pay off the loan without penalty—referred to as the "window period."

4. *Interest rate and mortgage payment caps.* To avoid what is known as "payment shock," most ARMs have adjustment and overall interest rate caps—a ceiling on annual and total rate increases. Although the loan contract will identify the specifics, the typical adjustments are a maximum of 1 percent every six months or 2 percent a year with a 4 to 6 percent total increase over the original starting rate or the fully indexed rate. For example, if an ARM starts out at 4 percent, the maximum increase in any one year might be 2 percent with a lifetime maximum of 6 percent, or a high of 10 percent for the life of the loan. ARM disclosures must also identify the "floor," the lowest rate to which the loan may adjust, in addition to the ceiling. This floor rate is usually a fixed number below which the loan can never adjust.

5. ARMs offer more flexible terms, maturities, and pricing than 30-year fixed-rate mortgages. Borrowers will find interest-only options with a wide range of margins, indexes, rate caps, pledged account options, prepayment options, and various modification privileges, depending on the lender.

A comprehensive list of questions that borrowers should ask when considering an ARM loan is located at the end of this section.

Negative Amortization and Adjustable Rate Mortgages

Negatively amortized loans become more popular during periods of high inflation, usually accompanied by rapid appreciation of home values. Rapid inflation can create a need to qualify a borrower at a low entry-level rate of interest even though the payments may later increase via regular rate adjustments and the loan, particularly if negatively amortized, will require re-amortization over a shorter term of years.

With negatively amortized loans, the initial monthly payments will likely be inadequate to pay the interest, let alone provide for any principal reduction. Whatever the amount of the interest shortfall, it is added to the existing principal balance of the loan, and the following month, the process is repeated. Since the interest shortfall is always added to the principal balance existing at the time, the borrower ends up paying interest on interest, and the principal balance grows with compounding effect.

Point of Reference: All negatively amortized ARM loans contain a provision limiting the amount of deferred interest that can be added to the loan balance before the loan must be recast, amortizing the new balance over the remaining term of the loan. The interest rate used to recast the loan is usually a fixed rate, often higher than the current ARM rate. The result is generally a higher monthly payment, many times creating a payment burden for the borrower.

Comparing ARMs to fixed rate loans can be confusing, so we've compiled a comprehensive list of questions that borrowers should ask when considering an ARM, located at the end of this section (p. 89).

To summarize, two changes can take place in connection with an ARM: a change in the interest rate and a change in the monthly payment. One can occur without the other. If changes in the payments are not made concurrently to accommodate the higher interest rates, negative amortization can take place, resulting in a debt increase rather than a decrease. There has been a definite movement by lenders away from granting real estate loans with negative amortization. It may be noted that many buyers were not concerned about negative amortization ("negam") during the housing frenzy that attracted buyers in large numbers seeking double and even triple digit returns on housing in the mid-2000s, as long as negam loans made qualifying for loans easier, based on the lower payments associated with negam financing.

Disclosure Requirements for ARMs

The technical aspects of the features of ARM loans can be confusing to borrowers. Therefore, lenders who issue ARMs must comply with Regulation Z of the Federal Truth in Lending Law. Regulation Z requires lenders who offer ARMs to give each potential borrower certain specific information about ARM loans. The major disclosure items are

1. The index used, where the index is found, and a 5-year history of the index.

2. How interest rates and margins interact to determine payments and what the current rates are.

3. If teaser rates are used, when they can change.

4. The interest and payment adjustment periods and how many days' warning will be provided before a change occurs.

5. Negative amortization features, if any.

6. Maximum caps on (1) the annual interest increase and (2) the total for the loan.

The lender may comply with Regulation Z by giving the potential borrower the *Consumer Handbook on Adjustable Rate Mortgages*, published by the Federal Reserve and the Federal Home Loan Bank Board. In addition, California lenders are required to have the borrower sign an adjustable rate loan rider to the promissory note (see Figure 4.2).

Advantages of an Adjustable Rate Mortgage to the Borrower

- Lower initial rates when compared with fixed rates (although the difference is slight unless the borrower elects to use a negatively amortized loan. Even then, depending upon the loan option, the fully indexed rate for qualifying purposes may not be much different than the fixed rate loan).

- Easier qualifying for home purchases in many cases.

- Initial costs of the loan are usually smaller (although this would depend upon how we interpret "initial costs").

- Ability to qualify for a larger loan at the lower interest rate.

- Potential for lower payments as the index comes down.

- Generally easier assumability upon resale.

ADJUSTABLE RATE LOAN RIDER
(CHANGE DATE LIMIT)

NOTICE: THIS DOCUMENT CONTAINS PROVISIONS FOR A VARIABLE INTEREST RATE. INCREASES IN THE INTEREST RATE WILL RESULT IN HIGHER PAYMENTS. DECREASES IN THE INTEREST RATE WILL RESULT IN LOWER PAYMENTS.

This Rider is made this . . . . day of . . . . , 19 . . . ., and is incorporated into and shall be deemed to amend and supplement the Mortgage, Deed of Trust, or Deed to Secure Debt (the "Security Instrument") of the same date given by the undersigned (the "Borrower") to secure Borrower's Note to . . . . SAVINGS & LOAN ASSOCIATION . . . . (the "Lender") of the same date (the "Note") and covering the property described in the Security Instrument and located at *(Property Address)* . . . .
. . . .

Modifications. In addition to the covenants and agreements made in the Security Instrument, Borrower and Lender further covenant and agree as follows:

A. INTEREST RATE AND MONTHLY PAYMENT CHANGES

The Note has an "Initial Interest Rate" of . . . . . . %. The Note interest rate may be increased or decreased on the . . . . . day of the month beginning on . . . . , 19 . . . . and on that day of the month every . . . . months thereafter. Each date on which the rate of interest may change is called a "Change Date".

Changes in the interest rate are governed by changes in an interest rate index called the "Index".

(A) The Index

Beginning with the first Change Date, the interest rate will be based on an Index. The "Index" is the "Monthly Weighted Average Cost of Funds Index for Eleventh District Savings Institutions" which is published monthly by the Federal Home Loan Bank of San Francisco. The most recent Index figure available as of the date 45 days before each Change Date is called the "Current Index".

If the Index is no longer available, the Lender will choose a new index which is based upon comparable information. The Lender will give notice of this choice.

(B) Calculation of Changes

Before each Change Date, the Lender will calculate the new interest rate by adding . . . . basis points (. . . . . . %)(this amount is called "Margin") to the Current Index. The Lender will then round the result of this addition to the nearest one-eighth of one percentage point (0.125%). This rounded amount will be the new interest rate until the next Change Date, subject to the limitations set forth in Section (C) below.

Based on the new interest rate, the Lender will determine the amount of the monthly payment that would be sufficient to reamortize the loan based on the unpaid principal balance of the loan expected to be owed on the Change Date plus interest at the new rate which will result in substantially equal payments over the remaining term of the loan.

(C) Limit on Interest Rate Changes

If the calculations set forth in Section (B) above result in a new interest rate of which is more than . . . . . higher or lower than the interest rate in effect immediately prior to the Change Date, the interest rate change will be limited to . . . . . . For the purpose of the first adjustment, the new interest will not be more than . . . . . higher or lower than . . . . %. Also, during the term of the loan the interest rate may never be higher than . . . . %, and may never be lower than . . . . %.

(D) Effective Date of Changes

Each new interest rate will become effective on the next Change Date. If Borrower's monthly payment changes as a result of a change in the interest rate, Borrower's monthly payment will change as of the first monthly payment date after the Change Date as provided in the Note.

(E) Notice to Borrower

The Lender will mail Borrower a notice by first class mail at least thirty and no more than forty-five days before each Change Date if the interest rate is to change. The notice will advise Borrower of:

    (i) the new interest rate on Borrower's loan;
    (ii) the amount of Borrower's new monthly payment; and
    (iii) any additonal matters which the Lender is required to disclose.

B. LOAN CHARGES

It could be that the loan secured by the Security Instrument is subject to a law which sets maximum loan charges and that law is interpreted so that the interest or other loan charges collected or to be collected in connection with the loan would exceed permitted limits. If this is the case, then: (A) any such loan charge shall be reduced by the amount necessary to reduce the charge to the permitted limit; and (B) any sums already collected from Borrower which exceeded permitted limits will be refunded to Borrower. Lender may choose to make this refund by reducing the principal owed under the Note or by making a direct payment to Borrower.

ADJUSTABLE RATE LOAN RIDER—CALIFORNIA   LN 164 0289

Figure 4.2 Sample adjustable rate loan rider.

C. PRIOR LIENS

If Lender determines that all or any part of the sums secured by this Security Instrument are subject to a lien which has priority over this Security Instrument, Lender may send Borrower a notice identifying that lien. Borrower shall promptly act with regard to that lien as provided in paragraph 4 of the Security Instrument or shall promptly secure an agreement in a form satisfactory to Lender subordinating that lien to this Security Instrument.

D. TRANSFER OF THE PROPERTY

If there is a transfer of the Property subject to paragraph 17 of the Security Instrument, Lender may require (1) an increase in the current Note interest rate, or (2) an increase in (or removal of) the limit on the amount of any one interest rate change (if there is a limit), or (3) a change in the Base Index figure, or all of these, as a condition of Lender's waiving the option to accelerate provided in paragraph 17.

By signing this, Borrower agrees to all of the above.

. . . . (Seal)
—Borrower

. . . . (Seal)
—Borrower

STATE OF CALIFORNIA

COUNTY OF _____ } ss.

On _____, 20 _____, before me, the undersigned, a Notary Public in and for said State, personally appeared _____

_____

personally known to me (or proved to me on the basis of satisfactory evidence) to be the person(s) whose name(s) _____

subscribed to the foregoing instrument and acknowledged that _____ executed the same.

WITNESS my hand and official seal.

(Reserved for offical seal)

_____
Notary Public in and for Said State

Figure 4.2 Sample adjustable rate loan rider (*continued*).

- No prepayment penalties. Although one can acquire an ARM without a prepay, in all but the "conforming ARMs" the borrower may end up paying a price, usually in the margin, which adds to the overall rate. Prepayment penalties are designated as either "soft" or "hard." Soft penalties allow the property to be sold without penalty but require that the penalty be paid if the property is refinanced within the noted time period. Hard penalties require the fee to be paid under all circumstances within the time frame. The kind of prepayment penalty and the time period for which the borrower is obligated are determined with the pricing/cost of the loan. For instance, a borrower selection of a soft prepay for a two-year period might cost an additional half point vs. a hard prepay for a two-year period at no additional cost.

- Lower interest charges during the early years. Given that the average life of a loan is only six years, the ARM may result in less

What Are Some Questions to Ask and Issues to Consider for Adjustable Rate Mortgages?

What is the beginning ("teaser") interest rate?

What index is used?

What is the formula that is used to set the rate?

What is the past performance of the index?

How much is the margin?

Is the beginning interest rate the sum of the index plus the margin? Is it fully indexed?

Do you qualify at the teaser rate or the fully indexed rate?

When could the first interest rate adjustment be made?

How often thereafter can the interest rate be adjusted?

By how much can the interest rate change at the time of adjustment?

Is there an interest rate cap for the life of the loan?

Is there an interest rate floor for the life of the loan?

Is the interest rate cap based on the starting interest rate or something else?

When can the monthly payment first change?

How often thereafter can the monthly payment change?

What is the largest monthly payment that can be charged?

By how much can the monthly payment change?

Is negative amortization involved?

Is there a limit on the amount of negative amortization?

If so, does the loan automatically recast?

Are changes in the monthly payments directly tied to interest rate changes?

Can you lock in interest rates, margin, and monthly payments at application?

What is the cost to originate the loan?

Is the loan assumable under the original terms?

Is the loan fully assumable, or does a new borrower have to qualify?

Can the loan be converted to a fixed rate loan?

How is the conversion rate determined?

If it can be converted, when? At what expense?

Note: The last five questions are related to assumability and conversion. Typically, a new borrower must "qualify" to assume the ARM loan and a fee is usually charged. The reality may be that after a couple of adjustments, and given the fact that the borrower must qualify, there is little incentive for said assumption when the new borrower could acquire a new adjustable at a lower rate. Depending upon the assumption fee charged, there could be some savings in the costs of acquiring the loan.

interest paid than might occur with a fixed rate loan during the same six-year period.

- Ability to make principal reduction payments. The ARM allows for principal payments that affect the monthly payment whereas principal reduction payments with a fixed rate merely affect the term of the loan.

Disadvantages of an Adjustable Rate Mortgage to the Borrower

- Income may not increase proportionately with increases in payments.

- In a slow real estate market, the rate of appreciation may be less than the rate of increase in the interest rates; that is, the spread between the value of the property and the outstanding loan balance could shrink each year, rather than increase.

- In some cases, the prospect for negative amortization means that borrowers may owe more than they would net out of the resale proceeds if the property is sold in the early years.

- The risk of rising interest rates is borne partly by the borrower, since the risk of change in the cost of funds can be shifted entirely to the borrower, within maximum caps allowed over the life of the loan.

4.3 Convertible Rate Loans

What Are Convertible Rate Loans?

There are times when prospective borrowers are torn between the initial low payments of the adjustable rate loan with the possibility of large increases in future payments, and a *fixed rate loan* with the initial higher, but certain, monthly payment. The ARM is low now but could increase to more than the present fixed rate loan. Borrowers ask themselves, Do I go adjustable or fixed? One answer may be a *convertible rate loan*.

A convertible rate loan is a hybrid that typically starts as an adjustable rate loan but contains the option to switch to a fixed rate loan at some later date. Or it may be the reverse: the loan starts as a fixed rate and later can be switched to an ARM. For this privilege, borrowers usually pay slightly higher initial rates than for conventional (i.e., nonconvertible) ARMs. There are many varieties of convertible rate loans. A borrower needs to ask, When can I convert? How much will it cost? Do I get the prevailing fixed interest rate or a higher-than-market fixed rate? Let's look at each, ARM to Fixed and Fixed to ARM, to answer some of these questions.

ARM to Fixed

A convertible loan that starts as a 30-year ARM may provide for conversion to a fixed rate at the election of the borrower on the first of each month for the first 37 months. Another may allow the election between the 13th and 60th month, which would be during the second, third, fourth, and fifth years of the loan. The time frame when a switch is allowed is called the "window period." In every case, advance notice must be given by the borrower to the lender prior to the switch. In some cases the lender can charge a fee for the switch. All terms are laid out at the time the loan is created.

Borrowers should be aware that, in the majority of cases, they will not be converting from the present low adjustable rate to the same rate on a fixed basis but to a higher fixed rate. The reason for converting is the borrower's fear that the existing ARM rate will eventually exceed the current fixed rate of interest.

The terms of the note will provide a mechanism for the conversion and the conversion interest rate. A normal conversion privilege might be to convert, at the option date, to a rate anywhere from .375 percent ($\frac{3}{8}$ percent) to 50 basis points ($\frac{1}{2}$ percent) above the "60-day Freddie Mac buy rate," available from the lender. In most circumstances, the fixed rate option produces an interest rate approximating the current fixed rate available from the lender.

The borrower may seek the lowest possible interest rate during the option period by inquiring as often as needed about the current rate available at conversion. Convertibles let home buyers enjoy the lower initial rates of adjustables (ARMs), but, if interest rates fall, the borrower has the option to lock in fixed monthly payments for the remaining term of the loan.

The costs of conversion should also be investigated. Some lenders may not charge for converting but may have a higher conversion interest rate than other lenders. Certain lenders may charge half a point for converting but may have a lower conversion interest rate. These alternatives should be sought out while you are seeking your original loan. After the loan is in place, it is too late to change these terms.

Convertible rate loans issued under proper guidelines can be resold in the secondary mortgage market, such as through FNMA or FHLMC (discussed in Chapter 7), thereby maintaining liquidity for lenders.

Figure 4.3 Convertible rate loans.

Fixed to Arm Rollovers

A wide variety of ARM loans are offered with fixed to ARM rollover (conversion) provisions. They may come with labels like 1/1 ARM, 3/1 ARM, 5/1 ARM, 7/1 ARM, and 10/1 ARM. The first number represents the number of years the rate is fixed, and the second number designates how frequently the rate adjusts after the rollover is exercised. For the 5/1 ARM, for instance, the rate is fixed for five years, and then converts to a one-year ARM, usually adjustable thereafter each year for the life of the loan. In general, the larger the first number (that is, the larger the fixed rate term), the higher the interest rate. For example, lenders may quote 6 percent interest for a 1/1, 6.25 percent for a 3/1, and 6.5 percent for a 5/1 ARM, with one discount point for each. Fixed to adjustable rates, and adjustable to fixed rates, can be visualized by reference to Figure 4.3.

4.4 Loans Amortized for 30 Years, but Due in 5 or 7 Years

In a **balloon mortgage** the amortization period is 30 years, but the entire unpaid balance is due at the end of the fifth or seventh year. A payment that is more than double the amount of a regular installment is, by Civil Code definition, a balloon payment.

The balloon payment mortgage, although used in financing commercial properties, has not met with huge success in financing homes because of the balloon feature. Unless the note calls for a rollover, there is no assurance that the loan will be rewritten with a new rate at maturity. Thus balloon payment home loans are frequently seller carryback loans used during tight, or high-interest, mortgage markets.

> ***Example:*** A balloon mortgage with an amortization schedule of
> 30 years, but with the note due and payable in 5 years, would work
> as follows: a $200,000 loan at 8%, amortized for 30 years but due in
> 5 years, will have monthly payments of principal and interest of
> $1,467.53. After 60 complete payments (5 years × 12 payments per
> year), the remaining loan balance due and payable will be
> $190,139.71.

The greatest problem confronting the borrower who uses a loan amortized in 30 years, but due in 5 or 7 years, is inability to meet the balloon at maturity. (We'll discuss a variety of ways to help overcome this problem in Chapter 11). Even if the borrower is able to arrange new financing, whether with the same or different terms and lender, the borrower will likely be subject to new expenses, including an origination fee/points and other closing costs for the refinanced amount.

4.5 Reverse Annuity Mortgage (RAM)

A reverse mortgage allows qualified homeowners to tap their home equity with no monthly repayments. It is not a financing plan for *buying* a home; on the contrary, it's designed to assist those who already own a home, often for many years. Hence we'll keep the discussion short and simple. For those wishing detailed information, several websites exist, including those for Fannie Mae [(800) 732-6643], the Department of Housing and Urban Development [(888) 466-3487], the nonprofit National Center for Home Equity Conversion, the AARP Home Equity Conversion Center, Financial Freedom [(800) 500-5150], and the National Reverse Mortgage Lenders Association [(888) 328-9171]. Links to these sites may be found at www.bond.swcollege.com and in Appendix A at the end of this book.

First, RAMs are available only for those 62 or older. The program is for single-family dwellings, condos, owner-occupied one-to-four dwelling unit apartment buildings, and manufactured homes on separate lots. Neither Fannie Mae nor FHA makes direct reverse loans. Instead, approved lenders make the loans with Fannie Mae and FHA backing. The Equity Guard RAM is a loan without Fannie Mae or FHA loan limits.

The three main programs are:

1. *Home Equity Conversion Mortgage.* FHA loan limits apply; this is an ARM loan, usually tied to 1-year T-bills with a certain cap above the starting interest rate.

2. *Home Keeper Program.* Fannie Mae loan limits apply; this is an ARM loan, usually tied to 1-month CD rates with a certain cap above the starting interest rate.

3. *Conventional Programs.* Lenders offering RAM loans not backed by FHA insurance or Fannie Mae secondary mortgage requirements can establish their own loan limits and other requirements.

Under all programs the maximum LTV ratio is determined by a formula based on the borrower's age, interest rates, and appraisal and/or maximum loan, as often found using the annuity principle. Payment options for the borrower usually include:

1. *Term option.* Equal monthly payments for a fixed number of years.

2. *Tenure option.* Equal monthly payments for as long as the borrower occupies the home.

3. *Line of credit option.* Funds drawn as needed (including a lump sum) up to the maximum loan amount that is calculated based on age of the borrower, interest rate, and location, since FHA sets maximum amounts on county-by-county basis around the country.

RAM Basics—FHA and Fannie Mae Programs

1. Borrower pays loan fees, closing costs, and a monthly servicing fee to issue the checks (approximately $30). In addition, under the FHA program, mortgage insurance premiums will be charged. Many of these fees can be financed as part of the loan. As long as the borrower continues to occupy the home as a principal residence, he or she cannot be forced to sell or vacate, even if the total payments received exceed the value of the home. If the borrower takes the *term option*, he or she cannot be forced to vacate the home when the term expires. According to the National Reverse Mortgage Lenders Association, approximately 90 percent of outstanding reverse mortgages are insured by the FHA, which sets the amount borrowers can borrow, based on their age, interest rates and value of the home.

2. The loan becomes due and payable upon death, or sale of the home, or if the borrower vacates the home for more than one year (including time spent in a rest home). The amount due consists of all payments made to the borrower, plus accrued interest. However, the amount payable shall not exceed the value of the home, even if the total payments received, plus interest owed, are more than the value of the home. If the home appreciates above the payoff amount, the borrower, or his or her heirs, get to keep the excess funds from the sale after paying off the loan and closing costs.

3. Because of past abuses, most reverse mortgage borrowers are required to attend an education session before a loan can be approved. This is designed to prevent relatives, so-called friends, or service providers such as home repair people from taking advantage of an elderly homeowner.

4. Fannie Mae's "Home Keeper for Home Purchase" program which, with a very large down payment, combined with a reverse mortgage, is used to acquire a home with no monthly payments. Although not as common as the other reverse mortgage programs where seniors stay in their existing home, this purchase program might be ideal for an older homeowner who wishes to move closer to relatives and loved ones. Contact Fannie Mae for details.

5. Funds received are tax-free because they represent a loan that must ultimately be repaid. One drawback: up-front fees, which can be twice the cost to secure a traditional purchase money mortgage.

4.6 Miscellaneous Alternative Plans

W e have discussed many different types of alternative mortgage programs. There are many others and still more to come. Some additional types are briefly described here.

Two-Step Mortgage

The purpose of a **two-step mortgage** is to allow home buyers to qualify for a loan based on lower interest rates and therefore lower payments. You will find that the two-step mortgage has many of the features of "loans amortized for 30 years but due in 5 or 7 years" discussed in Section 4.4. Its characteristics include the following:

- A fixed rate of interest is charged for the initial period, usually seven years, that is lower than the standard for 30-year, fixed rate loans.

- Amortization is based on a 30-year payment schedule.

- An automatic conversion following the initial period may be another fixed rate at the then-prevailing rate. It could be adjustable but with a lifetime interest ceiling set at the time of the loan, at no additional cost. The conversion feature assures the borrower that the otherwise large balloon due in seven years will come from the same lender, only at a different rate. Stated differently, the two-step guarantees fixed rate financing for the entire loan term without having to come up with a sizable balloon payment.

- Because they qualify for purchase by FNMA in the secondary market (discussed in Chapter 7), loan amounts vary according to the current limits set by FNMA.

The chief advantage of the two-step over a balloon mortgage or the previously discussed "amortized for 30 years, but due in 5 or 7 years" loan is that borrowers aren't forced to move or refinance—they simply endure a one-time adjustment to the interest rate.

Fifteen-Year Mortgage

In an effort to build up equity faster, to have a free and clear home sooner, and to obtain lower interest rates, a significant number of borrowers are signing up for 15-year, as opposed to 30-year, loans. Frequently, the borrower gets a 1/4% to 1/2% interest savings for a 15-year loan over a 30-year loan. See the Example for interest rate comparisons.

Biweekly Loan Payments

Traditionally, amortized real estate loans have been paid on a monthly basis. However, some lenders offer borrowers the option of biweekly, instead of monthly, loan payments.

A biweekly payment is made every two weeks, resulting in 26 biweekly payments per year. This is the equivalent of making 13 monthly payments. A biweekly payment is merely one-half of a monthly payment paid every 14 days. The extra payments apply more money against the principal loan amount, thereby greatly reducing the time it takes to pay off the loan.

How much faster is a loan paid off using biweekly instead of monthly payments? A rule of thumb is that it is one-third faster—a

Example: A $100,000 fixed rate loan at 9 percent, amortized for 30 years, requires a monthly principal and interest payment of $804.62. The same $100,000 loan at $8\frac{3}{4}$ percent, amortized for 15 years, requires a monthly payment of $999.45.

$999.45	per month for 15 years at $8\frac{3}{4}$%
−804.62	per month for 30 years at 9%
$194.83	per month more for a 15-year than for a 30-year loan program

This 15-year loan is especially attractive to high-income borrowers who wish to have their homes paid off prior to retirement. For the interest rate—conscious borrower, the amount of interest that is saved can be substantial. Using the above data (but ignoring pennies), we have:

$189,663	interest payable over 30 years at 9% ($999.45/ mo. × 360 pmts., less $100,000 loan amount)
−79,901	interest payable over 15 years at $8\frac{3}{4}$% ($804.62/ mo. × 180 pmts., less $100,000 loan amount)
$109,762	interest saved

Of course, no analysis of interest costs can be complete without comparing income tax consequences of one scheme over another, nor would we ignore the time value of money, but these aspects are well beyond the scope of this text.

traditional 30-year monthly amortized loan can be paid off in about 21 years using biweekly payments. Certain facilitating companies can set up this procedure for you, with fees in the range of $500.00 if your lender does not provide the opportunity.

Biweekly payment programs are approved by Fannie Mae and Freddie Mac; thus there is a secondary market for these loans. Some borrowers prefer the biweekly, as opposed to the traditional monthly payment loans, because of the savings in interest costs and faster loan payoff. More important to some borrowers is the fact that they are paid on an every two-week basis and paying half the loan payment each pay period may be easier for personal budgeting purposes. (We'll see how biweekly loan payments are computed in Chapter 13.)

For borrowers who do not wish to enter into a formal biweekly agreement—that is, for those who do not wish to tie themselves down to a binding commitment every two weeks—but who still want to reduce interest costs, there are solutions. For example, the borrower can accomplish similar results, though with a slightly longer payoff period, by making a 13th payment toward principal reduction each year. Or the borrower could increase each regular installment by 1/12 of the principal amount of the payment. Of course, these prepayments can be accomplished only if they are not prohibited under the terms of the promissory note. If the borrower makes the 13th monthly payment, he/she must make sure the lender is aware of its purpose: *principal reduction only*.

4.7 Epilogue

What we have discussed is just a sampling of mortgage alternatives. Only the lack of imagination and creativity will limit the infinite variety of possible variations, combinations and permutations in devising new plans. Of course, licensees must be cautious in recommending loan plans that may not be suitable for the client. Some of the options that were foisted upon buyers in earlier years are backfiring today because of poor assessment of the financial conditions of buyers.

Some variations on long-standing and proven types of loans can come to bite. For instance, an ARM known as an Option ARM lets borrowers pick how their monthly payments are calculated. Also called "Pick-a-payment" or "Cash flow ARM," monthly payments can be calculated as if the interest rate was only 1% or 2%, even though the market adjustable rate is 6%. Result: negative amortization necessitating interest added to the principal and repayments scheduled once the balance reaches 100 to 120 percent of the original loan. Borrowers will then face rescheduled payments increased by 50 percent and more, adding to the real possibility of foreclosure.

The financing smorgasbord offered in the mortgage cafeteria should provide alternatives paired with individual needs and abilities to repay. The real estate broker today is expected to be knowledgeable about financing alternatives, which means continuous exposure to and understanding of new financing vehicles, techniques, and choices.

SUMMARY

Financing of real estate is undergoing a revolution, and a host of innovative mortgages have been created, so that in theory, at least, loans can be matched to the borrower instead of tying all borrowers to just one loan type.

In the "good old days," applicants for real estate loans would be expected to ask six basic questions: How much of a loan can I get? At what rate? How much would my monthly payments be? How much will I have to pay for points and fees? Will I have to pay a penalty if I repay the loan before maturity? Could the loan be assumed?

Today, many loan applicants must ask these questions, plus many new ones: Is the loan based on a fixed or adjustable (fluctuating) interest rate? How often can increases in payments be made, and for how much? Is there a cap (ceiling) on the interest over the life of the loan? How are interest rate changes computed; that is, what index is being used by the lender? Is negative amortization involved? Is there a balloon payment? Will the lender extend or refinance the loan if I don't have the money at balloon time?

Adjustable rate mortgages (ARMs) are loans whose interest rate moves up and down based upon a neutral index. The distance between the borrower's rate and the index is called the margin. The maximum rate allowed is called the cap. A convertible loan allows the borrower to switch between an ARM and a fixed rate loan during a predetermined "window period." A balloon-type loan that is amortized for 30 years, with the entire unpaid balance due at the end of the fifth or seventh year, may be offered by some home lenders. A payment that is more than double the amount of a regular installment is, by Civil Code definition, a balloon payment.

A reverse annuity mortgage (RAM) allows homeowners aged 62 or older to tap their home equity with no monthly repayments. In essence, the homeowner receives a monthly payment from the lender and does not need to pay the loan back until he or she moves out, sells, or dies. The home must be free and clear, or have a low-balance existing loan. The program is for single-family dwellings only, except for FHA-approved condos. Neither Fannie Mae nor FHA makes direct reverse loans; instead, approved lenders make the loans with Fannie Mae and FHA backing.

Other alternative loan packages include two-step mortgages, fifteen-year loans, biweekly payment plans, and a host of other creative programs. Each of the alternative mortgage instruments discussed in this chapter is intended to answer borrowers' questions and to provide solutions to their dilemmas. None by themselves will provide the answer or the panacea to all of one's problems. But they do allow choices and alternatives to financing without which real estate would be limited to all-cash buyers only.

IMPORTANT TERMS AND CONCEPTS

Adjustable rate mortgage (ARM)

Alternative mortgage instruments

Balloon mortgage

Biweekly loan payments

Cap

Convertible rate loans

Fifteen-year loan

Fixed rate loan

Index

Margin

Negative amortization

Option ARMs

Reverse annuity mortgage (RAM)

Two-step mortgage

Window period

REVIEWING YOUR UNDERSTANDING

Questions for Discussion

1. **What are the key characteristics of ARM loans?**

2. **What is the main lender risk in granting loans amortized in 30 years, but due in 7 years?**

3. **List the main elements of a RAM loan.**

Multiple-Choice Questions

1. The principal objective of an Adjustable Rate Mortgage (ARM) loan is to
   a. reduce the risk of foreclosure.
   b. limit mortgage choices during periods of tight money.
   c. establish predictable cash flow during erratic real estate markets.
   d. share the risks of rising interest rates between lender and borrower.

d

2. Under an ARM loan, the distance between the actual rate paid by the borrower and the index is called the
   a. adjustment.
   b. cap.
   c. term.
   d. margin.

a 3. The maximum interest rate that a lender can charge under an ARM is called the
   a. cap.
   b. margin.
   c. term.
   d. adjustment.

b 4. In an ARM loan, when the initial interest rate is abnormally low it is known as the _____ rate.
   a. index.
   b. teaser.
   c. capped.
   d. basement.

a 5. Negative amortization can be associated with
   a. RAM loans.
   b. fully amortized loans.
   c. ARM loans.
   d. interest-only loans.

a 6. The first month's interest on a $200,000 loan at 9% payable at $1,800 per month is:
   a. $1,800
   b. $1,600
   c. $1,500
   d. $1,300

b 7. The first month's negative amortization (shortfall) amount on a $200,000 loan at 9% payable at $1,300 per month is:
   a. $600
   b. $500
   c. $300
   d. $200

c 8. The reverse annuity mortgage (RAM) is especially designed for
   a. poor families.
   b. younger borrowers.
   c. older borrowers.
   d. those unable to meet balloon payments.

9. The loan plan that offers borrowers an adjustable interest rate with the right to switch to a fixed rate at a later date is the
   a. dual rate, variable rate mortgage.
   b. rollover mortgage.
   c. reverse annuity mortgage.
   d. pledged account mortgage.

10. Under a convertible loan, the time period when the borrower is allowed to switch from an ARM to fixed rate or vice versa is called the _____ period.
    a. shift.
    b. crossover.
    c. section.
    d. window.

11. Which of these requires a substantial payment, one at least twice that of normal monthly installments, at maturity of the mortgage note?
    a. ARM.
    b. fully amortized.
    c. RAM.
    d. amortized for 30, but due in 7 years.

12. If a borrower is unable to meet a balloon payment, the borrower might arrange to
    a. obtain an extension of the loan with the existing lender.
    b. refinance the property.
    c. sell the property.
    d. do any of the above.

13. One option under a RAM program, where the borrower is scheduled to receive monthly payments for a fixed number of years, is called
    a. tenure option.
    b. set option.
    c. term option.
    d. line of credit option.

14. Which of the following will trigger a demand for payoff for a borrower under a RAM loan?
    a. moving to a second home for six months.
    b. staying in a rest home for more than one year.
    c. taking in a roommate.
    d. receiving a cash inheritance of more than $250,000.

15. A two-step mortgage is
    a. one in which the rate of interest is initially fixed below market with an automatic conversion to the prevailing fixed rate.
    b. the same as a RAM loan.
    c. another name for a FLIP loan.
    d. an equity kicker loan.

16. Mortgage interest rates that are subject to change according to a predetermined index, as stipulated in the promissory note, are labeled
    a. adjustable.
    b. nonvariable.
    c. fixed.
    d. fluctuating.

17. A 15-year loan, as opposed to a 30-year loan, will
    a. have no impact on annual interest deductions for income tax purposes.
    b. result in slower equity buildup.
    c. create a faster equity in the property, all other things being equal.
    d. initially generate lower monthly payments.

18. A biweekly payment program requires the borrower to make ____ payments per year.
    a. 12
    b. 13
    c. 24
    d. 26

19. When compared with a 30-year loan, the 15-year loan is especially attractive for borrowers who desire to reduce their
    a. monthly installment.
    b. total interest payments.
    c. principal payments.
    d. mortgage insurance premiums.

20. A homeowner will build up equity fastest during the first five years under which program?
    a. 15-year loan payable biweekly.
    b. 30-year ARM loan tied to the 11th District Cost of Funds Index.
    c. a fixed interest rate loan amortized for 30, but due in 7 years.
    d. 15-year two-step loan.

CHAPTER 5
CONVENTIONAL LOANS

PREVIEW

This chapter covers conventional loans, their advantages and disadvantages, and how to compare one lender with another. Buy-down loans are explained and several examples are given. The California Fair Lending Regulations are outlined and analyzed. This chapter concludes with a discussion of private mortgage insurance (PMI) companies.

After completing this chapter, you should be able to:

1. Define a conventional loan.

2. List several advantages and disadvantages of a conventional loan.

3. Describe what to look for when choosing a lender.

4. Demonstrate how the Community Home Buyers Program assists first-time buyers.

5. Give an example of a buy-down loan.

6. Outline the basic features of the California Financial Discrimination Act.

7. Explain how private mortgage insurance (PMI) works.

5.1 What Is a Conventional Loan?

There are two major categories of loans. One is ***government-backed loans***, which include the Federal Housing Administration (FHA), the U.S. Department of Veterans Affairs (DVA), the California Department of Veterans Affairs (Cal-Vet), and various other state, county, and city-backed subsidized home loan programs. Any loan that is not a government-backed loan is called a ***conventional loan***. The majority of loans originated on one-to-four-unit residential properties are conventional loans.

Conventional versus Government-Backed Loans

When someone buys a house, a decision must be made as to how to finance the purchase. The buyer has a choice of using conventional or government-backed financing. In order to make a wise decision, one must be able to compare one type of loan against the other. The advantages and disadvantages of conventional loans versus government-backed loans are outlined below.

Advantages of Conventional over Government-Backed Loans

1. *Processing time.* It *may* take less time to process a conventional loan. You can have a loan approved through a conventional lender in 30 days or less. If necessary, with automated (computerized) underwriting, a conventional loan can be approved in as little as one week and even less. It is difficult to get that type of quick service from government programs. Usually, government agencies do not have the flexibility in their procedures that a conventional lender enjoys; even though with "direct endorsements" and "DVA automatics," covered in Chapter 6, processing of government-backed loans has improved, it is unlikely that a government-backed loan can be completed in less than 30 days.

2. *Red tape.* Processing a conventional loan involves less red tape. There may be fewer forms to complete, and the routine of processing is more flexible, unless, as discussed in Chapter 7, the loan is to be sold to FNMA or FHLMC.

3. *Loan amounts.* There is no legal limitation on conventional loan amounts when the loan-to-value ratio is 80 percent or less,

unless the loan is sold off in the secondary market, as discussed in Chapter 7. But FHA sets maximum loan amounts on a home loan depending on geographical location. The DVA has no dollar loan maximum, but individual lenders do limit the veteran's loan amount because the DVA guarantees only part of the loan. Cal-Vet's maximum loan on a single-family dwelling is limited and can vary from year to year. Dollar limits on government-backed loans will be covered in Chapter 6.

4. *Number of lenders.* If you apply for a DVA-guaranteed loan and the loan is rejected by the DVA, you have no alternative lender. There is only one U.S. Department of Veterans Affairs, just as there is only a single FHA and one California Department of Veterans Affairs. On the other hand, if a loan is turned down by one conventional lender, there are other lenders who may approve the loan. No one conventional lender has a monopoly on the market: With different lenders come different under-writers and different attitudes, so that even though they are applying the same rules, results may differ due to compensating factors.

5. *Flexibility of portfolio lenders.* When a lender keeps a loan instead of reselling it in the secondary market, it is called a ***portfolio loan***. Many portfolio lenders offer an array of these loans with attractive provisions. Some loan choices require only minimum paperwork or documentation as evidenced by their names. . . . No Income-No Asset (NINA) documentation or a Stated Income-Stated Assets (SISA) loan. These loans generally require a larger down payment and rely heavily on a borrower's credit scores and the results of the property's appraisal.

Disadvantages of Conventional over Government-Backed Loans

1. *Higher down payments.* In certain lower price ranges, many buyers use government-backed financing because they usually require a smaller down payment than conventional loans. In affordable price ranges, DVA-backed loans do not require any down payment (although a lender may require a down payment if the sales price is higher than the appraised value); FHA and Cal-Vet programs only require a small down payment. However, during easy money markets, conventional real estate loans with no-to-low down payment may be offered and they come close to matching the government-backed loans.

2. *Prepayment penalties.* FHA, DVA, and Cal-Vet loans do not have a prepayment penalty. Some conventional loans contain prepayment penalties.

Sources of Conventional Money

One of the first questions that comes up after deciding to obtain a conventional loan is, "Where do I go to get the loan?" The main sources of conventional money are mortgage bankers and mortgage companies, commercial banks, and savings banks. Which one do you choose?

Before you choose, you must recognize that each conventional lender sets its own lending policy on loans it keeps. Every lender has to adhere to certain state or federal agencies' regulations; but beyond that, what a lender does is a matter of company policy. For example, no regulation dictates what interest rate a lender should charge. That decision is up to the lender. Besides interest rate, there are many other financing terms and conditions for which each lender sets its own policy, based on market (business) judgments. Again it must be stressed that this applies only if the lender is making a loan that it is going to keep in its inventory, the so-called portfolio loan.

But if a conventional lender wishes to resell the loan to the **Federal National Mortgage Association (Fannie Mae)** or the **Federal Home Loan Mortgage Corporation (Freddie Mac)**, the lender must stick to standards established by these major loan purchasers. In order to compare lenders, you have to know what items to look for. Here are some of the main items to check out and compare:

1. *Loan-to-value ratios.* Conventional lenders are able to make loans of 90 percent and up. Even 100 percent financing has become more common. Some loans may even include all or a portion of the borrower's closing cost, in effect making these 103 to 107 percent loans. The 125 percent loan, although still available, is seldom used (see the Special Interest Topic box later in this chapter).

   As a matter of company policy, some conventional lenders may even lower their LTV ratios on two-to-four-unit residential properties, nonowner occupied, raw land, and refinance loans.

2. *Type of property.* Lender policy determines the type and quality of property the lender is willing to accept as security for the loan. Does it lend on one-to-four-unit properties only, or does it lend on larger apartment houses, and commercial and industrial property? Will the lender make a loan on a steep hillside lot? Some lenders do not, because of the slide risk. There are other property standards that a lender sets, and these standards can vary greatly

from one lender to the next, as long as they are not illegally discriminatory.

3. *Maximum loan amounts.* Each lender sets its maximum loan amount. The loan amounts vary by type of property. For owner-occupied residential properties of one to four units, many lenders use the Fannie Mae/Freddie Mac loan maximums discussed in Chapter 7. These are "conforming" loans, based on the lenders' ability to sell the loans to FNMA/FHLMC, which set maximum loan limits. These loan limits change each year, and a borrower should call a loan officer or mortgage broker to determine the current limits. Other conventional lenders specialize in **jumbo loans** (loans greater than the Fannie Mae and Freddie Mac limits) for higher-priced homes.

4. *Interest rates.* The interest rate is the one item that immediately comes to mind when discussing differences between lenders. Interest rates frequently change for such reasons as demand, supply, risk, competition, and so on. There is no set pattern as to how often interest rates can change. They can change weekly or even daily. Interest rates also vary according to the type of property and loan-to-value ratio. For example, a 95 percent loan may command a higher rate than an 80 percent loan because of the higher risk.

5. *Loan fees.* The fee charged to charge for a loan is another item that each lender must determine. Loan fees on an 80 percent loan typically vary from 0 to 2 percent of the loan amount. Higher loan-to-value loans, such 90 percent and up, usually carry a higher loan fee. Most lenders offer tiered pricing, with loan fees (points) decreasing as interest rates offered increase. For example, if the prevailing market interest rate is 7 percent, a borrower may be required to pay a 1 percent loan fee (point), or the borrower may be offered an 8 percent interest rate at no points. The type of property also affects the loan fee. For instance, a lender may decide to charge a lower loan fee if the property will be owner-occupied versus a higher fee if the property is nonowner-occupied.

6. *Prepayment penalties.* As already noted, some conventional lenders charge prepayment penalties. When they do, the typical prepayment penalty on a conventional loan is six months' interest on the amount prepaid that exceeds 20 percent of the original amount of the loan. However, penalties vary with the lender. They can even be eliminated in some cases. For example, a lender may

waive the prepayment penalty if the seller has the new buyer finance the purchase with the same lender.

7. *Borrower qualifications.* There is no standard way to qualify a borrower, and each lender determines its own standards. Some lenders are very strict in qualifying a borrower, while others may be more lenient. Many conventional lenders use the Fannie Mae/Freddie Mac guidelines outlined in Chapter 9.

8. *Types of loans.* A few conventional lenders make only fixed rate loans. Other lenders offer adjustable rate loans, on which the interest rate is subject to change according to a specified index. Adjustable rate loans, for example, have been used since 1923 by the California Department of Veterans Affairs. Other types of loans are also available, such as convertible rate, buy-down loans, and, in some cases, reverse mortgages.

Policies and standards set by conventional lenders are not static. A conventional lender can change its property and borrower standards the same way it changes the interest rate. These changes are made to accomplish certain goals. If a lender has a surplus of money, it has to find a way to make more loans. It may lower its property or borrower standards. Or it can lower the interest rate or change some other policy that will enable it to make more loans. If the conventional lender wants to reduce loan demand, it could tighten up on its standards and increase the interest rate and loan fees, but its policies and standards cannot be discriminatory under fair housing laws.

5.2 Keeping Up with Lender Policies

Since conventional lender policies are subject to frequent changes, how do you keep up with these changes? Do you call every lender in town every time you want to borrow money? Successful real estate salespeople are aware of current financing because they realize how important financing is. Let's look at some of the methods they use to keep current.

1. *Communication with lenders.* Periodically, salespeople call various lenders to get their latest quotes. They usually do this when they are shopping for a loan on a specific property. Some real estate offices survey lenders periodically. This information is then distributed to all the salespeople within an office.

2. *Representatives* from lending institutions visit real estate offices and builders to solicit business and to inform them of their companies' current lending practices. Any changes in interest rate, loan programs, and so on are immediately brought to the attention of the real estate agents and builders.

3. *Other salespeople* who have recently secured a loan are a good source of loan information. Since they have recently secured a loan, they know which lenders are offering the best financing.

4. *Internet services.* A wide variety of Internet services are available for those seeking up-to-the-minute (or at least daily) rate quotes and other pertinent data for loans of all types. These online quotes can come from both local and national lenders.

5. *Newsletters and flyers* distributed by lenders show the current policy and rates. Other organizations such as title and escrow companies also mail out periodic reports on current financing.

6. *MLS.* Almost every area in California has a Multiple Listing Service (MLS) meeting each week, during which lenders will be permitted to quote their current programs and rates. In some areas, one designated person or committee member will quote ranges of rates for the local loan industry as a whole.

Which Lender to Use?

If you are trying to obtain a loan on a specific property, you have to decide which lender to use. Before you decide, you have to know the current lending practices of the various lending institutions. We have just discussed some of the ways you can do that. Your next step is to analyze the loan you are seeking. Are you looking for the lowest interest rate or the highest loan amount? Every loan is different because every property and borrower is different. *Deciding which lender to use is a matter of picking the best or the right lender for that specific loan.*

Quality of service is probably the major reason why one lender is chosen over another. A standard conventional loan on an average single-family dwelling can be obtained from many lenders. In all likelihood, the interest rate, fees, and other terms would be about the same. If that is the case, the lender you would choose would be the one with the best service and reputation for reliability.

When you analyze a lender's service, these are some of the questions you should ask: Is the lender dependable? If the lender's appraisers say they will be out to the property tomorrow, will they actually be there? Does the lender stand behind a loan commitment? How long will it guarantee a certain rate of interest? How fast does it process a loan? One lender may have your loan approved in a matter of days while another takes several weeks or more. Since time is of the essence in real estate transactions, processing time can be very important. Does the lender keep you advised regarding the status of your loan? Are the lender's employees customer oriented—are they helpful, courteous, and cooperative? The answers to these questions determine the quality of the service.

In many cases, the loan you are dealing with is not a standard conventional loan. Therefore, it is not just a matter of choosing the lender with the best service. This type of loan requires a more careful analysis before you are able to pick the best lender. The following cases are examples of how real estate transactions were closed because the real estate agent knew where to go to get the best financing. Without this knowledge, the sales would not have closed as rapidly and smoothly as they did.

Case 1

This case involved a small home in a rural California city. With a sales price of $325,000, the buyer was putting down 20 percent and needed an 80 percent loan. There was no problem with the house, but the buyer's income and credit rating were not up to typical lender standards. The salesperson who handled the transaction was aware of this problem. Her analysis concluded that the best lender for this loan was a local savings bank. This particular institution had a policy of being very lenient on borrower qualifications on loans of 80 percent or less on prime property. The institution approved the loan in their local area.

Case 2

A buyer was purchasing a $950,000 home and needed a 75 percent loan. The buyer wanted to get the lowest possible interest rate on the loan. The salesperson knew the buyer was self-employed and asked if the buyer had a strong banking relationship through the business. Although there was a strong relationship, the buyer wasn't going to apply for a loan with the business's bank because that bank usually did not make many real estate loans. The salesperson knew from past experience that banks are customer oriented and will make exceptions to their basic policy for a good customer, and accordingly advised the buyer to inquire. After checking with the bank, the buyer obtained an interest rate 1 percent lower than was available elsewhere.

Case 3

A young couple had enough saved for a 20 percent down payment and closing costs. Their offer to purchase a house was, as is common, contingent upon getting a 30-year fixed rate mortgage. Weeks later the couple learned that they could not qualify, despite a combined gross income of $178,000. All the income was from self-employment, with the net income only $60,000—roughly one third of gross—and the husband had been in business for only nine months. Since they could not qualify under normal underwriting guidelines (discussed in Chapter 9), they were turned down for the fixed rate loan. This would mean scaling down the amount of the mortgage, thus having to come up with more upfront money for the down payment. Contacting a mortgage broker, they found the solution: an adjustable rate mortgage with its lower initial rate, combined with a gift letter signed by their parents to help with the down payment. Result: Happy new homeowners, happy lender, happy mortgage broker, and, it is earnestly hoped, happy parents.

5.3 Buy-Down Loans

If you scan newspaper ads during tight-money periods, when interest rates on new home loans are high, you will see many home builders advertising new loans at below-market rates. Builders and other sellers are able to offer below-market rates by means of a **buy-down loan**. On a buy-down loan, the interest rate is reduced (bought down) by compensating the lender with a lump-sum payment at the time the loan is made. Sellers generally compensate the lender, but it can also be the borrower who pays the lender to reduce the rate.

Temporary Buy-Down Plans

Temporary buy-down loans are labeled "temporary" because interest rates are reduced for only part of the term of the loan, such as for two years. A typical temporary buy-down loan offers an initial rate at 2 percent below the note rate, and the interest rate increases are generally limited to 1 percent per year, sometimes called a "2/1" or "3/2/1" buy-down.

To illustrate the cost of a temporary buy-down, assume a $400,000 loan at a current market interest rate of 7 percent, amortized for 30 years, with a 2 percent buy-down for two years.

The total benefit to the buyer during the first two years of the loan is just over $9,300 in this case. This benefit is made possible in most cases by an upfront payment to the lender by a builder-seller, with the

BUY-DOWN ON A $400,000 LOAN AT 7% INTEREST

Months	Interest Rate	Monthly Payment @7%	Borrower's Payments	Monthly Buy-Down Amount			Total Buy-Down Amount
1–12	5%	$2,661.21	–$2,147.29 =	$513.92	× 12	=	$6,167.08
13–24	6%	$2,661.21	–$2,398.20 =	$263.01	× 12	=	$3,156.09
25–360	7%	$2,661.21	–$2,661.21 =	0	× 12	=	0
				Total		=	$9,323.17

"subsidy" being added to the price of the house, which then must reflect the added cost in the appraised value.

Permanent Buy-Down Plans

Some lenders offer a buy-down for the entire term of the loan. The fee paid to the lender is also calculated differently. The fee the seller pays the lender is a discount (points) that increases the lender's yield over the entire term.

> **Example:** A builder wishes to sell a new condo to a buyer, but subject to the buyer obtaining a $300,000 loan with a 30-year amortization and a 6 percent rate of interest. A lender is willing to make the loan; however, its rate of interest is 7 percent. The builder asks about buying the rate down to 6 percent. The lender states the rate can be bought down for a discount of about 5 points or $15,000, which increases the lender's effective yield to 6 percent. The builder agrees to pay the $15,000 (though it may increase the price by that amount and then the appraisal has to reflect the higher "value") and the sale is closed.

5.4 Low Down Payment Conventional Loans

Both the Federal National Mortgage Association and the Federal Home Loan Mortgage Corporation recognize that accumulating a down payment and the required closing costs keeps many people from buying a home. To help this situation, both have created several low down payment programs. Although there are minor differences between Fannie Mae and Freddie Mac, the gist of the popular Fannie/Freddie 97 programs is as follows:

- A down payment of only 3 percent is required, meaning a 97 percent loan-to-value (LTV) loan is granted.

- Income qualifying ratios are easier.

- Borrowers must have an excellent credit history.

- Borrowers must attend a home buyer educational seminar.

- In some cases there may be an income level requirement for the borrower (these limits are more generous in California than in most other states).

- The loan can be used to buy only single-family, principal residences, including condos, planned unit developments, and manufactured homes attached to a permanent foundation.

Another popular Fannie Mae/Freddie Mac offering is called the **Community Home Buyer's Program**. This plan is designed especially to help low- and moderate-income home buyers and features what is called the 3/2 option. The 3/2 Option provides for a low 5 percent down payment, but with a twist. It allows borrowers to put only 3 percent of their own money toward a down payment. The other 2 percent may be obtained from family gifts or by means of a grant or loan from the state, a local government agency, or a nonprofit organization.

Traditional credit standards are required, but other underwriting criteria are eased to qualify applicants, with greater emphasis on stable job history, steady rent and utility payments, and a ceiling on the qualifying income level, since the program is limited to those less affluent. Though creditworthiness is always important, a greater percentage of applicants' gross monthly income may be used to meet mortgage payments. Because of the high loan-to-value ratio, the 3/2 Option loans must be covered by private mortgage insurance, discussed later. But with what amounts to 97 percent financing, coupled with reduced closing costs and cash reserve requirements, more families may find the dream of homeownership affordable.

Special Interest Topic

Interest Deduction Limitations on 125 percent Loans. Watch Out!

In addition to questioning the economic soundness of sucking out the equity in a principal residence, there could be some income tax deductions problems. Contrary to what is advertised, as a general rule, homeowners cannot deduct the interest paid on any portion of home loan that exceeds the market value of the home, if the excess loan proceeds above the market value are used to pay off personal consumer debts. Possible exceptions: the interest may be deductible if excess proceeds are used for a business, investment, or in some instances medical or educational purposes. The IRS is discussing with lenders how to go about flagging the returns of homeowners who have taken out loans that exceed the market value of the property. Perhaps the information may some day appear on the lender's Form 1098 interest deduction filed with the IRS. Before taking any loan in excess of the property's market value, a borrower should consult a tax expert on recent IRS rulings.

5.5 California Fair Lending Regulations

The Housing Financial Discrimination Act (Anti-Redlining Law) applies to owner-occupied residential properties of one to four units. The act also includes nonowner-occupied loans on up to four units if 50 percent or more of the loan proceeds are to be used to improve the property.

The act states that financial institutions cannot deny or discriminate in fixing the amount, interest rate, or length of the loan based upon:

1. Neighborhood considerations as listed below unless the institution can prove that such considerations are necessary to avoid unsafe and unsound business practices.
   a. Age of other properties in the neighborhood
   b. Location of the property in the neighborhood
   c. Location of the property on or near land zoned industrial or commercial
   d. Other conditions, characteristics, or trends in the neighborhood

2. Race, color, religion, sex, marital status or registered domestic partnership, sexual orientation, national origin, handicap, ancestry, family size, or other characteristics of the borrower.

3. Racial, ethnic, religious, national origin, or income-level composition of a neighborhood or whether that composition is expected to change.

The act also prohibits *discrimination by effect*. That means that the institution cannot engage in a lending practice that has a discriminatory effect against a protected group, unless that practice is required to achieve a legitimate business purpose. If it is clear that a practice has a discriminatory effect, then the burden is on the institution to show that the practice is required. This is called the "Effects Test."

Some examples of discrimination by effect are rejecting a borrower because of an isolated credit difficulty or credit difficulties in the distant past; not including income from overtime or part-time work; or being overly restrictive on payment-to-income ratios when qualifying borrowers. These practices would discriminate against minority and lower-income groups.

It was previously indicated that the institution can adjust the terms of the loan, if necessary, to avoid unsafe and unsound business practices. The act has spelled out further regulations in regard to this.

4. If the institution can document that factors in the neighborhood are likely to cause the value of the property to decrease during the first five years, then it may make adjustments to the loan (reduce the loan amount, for example).

5. The institution may consider natural or other hazardous conditions surrounding the property. A steep, unstable site would be an example of a hazardous condition and reason for rejection of the property.

6. A loan does not have to be made if it is clearly evident that the physical condition of the property would create an imminent threat to the health or safety of the occupant.

7. Decisions on the loan security must be based solely on the value of the individual property, unless the institution can document specific neighborhood conditions that affect its present or short-range value (three to five years). Such conditions may include market trends based upon actual transactions involving comparable property and trends indicating increasing numbers of abandoned, vandalized, or foreclosed properties in the immediate vicinity of the property. A statement that there are abandoned, vandalized, or foreclosed properties in the neighborhood will not, by itself, support a conclusion that a neighborhood is declining. The evidence necessary to document a probable decline must be specific.

8. If pending or recent zoning would affect the short-term value of the property (three to five years), the loan may be denied or the terms may be altered. However, the fact that a property is located

on or near land zoned industrial or commercial will not, in itself, be an adequate basis for denying the loan. If the lender is reasonably sure that a building permit would not be issued in the event of a casualty loss due to zoning, the lender may be justified in denying the loan.

The act includes a number of regulations that affect a lender's policy on qualifying borrowers. The main ones are the following:

9. Supplemental income such as overtime, bonuses, and part-time employment must be considered, if stable. Not to consider stable supplemental income could be discriminatory because minority and low- and moderate-income families often rely on this type of income.

10. The combined income of husband and wife must be considered.

11. The lender cannot favor applicants who have previously owned homes.

12. Payment-to-income ratios should be flexible. Inflexible ratios could discriminate against low- or moderate-income persons who often devote a greater percentage of their income to housing. Additional general requirements of the act include these:

13. A lender may not deny a loan or require corrective work because of code violations or conditions of the property unless the cost of corrective work is more than 10 percent of the value before repairs or it is necessary to correct conditions that are a threat to the health and safety of the occupants.

14. A lender cannot use a rigid list of on-site characteristics as an automatic basis for rejecting a loan, such as a minimum square footage requirement.

15. Each lender must have written loan standards available to the public.

16. Upon submission of a written loan application, the applicant must be given a fair lending notice (see Figure 5.1).

5.6 Mortgage Insurance

Mortgage insurance is acquired to guarantee the payment of the upper portion of a conventional loan in case the lender forecloses and suffers a loss. Mortgage insurance is used primarily with loan-to-value ratios of more than 80 percent, as discussed in the next section.

THE HOUSING FINANCIAL DISCRIMINATION ACT OF 1977

FAIR LENDING NOTICE

It is illegal to discriminate in the provision of or in the availability of financial assistance because of the consideration of:

1. Trends, characteristics or conditions in the neighborhood or geographic area surrounding a housing accommodation, unless the financial institution can demonstrate in the particular case that such consideration is required to avoid an unsafe and unsound business practice: or

2. Race, color, religion, sex, marital status, domestic partnership, national origin or ancestry.

It is illegal to consider the racial, ethnic, religious or national origin composition of a neighborhood or geographic area surrounding a housing accommodation or whether or not such composition is undergoing change, or is expected to undergo change, in appraising a housing accommodation or in determining whether or not, or under what terms and conditions, to provide financial assistance.

These provisions govern financial assistance for the purpose of the purchase, construction, rehabilitation or refinancing of one- to four-unit family residences occupied by the owner and for the purpose of the home improvement of any one- to four-unit family residence.

If you have any questions about your rights, or if you wish to file a complaint, contact the management of this financial institution or the Department of Real Estate at one of the following locations:

2550 Mariposa Mall, Suite 3070
Fresno, CA 93721-2273

320 W. 4th Street, Suite 350
Los Angeles, CA 90013-1105

1515 Clay Street, Suite 702
Oakland, CA 94612-1462

2201 Broadway
P.O. Box 187000 *(mailing address)*
Sacramento, CA 95818-7000

1350 Front Street, Suite 3064
San Diego, CA 92101-3687

ACKNOWLEDGMENT OF RECEIPT

I (we) received a copy of this notice.

_____   _____
Signature of Applicant   *Date*

_____   _____
Signature of Applicant   *Date*

DEPARTMENT OF REAL ESTATE — Mortgage Lending Unit   RE 867 (Rev. 6/04)

Figure 5.1 Fair lending notice.

The insurance is sold by PMI (private mortgage insurance) companies. (FHA's Mortgage Insurance Premium [MIP] and Mutual Mortgage Insurance [MMI] are discussed in Chapter 6.) Before the depression of 1929–1934, a number of PMI companies were in operation. Most of them went into bankruptcy during the depression due to poor policies and inadequate regulations. The industry was dormant until the Mortgage Guarantee Insurance Corporation (MGIC) in Milwaukee began

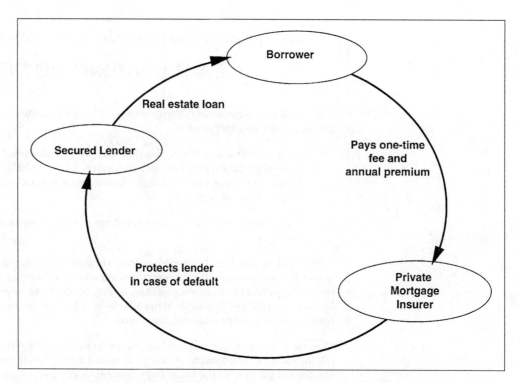

Figure 5.2 Mortgage insurance.

operations in 1957. Figure 5.2 shows the relationship between borrower, lender, and insurer.

The major growth of the PMI industry took place after 1970. One reason was that lenders and builders had become disenchanted with the Federal Housing Administration (FHA) because of the red tape and the artificially low interest rate set by the government. Due to the low FHA interest rate, builders in those days had to pay high discounts (points) to sell their houses. To avoid these problems, builders and lenders turned to conventional mortgages insured by private mortgage insurance companies. As a result, they were able to eliminate high discounts and costly red tape. In addition, the mortgage insurance allowed lenders to continue making loans with low down payments.

Private mortgage insurance companies began to skyrocket in 1971 when lending institutions were given the authority to make 95 percent loan-to-value loans. In the same year, the Federal Home Loan Mortgage Corporation (Freddie Mac) and Federal National Mortgage Association (Fannie Mae) were given the authority to purchase high-ratio conventional loans. However, one of their requirements was that all loans above 80 percent must have mortgage insurance. When Freddie Mac and Fannie Mae began buying high-ratio conventional loans, they sparked the secondary market for conventional loans. Since these loans required mortgage insurance, this accelerated the growth of private mortgage insurance companies.

PMI = If foreclosure occurs, the lender is reimbursed for any loss up to the maximum dollar coverage.

Credit Life Insurance = If borrower dies, the remaining loan balance is paid off by the insurance company.

Figure 5.3 The difference between private mortgage insurance and credit life insurance.

It should be noted that private mortgage insurance is not the same as **credit life insurance**. These two types of insurance are contrasted in Figure 5.3.

Coverage and Cost of Mortgage Insurance

Mortgage insurance is available on one-to-four-unit dwellings. Generally, the companies insure loans on one to two units up to 97 percent and on three to four units up to 90 percent. Figures can vary from company to company and the following examples are for illustration purposes only.

1. *Loans over 80 and up to 85 percent loan-to-value coverage:* The insurance ordinarily covers the top 12 percent of the loan amount. To keep it simple, if a home sold for $100,000 and the loan was 85 percent or $85,000, the coverage would be 12 percent of $85,000 = $10,200. The lender's exposure is $74,800, or 75 percent. *Cost:* If *annual* premiums are utilized, the fee due at close of escrow would be about .29 percent of $85,000, or about $246, and monthly collections thereafter would be $20.54. If *monthly* premiums are utilized, there may be no advance collection at COE, and the premiums based on .32 percent would be $22.67 per month.

2. *Loans above 85 and up to 90 percent loan-to-value coverage:* The insurance ordinarily covers the top 25 percent of the loan amount.

If a home sold for $100,000 and the loan was 90 percent or $90,000, the coverage would be 25 percent of $90,000 = $22,500. Lender's exposure is $67,800 or 68 percent. *Cost:* If *annual* premiums are utilized, the fee due at close of escrow would be about .49 percent of $90,000, or about $441, and monthly collections thereafter would be $36.75. If *monthly* premiums are utilized, there may be no advance collection at COE, and the premiums based on .52 percent would be $39 per month.

3. *Loans above 90 and up to 97 percent loan-to-value coverage:* The insurance ordinarily covers the top 30 percent of the loan amount. If a home sold for $100,000 and the loan was 95 percent or $95,000, the coverage would be 30 percent of $95,000 = $28,500. Lender's exposure is $66,500 or 67 percent. *Cost:* If *annual* premiums are utilized, the fee due at close of escrow would be about .75 percent of $95,000, or about $712, and monthly collections thereafter would be $59.38. If *monthly* premiums are utilized, there may be no advance collection at COE, and the premiums based on .78 percent would be $61.75 per month.

There are other variations of fees and annual premiums, as well as plans whereby you can pay one fee at the time of closing and no annual premium. Whether premiums are paid on the basis of $1/12$ of an annual premium or merely on a monthly premium basis, the amounts are ordinarily collected by the lender with monthly impounds of taxes and insurance.

Some lenders will, as an alternative, insure the loan using PMI that the lender pays for by increasing its loan interest rate. In this circumstance, the lender's quoted rate includes the PMI premiums, but since it is, in fact, an interest rate, it is deductible under IRS rules. If the lender charges an interest rate plus the PMI premium, then only the interest is deductible, and the insurance premium is not.

Offsetting this advantage or disadvantage (depending upon how long the borrower resides in the property) is the fact that when the lender includes the PMI in its rate, the payments will never change, even when the loan-to-value drops below 80 percent and the PMI coverage is dropped. At that point, the lender's yield increases by the amount of premium no longer paid. On the other hand, when the lender charges a rate plus a premium, the borrower's payment will decrease when loan-to-value declines to 78 percent or below, and PMI is no longer required. For short-term ownership, being able to deduct it all as interest may be advantageous. For long-term ownership, the likelihood that payments will someday decrease may be the better choice.

In California, the Civil Code allows residential borrowers to cancel PMI after two years if the loan-to-value ratio is 78 percent of the current market value. But better yet, under federal law, for all new insured loans originated after January 1999, all lenders on FHA-insured loans must cancel the MIP coverage when there is at least a 22 percent home equity. This 22 percent equity must be shown by an official appraisal, the borrower must have a good payment history, and the loan must be on the books for at least two years. Appreciation, not just principal pay down, counts to measure the 22 percent or more equity. Special note: Both the California and federal laws cover only new insured loans granted from January 1998 for the state law, and January 1999 for the federal law, but not loans already on record prior to those dates. In both cases, FHA mortgage insurance (MIP) cannot be cancelled.

How Is Mortgage Insurance Obtained?

Each PMI company sets its own policy regarding property and borrower standards. Generally, they follow the typical conventional lender standards set forth by FNMA/FHLMC. To obtain the insurance, an approved lender submits a loan package to the PMI company. After the package is received, the PMI company acts very quickly. The lender receives an answer by fax, e-mail, or telephone, usually the same day, and a written commitment follows later. This fast service is one of the main advantages of dealing with a PMI company. Some lenders are allowed to do in-house underwriting for PMI.

How Are Claims Handled?

If a foreclosure occurs on a property that is insured, the PMI company either:

- Pays off the lender in full and takes title to the property, or

- Pays the lender in accordance with the insurance, usually 20 to 25 percent of the principal balance plus certain expenses. The lender then keeps the property and is responsible for reselling it after foreclosure.

SUMMARY

Any loan that is not a government-backed loan is called a conventional loan. Some of the perceived advantages of a conventional loan are faster processing, high loan amounts, and *perhaps* less red tape. In some cases, the disadvantages include higher down payments and occasional prepayment penalties.

There are many sources of conventional loans. The main ones are thrift institutions, commercial banks, and mortgage companies. Each lender that keeps its paper (called portfolio loans), sets its own policy regarding loan-to-value ratio, type of property, interest rates, loan fees, and borrower qualifications as long as it is not discriminatory.

However, many lenders plan on reselling the loan in the secondary market to Fannie Mae or Freddie Mac. In doing so, the lender originating the loan loses flexibility and must abide by the Fannie Mae or Freddie Mac guidelines.

On a buy-down loan, the interest rate is reduced by paying the lender an up-front fee or discount. A standard buy-down loan allows the rate to be reduced no more than 2 percent. The California Housing Financial Discrimination Act forbids discrimination in residential loans based on neighborhood considerations or on race, color, religion, sex, marital status or registered domestic partnership, sexual orientation, handicap, national origin, family size, or ancestry of the borrower.

Mortgage insurance is used to guarantee the upper portion of conventional loans. It is used primarily on loans whose loan-to-value ratio exceeds 80 percent.

IMPORTANT TERMS AND CONCEPTS

Buy-down loans

Community Home Buyer's Program

Conventional loans

Credit life insurance

Discrimination by effect (Effects Test)

Federal Home Loan Mortgage Corporation (Freddie Mac)

Federal National Mortgage Association (Fannie Mae)

Government-backed loans

Jumbo loans

Low down payment conventional loans

Portfolio loan

Private mortgage insurance (PMI)

REVIEWING YOUR UNDERSTANDING

Questions for Discussion

1. **List five items of comparison when shopping with conventional lenders for a real estate loan.**

2. **Describe how private mortgage insurance (PMI) works, including coverage and costs.**

3. **The Housing Financial Discrimination Act (Anti-Redlining Law) prohibits discrimination based upon a variety of considerations. List at least five of these.**

Multiple-Choice Questions

1. A non-government-backed loan is best known as a _____ loan.
   a. portfolio.
   b. standard.
   c. conventional.
   d. normal.

2. Assume an application for a $450,000 loan is made and that the lender demands 1.5 points as a condition for granting the loan. The loan fee will be
   a. $6,750.
   b. $4,500.
   c. $67,500.
   d. none of the above.

3. Private mortgage insurance covers what portion of the loan amount?
   a. upper portion of the loan.
   b. middle portion of the loan.
   c. lower portion of the loan.
   d. entire loan.

4. The most flexible loan terms (not necessarily the lowest interest rate) are usually obtainable on what type of loan?
   a. portfolio.
   b. standard.
   c. conforming.
   d. FHA.

5. When prepayment penalties are charged by conventional lenders for an owner-occupied dwelling, the amount may not exceed
   a. one year's unearned interest.
   b. six months' interest, based on the excess over 20 percent of the original loan amount.
   c. an additional interest rate of $1/2$ percent on the unpaid balance.
   d. 10 percent of the loan balance.

6. In the event of foreclosure of a PMI-backed conventional loan, the insurer may
   a. pay off the lender in full and take back the property.
   b. pay the lender up to the amount of insurance.
   c. do either (a) or (b).
   d. do neither (a) nor (b).

7. When a seller or builder buys down the borrower's interest rate for the life of the loan, it is called
   a. a 3/2/1 buy-down.
   b. an adjustable buy-down.
   c. a fixed buy-down.
   d. a permanent buy-down.

8. Obtaining private mortgage insurance for a loan involves
   a. standards imposed by the private mortgage insurance company.
   b. lower interest rates.
   c. shorter processing time.
   d. lower loan-to-value ratios.

9. One might expect to find the shortest processing time in the case of
   a. government-backed loans.
   b. portfolio loans.
   c. loans that are to be sold in the secondary market.
   d. loans on which discount fees are charged.

10. Which of the following is often required for a Fannie Mae/ Freddie Mac low down payment first-time home buyer loan?
    a. educational seminar.
    b. sufficient rental income.
    c. five-year work history.
    d. tougher income qualifying ratios.

11. Once a loan has been denied by a conventional lender,
    a. the applicant is effectively barred from obtaining other financing.
    b. the best move is to apply for a jumbo loan.
    c. the applicant is entitled to apply through another conventional lender.
    d. the applicant can always get the seller to agree to a lease with option to buy.

12. The highest loan-to-value ratio permitted by regulation for insured conventional loans is
    a. 80 percent.
    b. 90 percent.
    c. 97 percent.
    d. 125 percent.

13. Conventional lenders who grant only portfolio loans
    a. are all the same and adhere strictly to the same set of rules.
    b. are closely regulated in the type and quality of property they will accept as security for loans.
    c. differ greatly in philosophy and can chart their own courses within the framework of their regulations.
    d. have no decision-making authority anymore.

14. Qualifying standards for borrowers using conventional loans that are to be sold to Fannie Mae/Freddie Mac
    a. differ widely, depending upon the particular lender.
    b. are usually the same throughout the range of lenders.
    c. are set by various government bodies.
    d. differ greatly, depending upon whether the lender is state or federally chartered.

15. An interest rate that is tied to an index that is subject to change is most commonly called:
    a. fluctuating.
    b. adjustable.
    c. changeable.
    d. irregular.

16. California's Housing Financial Discrimination Act allows lenders to discriminate in residential lending only in the case of
    a. loan applicant's low ratio of payment to income.
    b. location of the property near industrial property.
    c. a situation that would lead to unsafe and unsound business practices.
    d. ethnic or racial mix.

17. The Community Home Buyer's Program allows buyers to finance with as little as what percent of their own funds for the down payment?
    a. 5 percent.
    b. 3 percent.
    c. 2 percent.
    d. none of these.

18. The erosion in the purchasing power of money, and for which lenders may adjust interest rates under ARM loans, is labeled
    a. deflation.
    b. inflation.
    c. devaluation.
    d. stagflation.

19. The type of insurance that pays off the mortgage balance in the event of the borrower's death is called
    a. private mortgage insurance.
    b. standard life insurance.
    c. credit life insurance.
    d. disability insurance.

20. Of the buy-down loan plans, the type that's usually best for the buyer is the
    a. temporary buy-down for two years.
    b. temporary buy-down for five years.
    c. permanent buy-down plan.
    d. plan with full amortization.

CHAPTER 6
GOVERNMENT-BACKED FINANCING

PREVIEW

This chapter covers four major sources of government-backed loans: the Federal Housing Administration (FHA), U.S. Department of Veterans Affairs (DVA), California Department of Veteran Affairs (Cal-Vet), and the California Housing Finance Agency (CalHFA).

After completing this chapter, you should be able to:

1. List the main advantages and disadvantages of FHA-insured loans.

2. Calculate the maximum loan amount on various FHA programs.

3. Explain the key features of DVA guaranteed loans.

4. List the main characteristics of the Cal-Vet loan system.

5. Outline the CalHFA first-time home buyer program.

6.1 Federal Housing Administration

In this section, we discuss what the Federal Housing Administration (FHA) does and some of the advantages and disadvantages of an *FHA-insured loan*. Commonly used FHA programs are explained, with examples. Full details regarding FHA can be found at www.hud.gov.

What Is the FHA?

The FHA, part of the Department of Housing and Urban Development, was established in 1934 to improve the construction and the financing of housing. Since its creation, it has had a major influence on real estate financing. Some of today's loan features that are taken for granted were initiated by FHA. For example, before FHA, it was common practice to make real estate loans for short periods of time (one to five years). These loans were not fully amortized and every few years, borrowers had to renegotiate loans with their lender. This created problems, particularly during the Great Depression of the 1930s. During that time, when loans were due, many lenders were not willing or able to renew the loans and as a result there were massive foreclosures. Major loan reforms, spearheaded by the newly created Federal Housing Administration, included:

- Fully amortized loans

- Low down payment loans

- Low interest rates

- Mandatory collection of taxes and fire insurance premiums

- Minimum property standards

- Standards for qualifying the borrowers

What Does the FHA Do?

The FHA is not a lender—it does not make loans. Qualified mortgage companies, savings banks, and commercial banks make the loans. The FHA insures these lenders against loss in the event of foreclosure.

The FHA approves the property and the qualifications of the borrower. Later, a lender makes the loan, which, in turn, is insured by the FHA. The FHA charges the borrower a **Mortgage Insurance Premium (MIP)**, which the FHA-insured lender collects from the borrower and pays to the FHA. The borrower has a choice of paying the MIP in a lump sum up front or adding it to the loan amount and paying it over the term of the loan. In addition, the borrower pays a monthly MMI premiums (Mutual Mortgage Insurance) described under "FHA Guidelines."

This insurance should not be confused with credit life insurance. The FHA's insurance does not insure the borrower's life. The FHA insurance premiums go into a "pool" to be used by the FHA to cover losses on foreclosed properties. If a lender forecloses on an FHA-insured property, the lender then transfers title to the FHA, which in turn reimburses the lender if there is a loss.

Advantages of FHA Loans

It is important that you know when to use FHA financing. Knowing the advantages helps you decide.

1. Low down payment. The main advantage of an FHA loan is the low down payment required.

2. The maximum loan fee is 1 percent of the loan amount. The buyer normally pays this fee.

3. Secondary financing is allowed with a new FHA loan provided the combined FHA loan and second loan do not exceed the FHA maximum. However, this provision is rarely used.

4. The maximum loan term is 30 years or 75 percent of the remaining economic life of the property, whichever is less. The amount of remaining economic life is determined by the appraiser.

5. The FHA requires that monthly payments include principal and interest, taxes, fire insurance, and **Mutual Mortgage Insurance (MMI)**, often referred to as PITI + MMI. The monthly amounts paid toward taxes, insurance, and MMI are deposited in an impound account, also called an escrow account.

6. There is no maximum purchase price. The buyer can pay more than the FHA appraisal. However, the loan will be based on the FHA appraisal if it is lower than the purchase price.

7. The interest rates and discount points are completely negotiable between the lender and the borrower.

8. The borrower must occupy the property.

9. FHA appraisals (called "**conditional commitments**") are good for six months on existing property and one year on new construction. The FHA uses independent fee appraisers who are "FHA qualified."

10. The FHA requires that existing property must have no evidence of structural pest infestation. Certification must be obtained from a recognized structural pest inspection company.

11. As of 2006 borrowers must pay two mortgage insurance premiums. The first is identified by the initials MIP. It is an upfront fee measured by 1.5 percent of the loan amount in the case of a 30-year loan. It may be paid in cash through escrow or it can be financed by adding it to the loan amount.

    The second, MMI, is paid monthly, measured by $\frac{1}{2}$ percent (.5 percent) divided by 12, computed on the average annual loan balance, with this premium dropping slightly each year. For 15-year loans, the upfront fees are lower and monthly MMI drops to .25 percent. If the borrower attends a qualified homeowner education class the upfront fees can be lowered further. MMI premiums may be dropped when the remaining loan balance is 80 percent LTV or less. Due to the complexity and constantly changing rules, it is suggested that you check with local lenders for the latest insurance premium charges at the time the loan is applied for.

12. Direct Endorsement. A previous disadvantage was the length of time it took to approve an FHA loan. However, many lenders now have "direct endorsement" approval, which means the lender can underwrite the loans and do the FHA processing in-house.

It should be noted, as explained below, that the FHA does place a dollar-limit on the maximum insured loan.

How to Calculate FHA-Insured Loan Amounts

Like conventional lenders, FHA-insured loan amounts are based on a fixed percentage of the lower of the property's sales price or appraised value.

FHA multiplies the lesser of the two by a predetermined percentage to arrive at the maximum loan amount it will insure. This maximum will vary by state and counties within each state. In addition, the amount within each county can change each year. To determine the maximum FHA-insured loan for your area, you will need to ask a local FHA-approved lender or go to the HUD website at www.hud.gov and search for maximum FHA loan amounts. Then input the state and county and the current maximum FHA insured loan amount will appear.

Maximum Loan-to-Value Percentages for California Homes (as of 1/06)

Home Value	Percentage
$50,000 or less	98.75%
More than $50,000, up to $125,000	97.65%
More than $125,000, up to maximum allowed	97.15%

These loan-to-value ratios require the borrower to make a "cash investment" of at least 3 percent in the home. This 3 percent cash investment is composed of the required down payment, plus a portion of the **nonrecurring closing costs**. The allowable nonrecurring closing costs consist of items such as: loan origination fee, appraisal fee, credit report, and title and escrow fees. It should be mentioned that, as of January 2006, FHA was considering, but had not yet implemented, a no down payment feature, up to the maximum allowed loan.

Example 1: Over $50,000, up to $125,000 (California)

Sales price/value	$ 100,000
Maximum LTV ratio (97.65%)	× 0.9765
Maximum loan amount	$ 97,650
Sales price/value	$ 100,000
Maximum loan amount	− 97,650
Down payment	$ 2,350
Minimum qualifying closing costs to be paid	$ 650
3% investment needed	$ 3,000

Example 2: More than $125,000 (in a California higher-cost area)

Sales price/value	$ 300,000
Maximum LTV ratio (97.15%)	× 0.9715
Maximum loan amount	$ 291,450
Sales price/value	$ 300,000
Maximum loan amount	− 291,450
Down payment	$ 8,550
Minimum qualifying closing cost to be paid	450
3% investment needed	$ 9,000

FHA regulations originally stated that the required cash investment should come from the borrower's own funds. However, current FHA guidelines will allow the 3 percent cash investment to be a bona fide gift or a loan from a government agency or from a family member. If a loan, the said loan payment must be counted to determine whether the borrower is qualified for the FHA-insured loan. In addition, the junior loan must not require a balloon payment within the first five years.

The 3 percent cash investment cannot come from loans from other sources, such as the seller, the builder, or an outside private source. If the seller or builder attempts to circumvent this rule by offering a "decorating allowance" or any other inducements, the maximum FHA insured loan is decreased by said amounts.

FHA Programs

The National Housing Act of 1934 created the Federal Housing Administration. The act has eleven titles, or subdivisions, with further subdivisions called sections.

This chapter deals with only some of the sections under Title II of the act, since these are the most important to the average consumer or real estate agent. Title II authorizes the FHA to insure the financing on proposed or existing dwellings for one-to-four-family residences. The main sections are 203(b) and 245(a). Each of these programs is discussed below.

Section 203(b)

Under the 203(b) program:

1. Anyone 18 and over is eligible.

2. Loans are available on properties of from one to four units.

3. U.S. citizenship is not required; resident aliens are eligible.

4. The FHA establishes a range of maximum loan amounts for one-to-four-unit dwellings that vary according to area. In California, the maximum FHA loan amount varies by county. The cost of housing in a particular area determines the maximum loan amount, which is adjusted periodically to keep up with property values. As mentioned before; go to www.hud.gov to find the current loan amounts for your area.

Non-occupant borrower   The FHA requires the borrower to occupy the property. The only exception is if an investor purchases a HUD repossession.

Houses less than one year old   You cannot obtain a standard full-sized FHA loan on a house less than one year old which is not built under FHA or DVA inspections. This restriction also applies to houses that were moved onto the site less than one year earlier. The FHA penalizes these properties by reducing the loan to 90 percent of lower sales price or of appraised value.

FHA Adjustable Rate Loan—Section 245(a)

This loan is available on single-family dwellings. The maximum loan-to-value ratio is the same as for the 203(b) program.

Other features of the adjustable loan include:

1. *Index*. U.S. Treasury security constant maturity of one year.

2. *Margin*. Borrower may choose either 2 percent, 2.5 percent, or 2.75 percent.

3. *Adjustment period*. Adjustable once each year.

4. *Annual rate cap.* 1 percent.

5. *Lifetime cap.* 5 percent.

6.2 Department of Veterans Affairs

This section covers:

- Department of Veterans Affairs (DVA) Guaranteed Loans

- What the DVA does and some of the advantages and disadvantages and general features of a DVA loan

- Eligibility and partial entitlements

What Is the Department of Veterans Affairs (DVA)?

The U.S. Veterans Bureau was founded in 1916 to assist needy veterans of the Civil War and Spanish American War. Its name changed to the Veterans Administration in 1930, then again in 1989, when it was elevated to cabinet level with the designation Department of Veterans Affairs. We use DVA throughout the text, but most lenders and agents continue to use the shorter, long-used "VA" whenever dealing with veterans loans. Full details regarding DVA guaranteed loans can be found at www.homeloans.VA.gov.

Administration of DVA Home Loan Program

The Loan Guarantee Division of the Department of Veterans Affairs is responsible for the administration of the DVA home program. In many ways, the DVA home program operates like FHA. However, from a lender's point of view, the major differences are as follows:

1. DVA guarantees a loan, whereas FHA insures a loan.

2. DVA guarantees only a part of the loan, whereas FHA insures the entire loan.

The DVA-guaranteed amount is calculated as 25 percent of the current Freddie Mac conforming loan amount. Each year, if the Freddie Mac conforming loan amount increases, the DVA guarantee to an approved lender also increases. For example, as of January 2006, the maximum Freddie Mac conforming loan was $417,000, thus 25% × 417,000 = $104,250 maximum DVA lender guarantee.

Then, most DVA-approved lenders simply reverse the process and grant a no-money down loan to qualified veterans that is four times the DVA guarantee. For 2006, it would be $104,250 × 4 = $417,000 as the maximum no down payment DVA-guaranteed loan. Bottom line, the maximum DVA no money down loan amount is the same as maximum Freddie Mac conforming loan amount.

Whether a loan is insured or guaranteed is important only if a foreclosure occurs. If a foreclosure occurs, the DVA has two options:

1. It can pay the lender the loan balance and take back the property.

2. It can give the lender the property and pay it the amount of the deficiency, if any, up to the maximum amount of the DVA guarantee.

Advantages and Disadvantages of DVA Loans

In the discussion of FHA loans, the advantages and disadvantages were listed. Most of the advantages and disadvantages also apply to DVA loans. Some differences, however, are worth listing.

Advantages of DVA Loans

1. *No down payment.* DVA-guaranteed lenders ordinarily do not require any down payment on loans up to four times the DVA guarantee. This is the maximum that FHLMC and FNMA will purchase in the secondary market, as detailed in Chapter 7. The relatively high loan amount without a down payment requirement makes a DVA loan highly desirable. The "no down" feature is ideal not just for moderate-income people. Business and professional people are also attracted to DVA loans because they can use the money they save on a DVA loan in their business or other investments.

2. *No prepayment penalty.* The veteran-borrower may pay off the loan in full at any time without penalty.

3. *Possible assumability.* DVA loans recorded before March 1, 1988, are fully assumable, and without a rate increase. These DVA loans do not have alienation clauses; therefore, they are fully assumable. No approval from the lender or DVA is necessary. The lender can charge only a reasonable fee for changing the records. DVA loans recorded after February 29, 1988, can be assumed only if the new buyer meets DVA qualifications.

   However, the veteran who obtained the original loan remains personally liable to the DVA. If there is a foreclosure and subsequent loss to the DVA, the veteran can be charged for the amount of the loss.

A veteran can be released from liability by obtaining a Release of Liability from the DVA. There is a specific procedure set up by the DVA to obtain the release.

4. *Appraisal.* DVA appraisals, known as Certificate of Reasonable Value (CRVs), are made by independent licensed appraisers who work for the DVA on a fee basis. Appraisals are made to protect the veteran buyer. The DVA informs the buyer what it thinks is a reasonable value for the property. The buyer is allowed to pay more than that value if he or she agrees. But the veteran-buyer will be required to increase the down payment. This is protection for a buyer who is not aware of property values.

Disadvantages of DVA Loans

DVA loans have basically the same disadvantages as FHA loans.

1. *Red tape and processing time.* You run into the same problem with the DVA and the FHA. Processing time, inflexibility, paperwork, and the usual problems in dealing with a large government agency are disadvantages unless the lender is qualified to process DVA automatics, which are in-house approval programs.

2. *Repairs on existing property.* The DVA also requires repairs that it feels are necessary. In some cases, the DVA requires a certification from the city or county that the property meets current building codes.

3. *Lender limits.* DVA loans are usually not more than four times the guarantee. DVA itself does not prescribe a maximum, but lenders want saleable loans, hence their policy of limiting veteran loans to four times the DVA guarantee, according to FNMA/FHLMC "market" requirements.

4. *Discount points.* Though points are negotiable, from the borrower's point of view this may be a drawback. More often than not, buyer-borrowers end up paying all or part of these amounts, and the points may not be added to the loan.

Who Is Eligible for a DVA-Guaranteed Loan?
General Rules for Eligibility

As of January 2006, the general rules of eligibility state that a veteran is eligible for VA home loan benefits if he or she is currently serving or has served duty in the Army, Air Force, Marine Corps, or Coast Guard. If he or she has served in the past, the discharge must be for other than dishonorable reasons.

Specific requirements are broken down as follows:

<u>Wartime Service:</u>

WWII   09/16/40 to 07/25/47
Korean   06/27/50 to 01/31/55
Vietnam   08/05/64 to 05/07/75

The veteran must have spent at least 90 days on active duty and been discharged under other than dishonorable conditions.

<u>Peacetime Service:</u>

07/26/47   to 06/26/50
02/01/55   to 08/04/64
05/08/75   to 09/07/80 (enlisted)
            to 10/16/81 (officer)

The veteran must have served at least 181 days of continuous active duty and been discharged under other than dishonorable conditions.

<u>Service after 09/07/80 (enlisted) or 01/16/81 (officer)</u>
The veteran must have completed 24 months of continuous active duty or for the full period of at least 181 days, if called up for active duty, and discharged under conditions other than dishonorable.

<u>Gulf War Service from 08/02/90 to a date yet to be determined</u>
If the veteran service on active duty during the Gulf War, he or she must have completed 24 months of continuous duty or the full period of 90 days, if called or ordered to active duty, and been discharged under conditions other than dishonorable.

<u>Active-Duty Service Personnel</u>
If the veteran is now on active duty, he or she is eligible after having served 181 days (90 days during the Gulf War).

<u>Selected Reserves or National Guard</u>
If the reservist or National Guard member is not eligible in any of the aforementioned cases because he or she was not called up or ordered to active duty, he or she may be eligible if he or she has completed a total of six years in the Selected Reserves or National Guard while serving in an active unit, attended required weekend drills and two-week active duty for training, and is still serving or was discharged with an honorable discharge or was placed on the retired list or was transferred to a standby reserve.

Under all time frames noted, if the veteran was discharged for a service-connected disability before meeting the service time requirement, he or she may still be eligible for a DVA-guaranteed home loan.

There are other special rules for unmarried spouses of veterans who died in the service because of war or a service-connected accident, for spouses of veterans missing in action or prisoner of war, and for those who have served as a U.S. public health officer, as cadet in the U.S. Military academies, and so on. If there is a question regarding eligibility, contact the nearest DVA regional office for help.

Certificate of Eligibility

To establish eligibility for a DVA loan, a veteran must obtain a Certificate of Eligibility by filling out DVA Form 26-1880. To the form is attached a copy of the veteran's separation papers (DD214) and discharge. If still on active duty, the veteran submits a Statement of Service signed by the commanding officer. The form and attachments should be sent to the nearest DVA office, which will process the request and mail back the certificate.

The Certificate of Eligibility indicates the amount of the veteran's entitlement. The **entitlement** is the maximum number of dollars that the DVA will pay if the lender suffers a loss.

Reinstatement of Full Entitlement

A veteran will have full entitlement restored if the original loan has been paid in full and the property sold. Entitlement may also be restored if an eligible veteran agrees to assume the loan and substitute his or her entitlement for that of the original veteran. The new veteran must also qualify for the loan.

If a veteran sells a home with the new buyer assuming the loan, the veteran may be released from liability by the DVA if the new buyer is qualified. The veteran remains personally liable for any deficiency if the release is not obtained. The veteran must obtain both the *Reinstatement of Entitlement* and *Release of Liability*.

Partial Entitlements

The entitlement amount has been increased several times since the DVA program began, so veterans who have previously used their entitlement may have an unused partial entitlement. A veteran may purchase another home with a partial entitlement even if the previous DVA loan has not been paid off. The veteran can keep the first home and purchase another using DVA financing. Therefore, a veteran can technically have two or more DVA loans at the same time. To determine partial entitlements and their maximum loan amounts, veterans should contact their nearest DVA regional office.

General Information on DVA Loans

The FHA has a number of loan programs. In contrast, the DVA has only one program, offering either fixed or adjustable interest rates, and one set of rules that generally apply to all its loans.

1. *Type of property.* The DVA guarantees loans on properties from one to four units and units in planned unit developments and condominiums. The DVA approves new properties only if they were built under FHA or DVA inspections. If a property was not built with FHA or DVA inspections, you have to wait one year after the house has been completed. Then you can order the appraisal. Some exceptions to this one-year rule are (a) property located in a remote area where obtaining FHA or DVA inspections would be inconvenient; (b) property built by a small builder who does not normally use DVA loans to finance the sale of houses.

2. *Interest rate.* The interest rate and discount points are negotiable between lender and veteran-borrower. The seller may pay the discount points, the buyer and seller may split the payment, or these points can be paid by a third party.

3. *Loan origination and funding fees (as of January 2006).* The loan fee cannot exceed 1 percent of the loan amount. This 1 percent loan fee goes to the lender. Then the veteran is charged a funding fee that goes to DVA to help cover the cost of the government program.

   This funding fee is calculated as a percentage of the loan amount and the veteran has the option of paying the fee up front or financing it as part of DVA-guaranteed loan. The funding fee schedule for a home purchase is given below:

Type of Veteran	Down Payment	First Time Use	Subsequent Use
Regular Military	None	2.15%	3.30%
	5%–9%	1.50%	1.50%
	10% or more	1.25%	1.25%
Reserves/National Guard	None	2.4%	3.30%
	5–9%	1.75%	1.75%
	10% or more	1.50%	1.50%

Note: There are different funding fees for a DVA-guaranteed refinance and for manufactured home loans and loan assumptions.

4. *Term of loan.* The term cannot exceed the remaining economic life of the property, with a maximum term of 30 years.

5. *Down payment.* The DVA does not require a down payment—the veteran is allowed to borrow the full amount of the purchase price up to the maximum allowed by the DVA approved lender. What happens if the DVA appraises the property for less than the purchase price? At one time, the DVA would not allow the veteran to pay more than its appraisal. This caused real problems, since many veterans were willing and able to do so. This regulation prevented these veterans from purchasing a house of their choice. The regulation has since been eliminated. Now, the DVA will allow a veteran to pay more than the appraisal, but the loan amount cannot exceed the appraisal. The difference between the purchase price and the appraisal has to be in cash, and the money cannot be borrowed.

6. *Maximum loan.* There is no maximum loan amount under DVA rules. This does not mean you can obtain a no-down DVA loan in any amount. Since the DVA guarantees only a portion of the loan, lenders limit the amount they will lend on DVA loans. Most lenders use the maximum loan amount set in the secondary market.

   As stated earlier, since the bulk of DVA loans are sold to Fannie Mae or Freddie Mac, lenders follow FNMA or FHLMC rules. Both agencies limit the maximum loan to four times the entitlement. When the entitlement is increased, the maximum loan is thereby increased. The main point to remember is that the DVA does not set the maximum loan amount; it is the lender that determines the amount. Regardless of the loan amount, the DVA will not reimburse the lender for more than the amount of entitlement, regardless of what the lender's loss may be upon foreclosure.

7. *Occupying the property.* The veteran must occupy the property. The DVA does not have a program for veterans who do not intend to occupy the property.

8. *Monthly installments.* Technically, the DVA requires only monthly principal and interest payments. It does not require property taxes and insurance to be included. However, the DVA recommends that these be included, and the deed of trust provides lender authority to collect them. As a practical matter, all DVA loans include the taxes and insurance in the monthly payment.

9. *Appraisal.* The DVA-completed appraisal is turned in to the regional office to be checked and reviewed. The next step is to issue a **Certificate of Reasonable Value (CRV)**. Reasonable value means current market value, which the certificate states. In

practice, the DVA never issues a certificate showing a value greater than the sales price. If a home sells for $400,000, but the appraisal comes in at $425,000, the CRV will be for the $400,000 sales price, not the $425,000 appraised value. However, if the sales price is $400,000, but the appraisal comes in a $375,000, the CRV will be for $375,000 appraisal.

10. *Secondary financing.* It is commonly believed that a second loan on a DVA transaction is prohibited. This is not technically correct. Seconds are allowed but rarely used because they are not practical or not understood.

    Secondary financing can be approved on a case-by-case basis. The DVA Regional Office will determine on what basis it is acceptable. Generally, it is desirable that the second carry the same interest rate and terms as the first loan. The first and second loans added together cannot under any circumstances be more than the CRV. An example where a second can be used is as follows:

Sales price/CRV	$450,000
Maximum loan available from lender	−417,000
Down payment from buyer	−20,000
Second mortgage	$13,000

    In this example, we need an additional $13,000 to complete the transaction. If the seller is willing to carry back a second loan at the same rate and terms as the first, the sale can be made.

11. *Termite reports.* The DVA requires that a structural pest report be obtained from a recognized inspection company. Necessary work must be done, and both the veteran and an inspector must certify that the work is done satisfactorily.

    The DVA requires the structural clearance to state, "There is no evidence of termite, wet rot, dry rot, or fungus in the property." The DVA also requires inspection of all detached buildings, not just the house. For example, detached garages and cottages must be inspected. The veteran cannot waive this requirement.

    On older properties this can be a problem. A detached garage may cost more to repair than it is worth. If it is not economical to repair the garage, then it may be torn down and the value of the property adjusted accordingly. For example, assume that it costs $25,000 to repair a garage and the DVA has appraised it at only $23,000. You would be better off removing the garage and reducing the value by $23,000. Always consult with the DVA first in such situations.

Structural pest reports include the cost of corrective work. On the detached garage in the preceding example, it may be possible to meet DVA requirements merely by chemically spraying the garage at a lower cost. This applies only to detached buildings. DVA requirements in this area are greatly misunderstood and vary from one regional DVA office to another. Be sure that the inspection company understands what is required before it proceeds with the work. For other repairs, doing much of the work yourself, if you fancy yourself a do-it-yourselfer, might save money.

12. *Closing costs*. The DVA has several rules that are unusual. The DVA will not allow the veteran to pay for nonrecurring closing costs, such as termite reports, escrow fees, tax service fees, document preparation fees, notary fees, or a certificate of reasonable value that was ordered before the veteran agreed to purchase the property.

    The DVA allows the seller to pay all of the closing costs, including prepaid expenses and **recurring closing costs** such as tax impounds, fire insurance, and so on. Most lenders require buyers to pay for prepaid items. A "seller pay all" is often referred to as a "VA no-no"—no down, no closing costs.

13. *Internet underwriting*. If the lender is "LAPP" approved (**Lender Appraisal Processing Program**), the processing time for approval is greatly reduced because it takes place through the Internet.

Choosing a Lender for FHA and DVA Loans

Many lenders, such as commercial banks, savings banks, and mortgage companies, are authorized to process FHA and DVA loans. Because they have authorization does not automatically mean they do a good job. Processing FHA and DVA loans can be very complex, technical, and time consuming. Certain lenders specialize in processing government loans. They are experienced, they know what to do, and they keep up to date. Choose a lender that has this type of experience—otherwise, it can be very frustrating and costly.

6.3 Cal-Vet Loans

The Cal-Vet program is administered by the California Department of Veterans Affairs, Division of Farm and Home Purchases. Applicants can apply directly to Cal-Vet or apply through a

Cal-Vet certified mortgage broker and pay a one-point loan origination fee (which can go to the mortgage broker). The money that funds the loans is obtained from the sale of general obligation bonds and revenue bonds. There is also a program using what are designated as **un-restricted funds** for qualified veterans with wartime service. This can be used only as funds are available. Full details regarding Cal-Vet loans can be found at www.cdva.ca.gov.

Who is Eligible for Cal-Vet Loans?

Cal-Vet eligibility rules are more liberal than the federal DVA rules. Assuming the veteran has the required income and credit rating, under Cal-Vet rules, if a veteran received an honorable discharge or is currently on active duty, the veteran is eligible provided he or she served for a minimum of 90 days, not counting basic training. It makes no difference if the service was during war or peacetime.

Veterans who served for fewer than 90 days are also eligible for a Cal-Vet loan if the shorter time was the result of a service-connect disability or was spent in active duty that was eligible to receive a U.S. campaign or expeditionary medal, or the direct result of a call up to active duty from the Reserves or National Guard as the result of a Presidential Executive Order.

Current members of the U.S. Military Reserves and the California National Guard—who do not otherwise qualify under the aforementioned rules—become eligible after they serve a minimum of one year of a six-year obligation, provided they qualify as a first-time home buyer or purchase a home in certain targeted areas.

It should be noted that if the veteran is currently in the military, Cal-Vet does have a rule that requires that the veteran or a member of the immediate family must occupy the home until the Cal-Vet loan is paid off. Therefore, a change in active duty station would require a pay off of the Cal-Vet loan unless the veteran's family remains in the home. This required resale could result in a loss if a veteran is transferred after a short period of time, in that the veteran seller's closing costs could exceed any short-term appreciation.

General Information about Cal-Vet Loans

1. *Property.* Cal-Vet has basically the same property standards as FHA and DVA. The property must be an owner-occupied, single-family dwelling or a unit in a condominium or planned unit development. Owner-occupied farms and mobile homes are also acceptable.

2. *Maximum loan.* The maximum Cal-Vet loan amounts can vary each year. There are separate maximums for single-family dwellings, farms, and mobile homes. To find the current maximum for each go to the Cal-Vet website, www.cdva.ca.gov.

3. *Down payment and loan fees.* Cal-Vet loans guaranteed by the DVA are called Cal-Vet/VA loans and are available for no money down up to the current maximum DVA guaranteed loan, which is usually four times the maximum DVA guarantee discussed earlier in the chapter.

   On straight Cal-Vet loans, without a DVA guarantee, the down payment is 3 percent of the purchase price or appraised value, whichever is the lesser amount.

   Cal-Vet charges a 1 percent loan origination fee, plus a loan guarantee fee that ranges 1.25 percent to 2 percent of the loan amount. Under certain circumstances, the loan guarantee fee may be financed, but the 1 percent loan origination fee must be paid in escrow. If a veteran puts 20 percent or more down, only the 1 percent loan-origination fee applies. The 1.25 to 2 percent loan guarantee fee is waived.

4. *Term of loan.* Cal-Vet loans are set up as 30-year loans. A veteran is allowed to make additional principal payments to shorten the length of the loan. There is no prepayment penalty for paying off the loan early.

5. *Interest rate.* All Cal-Vet loans have a variable interest rate. The initial interest rate is set at the time of the loan based on the cost of bond funds and market conditions. Once set, the interest rate has a cap of only a half percent over the start rate.

6. *Secondary financing.* At the time of purchase, secondary financing is permitted. However, the two loans together cannot exceed 98 percent of the Cal-Vet appraisal. In addition, some lenders are unwilling to make a loan behind a land contract of sale.

7. *Occupancy.* The veteran or an immediate member of the family who qualifies as a dependent must occupy the property.

8. *Insurance.* All properties are covered by Cal-Vet's Disaster Indemnity program, which provides protection against loss from floods and earthquakes (with limitations). All Cal-Vet contract holders under age 62 must carry basic life insurance. Based on health status at time of application, coverage provides payments of principal and interest for up to five years following the death of the

insured—but "substandard risks" are covered for only 36 months and "highly substandard risks" are covered for only 12 months. Under certain circumstances, optional life insurance, spouse life insurance, and disability insurance may be obtainable. Disability insurance terminates at age 62. All life insurance coverage terminates at age 70.

9. *Monthly payments.* Included in monthly mortgage payments are principal, interest, property taxes, and fire, disability, and life insurance premiums.

10. *Title to property.* When a property is being financed with a Cal-Vet loan, the title is first conveyed to the Department of Veterans Affairs of the State of California by the seller. The department then sells the property to the veteran under a **land contract of sale**. The department continues to hold the legal title until the veteran has paid the loan in full, after which the buyer gets a grant deed. The department uses a standard CLTA joint protection policy, rather than a "lender's" ALTA policy.

11. *Application fee.* A small application fee and appraisal fee is paid by the applicant.

12. *Construction loan.* All other qualifications remain the same. Cal-Vet usually uses a five-draw system, with the construction period ordinarily nine months, followed by 29-year/3-month amortization.

13. *Refinancing.* No refinancings are available, with a possible exception in which a Cal-Vet take-out is arranged prior to obtaining an "outside" construction loan and prior to the transfer of title to property. However, if your old loan is paid off, a new Cal-Vet loan is available. Cal-Vet loans may be paid off without penalty and may be used over and over.

For additional information about your area and qualifications, contact the California Department of Veterans Affairs website.

Advantages and Disadvantages of Cal-Vet Loans

The main advantages of the Cal-Vet loan are its relatively low interest rate; inexpensive life, fire, and disaster (flood, quake) insurance; and low closing costs.

Disadvantages include lack of refinancings and occasional shortage of available funds for the program. For unmarried couples who are not registered as domestic partners, another disadvantage might be that

Cal-Vet can refuse to allow assignment of the veteran's contract of sale to the couple as joint tenants.

6.4 California Housing Finance Agency Program (CalHFA)

T he CalHFA program is designed to help first-time home buyers acquire a home in California's expensive housing market. This state agency sells mortgage revenue bonds to investors, and then uses the funds to buy loans from approved lenders who make loans under CalHFA guidelines. Thus, like FHA, DVA, Fannie Mae, and Freddie Mac, CalHFA does not make loans directly to borrowers. Instead, this state agency purchases the loans made by approved lenders. CalHFA prides itself by not using state funds and taxpayer dollars to operate its program. Full details regarding CalHFA can be found at www.calhfa.ca.gov.

Two Main Programs

CalHFA offers a 30-year fixed-rate conventional loan program and what it calls an interest-only plus plan.

30-Year Fixed Rate Conventional Loan Program

This program features a below-market fixed interest rate amortized loan for 30 years and a maximum loan-to-value ratio of 100 percent. In special circumstances the loan can be as high as 107 percent loan-to-value ratio! The loan origination fee cannot exceed 1.5 percent of the loan amount. Mortgage insurance is required and CalHFA provides this coverage at a very low fee.

Property Eligibility. The property must meet all of the following requirements:

1. Sales price of the home cannot exceed CalHFA price limits. Said price limits vary by counties (see www.calhfa.ca.gov for your area).

2. Must be an owner-occupied single family, one-unit home, condo, or PUD.

3. Manufactured homes are allowed if they meet CalHFA construction standards.

Borrower eligibility. The borrower must meet the following requirements:

1. Be a U.S. citizen, permanent resident alien, or qualified alien.

2. Be a first-time home buyer, unless the home is located in a federally designated targeted area that is deemed to need an infusion of investment.

3. Occupy the home as a principal or primary residence; nonowner-occupied loans are not allowed.

4. Borrower's income cannot exceed CalHFA income limits established for the county where the home is located.

5. Meet CalHFA credit requirements.

There are certain special circumstances in which a home or borrower may still qualify even if they cannot quite meet all of the requirements listed. See CalHFA for additional details.

Interest Only PLUS Program

This CalHFA plan features a conventional loan with (1) a below-market fixed interest rate, (2) a 35-year term, and (3) interest-only payments for the first five years. Then, the payments switch to an amortized loan for the remaining 30 years. The interest rate remains fixed for the entire 35-year term. The loan-to-value ratio is 100 percent, increasing to 107 percent under special circumstances. Mortgage insurance is required and is provided by CalHFA at very low rates. The property and borrower eligibility requirements are identical to the ones listed previously for the 30-year fixed rate program.

For more information about this first-time home buyer program, contact CalHFA at their website, www.calhfa.ca.gov.

SUMMARY

The FHA, DVA, and CalHFA are government agencies that do not make loans; they either insure, guarantee, or purchase loans made by approved lenders using their agency's guidelines. FHA-insured loans are made to any qualified borrower, whereas DVA-guaranteed loans are made to qualified veterans. CalHFA backed loans focus on California first-time home buyers. Contrary to the FHA, DVA, and CalHFA programs, the Cal-Vet program is a direct loan made to qualified veterans. Table 6.1 compares the major features of the FHA, DVA, and Cal-Vet programs.

Table 6.1 Comparison of government-backed loans (January 2006).

Feature	Federal Housing Administration	U.S. Department of Veterans Affairs (GI)	Cal-Vet
Purpose of loan	1—4 units	1—4 units	Single dwellings, condominiums
Eligibility	Any U.S. resident	U.S. veteran	Qualified veterans
Expiration of eligibility	Indefinite	Indefinite	Must apply within 30 years from date of discharge
Maximum purchase price	None	None	None
Maximum loan	Varies by counties	None by DVA; lenders limit loan amount	Varies for homes, farms, and mobile homes
Down payment	Section 203(b) Minimum 3%	None, but loan limited to CRV	0 to 3%
Maximum term	30 years	30 years	30 years
Secondary financing	Allowed with limitations	Allowed with limitations	Allowed with limitations
Interest rate	Fixed	Fixed	Floating (variable) rate
Prepayment penalty	None	None	None

IMPORTANT TERMS AND CONCEPTS

CalHFA

Cal-Vet loans

Certificate of Eligibility

Certificate of Reasonable Value (CRV)

Conditional commitment

DVA-guaranteed loan

FHA-insured loan

FHA 203(b) program

FHA 245 program

Land contract of sale

Lender Appraisal Processing Program (LAPP)

Mortgage Insurance Premium (MIP)

Mutual Mortgage Insurance (MMI)

Nonrecurring closing costs

Recurring closing costs

REVIEWING YOUR UNDERSTANDING

Questions for Discussion

1. List three advantages and three disadvantages of an FHA-insured loan.

2. Compare the borrower requirements for an FHA, DVA, Cal-Vet, and CalHFA loan. What are the down payment requirements for each?

3. What are the maximum loan fees a lender can charge for FHA, DVA, Cal-Vet, and CalHFA loans?

4. In your area, which of the four programs listed in Question #3 will allow the greatest loan amount?

Multiple-Choice Questions

1. Assume a condo purchase price of $500,000. Under FHA Title II, Section 203(b), the maximum loan for an owner-occupied dwelling in a high-cost area would be
   a. $417,000.
   b. $144,336.
   c. $151,050.
   d. $253,650.

2. The maximum entitlement under the DVA loan program can be as high as 50 percent of the loan balance, but not to exceed
   a. $22,500.
   b. $36,000.
   c. $104,250.
   d. $60,000.

3. A veteran purchased a home for $200,000 five years ago with DVA 100 percent financing. Three months ago the property went into foreclosure and there was a balance of $195,000 owing on the loan. The sale price at the time of foreclosure is $178,000. The maximum amount of liability, excluding costs of sale, is
   a. $50,750.
   b. $46,000.
   c. $17,000.
   d. none of these.

4. Cal-Vet financing
   a. requires no down payment.
   b. has no prepayment penalties.
   c. cannot be used for construction.
   d. uses a mortgage as security for the loan.

5. Which program is specifically designed for first-time home buyers?
   a. FHA.
   b. DVA.
   c. Cal-Vet.
   d. CalHFA.

6. Which of the following would generally offer the highest loan for the purchase of a $250,000 home?
   a. DVA guaranteed.
   b. FHA insured.
   c. Cal-Vet loan.
   d. conventional lender.

7. If a government-backed and conventional loan are for the same amount, the government loan would most likely
   a. offer greater flexibility.
   b. require a similar monthly payment for principal and interest.
   c. be useful only for higher-priced homes.
   d. require larger loan fees, or points, to the borrower.

8. One advantage of Cal-Vet financing is the
   a. requirement for purchase of life and disability insurance.
   b. zero down payments.
   c. lower property tax rate for Cal-Vet properties.
   d. relatively low interest rate.

9. The Federal Housing Administration
   a. makes most of the nation's single-family dwelling loans.
   b. insures loans made by approved lenders.
   c. does not require a down payment on approved loans.
   d. all of the above are correct.

10. The rules under which the FHA operates provide that
    a. loans can be insured only for owner-occupied, single-family dwellings.
    b. loan origination fees cannot be more than 1 percent.
    c. secondary financing may not exceed 50 percent of the down payment.
    d. the borrower may purchase the property in "as is" condition.

11. Eligible for FHA loans are
    a. any U.S. residents.
    b. only naturalized citizens.
    c. qualified veterans.
    d. those meeting the 10 percent required down payment.

12. The Lender Appraisal Processing Program is associated with
    a. automatic underwriting standards.
    b. conventional appraisals.
    c. loan processing via the Internet.
    d. in-house appraisals.

13. FHA requires a 3 percent cash investment that must come from the borrower's own funds, or from
    a. a bona fide gift.
    b. a loan from a family member.
    c. a governmental agency or instrumentality.
    d. any of the above sources.

14. The U.S. Department of Veterans Affairs
    a. guarantees loans made to qualified veterans by approved lenders.
    b. permits interest rates to be set by mutual agreement with the lender.
    c. operates its real estate loan program under the GI Bill of Rights, passed by Congress in 1944.
    d. does all of the above.

15. If special circumstances exist, under which home loan program is it possible to obtain more than 100 percent financing?
    a. CalHFA.
    b. FHA.
    c. DVA.
    d. Cal-Vet.

16. Which of the following is a recurring closing cost?
    a. Cal-Vet hazard insurance policy.
    b. FHA loan origination fee.
    c. DVA funding fee.
    d. CalHFA credit report.

17. The initials *CRV* refer to
    a. certified regional valuations.
    b. a DVA appraisal.
    c. a loan guaranteed by the Department of Veterans Affairs.
    d. a real estate agent who specializes in GI loans.

18. The following is used as the security instrument to finance a Cal-Vet loan:
    a. deferred deed.
    b. land contract.
    c. mortgage.
    d. trust deed.

19. FHA-insured loans insure lenders against
    a. decline in real estate values.
    b. loss due to foreclosure.
    c. loss due to borrowers losing their jobs.
    d. late payments by borrowers.

20. The stated goal of all government home loan programs is to
    a. encourage speculation in housing.
    b. assist struggling real estate agents during down markets.
    c. offer subsidized interest rates to minority groups.
    d. foster homeownership.

CHAPTER 7
POINTS, DISCOUNTS, AND THE SECONDARY MORTGAGE MARKET

PREVIEW

This chapter explains points, discounts, and two other terms called *price* and *yield*. All these are used in the secondary mortgage market, where existing loans are bought and sold. The main purpose of the secondary market is to shift funds from capital surplus areas to capital shortage areas. This is accomplished in part by lenders selling loans to each other. Capital is brought into the mortgage market by the operations of large corporations, including the Federal National Mortgage Association (Fannie Mae) and the Federal Home Loan Mortgage Corporation (Freddie Mac), and by the use of mortgage-backed securities.

After completing this chapter, you should be able to:

1. Explain the difference between the terms *points* and *discounts*.

2. Define the term *premium* and contrast this to *discount*.

3. Differentiate between secondary financing and secondary mortgage market.

4. Describe the purpose of Fannie Mae and Freddie Mac.

5. Explain how a Ginnie Mae mortgage-backed security works.

6. Discuss the role of investment bankers in mortgage-backed securities and the secondary market.

7.1 Points and Discounts

A *point* is 1 percent of the loan amount. It is used because it is easier to say one point than it is to say 1 percent of the loan amount. A point is not 1 percent of the sales price; it is always a percentage of the loan amount.

A *discount* is the amount of money a lender deducts from the loan amount when loan proceeds are funded.

Example:

Loan amount	$150,000
Less 2-point discount	−3,000
Net funds	$147,000 excluding appraisal and other fees

The size of a discount is expressed in points. In the real estate business, many people use the words points and discounts interchangeably, often using the expression *discount points*.

Points are also used to measure loan fees. Suppose the loan origination fee is 1 percent of the loan amount. People in real estate would call this a one-point loan fee. If we were dealing with a conventional loan with a 1.5 percent loan fee, we would call it a 1.5-point loan fee.

A *premium*, on the other hand, involves a loan sold for more than the face amount or balance of the loan. A $100,000 loan sold at a premium of 2 percent is sold for $102,000. Why would a loan sell for more than its face amount? Because of the higher interest rate and higher yield to the lender that the loan carries in the marketplace, this premium is referred to as a "service release premium" (SRP) or "rebate pricing." Lenders in some cases pass this savings along to the consumer-borrower in the form of zero-point loans or a reduction in the loan fee. Investors sometimes find that even by paying premiums for certain loans, they can realize a better yield than they could obtain elsewhere in the marketplace. It should be noted that premiums paid for loans, although becoming more popular in recent years, remain a concern to lenders for two reasons. First, these loans carry a higher-than-market-interest rate, making them more likely to be paid off early through refinancing at a lower rate. Second, there has been controversy over the proper disclosure to borrowers regarding the premiums paid.

Why Discounts Are Used

Lenders use discount points to increase their actual return, which is called the **yield**. Some also call it **effective interest rate**, though this generally describes the **Annual Percentage Rate (APR)**.

Example: Assume you borrowed $100,000 for one year at a 10 percent interest rate. At the end of the year, you would repay the lender the $100,000 plus $10,000 in interest. The lender's yield would be calculated as follows:

$$\frac{\text{Interest}}{\text{Money received}} = \frac{\$10,000}{\$100,000} = 10\%$$

If the lender charged you a loan fee, the result would be different. If the fee were five points, or $5,000, you would receive only $95,000, because the lender subtracts the points from the loan amount and remits the difference. At the end of the year, you would pay the lender the $100,000 principal balance plus $10,000 in interest. In addition to the interest, the lender also collects the $5,000 in points. The effective interest rate that the lender has achieved is 15.8 percent, calculated as follows:

$$\frac{\text{Interest} + \text{Discount}}{\text{Money Disbursed}} = \frac{\$15,000}{\$95,000} = 15.8\%$$

To determine yields at various discounts, lenders use a table such as the one shown in Table 7.1.

Table 7.1 shows yields on 11 percent, 30-year loans at fees ranging from one to ten points. Yields are also determined by the date the loan is paid off. Even though the term is 30 years, the average life of a loan is considerably less. Industry studies show the average life to be approximately 12 years. This assumption is always subject to change and it varies among lenders, by type of loan, and by geographical location.

An 11 percent loan with a discount of two points, prepaid in 12 years, would have an effective yield of 11.31 percent. What would the effective rate be if the fees were ten points? (Answer: 12.67 percent)

Table 7.1 and the two that follow, 7.2 and 7.3, are for demonstration purposes only, to show that such tools exist. The formulas required for performing the calculations are beyond the scope of this text, but readers may find the topic to be of at least marginal interest.

Table 7.1 Yields on an 11 percent, 30-year loan at various discounts prepaid in 12 years.

Discount (# of points)	Effective Yield (%)
0	11.00
1	11.16
2	11.31
3	11.48
4	11.64
5	11.81
6	11.97
7	12.14
8	12.00
9	12.49
10	12.67

Price and Yield

When real estate salespeople deal with lenders, they use the terms *points* and *loan fees*. When lenders *sell* loans to other lenders or investors, they deal in terms of *price* and *discount*. Price + Discount = Face Value, or par.

Price is another way of quoting the discount. A lender selling a loan at a five-point discount would quote a price of 95. The lender is saying that it will sell the loan for 95 percent of the loan amount. Therefore, an existing $100,000 loan would be sold to another lender for $95,000 (95 percent × $100,000). Price and discount added together always equal 100, which is called **par** (face value). To determine price, you deduct the discount from 100. For example, if the discount is three points, what is the price?

Par	100
Discount	−3
Price	97

If you know the price and you want to determine the discount, you reverse the process. If the price is 97, what is the discount?

Par	100
Price	−97
Discount	3

If you know the price, it is simple to determine the effective return, which lenders call yield. When a loan is sold with no discount, at par, the return on the loan and the yield are the same. With a discount, the yield

Table 7.2 Desired yield on a 10 percent, 30-year loan at various prices prepaid in 12 years.

Price	Effective Yield (percent)
90	11.61
91	11.43
92	11.26
93	11.10
94	10.93
95	10.77
96	10.61
97	10.46
98	10.30
99	10.15
100	10.00

will be higher than the interest rate on the loan. To determine yields at various prices, lenders use tables similar to the one in Table 7.2.

At a price of 97, based on a 12-year payoff, the yield is 10.46 percent. Investors who purchase existing loans use such tables or financial calculators to determine the price they can pay to achieve a certain yield. They are usually comparing mortgage loans with other competing investments, such as corporate bonds; these are compared on the basis of yield. For example, if an investor wants to achieve a yield of 11.10 percent on the purchase of an existing $100,000 mortgage, what price should the investor pay? Looking at Table 7.2 and assuming the loan will be prepaid in 12 years, the investor would pay a price of 93, or $93,000 (93 percent × $100,000).

For those skilled with the use of financial calculators, tables such as these can be constructed for virtually any interest rate, term, and prepayment period. Chapter 13 examines TI-BA and HP-12C applications to real estate problems.

Where Are Discounts Used?

A mortgage or deed of trust recorded after the first mortgage is called a ***junior mortgage***. If the junior mortgage is recorded after the first mortgage, it is called a *second mortgage*. A mortgage recorded after the first and second mortgages is called a *third mortgage*. (There is no limit on how many liens can be placed on a property: one author, Robert Bond attended a foreclosure auction in which the *9th* trust deed was being foreclosed!) A detailed discussion of junior mortgages and deeds of trust is presented in Chapter 14.

Table 7.3 Discount required for various yields on a loan with a 15 percent interest rate with the balance due in five years.

DESIRED YIELD (%)	MONTHLY PAYOFF RATE		
	1.25%	1.5%	2%
15	0.0	0.0	0.0
17	6.7	6.2	5.1
19	12.9	11.8	9.8
21	18.5	17.1	14.2
23	23.7	21.9	18.3
25	28.4	26.3	22.1
27	32.8	30.4	25.7

Junior loans are bought and sold by investors. For example, sellers of a property may need to carry back a second deed of trust to sell their house. After the sale, the sellers may want to sell the second to obtain cash. To sell, they probably have to offer the second deed of trust at a discount. Discounts on junior loans vary widely—sometimes from 10 to 50 percent depending on note rate, size of monthly payments (rate of payoff), due date, borrower payment history, amount of equity in the property, and prevailing yields in the marketplace. As the risk increases, the discount increases, resulting in a higher yield. Stated differently, the lower the discount, the lower the yield.

Yields at various discounts can be determined from published tables, as shown in Table 7.3, or by financial calculators like the two applied in Chapter 13.

Assume that in the real estate market, interest rates increase and seller-carried seconds at 15 percent interest become common. (Yes, even first mortgages were charging 18 percent and more in 1980–1982, with junior liens commanding more than 15 percent!) Table 7.3 indicates yields and discounts for mortgages at a 15 percent interest rate, with the entire remaining balance due in five years. Note that the rate of monthly payoff has an effect on the discount. To obtain a 21 percent yield, you would need an 18.5 percent discount if the loan pays off at a rate of 1.25 percent per month; the discount drops to 17.1 percent at a payoff rate of 1.5 percent per month, and only a 14.2 percent discount if the loan pays off at a 2 percent rate.

The monthly payoff rates are derived by dividing monthly payment by principal balance, for example:

Monthly payment ÷ Principal balance = Rate of payoff
$200 ÷ $10,000 = 2% per month

Example: If a 15 percent second loan due in five years has a balance of $50,000, and monthly payments of $1,000, how much of a discount would be required to yield 25 percent?

Solution:

$$\frac{\text{Monthly payment}}{\text{Principal balance}} = \frac{\$1,000}{\$50,000} = 2\% \text{ rate of payoff}$$

To achieve a 25 percent yield, the last column in the table shows that a discount of 22.1 percent will be required. The purchase price of the junior lien is calculated as follows:

Principal balance	$50,000
Less: 22.1% of 50,000	−11,050
Purchase price	$38,950

7.2 Secondary Mortgage Market

When lenders speak about the secondary mortgage market, they are not referring to second mortgages or deeds of trust. They are talking about a market where existing loans are bought and sold. The difference between a secondary mortgage market and secondary financing is illustrated in Figure 7.1.

When a lender makes a loan directly to a borrower, that action takes place in the ***primary mortgage market***. Later, that loan may be sold to a bank, pension fund, or some other investor. The sale of that loan takes place in the secondary market. For example, if a savings bank makes a loan directly to a borrower, it is involved in the primary market. If the loan is subsequently sold to the Federal Home Loan Mortgage Corporation, that sale takes place in the secondary market.

The secondary market consists of private and institutional lenders, investors, and government agencies that buy and sell mortgages to each other. In the secondary market, discounts are used constantly. Buyers and sellers of mortgages negotiate on the basis of yield. Discounts are used to adjust yields so agreements can be reached and sales made.

Purpose of the Secondary Market

Why do lenders need a secondary market? Why don't they just make loans and keep them? That would work well if every lender had a perfect balance between demand for loans and supply of money. However, such a perfect balance rarely exists. The main purpose of the

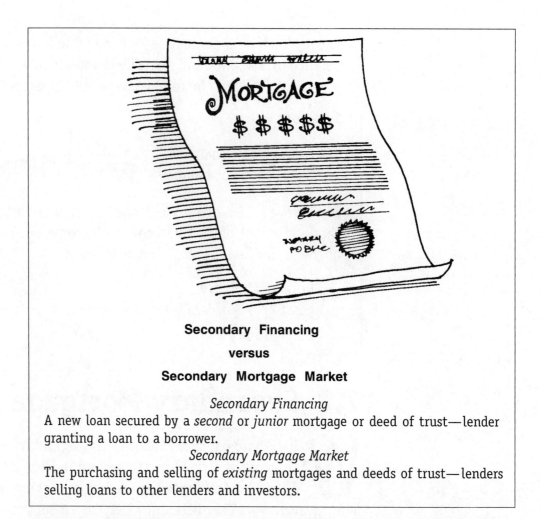

Secondary Financing
versus
Secondary Mortgage Market

Secondary Financing
A new loan secured by a *second* or *junior* mortgage or deed of trust—lender granting a loan to a borrower.

Secondary Mortgage Market
The purchasing and selling of *existing* mortgages and deeds of trust—lenders selling loans to other lenders and investors.

Figure 7.1 The difference between secondary financing and secondary mortgage market.

secondary market is to shift money from areas where there is a surplus to areas where there is a shortage.

In the early 1970s, depository institutions sold only a small portion of the loans they originated. They were able to rely on their savings inflow to finance the loans they made. During this time, interest rates and the flow of deposits were relatively stable. As the 1970s progressed, the institutions were forced to sell more loans in the secondary market because loan volume had increased greatly. A slow rate of new deposits, typically referred to as "rate of savings inflow," was not sufficient to take care of the higher demand for loans.

In the 1980s, institutions found their cost of acquiring deposits increasing dramatically. They also experienced a major outflow of deposits due to higher rates offered by competing investments, such as mutual funds and certain bonds. Recall from Chapter 1 that this is labeled "disintermediation." With less money to support the demand for loans, the institutions have increasingly turned to the secondary market for funds.

One industry that has always operated in the secondary mortgage market is mortgage banking. Mortgage bankers do not have deposits to lend; therefore, they have to sell the loans they make to other investors. They operate as a conduit between the primary market and the secondary market. Today, almost all mortgage lenders operate in the secondary market to maintain liquidity and to stabilize the supply and demand for mortgage money.

Additional Sources for the Secondary Market

On a nationwide basis, deposits in institutions are not sufficient to meet the demand for mortgages. Therefore, to obtain additional funds for mortgages, lenders have had to revert to the capital market. The capital market is the market for long-term investments, which include government and corporate bonds as well as mortgage loans. Some of the investors in the capital market that buy long-term investments are insurance companies, trusts, pension funds, and individuals.

How Are Mortgage Funds Shifted?

There are a number of methods used in the marketplace to shift funds to where they are needed. One method is lenders selling loans to each other. For example, a savings bank in California may have more demand for loans than it can meet. A savings bank in Florida may have the opposite problem. The solution is to have the California savings bank sell loans to the Florida savings bank. The California savings bank would thereby obtain additional funds to use to make new loans, and the Florida savings bank would be investing surplus funds.

Another method to move funds from one source to another is called ***participation***. Participation occurs when one institution sells a part interest in a block of loans to another institution. For example, assume the California savings bank wanted to sell $10,000,000 in loans to the Florida savings bank. Rather than sell the entire block of loans, it could sell a 90 percent interest, or $9,000,000. The other 10 percent share, $1,000,000, would be retained by the lender. The California bank would continue to service the loans and pass on 90 percent of the mortgage payments to the Florida bank. FNMA and FHLMC are also actively involved with participations in 5 percent increments, purchasing 90 or 95 percent of a loan. This enables the loan seller to leverage its funds. However, FNMA and FHLMC are more often involved in the sale of "whole" loans.

Mortgage-Backed Securities

Today the most common method used to move funds is by the use of mortgage-backed securities, which are backed by a pool of mortgages.

They were created to make investing in mortgages as simple as buying stocks or bonds. Before then, lending institutions sold and purchased loans among themselves. This was not an efficient method—it was time consuming and involved a lot of paperwork. In addition, each lender had its own property and borrower standards, which further complicated transactions. More importantly, there was no system to obtain money from the capital markets. Lenders had to depend on deposits, which had proven to be volatile. The invention of the mortgage-backed security revolutionized the operation of the secondary market.

Three agencies play an important role in the secondary market: the *Government National Mortgage Association (GNMA)*, the *Federal Home Loan Mortgage Corporation (FHLMC)*, and the *Federal National Mortgage Association (FNMA)*. The GNMA is a government agency; the FHLMC is a quasi-government agency; and the FNMA is a former government agency that became a private corporation in 1968. The function of these agencies is to support the secondary market through the purchase of loans or the guarantee of *mortgage-backed securities* issued by lenders. These agencies, along with other minor players such as the Federal Agricultural Mortgage Corporation, or Farmer Mac, and the Student Loan Marketing Association, or Sallie Mae, are collectively known as *government-sponsored enterprises*, or GSE for short.

Government National Mortgage Association (GNMA)

The first mortgage-backed security was developed by the Government National Mortgage Association, commonly called Ginnie Mae. It was established in 1968 as a government agency within the Department of Housing and Urban Development (HUD). Its basic mission was to create and operate a mortgage-backed security program for FHA and DVA mortgages. It took over duties formerly performed by FNMA, after FNMA was given private status.

In 1970 Ginnie Mae issued the first security backed by a pool of FHA and DVA mortgages. It was called a *pass-through security* because the monthly principal and interest payments collected from the borrowers were passed through to the investor. Ginnie Mae does not purchase mortgages. Its function is to guarantee that principal and interest will be paid every month. Since it is a government agency, the guarantee is backed by the "full faith and credit" of the U.S. government. For this guarantee, Ginnie Mae receives a small fee from the lender, which is collected monthly. The minimum amount that can be placed in a pool is $1,000,000. The mortgages cannot be more than one year old and must have met predetermined average yields for the pool of loans. The pool can contain any combination of FHA and DVA mortgages. The lender can apply to Ginnie Mae for a commitment to issue a certificate at any time. When applying, it must indicate the size of the pool and the rate of interest on the mortgages. If Ginnie Mae approves the request, it issues a commitment that is good for one year.

Before the certificate is sold, Ginnie Mae requires that the mortgages be in the hands of a third party. This party acts as a trustee for Ginnie Mae and is called the *custodian*. The custodian is usually a bank, but it could be any federal or state financial institution acceptable to Ginnie Mae. The lender delivers the mortgage documents to the custodian, who checks the information carefully. Once the custodian is satisfied that it has all the documents, it notifies Ginnie Mae. The certificate is then issued to the lender.

With the certificate in hand, the lender is able to sell the mortgages to an investor. When the investor buys the mortgages, it receives the certificate. Typically, the securities are purchased by securities dealers who trade in Ginnie Mae securities. They in turn sell the securities to other investors such as insurance companies, pension funds, other lenders who need mortgages, and individuals. The securities can be broken down into smaller denominations to satisfy the demands of the various investors (the smallest denomination is $25,000). The securities are traded on Wall Street just like stocks and bonds. There is an active market for the securities, which makes them a liquid investment.

Readers wishing more information on the GNMA can access its website through a link at http://bond.swlearning.com.

Federal Home Loan Mortgage Corporation (FHLMC)

Because Ginnie Mae included only FHA and DVA mortgages in its securities, there was a great need to develop a mortgage-backed security for conventional loans. In 1971, the Federal Home Loan Mortgage Corporation, also known as Freddie Mac, introduced the first security backed by conventional loans. Freddie Mac is a subsidiary of the Office of Thrift Supervision (OTS), which supervises the federally chartered thrifts. As a government-chartered stockholder-owned corporation, FHLMC buys mortgages and sells them in the secondary market.

Freddie Mac buys conventional loans from lenders such as savings banks, commercial banks, and mortgage companies. It then assembles a pool of mortgages and issues a security backed by the mortgages. The security is called a *Participating Certificate* (PC) or Guaranteed Mortgage Certificate. The agency guarantees the full payment of principal and the timely payment of interest. The security is later sold to investors in the capital markets. For the guarantee, Freddie Mac receives a monthly fee paid by the investors.

For more information on FHLMC, access its website through a link at bond.swcollege.com/.

Federal National Mortgage Association (FNMA)

The Federal National Mortgage Association, known as Fannie Mae, was established by Congress in 1938 to provide a secondary market for mortgages. It remained a part of the federal government until 1968, when it became a private corporation. Even though it is private, the corporation has a public purpose and maintains strong government ties. It is subject to some regulations by the Department of Housing and Urban Development (HUD). It also has the ability to tap the U.S. Treasury if necessary.

Fannie Mae issues a security backed by conventional loans and operates the issuance of its securities much like Freddie Mac. It buys mortgages from lenders, places them in a pool, and issues a security. The security is sold to investors, who receive a guarantee that principal and interest will be paid monthly, whether or not payments have been collected from the borrowers. Fannie Mae charges a monthly fee for the guarantee.

Collateralized Mortgage Obligations

Fannie Mae issues mortgage-backed securities called ***collateralized mortgage obligations (CMO)***. They were designed to limit prepayment risk to investors. Prior to this time, mortgage-backed securities were pass-throughs, which means that all the principal and interest collected were passed on to the investor. The investor had no protection from the early prepayment of principal. If borrowers in the pool decided to pay their mortgages in full, the proceeds were passed on to the investors.

When investors calculate yield, they make assumptions regarding the repayment of principal. When mortgages are paid early, the yield will change. Therefore investors are looking for a security that can provide some protection against early prepayment.

A CMO is divided into classes. For example, the first CMO had three classes. Each class paid interest on the outstanding balance. However, all collections of principal from the pool were first applied to class one. After that class had been paid in full, all principal collections went to class two. After class two had been paid in full, the remaining principal payments went to class three. The CMO gives investors opportunities to choose classes that offer different rates and maturities. The creation of the CMO attracted investors that were not normally mortgage investors.

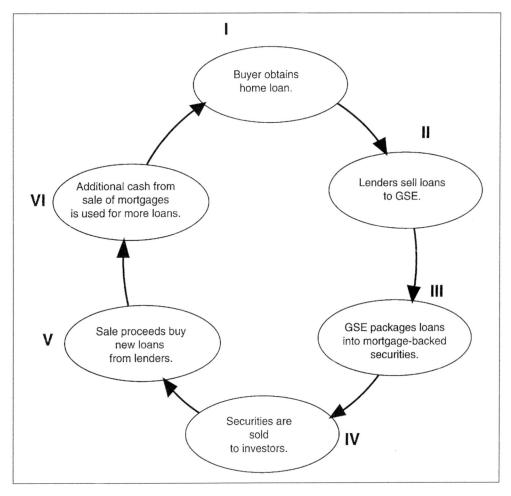

Figure 7.2 Contribution of secondary markets to home loans.

For readers wishing more information on the FNMA and on Fannie Mae Foundation, which offers information on finding and financing homes, access their websites through links at bond.swcollege.com/.

Nonconforming Loans

The U.S. Congress sets the maximum loan amount on conventional loans purchased by Freddie Mac and Fannie Mae. The 2006 maximum for single-family loans was $417,000. The maximum loan amount changes regularly based on economic conditions, usually adjusted each year by FNMA and Freddie Mac, who bundle these loans to resell to investors, to reflect local price trends. The interest rate on these conforming loans typically is a quarter percent lower than those on jumbo loans. One can access the latest numbers on sites such as KiplingerForecasts.com/ahead/loans. Loans that meet these limits are called **conforming loans**. Interest rates for nonconforming loans are often higher than rates for conforming loans.

In many areas of the United States, particularly in California, there is a high demand for loans that exceed these loan limits. These loans are commonly referred to as **jumbo loans**, **nonconforming loans**, or *high balance loans*. Because of the demand, private corporations were formed to issue mortgage-backed securities backed by these loans. The corporations are usually subsidiaries of large financial institutions and operate in much the same manner as Freddie Mac and Fannie Mae. They purchase loans, put them into pools, issue securities, and sell these securities to investors.

Investment Bankers

Investment bankers make a market for both new and seasoned mortgage-backed securities. These firms, called *securities dealers*, buy and sell securities from lenders and investors. In the financial section of your daily newspaper you will find information, such as price and yield, on the various securities. Mortgage bankers, savings banks, pension funds, insurance companies, and mutual funds generally conduct their secondary market transactions with investment bankers.

Standardization

One major benefit brought about by the creation of mortgage-backed securities by Freddie Mac and Fannie Mae is the standardization of conventional loan forms and property and borrower standards. FHA and DVA loans have been readily sold in the secondary market for years. One of the reasons is that their forms are standardized. As an investor you could buy an FHA or DVA loan anywhere in the United States and know the exact loan provisions. Previously this could not be done with a conventional loan.

To have a functional secondary market for conventional loans, you must also have standardization. Freddie Mac and Fannie Mae have accomplished this by using the same forms and by having basically the same property and borrower standards. Almost all lenders today use the standard forms, and many adhere to the property and borrower standards set forth by the agencies. This gives the lenders great flexibility in ensuring that their loans can be sold in the secondary market.

Mortgage Revenue Bonds

The State of California and local governments—cities and counties—have the authority to issue bonds. Interest paid on the bonds is tax exempt to the investors. Bonds sold by state and local governments and used to finance mortgages are called ***mortgage revenue bonds***. Because the bonds are tax exempt, the interest rate is less than on a standard bond and, as a result, mortgage loans can be made at rates that are below market rate. The government agencies do not guarantee the bonds. The bonds are backed by the mortgages created by the bond funds. The issuer of the bond merely acts as a conduit; local lenders process, close, and then service the loans for the government. These bond issues generally work the same way as other mortgage-backed securities, but the paperwork is much more complex.

Local bond issues typically are used to promote lower-income or affordable housing ventures. Borrower requirements usually include income and/or price limits, length of time ownership requirements, and limitations on the amount of equity to be retained upon resale.

SUMMARY

A point, by definition, is 1 percent of the loan amount. Points are used to measure discounts, loan origination fees, and premiums. Lenders charge discounts to increase the effective yield they receive on a loan. When lenders sell loans to investors, they sell on the basis of price. Price is another way of quoting discount. A loan with a discount of three points would have a price of 97; price and discount added together equal 100, or par. When lenders buy or sell loans, they look at the *yield*, or effective interest rate. Yield on a loan can be adjusted by varying the discount. On a given loan, as the discount increases, the yield will increase, and lenders use discounts to increase the yield. Discounts are also used on conventional loans, government loans, and junior mortgages and in the secondary mortgage market.

Existing loans are bought or sold in the secondary market. The purpose of the secondary market is to shift funds from capital surplus areas to capital short areas. One method involves lenders selling loans to each other. Lenders also sell participating interests in blocks of loans to other lenders. Mortgage-backed securities are another tool used to obtain money from the capital market. There are securities backed by FHA and DVA loans and others backed by conventional loans. Since 1978, tax-exempt bonds have been widely used by state and local governments to finance housing.

IMPORTANT TERMS AND CONCEPTS

Annual percentage rate (APR)

Collateralized mortgage obligation (CMO)

Conforming loan

Discounts

Effective interest rate

Federal Home Loan Mortgage Corporation (FHLMC)

Federal National Mortgage Association (FNMA)

Government National Mortgage Association (GNMA)

Government-sponsored enterprise (GSE)

Jumbo loans

Junior mortgage

Mortgage-backed securities

Mortgage revenue bonds

Nonconforming loans

Par

Participations

Pass-through securities

Points

Premium

Price

Primary mortgage market

Secondary financing

Secondary mortgage market

Standardization

Yield

REVIEWING YOUR UNDERSTANDING

Questions for Discussion

1. Describe what *price* means when one lender sells existing real estate loans to another lender. How is yield computed?

2. Explain why borrowers pay loan origination fees when obtaining a loan.

3. What is the difference between secondary financing and the secondary mortgage market?

4. What is a mortgage-backed security?

Multiple-Choice Questions

1. Securities that are usually exempt from federal and state income taxation are popularly labeled
   a. conventional mortgage-backed securities.
   b. mortgage revenue bonds.
   c. private mortgage-backed certificates.
   d. participation loans.

2. Interest rates on FHA and DVA loans are set by
   a. HUD.
   b. Department of Veterans Affairs.
   c. an agreement between the borrower and lender.
   d. the lender solely.

3. A lender selling a loan at a six-point discount would quote a price of
   a. 106.
   b. 94.
   c. 100.
   d. none of the above.

4. Which of the following parties would likely not sell mortgage loans to Freddie Mac?
   a. mortgage companies.
   b. commercial banks.
   c. individuals.
   d. savings banks.

5. A condo is listed for $100,000 and sells for $95,000. The buyer applies for a loan of $70,000. The lender quotes three points to make a commitment. The proceeds to be disbursed, ignoring fees and costs, will be
   a. $92,150.
   b. $67,900.
   c. $72,100.
   d. none of the above.

6. The amount of principal to be repaid in the previous transaction that will be shown on the promissory note is
   a. $95,000.
   b. $70,000.
   c. $100,000.
   d. none of the above.

7. Which of the following is a major buyer and seller in the secondary mortgage market?
   a. FHA.
   b. FNMA.
   c. DVA.
   d. Cal-Vet.

8. Which of the following is also significantly involved in the secondary mortgage market?
   a. Federal Reserve Board.
   b. Federal Housing Administration.
   c. California Housing Finance Agency.
   d. Federal Home Loan Mortgage Corporation.

9. Fannie Mae is the popular name for
   a. Federal National Mortgage Association.
   b. Federal National Marketing Association.
   c. Federal Home Loan Mortgage Corporation.
   d. Federal Housing Administration.

10. Discounts and loan origination fees
   a. are both measured in points.
   b. describe exactly the same thing.
   c. can be paid by the borrower-buyer.
   d. both (a) and (c) are true.

11. When forwarding loan proceeds to the escrow holder, lenders generally
   a. forward the loan amount, and look to the escrow holder to disburse the discount and lender's fees.
   b. deduct the amount of the discount and its fees.
   c. insist on having a check for the amount of any discount or fee.
   d. none of the above.

12. When dealing in the secondary market, price and discount
   a. are synonymous with points and discounts.
   b. when added together, equal 100 percent, or par.
   c. actually describe "sales price" and "effective yield."
   d. none of the above.

13. Conforming loans are periodically adjusted by the
   a. U.S. Treasury.
   b. Federal Reserve Board.
   c. Real Estate Commissioner.
   d. Government-Sponsored Enterprises.

14. The term *secondary market*
    a. describes any junior lien, whether second or lower in priority.
    b. is where loans are actually made to the borrower.
    c. describes a market where existing loans are bought and sold.
    d. involves FNMA, GNMA, and FHLMC as the only participants.

15. Mortgage-backed securities
    a. can be issued only in multiples of $1,000,000.
    b. are very complicated, but lenders have become sophisticated enough to understand them.
    c. are available only for pools of FHA mortgages.
    d. none of the above.

16. Investment bankers
    a. make a market for both new and seasoned securities.
    b. buy and sell securities from lenders and investors.
    c. are very active in the secondary market.
    d. are involved in each of the foregoing activities.

17. If you were selling a loan at a two-point premium, you would quote a price of
    a. 2.
    b. 102.
    c. 98.
    d. 100.

18. The objectives and mechanics of the secondary mortgage market are many and varied, including
    a. making below-market interest rate loans to home buyers.
    b. buying and selling existing mortgages.
    c. providing funds for needy sellers.
    d. insuring loans for home buyers.

19. Which of the following is the popular name for the Federal Home Loan Mortgage Corporation?
    a. Fannie Mae.
    b. Freddie Mac.
    c. Ginnie Mae.
    d. Fed Mae.

20. You list a home for $220,000, and then the real estate market begins to decline. A young couple offers to purchase the home for $175,000, and after a series of counteroffers it sells for $180,000. The couple apply for a $150,000 loan, and the lender commits to a two-point fee. Ignoring other charges, the amount of proceeds to be disbursed will be
    a. $147,000.
    b. $176,000.
    c. $196,000.
    d. $150,000.

CHAPTER 8
QUALIFYING THE PROPERTY

PREVIEW

This chapter describes the procedures lenders use in qualifying or appraising a property for loan purposes: The neighborhood is analyzed, the property is inspected, and a value is determined so that a loan may be arranged. The chapter also reviews the use of an appraisal form in depth and lists special considerations by lenders on planned unit developments and condominiums.

After completing this chapter, you should be able to:

1. Discuss the influence of Freddie Mac and Fannie Mae on a lender's qualifying standards.

2. Describe what an appraiser looks for when analyzing a neighborhood.

3. Outline the steps used in the market data approach to estimating loan value.

4. Demonstrate why sales price is not the same as fair market value.

5. Differentiate the formal classifications of real estate appraisers in California.

6. Suggest possible ways for working more smoothly with an appraiser.

8.1 What Does Qualifying the Property Mean?

The expression "qualifying the property" often is used inter-changeably with the term "appraising the property." When making a loan, one of the lender's early actions is to obtain an appraisal to determine whether the property is sufficient collateral for the requested amount loan.

Although state and federal laws prohibit a lender from "redlining" an area based on neighborhood, ethnic, racial, or other illegal reasons, a lender is allowed to demand that the value of the property be high enough to justify the loan. A lender will base the loan amount on the market value of the property or the purchase price, *whichever is the lesser*. This, coupled with the borrower's income and credit profile, determines the maximum loan-to-value ratio the lender will allow as a condition for making the loan.

Lenders' Property Standards

Lenders' property standards are somewhat flexible. There are basic guidelines for Fannie Mae or Freddie Mac loans. But lenders granting loans that are not to be sold to Fannie Mae or Freddie Mac can establish their own guidelines. For example, it may be lender policy not to make loans on any property over two units. But what if a 60 percent LTV loan on a good four-unit dwelling was requested? Because of the large down payment, the lender probably would make an exception to its basic policy and approve the loan. Again, this could result in illegal discrimination unless the lender's basic policy provides for such exceptions.

Lenders' basic property standards change periodically due to fluctuating money situations and market conditions. If a lender is having a problem finding loans, the lender will almost certainly loosen its standards. If a lender does not have enough money for the loans being requested, the lender will stiffen property standards. During tight money periods, lenders become very selective on property, while during easy money periods they become less selective. As noted in the next section, a lender's attitude will also be influenced by whether the loan will be sold in the secondary market or kept in its own portfolio.

Influence of Freddie Mac and Fannie Mae

Freddie Mac and Fannie Mae influence a conventional lender's property standards. A lender that intends to sell its loans to either agency must follow the particular agency's standards. Some lenders, such as mortgage companies, sell most of their loans to Fannie Mae. Thus a mortgage company will not approve a loan on a property unless the property is acceptable to Fannie Mae. If the property was not acceptable to Fannie Mae, the mortgage company would be stuck with the loan. There are other lenders, such as savings banks, that sell many loans. However, they may still want to use Freddie Mac or Fannie Mae property standards for all of their loans. This ensures that their loans are saleable to these agencies, giving the lender more flexibility in managing its funds. Therefore more lenders are being influenced and governed by the property requirements of both Fannie Mae and Freddie Mac.

FHA and DVA Property Standards

The Federal Housing Administration and the Department of Veterans Affairs do not operate like conventional lenders; they *insure* or *guarantee* loans. They have minimum property standards known as habitability standards that all properties have to meet. Beyond that, the FHA and the DVA have no specific property requirements. They do not adjust the loan-to-value ratio because of the property—if the property meets the minimum standards, it will be entitled to the maximum loan amount under existing FHA and DVA guidelines. Likewise, the interest rate is not affected by the property. Lenders' rates and points for FHA and DVA are entirely negotiable.

Procedure for Qualifying a Property

How do lenders qualify or appraise a property? FHA and DVA requirements differ from most requirements for conventional loans. First let's discuss how the FHA and the DVA qualify property.

Qualifying for FHA and DVA

The primary responsibility of the FHA and the DVA is to ensure that a property meets their minimum property standards. In addition, they must establish a market value for the property. An FHA appraisal must be ordered through an approved FHA lender (commercial banks, savings banks, and most mortgage companies can be approved lenders). The lender orders an appraisal by filling out an FHA appraisal request form. On receipt of the request, the FHA will assign it to a licensed FHA-qualified fee appraiser, an independent appraiser who works with lenders and the public.

After the appraiser has inspected and appraised the property, a **conditional commitment** is issued. The "conditional" includes any other conditions that the FHA is requiring, such as termite work and repairs, all of which must be completed before FHA insurance will be issued. A copy of the conditional commitment is sent back to the lender who ordered the appraisal.

The DVA operates in much the same way as the FHA. A DVA appraisal is ordered by filling out an appraisal request form. The appraisal can be ordered by anyone, but in practice is usually ordered by a DVA-qualified lender. The appraisal request is sent to the DVA, which in turn gives it to a licensed independent fee appraiser who is DVA qualified. The DVA uses fee appraisers for all of its field work. It does have full-time staff appraisers, but their function is to act as reviewers and supervisors. Once the fee appraiser has completed the appraisal, it is sent to the DVA office for review. If it is approved, the next step is to issue a ***Certificate of Reasonable Value (CRV)***, which also includes other conditions and repairs that the DVA requires on the property. A copy of the CRV is mailed to the person who ordered it and to the veteran-buyer.

Conventional Lenders

Conventional lenders use a less formal process than FHA or DVA in appraising the property. Typically, the borrower completes a loan application, which is reviewed by the lender or its loan correspondent. After determining that the application has been property completed, loan terms usually are discussed and, if the parties agree to continue, a credit report and appraisal are ordered.

Conventional lenders can use either licensed staff or fee appraisers. After an appraisal is completed, the lender reviews it for completeness as well as to determine whether the value of the property is sufficient for the loan request. While the appraisal is being done, the lender uses this time to qualify the borrower.

If the loan request was based on a sales price of $580,000 and the appraised value is only $550,000, the lender will base the maximum loan on the lower $550,000 figure. If the appraisal came in at a value of $600,000, then the lender would base the maximum loan on the lower sales price of $580,000.

Assuming that the appraisal issue is settled and the borrower is qualified, the entire loan package is submitted to a loan committee, or underwriter, who reviews the package and makes the final approval or rejection. If the loan committee or underwriter needs additional information prior to making a final decision, the request for additional information is sent back down the chain to the loan officer or correspondent.

8.2 Appraising a Property

We have discussed in general terms what a lender does when it qualifies a property. The appraisal of the property by the appraiser is one of the most critical phases of the whole process. (Qualifying the borrower is another, covered in the next chapter.) It is the appraisal report that the lender relies on to determine the acceptability of the property as collateral. The main purpose of an appraisal is to estimate *fair market value (FMV)*, defined as "the most probable price in terms of money that a property should bring in a competitive and open market under all conditions requisite to a fair sale, the buyer and seller acting prudently, knowledgeably and assuming the price is not affected by undue stimulus." There are many reasons for appraisals—lending, insurance, income taxes, property taxation, probates to settle estates, divorce, bankruptcy, and other legal concerns. The reason for the appraisal will affect the appraiser's approach to the task. For example, insurance appraisals are done to estimate replacement value of the improvements and therefore are not concerned with land value.

In this chapter we're concerned with appraisals only for loan purposes. Because what the appraiser does is so important, let's find out how the value of properties is determined.

Location

What is the first thing the appraiser does when assigned an appraisal request? The appraiser checks out the location of the property, knowing that location has a major influence on the value of the property. In analyzing the location, both city and neighborhood influences must be considered. But appraisers must not be influenced by lenders who may attempt to systematically exclude certain neighborhoods under a prohibited, discriminatory practice called *redlining*, discussed in Chapter 11.

City Influence

The following case history will demonstrate why city location is important. Some years ago, a developer built a subdivision in the Central Valley area. Part of the subdivision was located in a city that had a reputation for being a desirable place to live. The rest of the subdivision was in a city that was considered an average place to live. The houses in the subdivision consisted of just a few models. Walking around the subdivision, you could not tell that the houses were located in two different cities. Yet the sales results were dramatically different. The houses in the city with the better reputation sold quickly. The same houses in the other city were not selling nearly as well. The only difference was the city address. The developer recognized the difference in sales results and increased the prices of the homes with the prestige city address. They still sold readily at the high price because people were willing to pay more for a good address. The same houses on the same street sold for different prices for one single reason: *location*.

Neighborhood Influence

Within a given city, there are many neighborhoods, each of which can vary greatly in quality and desirability. How do you check a neighborhood? In most cases, an appraiser looks for the same items a cautious buyer might look for. The main items that buyers and appraisers check when considering a neighborhood's influence are the following:

1. *Approach to the property*. To get to the property, do you drive through a pleasant neighborhood, or do you have to drive through a run-down area? The approach to the property is important to a buyer, and therefore the appraiser considers this.

2. *Appeal of neighborhood*. Does the neighborhood have sales appeal? For example: Is it attractive? Does it have tree-lined streets? Is it laid out in a grid pattern, or does it have winding streets with cul-de-sacs?

3. *Neighborhood homogeneity*. Are the properties all single-family dwellings, or is there a mixture of apartment houses and commercial buildings? Are the properties of about the same age and same price range? Homogeneous neighborhoods are considered more desirable by most buyers and therefore more desirable to lenders.

4. *Neighborhood condition*. Do the neighbors take care of their homes? Many appraisers identify this characteristic as pride of ownership. You can easily determine pride of ownership by driving through the area and checking the landscaping and the exterior of the homes. Homes in well-maintained neighborhoods have greater value and marketability.

5. *Neighborhood trend*. An appraiser will carefully analyze the trend of the neighborhood. Is it stable, improving, or declining? Since the lender is concerned about the future of the property, this determination is very important. Some neighborhoods are in a state of transition where single-family homes are being replaced by apartment houses. This has an effect on the desirability of the

neighborhood. Again, appraisers and lenders must guard against redlining.

6. *Adverse influences.* An example of an adverse influence would be property located next to a noisy freeway. Any adverse influence will affect the value of the property. Other adverse influences that appraisers watch out for are airport flight patterns, slide and flood areas, climate (too foggy or windy) and obnoxious odors.

7. *Schools and shopping.* Buyers who have school-age children are interested in the proximity of schools. Proximity to shopping facilities is also important to a potential buyer.

8. *Other items.* Appraisers also look for such items as curbs and gutters, libraries, and police and fire protection.

An experienced appraiser may already know the quality of the neighborhood. Usually the appraiser checks the area while driving to the property. Upon arriving at the property, the appraiser probably already has a good idea of the quality of the neighborhood.

There are other location features that the appraiser must check—see the sample appraisal form (Figure 8.1). Many appraisal forms are used, but they all contain the same basic information.

At the Property

At the property, the appraiser remains outside and asks, Does the house fit in with the rest of the neighborhood? Is it in about the same price range or is it overimproved or underimproved? What is the sales appeal of the house? Are the exterior and landscaping well maintained? The answers to these questions will have a significant bearing on the value of the property.

8.3 Using a Standard Appraisal Form

A completed appraisal form is used by the lender to determine the acceptability of the property as security and to set the amount of the loan. The form shown in Figure 8.1 is the standard used by Fannie Mae and Freddie Mac. Since its adoption by the agencies, most lenders have come to use it as well, with some exceptions that we need not go into here (e.g., lenders participating in FNMA's *Desktop* Underwriter program). The following is a discussion of the three basic sections of the appraisal form (Figure 8.1) which

Uniform Residential Appraisal Report   File

The purpose of this summary appraisal report is to provide the lender/client with an accurate, and adequately supported, opinion of the market value of the subject property.

SUBJECT				
Property Address		City	State	Zip Code
Borrower	Owner of Public Record		County	
Legal Description				
Assessor's Parcel #		Tax Year	R.E. Taxes $	
Neighborhood Name		Map Reference	Census Tract	
Occupant ☐ Owner ☐ Tenant ☐ Vacant	Special Assessments $	☐ PUD HOA $	☐ per year ☐ per month	
Property Rights Appraised ☐ Fee Simple ☐ Leasehold ☐ Other (describe)				
Assignment Type ☐ Purchase Transaction ☐ Refinance Transaction ☐ Other (describe)				
Lender/Client	Address			

Is the subject property currently offered for sale or has it been offered for sale in the twelve months prior to the effective date of this appraisal? ☐ Yes ☐ No
Report data source(s) used, offering price(s), and date(s).

CONTRACT

I ☐ did ☐ did not analyze the contract for sale for the subject purchase transaction. Explain the results of the analysis of the contract for sale or why the analysis was not performed.

Contract Price $ Date of Contract   Is the property seller the owner of public record? ☐ Yes ☐ No   Data Source(s)
Is there any financial assistance (loan charges, sale concessions, gift or downpayment assistance, etc.) to be paid by any party on behalf of the borrower? ☐ Yes ☐ No
If Yes, report the total dollar amount and describe the items to be paid.

NEIGHBORHOOD

Note: Race and the racial composition of the neighborhood are not appraisal factors.

Neighborhood Characteristics			One-Unit Housing Trends			One-Unit Housing		Present Land Use %	
Location ☐ Urban	☐ Suburban	☐ Rural	Property Values ☐ Increasing	☐ Stable	☐ Declining	PRICE	AGE	One-Unit	%
Built-Up ☐ Over 75%	☐ 25–75%	☐ Under 25%	Demand/Supply ☐ Shortage	☐ In Balance	☐ Over Supply	$ (000)	(yrs)	2-4 Unit	%
Growth ☐ Rapid	☐ Stable	☐ Slow	Marketing Time ☐ Under 3 mths	☐ 3–6 mths	☐ Over 6 mths	Low		Multi-Family	%
Neighborhood Boundaries						High		Commercial	%
						Pred.		Other	%

Neighborhood Description

Market Conditions (including support for the above conclusions)

SITE

Dimensions	Area	Shape	View
Specific Zoning Classification	Zoning Description		

Zoning Compliance ☐ Legal ☐ Legal Nonconforming (Grandfathered Use) ☐ No Zoning ☐ Illegal (describe)
Is the highest and best use of the subject property as improved (or as proposed per plans and specifications) the present use? ☐ Yes ☐ No If No, describe

Utilities	Public	Other (describe)		Public	Other (describe)	Off-site Improvements—Type	Public	Private
Electricity	☐	☐	Water	☐	☐	Street	☐	☐
Gas	☐	☐	Sanitary Sewer	☐	☐	Alley	☐	☐

FEMA Special Flood Hazard Area ☐ Yes ☐ No FEMA Flood Zone   FEMA Map #   FEMA Map Date
Are the utilities and off-site improvements typical for the market area? ☐ Yes ☐ No If No, describe
Are there any adverse site conditions or external factors (easements, encroachments, environmental conditions, land uses, etc.)? ☐ Yes ☐ No If Yes, describe

---

IMPROVEMENTS

General Description		Foundation		Exterior Description	materials/condition	Interior	materials/condition
Units ☐ One ☐ One with Accessory Unit		☐ Concrete Slab ☐ Crawl Space		Foundation Walls		Floors	
# of Stories		☐ Full Basement ☐ Partial Basement		Exterior Walls		Walls	
Type ☐ Det. ☐ Att. ☐ S-Det./End Unit		Basement Area sq. ft.		Roof Surface		Trim/Finish	
☐ Existing ☐ Proposed ☐ Under Const.		Basement Finish %		Gutters & Downspouts		Bath Floor	
Design (Style)		☐ Outside Entry/Exit ☐ Sump Pump		Window Type		Bath Wainscot	
Year Built		Evidence of ☐ Infestation		Storm Sash/Insulated		Car Storage ☐ None	
Effective Age (Yrs)		☐ Dampness ☐ Settlement		Screens		☐ Driveway # of Cars	
Attic ☐ None		Heating ☐ FWA ☐ HWBB ☐ Radiant		Amenities ☐ Woodstove(s) #		Driveway Surface	
☐ Drop Stair ☐ Stairs		☐ Other Fuel		☐ Fireplace(s) # ☐ Fence		☐ Garage # of Cars	
☐ Floor ☐ Scuttle		Cooling ☐ Central Air Conditioning		☐ Patio/Deck ☐ Porch		☐ Carport # of Cars	
☐ Finished ☐ Heated		☐ Individual ☐ Other		☐ Pool ☐ Other		☐ Att. ☐ Det. ☐ Built-in	

Appliances ☐ Refrigerator ☐ Range/Oven ☐ Dishwasher ☐ Disposal ☐ Microwave ☐ Washer/Dryer ☐ Other (describe)
Finished area **above** grade contains: Rooms   Bedrooms   Bath(s)   Square Feet of Gross Living Area Above Grade
Additional features (special energy efficient items, etc.)

Describe the condition of the property (including needed repairs, deterioration, renovations, remodeling, etc.).

Are there any physical deficiencies or adverse conditions that affect the livability, soundness, or structural integrity of the property? ☐ Yes ☐ No If Yes, describe

Does the property generally conform to the neighborhood (functional utility, style, condition, use, construction, etc.)? ☐ Yes ☐ No If No, describe

---

Freddie Mac Form 70   March 2005   Page 1 of 6   Fannie Mae Form 1004   March 2005

Figure 8.1 Residential appraisal report.

Uniform Residential Appraisal Report   File

There are ____ comparable properties currently offered for sale in the subject neighborhood ranging in price from $ ____ to $ ____.						
There are ____ comparable sales in the subject neighborhood within the past twelve months ranging in sale price from $ ____ to $ ____.						

FEATURE	SUBJECT	COMPARABLE SALE # 1		COMPARABLE SALE # 2		COMPARABLE SALE # 3	
Address							
Proximity to Subject							
Sale Price	$		$		$		$
Sale Price/Gross Liv. Area	$	sq. ft.	$	sq. ft.	$	sq. ft.	$	sq. ft.
Data Source(s)							
Verification Source(s)							
VALUE ADJUSTMENTS	DESCRIPTION	DESCRIPTION	+(-) $ Adjustment	DESCRIPTION	+(-) $ Adjustment	DESCRIPTION	+(-) $ Adjustment
Sale or Financing Concessions							
Date of Sale/Time							
Location							
Leasehold/Fee Simple							
Site							
View							
Design (Style)							
Quality of Construction							
Actual Age							
Condition							
Above Grade Room Count	Total / Bdrms. / Baths	Total / Bdrms. / Baths		Total / Bdrms. / Baths		Total / Bdrms. / Baths	
Gross Living Area	sq. ft.	sq. ft.		sq. ft.		sq. ft.	
Basement & Finished Rooms Below Grade							
Functional Utility							
Heating/Cooling							
Energy Efficient Items							
Garage/Carport							
Porch/Patio/Deck							
Net Adjustment (Total)		☐ + ☐ -	$	☐ + ☐ -	$	☐ + ☐ -	$
Adjusted Sale Price of Comparables		Net Adj. ___% Gross Adj. ___%	$	Net Adj. ___% Gross Adj. ___%	$	Net Adj. ___% Gross Adj. ___%	$

I ☐ did ☐ did not research the sale or transfer history of the subject property and comparable sales. If not, explain

My research ☐ did ☐ did not reveal any prior sales or transfers of the subject property for the three years prior to the effective date of this appraisal.

Data source(s)

My research ☐ did ☐ did not reveal any prior sales or transfers of the comparable sales for the year prior to the date of sale of the comparable sale.

Data source(s)

Report the results of the research and analysis of the prior sale or transfer history of the subject property and comparable sales (report additional prior sales on page 3).

ITEM	SUBJECT	COMPARABLE SALE # 1	COMPARABLE SALE # 2	COMPARABLE SALE # 3
Date of Prior Sale/Transfer				
Price of Prior Sale/Transfer				
Data Source(s)				
Effective Date of Data Source(s)				

Analysis of prior sale or transfer history of the subject property and comparable sales

Summary of Sales Comparison Approach

Indicated Value by Sales Comparison Approach $

Indicated Value by: Sales Comparison Approach $ ____   Cost Approach (if developed) $ ____   Income Approach (if developed) $ ____

This appraisal is made ☐ "as is", ☐ subject to completion per plans and specifications on the basis of a hypothetical condition that the improvements have been completed, ☐ subject to the following repairs or alterations on the basis of a hypothetical condition that the repairs or alterations have been completed, or ☐ subject to the following required inspection based on the extraordinary assumption that the condition or deficiency does not require alteration or repair:

Based on a complete visual inspection of the interior and exterior areas of the subject property, defined scope of work, statement of assumptions and limiting conditions, and appraiser's certification, my (our) opinion of the market value, as defined, of the real property that is the subject of this report is
$ ____ , as of ____ , which is the date of inspection and the effective date of this appraisal.

Figure 8.1 Residential appraisal report *(continued).*

Uniform Residential Appraisal Report

File #

ADDITIONAL COMMENTS

COST APPROACH TO VALUE (not required by Fannie Mae)

Provide adequate information for the lender/client to replicate the below cost figures and calculations.

Support for the opinion of site value (summary of comparable land sales or other methods for estimating site value)

COST APPROACH

ESTIMATED ☐ REPRODUCTION OR ☐ REPLACEMENT COST NEW	OPINION OF SITE VALUE .... = $
Source of cost data	Dwelling Sq. Ft. @ $ .... =$
Quality rating from cost service Effective date of cost data	Sq. Ft. @ $ .... =$
Comments on Cost Approach (gross living area calculations, depreciation, etc.)	
	Garage/Carport Sq. Ft. @ $ .... =$
	Total Estimate of Cost-New .... = $
	Less Physical Functional External
	Depreciation =$( )
	Depreciated Cost of Improvements...................................=$
	"As-is" Value of Site Improvements.................................=$
Estimated Remaining Economic Life (HUD and VA only) Years	Indicated Value By Cost Approach ....=$

INCOME APPROACH TO VALUE (not required by Fannie Mae)

INCOME

Estimated Monthly Market Rent $ X Gross Rent Multiplier   = $ Indicated Value by Income Approach

Summary of Income Approach (including support for market rent and GRM)

PROJECT INFORMATION FOR PUDs (if applicable)

PUD INFORMATION

Is the developer/builder in control of the Homeowners' Association (HOA)? ☐ Yes ☐ No   Unit type(s) ☐ Detached ☐ Attached

Provide the following information for PUDs ONLY if the developer/builder is in control of the HOA and the subject property is an attached dwelling unit.

Legal name of project

Total number of phases   Total number of units   Total number of units sold

Total number of units rented   Total number of units for sale   Data source(s)

Was the project created by the conversion of an existing building(s) into a PUD? ☐ Yes ☐ No   If Yes, date of conversion

Does the project contain any multi-dwelling units? ☐ Yes ☐ No   Data source(s)

Are the units, common elements, and recreation facilities complete? ☐ Yes ☐ No   If No, describe the status of completion.

Are the common elements leased to or by the Homeowners' Association? ☐ Yes ☐ No   If Yes, describe the rental terms and options.

Describe common elements and recreational facilities

Freddie Mac Form 70   March 2005   Page 3 of 6   Fannie Mae Form 1004   March 2005

Figure 8.1 Residential appraisal report *(continued)*.

Uniform Residential Appraisal Report   File

This report form is designed to report an appraisal of a one-unit property or a one-unit property with an accessory unit; including a unit in a planned unit development (PUD). This report form is not designed to report an appraisal of a manufactured home or a unit in a condominium or cooperative project.

This appraisal report is subject to the following scope of work, intended use, intended user, definition of market value, statement of assumptions and limiting conditions, and certifications. Modifications, additions, or deletions to the intended use, intended user, definition of market value, or assumptions and limiting conditions are not permitted. The appraiser may expand the scope of work to include any additional research or analysis necessary based on the complexity of this appraisal assignment. Modifications or deletions to the certifications are also not permitted. However, additional certifications that do not constitute material alterations to this appraisal report, such as those required by law or those related to the appraiser's continuing education or membership in an appraisal organization, are permitted.

SCOPE OF WORK: The scope of work for this appraisal is defined by the complexity of this appraisal assignment and the reporting requirements of this appraisal report form, including the following definition of market value, statement of assumptions and limiting conditions, and certifications. The appraiser must, at a minimum: (1) perform a complete visual inspection of the interior and exterior areas of the subject property, (2) inspect the neighborhood, (3) inspect each of the comparable sales from at least the street, (4) research, verify, and analyze data from reliable public and/or private sources, and (5) report his or her analysis, opinions, and conclusions in this appraisal report.

INTENDED USE: The intended use of this appraisal report is for the lender/client to evaluate the property that is the subject of this appraisal for a mortgage finance transaction.

INTENDED USER: The intended user of this appraisal report is the lender/client.

DEFINITION OF MARKET VALUE: The most probable price which a property should bring in a competitive and open market under all conditions requisite to a fair sale, the buyer and seller, each acting prudently, knowledgeably and assuming the price is not affected by undue stimulus. Implicit in this definition is the consummation of a sale as of a specified date and the passing of title from seller to buyer under conditions whereby: (1) buyer and seller are typically motivated; (2) both parties are well informed or well advised, and each acting in what he or she considers his or her own best interest; (3) a reasonable time is allowed for exposure in the open market; (4) payment is made in terms of cash in U. S. dollars or in terms of financial arrangements comparable thereto; and (5) the price represents the normal consideration for the property sold unaffected by special or creative financing or sales concessions* granted by anyone associated with the sale.

*Adjustments to the comparables must be made for special or creative financing or sales concessions. No adjustments are necessary for those costs which are normally paid by sellers as a result of tradition or law in a market area; these costs are readily identifiable since the seller pays these costs in virtually all sales transactions. Special or creative financing adjustments can be made to the comparable property by comparisons to financing terms offered by a third party institutional lender that is not already involved in the property or transaction. Any adjustment should not be calculated on a mechanical dollar for dollar cost of the financing or concession but the dollar amount of any adjustment should approximate the market's reaction to the financing or concessions based on the appraiser's judgment.

STATEMENT OF ASSUMPTIONS AND LIMITING CONDITIONS: The appraiser's certification in this report is subject to the following assumptions and limiting conditions:

1. The appraiser will not be responsible for matters of a legal nature that affect either the property being appraised or the title to it, except for information that he or she became aware of during the research involved in performing this appraisal. The appraiser assumes that the title is good and marketable and will not render any opinions about the title.

2. The appraiser has provided a sketch in this appraisal report to show the approximate dimensions of the improvements. The sketch is included only to assist the reader in visualizing the property and understanding the appraiser's determination of its size.

3. The appraiser has examined the available flood maps that are provided by the Federal Emergency Management Agency (or other data sources) and has noted in this appraisal report whether any portion of the subject site is located in an identified Special Flood Hazard Area. Because the appraiser is not a surveyor, he or she makes no guarantees, express or implied, regarding this determination.

4. The appraiser will not give testimony or appear in court because he or she made an appraisal of the property in question, unless specific arrangements to do so have been made beforehand, or as otherwise required by law.

5. The appraiser has noted in this appraisal report any adverse conditions (such as needed repairs, deterioration, the presence of hazardous wastes, toxic substances, etc.) observed during the inspection of the subject property or that he or she became aware of during the research involved in performing this appraisal. Unless otherwise stated in this appraisal report, the appraiser has no knowledge of any hidden or unapparent physical deficiencies or adverse conditions of the property (such as, but not limited to, needed repairs, deterioration, the presence of hazardous wastes, toxic substances, adverse environmental conditions, etc.) that would make the property less valuable, and has assumed that there are no such conditions and makes no guarantees or warranties, express or implied. The appraiser will not be responsible for any such conditions that do exist or for any engineering or testing that might be required to discover whether such conditions exist. Because the appraiser is not an expert in the field of environmental hazards, this appraisal report must not be considered as an environmental assessment of the property.

6. The appraiser has based his or her appraisal report and valuation conclusion for an appraisal that is subject to satisfactory completion, repairs, or alterations on the assumption that the completion, repairs, or alterations of the subject property will be performed in a professional manner.

Freddie Mac Form 70 March 2005	Page 4 of 6	Fannie Mae Form 1004 March 2005

Figure 8.1 Residential appraisal report *(continued)*.

Uniform Residential Appraisal Report

File #

APPRAISER'S CERTIFICATION: The Appraiser certifies and agrees that:

1. I have, at a minimum, developed and reported this appraisal in accordance with the scope of work requirements stated in this appraisal report.

2. I performed a complete visual inspection of the interior and exterior areas of the subject property. I reported the condition of the improvements in factual, specific terms. I identified and reported the physical deficiencies that could affect the livability, soundness, or structural integrity of the property.

3. I performed this appraisal in accordance with the requirements of the Uniform Standards of Professional Appraisal Practice that were adopted and promulgated by the Appraisal Standards Board of The Appraisal Foundation and that were in place at the time this appraisal report was prepared.

4. I developed my opinion of the market value of the real property that is the subject of this report based on the sales comparison approach to value. I have adequate comparable market data to develop a reliable sales comparison approach for this appraisal assignment. I further certify that I considered the cost and income approaches to value but did not develop them, unless otherwise indicated in this report.

5. I researched, verified, analyzed, and reported on any current agreement for sale for the subject property, any offering for sale of the subject property in the twelve months prior to the effective date of this appraisal, and the prior sales of the subject property for a minimum of three years prior to the effective date of this appraisal, unless otherwise indicated in this report.

6. I researched, verified, analyzed, and reported on the prior sales of the comparable sales for a minimum of one year prior to the date of sale of the comparable sale, unless otherwise indicated in this report.

7. I selected and used comparable sales that are locationally, physically, and functionally the most similar to the subject property.

8. I have not used comparable sales that were the result of combining a land sale with the contract purchase price of a home that has been built or will be built on the land.

9. I have reported adjustments to the comparable sales that reflect the market's reaction to the differences between the subject property and the comparable sales.

10. I verified, from a disinterested source, all information in this report that was provided by parties who have a financial interest in the sale or financing of the subject property.

11. I have knowledge and experience in appraising this type of property in this market area.

12. I am aware of, and have access to, the necessary and appropriate public and private data sources, such as multiple listing services, tax assessment records, public land records and other such data sources for the area in which the property is located.

13. I obtained the information, estimates, and opinions furnished by other parties and expressed in this appraisal report from reliable sources that I believe to be true and correct.

14. I have taken into consideration the factors that have an impact on value with respect to the subject neighborhood, subject property, and the proximity of the subject property to adverse influences in the development of my opinion of market value. I have noted in this appraisal report any adverse conditions (such as, but not limited to, needed repairs, deterioration, the presence of hazardous wastes, toxic substances, adverse environmental conditions, etc.) observed during the inspection of the subject property or that I became aware of during the research involved in performing this appraisal. I have considered these adverse conditions in my analysis of the property value, and have reported on the effect of the conditions on the value and marketability of the subject property.

15. I have not knowingly withheld any significant information from this appraisal report and, to the best of my knowledge, all statements and information in this appraisal report are true and correct.

16. I stated in this appraisal report my own personal, unbiased, and professional analysis, opinions, and conclusions, which are subject only to the assumptions and limiting conditions in this appraisal report.

17. I have no present or prospective interest in the property that is the subject of this report, and I have no present or prospective personal interest or bias with respect to the participants in the transaction. I did not base, either partially or completely, my analysis and/or opinion of market value in this appraisal report on the race, color, religion, sex, age, marital status, handicap, familial status, or national origin of either the prospective owners or occupants of the subject property or of the present owners or occupants of the properties in the vicinity of the subject property or on any other basis prohibited by law.

18. My employment and/or compensation for performing this appraisal or any future or anticipated appraisals was not conditioned on any agreement or understanding, written or otherwise, that I would report (or present analysis supporting) a predetermined specific value, a predetermined minimum value, a range or direction in value, a value that favors the cause of any party, or the attainment of a specific result or occurrence of a specific subsequent event (such as approval of a pending mortgage loan application).

19. I personally prepared all conclusions and opinions about the real estate that were set forth in this appraisal report. If I relied on significant real property appraisal assistance from any individual or individuals in the performance of this appraisal or the preparation of this appraisal report, I have named such individual(s) and disclosed the specific tasks performed in this appraisal report. I certify that any individual so named is qualified to perform the tasks. I have not authorized anyone to make a change to any item in this appraisal report; therefore, any change made to this appraisal is unauthorized and I will take no responsibility for it.

20. I identified the lender/client in this appraisal report who is the individual, organization, or agent for the organization that ordered and will receive this appraisal report.

Freddie Mac Form 70 March 2005   Page 5 of 6   Fannie Mae Form 1004 March 2005

Figure 8.1 Residential appraisal report *(continued).*

Uniform Residential Appraisal Report

File #

21. The lender/client may disclose or distribute this appraisal report to: the borrower; another lender at the request of the borrower; the mortgagee or its successors and assigns; mortgage insurers; government sponsored enterprises; other secondary market participants; data collection or reporting services; professional appraisal organizations; any department, agency, or instrumentality of the United States; and any state, the District of Columbia, or other jurisdictions; without having to obtain the appraiser's or supervisory appraiser's (if applicable) consent. Such consent must be obtained before this appraisal report may be disclosed or distributed to any other party (including, but not limited to, the public through advertising, public relations, news, sales, or other media).

22. I am aware that any disclosure or distribution of this appraisal report by me or the lender/client may be subject to certain laws and regulations. Further, I am also subject to the provisions of the Uniform Standards of Professional Appraisal Practice that pertain to disclosure or distribution by me.

23. The borrower, another lender at the request of the borrower, the mortgagee or its successors and assigns, mortgage insurers, government sponsored enterprises, and other secondary market participants may rely on this appraisal report as part of any mortgage finance transaction that involves any one or more of these parties.

24. If this appraisal report was transmitted as an "electronic record" containing my "electronic signature," as those terms are defined in applicable federal and/or state laws (excluding audio and video recordings), or a facsimile transmission of this appraisal report containing a copy or representation of my signature, the appraisal report shall be as effective, enforceable and valid as if a paper version of this appraisal report were delivered containing my original hand written signature.

25. Any intentional or negligent misrepresentation(s) contained in this appraisal report may result in civil liability and/or criminal penalties including, but not limited to, fine or imprisonment or both under the provisions of Title 18, United States Code, Section 1001, et seq., or similar state laws.

SUPERVISORY APPRAISER'S CERTIFICATION: The Supervisory Appraiser certifies and agrees that:

1. I directly supervised the appraiser for this appraisal assignment, have read the appraisal report, and agree with the appraiser's analysis, opinions, statements, conclusions, and the appraiser's certification.

2. I accept full responsibility for the contents of this appraisal report including, but not limited to, the appraiser's analysis, opinions, statements, conclusions, and the appraiser's certification.

3. The appraiser identified in this appraisal report is either a sub-contractor or an employee of the supervisory appraiser (or the appraisal firm), is qualified to perform this appraisal, and is acceptable to perform this appraisal under the applicable state law.

4. This appraisal report complies with the Uniform Standards of Professional Appraisal Practice that were adopted and promulgated by the Appraisal Standards Board of The Appraisal Foundation and that were in place at the time this appraisal report was prepared.

5. If this appraisal report was transmitted as an "electronic record" containing my "electronic signature," as those terms are defined in applicable federal and/or state laws (excluding audio and video recordings), or a facsimile transmission of this appraisal report containing a copy or representation of my signature, the appraisal report shall be as effective, enforceable and valid as if a paper version of this appraisal report were delivered containing my original hand written signature.

APPRAISER

Signature_____
Name _____
Company Name _____
Company Address_____

Telephone Number _____
Email Address_____
Date of Signature and Report_____
Effective Date of Appraisal _____
State Certification #_____
or State License # _____
or Other (describe) _____ State # _____
State _____
Expiration Date of Certification or License _____

ADDRESS OF PROPERTY APPRAISED

_____
_____

APPRAISED VALUE OF SUBJECT PROPERTY $ _____

LENDER/CLIENT

Name _____
Company Name _____
Company Address_____
_____
Email Address_____

SUPERVISORY APPRAISER (ONLY IF REQUIRED)

Signature _____
Name_____
Company Name _____
Company Address_____
_____

Telephone Number _____
Email Address _____
Date of Signature _____
State Certification #_____
or State License # _____
State _____
Expiration Date of Certification or License _____

SUBJECT PROPERTY

☐ Did not inspect subject property
☐ Did inspect exterior of subject property from street
   Date of Inspection _____
☐ Did inspect interior and exterior of subject property
   Date of Inspection _____

COMPARABLE SALES

☐ Did not inspect exterior of comparable sales from street
☐ Did inspect exterior of comparable sales from street
   Date of Inspection _____

Freddie Mac Form 70   March 2005   Page 6 of 6   Fannie Mae Form 1004   March 2005

Figure 8.1 Residential appraisal report *(continued).*

include neighborhood characteristics and trends, property description and information, and valuation.

Neighborhood

Following the identification of the property at the top of the page is the neighborhood section. A neighborhood is a group of properties relatively similar in land use and value. It can be large or as small as a single block or street. Some of the items that are important when analyzing a neighborhood are listed on the form and are discussed below.

Supply and Demand

If supply and demand are not in balance, it can affect prices in the neighborhood. For example, if there were an oversupply of houses, a buyer's market could exist and forced sales could result, which would depress property values.

Price Range

The price range of properties in a neighborhood are important because, with that information, we can determine if the subject property is over- or underimproved. If the sales price of the property exceeded the upper price level, it would be an overimprovement. Overimprovements have less marketability, because they may not be acceptable to the average buyer. A property with a sales price below the lower price level (underimprovement) generally has good marketability because it provides buyers an opportunity to live in a neighborhood they want but could not otherwise afford.

Neighborhood Description

The appraiser will summarize the items in a neighborhood that buyers consider to be of importance. A few of the main items are these:

1. *Employment stability.* An area where employment is provided primarily by just one industry would not have good employment stability. Small towns built around a lumber mill are a good example. Another recent example is communities that depended on the computer and software industry. Severe depression of that industry caused widespread unemployment in some California areas in the early 2000s.

2. *Convenience to employment, shopping, and schools.* Buyers care about these convenience factors, in terms of both time and mileage. As the cost of operating an automobile increases, these factors become more important.

3. *Protection from detrimental conditions.* A detrimental condition in a neighborhood affects the marketability and, therefore, the value

of the property. Examples of detrimental conditions the appraiser checks for are high vacancy rate, poorly maintained properties, abandoned properties, obnoxious odors, poor climate, and annoying airport flight patterns.

Property

After the neighborhood has been analyzed, the appraiser inspects the site and the physical property. This portion of the report is divided into various sections: site, improvements, room list, interior finish and equipment, and a property rating.

Site

As the appraiser checks the site, these are some of the items that are carefully analyzed:

1. *Zoning.* It is important to know if the improvements conform to the current zoning of the site. If they do not, there may be a problem, since nonconforming properties generally cannot be reconstructed if destroyed. If the lender is positive that a new building permit would not be issued, it may deny the loan.

2. *The lot.* The topography and drainage on a lot could be very important. A home built on a steep hillside could be subject to earth slides, particularly if there are drainage problems.

3. *Flood area.* If the property is located in a HUD-identified flood area, the property must carry flood insurance if a loan is made. It is the responsibility of the lender to make sure flood insurance is obtained if required.

Improvements, Room List, Interior Finish and Equipment, Property Rating

These sections of the report serve as a good checklist while the appraiser is inspecting the property. The appraiser starts by checking the exterior of the improvements. The number and type of rooms and the floor plan are the next items noted.

The appraiser carefully checks for poor structural designs or unusual floor plans that could affect marketability of the property. This is referred to as **functional obsolescence**, a loss in value from sources *within* the property. In contrast, **economic obsolescence** is a loss in value from forces *outside* of the property, such as adverse zoning or a freeway behind the property.

Examples of functional obsolescence include houses with unusual floor plans. To illustrate, a house located in a prime San Francisco Bay area was well built, in excellent condition, and nearly 3,500 square feet in living space. The problem? The home had only one bedroom, which seriously affected its marketability. As a result the loan request was substantially reduced.

Other examples of problem floor plans include five bedrooms with one bath; access to bath through another bedroom; and a bathroom opening into the kitchen, as was common for homes built in the 1920s.

While inspecting the interior of the building, the appraiser notes the condition of the paint, floor, kitchen equipment, and garage. The appraiser looks for signs of problems; water stains or moisture could be evidence of a roof or plumbing leak. Structural problems are far more serious than cosmetic problems; sagging floors, sticky doors, and large cracks could be caused by a settling foundation or a shifting of the structure—all forms of *physical depreciation*.

Photographs and Square Footage Measurement

In addition to the appraisal, lenders require a photograph of the front of the property, the street it is located on, and the side and back yards. The appraiser must also obtain the square footage of the house, since this information is used in calculating the value.

To obtain the square footage, the appraiser measures the house from the outside and draws a sketch as shown in Figure 8.2. The photographs and the sketch are attached to the report when it is completed.

Valuation

The valuation section outlines market data, cost, and income approaches that will aid in determining market value.

Sales Comparison Approach

The basis of the *sales comparison approach* to value, also popularly called *market data approach*, is that a buyer will not pay more for a property than the cost of acquiring an equally desirable substitute property. This is what economists refer to as the "principle of substitution." For example, assume a property is for sale at $500,000. In the same neighborhood, there are two other properties with the same amenities that are for sale at $475,000. A buyer will not pay $500,000 when an equally desirable property is available at $475,000. Therefore, the first property is not worth $500,000, because knowledgeable buyers will not pay that much.

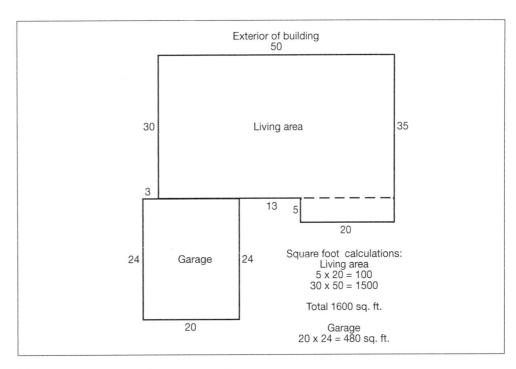

Figure 8.2 Computing square footage.

Buyers and real estate salespeople use a simplified market data approach when appraising property. To arrive at a value of a property, they seek answers to these questions: What properties have sold recently that are similar to the subject property? How did these properties compare with the subject? How much are those differences worth? After subtracting or adding for the differences, called ***adjustments***, they arrive at a value for the subject property. Appraisers use the same procedure; however, they do it in a more systematic and precise manner, utilizing such specialized types of appraisal resources as *Marshall and Swift* to identify home component cost values.

Determining value through the sales comparison approach involves a four-step procedure:

1. Obtain recent sales of properties that are comparable to the subject property.

2. Analyze these sales.

3. Adjust for differences between these sales and the subject property.

4. Arrive at an estimate of market value.

In the market data analysis section of the appraisal report, the subject property is listed in the first column and comparable sales in the next three columns. Note that the properties have been rated on various items such as location, design and appeal, condition, and so on. When an item on a comparable property differs from the subject, a dollar adjustment appears.

Comparables chosen by the appraiser should be as similar to the subject property as possible, because this minimizes the need for and size of dollar adjustments, which ordinarily should not exceed 15 percent. The appraiser attempts to obtain comparables that have sold recently and are in the same neighborhood. This reduces the need for time and location differences. Dollar adjustments should reflect the market reaction to the differences, not necessarily the cost of the differences. For example, swimming pools, intercom systems, and elaborate landscaping may not increase market value to the full extent of their cost.

Appraisers must pay particular attention to the "Sales or Financing Concessions" item. This item includes adjustments for different types of financing that can affect the sales price. Examples include the seller carrying back a loan at a lower rate than the market, the buyer assuming a loan at a low rate, and the seller paying points to enable the buyer to obtain an interest buy-down loan. When sellers pay points, they usually increase the price of the property to cover the cost of the points. The appraisal must then reflect the increased price. Examples of sales concessions are gifts of merchandise such as a new car with the purchase of a home.

Because choosing good comparables is so important, appraisers use many sources in obtaining information on comparable sales, including the following:

1. The appraiser's own files.

2. Multiple listing service of real estate boards.

3. Real estate agents.

4. Public records (county assessor and recorder via documentary transfer tax shown on deeds).

5. Appraisal Institute, composed of the former Society of Real Estate Appraisers (SREA) and the American Institute of Real Estate Appraisers (AIREA), a nonprofit corporation that publishes sales by county, region, and other criteria.

Note how the adjustments are handled: If the item on the comparable property is *superior* to the subject property, a *minus* (−) adjustment is made. If *inferior*, a *plus* (+) adjustment is made. After the adjustments have been made for each comparable, they are totaled at the bottom of the column. This plus or minus total is applied to the sales price of the comparable to arrive at an indicated value of the subject property.

The appraiser's next task is to arrive at one figure, which represents the "indicated value by sales comparison approach." There is no formula that the appraiser can use. You cannot average the three results and come up with a figure. It is a matter of exercising good judgment. Typically, appraisers give the greatest weight to the comparable sale that required the least adjustments.

Cost Approach

Cost approach is based on the principle that property is worth what it would cost to duplicate. Adjustments to cost are made to allow for any loss in value due to economic age, condition, and other factors that reduce marketability.

Determining value through the cost approach involves a three-step procedure:

1. Estimate the total cost to reproduce the structure at current prices.

2. Subtract the estimated depreciation from all sources.

3. Add the estimated value of the land, based on the comparison or market data approach.

Income Approach

The principle of the income approach is that there is relationship between the income the property can earn and the property's value. On owner-occupied homes, an appraiser may omit the income approach on the theory that an owner-occupied home will not be rented. But if an income approach is used on a home, the appraiser will usually use **gross rent multipliers (GRM)**, instead of the standard income approach to value.

Gross rent multipliers are ratios that state the relationship between gross rental income and sales price. The can be use on a monthly or annual basis. GRMs typically provide a ballpark amount and not a precise figure of value.

The formula for the gross rent multiplier is:

$$\frac{\text{Sales Price}}{\text{Gross Monthly Rent}} = \text{Gross Rent Multiplier (GRM) on a monthly basis}$$

Or

$$\frac{\text{Sales Price}}{\text{Gross Annual Rent}} = \text{Gross Rent Multiplier (GRM) on a annual basis}$$

Example: A single family home sold for $500,000. The property could be rented for $2,500 per month. What is the GRM?
Solution:

$$\text{Monthly basis}: \frac{\$500,000}{\$2,500} = 200 = GRM$$

$$\text{Annual basis}: \frac{\$500,000}{\$30,000(\$2,500\ \text{month} \times 12\ \text{months})} = 16.67 = GRM$$

To establish a valid market GRM, the appraiser must locate similar properties in comparable neighborhoods that were recently sold or rent at the time of the appraisal. Sometimes it may be difficult to establish a market GRM because of the lack of recent information. However, once a valid market GRM is established, the appraiser uses the following formula to arrive at indicated value.

Subject Property's Monthly Rent × Market GRM = Indicated Value
Or
Subject Property's Annual Rent × Market GRM = Indicated Value

Example: On another property, an appraiser determines that the market rent should be $2,000 per month and that the monthly market GRM is 200. What is the indicated value?
Solution: $2,000 monthly rent × 200 GRM = $400,000 Indicated Value

On larger-income properties such as apartment houses, office buildings, and shopping centers, the standard income approach—often called the ***capitalization*** method—is used. This approach determines the present value of a property based on the net operating income of the property.

The standard income approach uses this procedure:

1. Calculate scheduled gross annual income, which is income from all sources, assuming 100 percent occupancy.

2. From gross annual income, deduct reasonable vacancy and collection losses to arrive at *effective gross income*.

3. Estimate all expenses such as taxes, wages, utilities, insurance, repairs, and management, and then deduct these operating expenses from effective gross income to determine the ***net***

operating income (NOI). It is important to note that mortgage payments, called debt service, are not considered an operating expense.

4. Select an appropriate **capitalization rate.** The methods for calculating the capitalization rate are technical but, basically, a capitalization rate is the rate of return that an investor would seek as a reasonable return on an investment.

5. Divide the market capitalization rate into the subject property's net operating income.

$$\frac{\text{Subject Property's Net Operating Income}}{\text{Market Capitalization Rate}} = \text{Indicated value}$$

Example: Small Rental Property:

Gross Scheduled Annual Income	$100,000
Less: Vacancy and Collection Losses	−5,000
Equals: Effective Gross Income	$95,000
Less: Annual Operating Expenses	−35,000
Equals: Net Operating Income	$60,000

Assume Market Capitalization Rate (Cap Rate) @ 8 percent

$$\frac{\$60,000 \text{ Net Operating Income}}{8 \text{ percent Market Capitalization Rate}} = 750,000 \text{ } \textit{Indicated Value}$$

Final Market Value

The appraiser's approach to determine value, called a final reconciliation, depends on the type of property being appraised.

In the appraisal of single-family properties, more weight is given to the sales comparison or market approach because it is the most reliable. The cost approach is not as reliable, because it is difficult to estimate depreciation and to determine the value of land in a built-up neighborhood. The cost approach is best used for special-purpose properties such as churches, schools, government buildings, and anything unusual that does not sell routinely in the marketplace. The use of a gross rent multiplier may not be used in appraising a single-family owner-occupied property, because typical buyers do not buy them for income purposes.

Next, the appraiser analyzes the data used in the report for completeness and reliability. The final step is to arrive at market value.

Again, this is not an averaging process, but one in which the appraiser evaluates each approach, then selects a single estimate of value.

Sales Price versus Fair Market Value

The sales price and the fair market value of a property are not always the same. Some reasons for the differences may be an unknowledgeable buyer or seller, financing concessions (seller paying fees or points or carrying a loan), personal property included in the sale, or a seller under pressure to sell.

Appraisers realize that appraising is not an exact science and that a lot of judgment is involved. Although the value of a property cannot be pinpointed, appraisers know that the sales price is one of the best indications of value. If the data in the appraisal report are adequate and reliable, then the appraiser should have no problem accepting the sales price as market value. If the figures are different, the lender bases the loan on the sales price or the appraised value, whichever is lower.

8.4 Underwriting the Loan

After the appraisal has been completed, and any other requirements have been met, it is ready for underwriting by the lender. The purpose of underwriting is to determine if the property is acceptable by lender standards, if the market value supports the loan requested, and if the loan meets the lender's policies. The lender may alter the terms or conditions of the loan to comply with standards and policies. For example, if the appraisal indicates that the roof leaks, the lender may add a condition to the loan approval that the roof be repaired.

The lender also has an interest in the future value of the property, because, in case of foreclosure, there must be sufficient value to cover the loan. For one-to-four-unit properties, estimating future value becomes very subjective and imprecise. Therefore, lenders are concerned about only the early years of the mortgage. If the underwriter is certain, and able to document, that value will likely decrease during the first one to five years, then the terms of the loan may be adjusted (such as reducing the loan amount). The adjustments should not exceed the minimum required for the property to be an adequate security. Underwriters are very careful not to violate State of California regulations (see Chapter 2) when making adjustments or in their general underwriting.

8.5 Planned Unit Developments and Condominiums

In recent years, many ***planned unit developments (PUDs)*** and ***condominiums*** have been built in the United States. As more are built and resales occur, it is important that you know what they are and how they are appraised. It is important because some lenders have different loan policies on PUDs and condominiums as opposed to single-family homes.

A PUD or condominium is a type of property ownership, not a type of structure. A PUD refers to separate, individual fee ownership of a lot and home or townhouse. In addition, you own a proportionately undivided interest jointly with others in the development of the common areas and recreational facilities, if any. A typical PUD is illustrated in Figure 8.3. It is sometimes called a townhouse development. However, the term *townhouse* refers to the architecture and not the type of ownership. A PUD could be a group of single-family homes if there were joint ownership of a common area. In a PUD, there is no one living in the "airspace" above anyone else.

A condominium (see Figure 8.3) is a type of development in which a person owns a specified residential unit (three-dimensional airspace), together with an undivided interest in all the land including recreational facilities. A condominium may be part of a high rise, attached rowhouse, or even a single-family detached development. In a legal sense, a condominium owner acquires a fee title interest in the airspace of the particular unit and an undivided interest (with the other condominium owners) in the land plus all other common areas such as hallways, elevators, utility rooms, carports, and recreational facilities.

Both PUDs and condominiums have homeowner association groups that are responsible for the management of the development. These groups meet regularly and are governed by specific regulations. It is the association's responsibility to maintain the common areas. It also sets the dues that each owner must pay in order to maintain the common areas and the exteriors of the individual structures.

A lender appraising a PUD or condominium unit is interested in more than just that particular unit. The lender is interested in the overall project, because the value of one unit is affected by the quality and the operation of the entire project. When a lender appraises a PUD or condominium, these are some of the items checked:

Figure 8.3 (a) A typical PUD. (b) A typical condominium.

1. General appearance of project.

2. Recreational facilities that are adequate and well maintained.

3. Adequate parking for owners and guests.

4. Maintenance of common areas.

5. Amount of monthly homeowner dues, which should include reserves.

A unit in a PUD or condominium is appraised basically the same way as a single-family dwelling. The appraiser uses the three approaches to value and relies primarily on the market data approach in arriving at a final value.

Figure 8.4 is the uniform FNMA/FHLMC rider attached to condominium loans.

Figure 8.5 is the FNMA/FHLMC rider for PUD loans.

8.6 The Licensing of Real Estate Appraisers

Federal law has created the requirement that real estate appraisers must be licensed if the property transaction requires financing by a lender that is insured or backed by a federal agency, such as the Federal Deposit Insurance Corporation and similar such agencies. Under federal law, each state is charged with enforcing the law within their borders. In California, the Office of Real Estate Appraisers (OREA) is the enforcement agency.

As of 2006, there are four levels of real estate appraiser licensing. They are:

1. *Trainee License.* A trainee cannot do an appraisal on his/her own. He/she can only work under the technical supervision of a licensed appraiser.

2. *Residential License.* This license allows a person to appraise non-complex 1-to-4-unit residential property up to a transaction value of $1 million, and complex 1-to-4-unit and nonresidential property up to a transaction value of $250,000.

3. *Certified Residential License.* This license allows a person to appraise all 1-to-4-unit residential property without regard to complexity or value, and nonresidential property up to a transaction value of $250,000.

4. *Certified General License.* This license allows a person to appraise all types of property without any value or complexity restrictions. Certified General is currently the highest level of licensed appraiser.

There are various educational and experience requirements for each license level, and these requirements are subject to change. For the latest requirements, contact the Office of Real Estate Appraisers website at www.orea.ca.gov.

It is important to note that a real estate licensee may provide what is called a *comparative market analysis (CMA)* outlining what other similar properties have sold for, but under no circumstance can the

CONDOMINIUM RIDER

THIS CONDOMINIUM RIDER is made this   day of   ,
and is incorporated into and shall be deemed to amend and supplement the Mortgage, Deed of Trust or Security Deed (the "Security Instrument") of the same date given by the undersigned (the "Borrower") to secure Borrower's Note to

(the "Lender")
of the same date and covering the Property described in the Security Instrument and located at:

[Property Address]

The Property includes a unit in, together with an undivided interest in the common elements of, a condominium project known as:

[Name of Condominium Project]

(the "Condominium Project"). If the owners association or other entity which acts for the Condominium Project (the "Owners Association") holds title to property for the benefit or use of its members or shareholders, the Property also includes Borrower's interest in the Owners Association and the uses, proceeds and benefits of Borrower's interest.

CONDOMINIUM COVENANTS. In addition to the covenants and agreements made in the Security Instrument, Borrower and Lender further covenant and agree as follows:

A. Condominium Obligations. Borrower shall perform all of Borrower's obligations under the Condominium Project's Constituent Documents. The "Constituent Documents" are the: (i) Declaration or any other document which creates the Condominium Project; (ii) by-laws; (iii) code of regulations; and (iv) other equivalent documents. Borrower shall promptly pay, when due, all dues and assessments imposed pursuant to the Constituent Documents.

B. Hazard Insurance. So long as the Owners Association maintains, with a generally accepted insurance carrier, a "master" or "blanket" policy on the Condominium Project which is satisfactory to Lender and which provides insurance coverage in the amounts, for the periods, and against the hazards Lender requires, including fire and hazards included within the term "extended coverage," then:

(i) Lender waives the provision in Uniform Covenant 2 for the monthly payment to Lender of one-twelfth of the yearly premium installments for hazard insurance on the Property; and

(ii) Borrower's obligation under Uniform Covenant 5 to maintain hazard insurance coverage on the Property is deemed satisfied to the extent that the required coverage is provided by the Owners Association policy.

Borrower shall give Lender prompt notice of any lapse in required hazard insurance coverage.

In the event of a distribution of hazard insurance proceeds in lieu of restoration or repair following a loss to the Property, whether to the unit or to common elements, any proceeds payable to Borrower are hereby assigned and shall be paid to Lender for application to the sums secured by the Security Instrument, with any excess paid to Borrower.

C. Public Liability Insurance. Borrower shall take such actions as may be reasonable to insure that the Owners Association maintains a public liability insurance policy acceptable in form, amount, and extent of coverage to Lender.

D. Condemnation. The proceeds of any award or claim for damages, direct or consequential, payable to Borrower in connection with any condemnation or other taking of all or any part of the Property, whether of the unit or of the common elements, or for any conveyance in lieu of condemnation, are hereby assigned and shall be paid to Lender. Such proceeds shall be applied by Lender to the sums secured by the Security Instrument as provided in Uniform Covenant 10.

E. Lender's Prior Consent. Borrower shall not, except after notice to Lender and with Lender's prior written consent, either partition or subdivide the Property or consent to:

(i) The abandonment or termination of the Condominium Project, except for abandonment or termination required by law in the case of substantial destruction by fire or other casualty or in the case of a taking by condemnation or eminent domain;

(ii) any amendment to any provision of the Constituent Documents if the provision is for the express benefit of Lender;

(iii) termination of professional management and assumption of self-management of the Owners Association; or

(iv) any action which would have the effect of rendering the public liability insurance coverage maintained by the Owners Association unacceptable to Lender.

F. Remedies. If Borrower does not pay condominium dues and assessments when due, then Lender may pay them. Any amounts disbursed by Lender under this paragraph F shall become additional debt of Borrower secured by the Security Instrument. Unless Borrower and Lender agree to other terms of payment, these amounts shall bear interest from the date of disbursement at the Note rate and shall be payable, with interest, upon notice from Lender to Borrower requesting payment.

BY SIGNING BELOW, Borrower accepts and agrees to the terms and provisions contained in this Condominium Rider.

_____ (Seal)   _____ (Seal)
                                          -Borrower   -Borrower

_____ (Seal)   _____ (Seal)
                                          -Borrower   -Borrower

MULTISTATE CONDOMINIUM RIDER -- Single Family -- **Fannie Mae/Freddie Mac UNIFORM INSTRUMENT**   **Form 3140 9/90**
ITEM 1623L0 (9102)   Great Lakes Business Forms, Inc. ■ To Order Call: 1-800-530-9393 ☐ FAX 616-791-1131

Figure 8.4 FNMA/FHLMC condominium rider.

PLANNED UNIT DEVELOPMENT RIDER

THIS PLANNED UNIT DEVELOPMENT ("PUD") RIDER is made this . . . . .day of
. . . . , 20 . . . ., and is incorporated into and shall be deemed to amend and supplement
a Mortgage, Deed of Trust or Deed to Secure Debt (herein "security instrument") dated of even date herewith, given by
the undersigned (herein "Borrower") to secure Borrower's Note to . . . .
. . . .(herein "Lender") and covering the Property described in the
security instrument and located at . . . .
(Property Address)
. . . . The Property comprises a parcel of land improved with a dwelling, which, together with
other such parcels and certain common areas and facilities, all as described in . . . .
. . . .
. . . .
(herein "Declaration"), forms a planned unit development known as . . . .
. . . .
(Name of Planned Unit Development)
(herein "PUD").

PLANNED UNIT DEVELOPMENT COVENANTS. In addition to the covenants and agreements made in the security
instrument, Borrower and Lender further covenant and agree as follows:

A. PUD Obligations. Borrower shall perform all of Borrower's obligations under the: (i) Declaration; (ii)
articles of incorporation, trust instrument or any equivalent document required to establish the homeowners
association or equivalent entity managing the common areas and facilities of the PUD (herein "Owners Association");
and (iii) by-laws, if any, or other rules or regulations of the Owners Association. Borrower shall promptly pay, when
due, all assessments imposed by the Owners Association.

B. Hazard Insurance. In the event of a distribution of hazard insurance proceeds in lieu of restoration or repair
following a loss to the common areas and facilities of the PUD, any such proceeds payable to Borrower are hereby
assigned and shall be paid to Lender for application to the sums secured by the security instrument, with the excess,
if any, paid to Borrower.

C. Condemnation. The proceeds of any award or claim for damages, direct or consequential, payable to
Borrower in connection with any condemnation or other taking of all or any part of the common areas and facilities
of the PUD, or for any conveyance in lieu of condemnation, are hereby assigned and shall be paid to Lender. Such
proceeds shall be applied by Lender to the sums secured by the security instrument in the manner provided under
Uniform Covenant 9.

D. Lender's Prior Consent. Borrower shall not, except after notice to Lender and with Lender's prior written
consent, consent to:

(i) the abandonment or termination of the PUD;

(ii) any material amendment to the Declaration, trust instrument, articles of incorporation, by-laws of the
Owners Association, or any equivalent constituent document of the PUD, including, but not limited to, any
amendment which would change the percentage interests of the unit owners in the common areas and facilities of
the PUD;

(iii) the effectuation of any decision by the Owners Association to terminate professional management and
assume self-management of the PUD; or

(iv) the transfer, release, encumbrance, partition or subdivision of all or any part of the PUD's common areas
and facilities, except as to the Owners Association's right to grant easements for utilities and similar or related purposes.

E. Remedies. If Borrower breaches Borrower's covenants and agreements hereunder, including the covenant
to pay when due planned unit development assessments, then Lender may invoke any remedies provided under the
security instrument, including, but not limited to, those provided under Uniform Covenant 7.

IN WITNESS WHEREOF, Borrower has executed this PUD Rider.

Figure 8.5 FNMA/FHLMC planned unit development rider.

real estate licensee call this a certified appraisal, unless the real estate
licensee also hold an appropriate separate appraisal license.

A *certified appraisal report* is any written communication of an
analysis, opinion, or conclusion relating to the value that is termed
certified. For property containing one to four residential units, almost
all appraisers use the standard FNMA/FHLMC appraisal form, illustrated in Figure 8.1. The details go beyond the scope of this text but
are thoroughly covered in any appraisal course.

8.7 Working with Appraisers: The Do's and Don'ts

People in the real estate business who are involved in buying or selling will come into contact with appraisers. A lot of advice is given regarding how to work with appraisers. Some of the advice is good, but much of it is incorrect. It pays to know the "do's and don'ts" in dealing with appraisers.

1. *Access to property*. Make it easy for the appraiser to see the property. Make sure your instructions on how to see the property are correct. Nothing irritates an appraiser more than to be told to go directly to the property because "the owner is always home." Then, when the appraiser arrives, no one is there. Be considerate of his or her time, and make it convenient to see the property.

2. *At the property*. In most cases, the owner or salesperson is at the property when the appraiser is there. Do not follow the appraiser around the property. Some people do this while talking constantly about all the good features of the property. Do not distract the appraiser; however, most appraisers welcome any information on the property that would be helpful to them.

3. *Comparable sales*. If you have information on comparable houses that have sold, give it to the appraisers. They appreciate any data that will help them in their appraisal. If you do give them information, make it as complete as possible. On comparable sales the appraisers need to know such things as the date of sale, number of bedrooms and baths, square footage, age of property, and so on.

4. *Influencing the appraiser*. Don't try to influence appraisers by giving them a sales talk. Most appraisers are experienced and knowledgeable. They are not influenced by a sales pitch—in fact, it may backfire on you. Appraisers try to be objective; however, if they are irritated while at the property by an overaggressive individual, it may affect their outlook on the property.

SUMMARY

It is the future, not the past, that will determine whether a loan is good or bad. That is why conventional lenders emphasize the future resale potential of a property. Lenders want to make sure that if they must foreclose, they can resell the property quickly and recover the loan amount. Conventional lenders set up specific property standard policies. These standards vary with each lender, are flexible, and vary with market conditions. But, if the loan is to be resold to Fannie Mae or Freddie Mac, the lender must follow their appraisal standards and forms.

Real estate appraisers evaluate a neighborhood with great care because location has a great influence on the value of a property. Appraisers also pay particular attention to the condition and quality of the property. It is important to note, however, that redlining is illegal.

In determining market value, the appraiser can use three approaches: the cost, sales comparison, and income approaches. On one-to-four-unit properties, the sales comparison approach is the most reliable.

PUDs and condominiums present special appraising and lending problems. Lenders are concerned about the entire project as well as the value of a single unit within the project.

IMPORTANT TERMS AND CONCEPTS

Adjustments

Capitalization

Capitalization rate

Certificate of Reasonable Value (CRV)

Certified appraisal report

Comparables

Comparative market analysis (CMA)

Conditional commitment

Condominium

Cost approach

Economic obsolescence

Fair market value (FMV)

Functional obsolescence

Gross rent multiplier (GRM)

Income approach

Market data approach

Neighborhood data

Net operating income (NOI)

Physical depreciation

Planned unit development (PUD)

Redlining

Sales comparison approach

REVIEWING YOUR UNDERSTANDING

Questions for Discussion

1. "The sales price and the fair market value of a property are not always the same." Explain this statement.

2. Discuss how property standards for local lenders are influenced by Freddie Mac and Fannie Mae.

3. List five characteristics an appraiser looks for when checking a neighborhood.

4. What are the basic steps in the cost approach to value?

5. Explain the sales comparison (market data) approach to value.

6. When appraising single-family homes and large apartments, do appraisers use the same income approach techniques? Explain the techniques used.

7. How does a planned unit development (PUD) differ from a condominium?

8. List some "do's and don'ts" for establishing a good working relationship with a real estate appraiser.

Multiple-Choice Questions

1. Adverse influences that tend to reduce property values include
   a. gentle curving in street pattern.
   b. noisy freeways.
   c. acceptable school system.
   d. presence of recreational facilities.

2. The loss in value due to negative neighborhood influences is called:
   a. physical deterioration.
   b. economic obsolescence.
   c. functional obsolescence.
   d. structural obsolescence.

3. To arrive at total square footage of a structure, appraisers measure the
   a. exterior of the structure.
   b. interior dimensions of the house, plus the garage.
   c. interior dimensions of the house, excluding the garage.
   d. length, width, and height of the building.

4. Loss in value from poor structural design is referred to by appraisers as
   a. physical deterioration.
   b. economic obsolescence.
   c. functional obsolescence.
   d. structural obsolescence.

5. Buyers will not pay more for a property than the cost of acquiring an equally desirable substitute property. Economists refer to this as the principle of
   a. conformity.
   b. desirability.
   c. acquisition.
   d. substitution.

6. The cost per square foot would usually be the least for:
   a. garages.
   b. homes.
   c. PUD buildings.
   d. condo buildings.

7. The most reliable approach to establishing values of single-family dwellings is the
   a. cost approach.
   b. income approach.
   c. gross multiplier.
   d. sales comparison approach.

8. When comparing properties with one that is being appraised, certain adjustments are made for differences in construction, quality, and other characteristics. In the event a comparable house is exactly the same as the subject house, except that the comparable or "comp" is in better condition, the appraiser will
   a. deduct from the "comp."
   b. deduct from the subject property.
   c. make no adjustments.
   d. find that insufficient information is given to accurately determine the kind of adjustments required, if any.

9. The organization that publishes periodic summaries of sales in a designated area and available to real estate agents is:
   a. Multiple Listing Service.
   b. County Recorder.
   c. County Assessor.
   d. Institute of Continuing Education.

10. To arrive at "value" using the monthly gross rent multiplier, one would apply which formula?
    a. monthly rent × gross multiplier
    b. monthly rent ÷ gross multiplier
    c. sales price ÷ monthly rent
    d. monthly rent + sales price

11. A dollar amount, subtracted from depreciation to arrive at the present value of the improvements, is used in the _____ approach to value.
    a. cost.
    b. income.
    c. market.
    d. GRM.

12. The location of a particular property is
    a. no longer considered a determinant of value as a result of anti-redlining legislation.
    b. of considerable importance in determining the value of property.
    c. relevant only on commercial properties.
    d. relevant on all properties except owner-occupied SFDs.

13. When using the FHLMC/FNMA appraisal report form for single-family dwellings appraisers
    a. normally use three comparable sales.
    b. make note of off-site improvements.
    c. consult available sources like Marshall & Swift to arrive at a cost per square foot.
    d. do all of the above.

14. The terms PUD, condo, and townhouse
    a. are different ways to describe the same thing.
    b. grew out of a need to better describe apartment living.
    c. define two types of single-family dwellings and one type of apartment.
    d. differ either by ownership or by structural development.

15. A GRM is
    a. a gross rent maintenance plan.
    b. applied on a strictly monthly rental basis.
    c. a shortcut method used to arrive at value of income property.
    d. all of the above.

16. The licensing designation limiting appraisers to noncomplex one-to-four-unit residential properties is
    a. Certified Appraiser–Residential.
    b. Licensed Appraiser–Residential.
    c. Certified Appraiser–General.
    d. none of the above.

17. The designation permitting appraisers to appraise all real estate without regard to value or complexity is
    a. Certified Appraiser–Residential.
    b. Licensed Appraiser–Residential.
    c. Certified Appraiser–General.
    d. none of the above.

18. When a lender hires an appraiser, the lender is usually looking for the property's:
    a. book value.
    b. market value.
    c. adjusted cost value.
    d. depreciated value.

19. Given an annual gross multiplier of 8 for a given rental market where the gross rents are $80,000 and the net operating income is $50,000, the indicated value of the property is
    a. $640,000.
    b. $400,000.
    c. $1,000,000.
    d. none of the above.

20. Which of the following regarding the income approach to value is true?
    a. The lower the capitalization rate, the lower the property value.
    b. The lower the gross rent multiplier, the higher the property value.
    c. The lower the capitalization rate, the higher the property value.
    d. The lower the net operating income, the higher the property value.

CASE & POINT
Appraisals on the Internet

Potential home buyers can be preapproved for loans predicated, in part, on property valuations. The Internet continues to grow as a significant source of information for determining property values. If you'd like to know what your neighbors paid for their home, for example, click on www.homes.wsj.com and follow the step-by-step instructions. Another home price comparison site is www.homeprice check.com, where you can search for homes by street, block, price range, or other criteria. Here are some other useful websites to assist you in finding recent home sale prices: www.homepricecheck.com and www.appraisers.org.

Being preapproved for a mortgage helps potential buyers determine the maximum loan they can qualify for and, thereby, their maximum price range. Also, local property tax assessments are helpful: www.domania.com lets you check sales prices and tax assessments for most recent sales since 1987. In very remote regions, or small towns and cities where there is not enough sales activity, however, you may not find sales data to help establish market value or appraisals for financing and other purposes.

Freddie Mac, the nation's second-largest secondary market, has been experimenting with an electronic valuation ("collateral assessment") instead of a full-blown appraisal to determine market values. It does this by accessing on-line databases that it already accesses for a variety of information about housing prices and values. The rationale is the savings for home buyers, as much as 50 percent and more of the cost of a standard appraisal. Freddie Mac also states that electronic appraisals will shorten the loan approval process, since standard or manual appraisals can get bogged down when appraisers are overextended with applications that may require weeks to get to. Not all types of housing qualify, including, for now, condominiums and cooperatives. Also, homes that have changed hands within a designated period preceding application, and refinancing, are not eligible. Fannie Mae, the largest secondary market, is also experimenting with electronic appraisals, so stay tuned for any developments.

CHAPTER 9
QUALIFYING THE BORROWER

PREVIEW

The process of qualifying borrowers for real estate loans continues to change. Lenders have traditionally looked at prospective borrowers and determined the 3 Cs of lending: Credit/Stability, Capacity/Ability, and Collateral—in other words, a credit file that indicates the likelihood of continued loan payments, the ability and willingness to pay the loan, and a property with sufficient equity to protect the lender in the event of default. Although the 3 Cs still apply, in many situations the focus has shifted primarily to addressing the issue, "Can we qualify the buyer?" As home values increased, lenders relaxed qualifying standards, resulting in a plethora of "alternative" loan instruments such as interest only and stated income loans and the more recent introduction of "negatively amortized" option ARM loans. This latter loan option features low initial payments designed to qualify buyers but that are insufficient to pay the interest due on the loan. The deferred interest is added to the loan balance where interest is charged on the increasing loan amount. At the same time, lenders came to rely more heavily upon borrower credit score as used in lenders' automated qualifying models. These automated systems, Fannie Mae's "desktop underwriting" (DU) and Freddie Mac's "loan prospector" (LP), have stretched qualifying ratios to nearly 50 percent of gross income, especially for high credit score borrowers or those with acceptable compensating factors. Although the systems attempt to balance credit, income, assets and evaluate a borrower's profile, many now argue that the process emphasizes "making sure a borrower qualifies" rather than truly evaluating the borrower's ability to borrow.

Although lenders retain their desire to avoid making loans that could result in foreclosures, the recent rapid appreciation rates have tended to provide what might turn out to be a false sense of security with new loan guidelines as, for instance, loans made to high credit score applicants on a stated income or no income verified basis. With no knowledge of a borrower's income, these loans are made strictly on the expectation that the borrower's good credit "suggests" that the loan will be repaid. But, if not, the high appreciation rates for property will allow the borrower to sell, if necessary, or for the lender to be protected should they have to foreclose. Lenders likely recognize the risks involved in these alternative loan options for which the borrower usually pays by way of higher interest rates, terms, and often prepayment penalty requirements. Only time will tell whether these changes and expectations with the qualifying process will prove to be accurate. Despite these changes, many loans are still qualified under the more normal guidelines or the tried and true methods of evaluating a borrower's ability and willingness to pay a loan. Let's start by analyzing a case history and reviewing how a lender would typically evaluate the borrower.

After completing this chapter, you should be able to:

1. Discuss income requirements to qualify for different types of loans.

2. Explain what effect debts have on a prospective borrower's qualifications.

3. Describe how lenders analyze stability of income.

4. Explain why lenders are concerned about borrowers' credit history and credit score.

5. Draw up a list of things that real estate agents can do to help clients obtain financing.

9.1 Ability or Capacity to Pay: A Case History

A young mother contacted a loan officer in a local savings bank. Their conversation revealed the facts that her husband had recently died and she wanted to buy a home to provide housing more permanent than a rental unit would furnish for herself and her three children, ages 6, 9, and 12.

The discussion further indicated that she had just returned to work for the first time in a dozen years, at age 38. The woman had a bachelor's degree in liberal arts and had been an executive secretary before having children. For the past 12 years, her husband had been the sole provider, but the borrower had just been hired as an executive secretary with a take-home salary of $3,400 per month.

Her search efforts resulted in finding a small but suitable home listed at $220,000. Her intent to put a 20 percent down payment would result in a need for a loan of $176,000. A 30-year loan at 6.25 percent per annum would require monthly payments of $1,083.67 principal and interest plus taxes and insurance of $235 for a total monthly payment of $1,318.67.

A quick computation demonstrates that her "top" payment ratio was 38.8 percent. Her long-term debt was approximately $275 per month, producing a "bottom" ratio of 46.9 percent. Under general FNMA/FHLMC standards, she is "pushing" the qualifying loan limits.

As the interview continued, the loan officer discovers that her credit was mostly combined with her deceased husband's. Her debt consisted of two credit card accounts in her own name plus a $150 auto payment that will continue for four years. Her mid-credit score was 668. Other disclosures indicated that she had received $150,000 in life insurance policy proceeds. The couple had also accumulated $40,000 in the form of savings deposits, stock, and CD investments during their 14-year marriage.

This additional information allowed the loan officer to strengthen the loan file by using the concept of "compensating factors." These involved consideration of the fact that the woman's employer indicated that her likelihood of continued employment was excellent. Her low credit debt demonstrated a commitment to retaining a low debt total. Her money in the bank represented reserves, a financial cushion that would protect the lender from a threat of future loan default. And the substantial 20 percent down payment was viewed as protection for the lender.

The application was taken, and a fixed rate loan was approved.

What Does This Case Illustrate?

Lenders typically have general guidelines upon which to base their lending decisions. Although expanded guidelines as indicated in the Preview are sometimes used, it is wise to depend upon these more typical loan-qualifying guidelines. Thus, real estate licensees are urged to suggest to prospective buyers that lenders require stable income, sufficient assets, and acceptable credit.

Although compensating factors can be used under some circumstances, it is recommended that only lenders use these expanded guidelines (compensating factors) in qualifying potential buyers.

Why Qualify Borrowers?

Some people ask, Why bother qualifying borrowers? If the borrower doesn't make the payment, the lender can just take back the property! There are several reasons why a lender qualifies a borrower.

First, lenders are not in the business of foreclosing and taking back properties. That is the last thing a lender wants to do. Lenders are in the money business, not the real estate business. In most cases when lenders foreclose, they suffer a loss in both time and money.

In earlier years, when a 50 percent down payment was required, qualifying the borrower was not as important as today. With large down payments there was less need to worry about the borrower's qualifications. Few borrowers were willing to allow a loan to default and lose a large equity. With a large equity, borrowers in financial trouble could simply sell the property, pay the lender, and salvage what they could. Today, the situation is different—lenders are making high-ratio conventional loans or government-backed loans that require little, if any, down payment. With these loans, lenders must rely heavily on borrower qualifications because there is little if any equity in the property. With expanded criteria type loans (e.g., stated income or no-income verification) the lender's risk is even greater, especially with high Loan-to-Value ratio loans. The criteria remains: the greater the equity, the greater the incentive to make mortgage payments. The less the equity, the less the incentive. In falling markets, values can actually drop below remaining loan balances.

There is another reason that lenders go through the trouble to qualify borrowers. It is a disservice to approve a loan beyond the borrower's financial capabilities. Some buyers are not aware of what it takes to own a house and to support a family. They get carried away and attempt to buy homes that are clearly too expensive. By turning down this type of buyer, the lender is actually doing the buyer a favor. It is axiomatic that *if a loan is not sound for the borrower, it is not sound for the lender, and vice versa*. In this regard, the creative financing options mentioned earlier are causing some alarm for lenders. The term "abusive lending practices" has entered the lexicon, and oversight agencies indicate that penalties may be imposed in cases in which lenders arrange financing for borrowers who are found unable to comply with the loan's requirements, including excessive negative amortization and fast-rising mortgage payments, to name a few. The low- or no-documentation loans are under particular scrutiny as charges of fraud mount. This is a perfect example of how lending practices change and evolve as lenders determine not only what lending instruments the market may need but what actually works.

9.2 How Lenders Qualify Prospective Borrowers

Using the typical methods for qualifying a borrower, the lender attempts to answer the question, "Do we expect the borrower to make timely payments on the mortgage?" To answer this question, the lender analyzes two general areas: the borrower's capacity and willingness to pay.

1. *Ability or Capacity to Pay.* To determine ability or capacity to repay loans, lenders seek answers to these questions: Do the borrowers earn enough to make the required payments? If so, is it a steady source of income? Do the borrowers have enough cash to buy the property? What other assets do they have?

2. *Desire or Willingness to Pay.* A person may have the ability to pay but lack the desire or willingness to do so. The desire to pay is just as important, but more difficult to measure. Lenders use a number of methods to determine a person's desire, discussed later in the chapter.

Each of these areas will be examined in detail. It should be emphasized that qualifying a borrower is not a strict, precise operation. It is a process in which flexibility and judgment are very important. There are rules that are used to qualify borrowers, but they are merely guidelines and are meant to be flexible. Each borrower is qualified on a case-by-case basis. All aspects of the loan must be weighed before a decision can be made.

9.3 Capacity to Pay

Whether the borrower earns enough to make the monthly payments is the first consideration in determining the applicant's ability or capacity to repay the loan. There is no one answer because various lenders use different formulas, depending upon the type of loan. Conventional lenders, FHA, DVA, and Cal-Vet each have their own distinctive method of qualifying a borrower. To compare the qualifying methods used, we'll look at one set of borrowers. Figure 9.1 provides hypothetical information on the borrowers, a couple whom we'll use as applicants for a conventional loan, then compare this type to FHA and DVA requirements.

Income Ratios

Lenders use the monthly payment on a property in determining a borrower's qualifications. The payment includes principal, interest, property taxes, and insurance—commonly referred to as *PITI*. Even if the borrowers are paying their own taxes and insurance, the lender adds them all together in qualifying the borrowers. For FHA, Mutual Mortgage Insurance (MMI) is also included. Lenders also include homeowner association dues (HOA) and assessments (PITIA).

Lenders use ratios in qualifying borrower income. The "housing ratio" is quoted as the total monthly payment divided by the borrower's gross monthly income. The "qualifying ratio" is calculated by adding the housing expense plus all other credit debt divided by the borrower's gross monthly income.

Some years ago, a 25 percent housing ratio was common. Today, borrowers pay a third or more of their income for housing.

The current published qualifying housing ratio used by the agencies is 33 percent, indicating that a borrower's monthly housing payments should not exceed 33 percent of their gross monthly income. Expressing it as a multiplier, we would say the borrower should earn approximately three times the monthly payment. Qualifying ratios used by the agencies change depending upon various circumstances: as the cost of housing increases, borrowers must allocate more of their income to housing; compensating factors may allow an expansion of the ratios; and high credit score buyers are granted greater flexibility in their ratios. Thus, although the 33/42 ratios are identified in "policy" manuals, the agencies accommodate some flexibility.

As indicated, the qualifying ratios are merely a guide, and many loans are approved with higher ratios, especially when "compensating factors" exist, serving as potential protection for the lender in case

Name	John and Janet Smith
Dependents	Two, aged 4 and 6
Employment	
John Smith	
Employer	Self-Employed
Position	Consultant
Years on job	6 years
Income	$3,000 per month
Janet Smith	
Employer	Citybank
Position	Administrative Assistant
Years on job	3 years
Income	$2,000 per month
Cash in bank	$60,000

Debts:	Payment	Balance
Car	$350	$5,000
Furniture	75	1,000
Dept. Store	20	100

Loan Information:	
Purchase price of home	$250,000
Loan amount	200,000
Interest rate	7%
Term	30 years

Monthly Payment:	
Principal and interest	$1,331
Taxes	260
Insurance	55
Total PITI	$1,646

Figure 9.1 Basic information about sample borrowers.

the borrowers encounter difficulty in meeting payments. The following are some examples of when a lender might feel justified in approving a higher loan ratio.

- Borrowers have a substantial cushion. If the net worth is liquid, it can be used to make the mortgage payments if necessary.

- Borrower has a credit-worthy co-borrower with additional income.

- Borrowers have excellent potential for higher earnings due to education or training, and current income is stable.

- Borrowers are making a large down payment.

- Borrowers have no "payment shock" as they have been making the mortgage or rent payments at about the same level as the new loan.

Let's look at our sample borrowers, the Smiths from Figure 9.1, to determine how they qualify. Their monthly PITI payment is $1,646, and their monthly income is $5,000.

$$\frac{\text{Mortgage payment}}{\text{Gross income}} = \frac{\$1,646}{\$5,000} = 32.9\%$$

This ratio is frequently referred to as the top ratio or *front-end* or *front-door ratio*. The Smiths would qualify based on current income guides.

Buy-down loans, graduated-payment mortgages, and adjustable rate loans require special handling. With these loans, the initial payment is lower and then increases. The problem is, what payment do you use in qualifying the borrower? Lenders' choices vary. Some use the initial payment, provided there is a reasonable expectation that the borrower's income will increase to cover the yearly increases in payments. By using the initial payment, borrowers are able to qualify for a larger loan. This is one of the major advantages of buy-downs, graduated-payment mortgages, and adjustable rate loans. However, in some cases, lenders have tightened their standards and qualify borrowers based only on the "fully indexed" payments, that is, the index plus the margin at time of qualifying.

Debts

So far, we have discussed only a borrower's housing ratio. Lenders must also take into account the borrower's debts. Lenders break debts down into two categories, short term and long term. The short-term debts are generally ignored, and only **long-term debts** are considered in qualifying a borrower. How are long-term debts defined? Conventional lenders follow the standards of Fannie Mae, Freddie Mac, FHA, and PMI companies, which define a long-term debt as a debt that will take 10 months or longer to pay off. Alimony and child support payments are also considered long-term debts if they will continue for more than 10 months.

Once long-term debts have been determined, the lender adds the total to the monthly payment. The two, added together, are called **total monthly expenses**. The total monthly expenses are divided by the borrower's gross monthly income, coming up with another ratio, called the *bottom ratio* or **back-end ratio** or *back-door ratio*. Conventional lenders again use Fannie Mae and Freddie Mac current standards, which state that this ratio should not exceed 42 percent, including PMI.

Our borrowers, the Smiths, have three debts. Their car and furniture payments will take more than one year to pay off. Therefore, they are long-term debts. The department store debt is a short-term debt. Long-term debts total $425 per month, which, added to the mortgage payment of $1,646, gives us a total monthly expense of $2,071.

$$\frac{\text{Total monthly expense}}{\text{Gross income}} = \frac{\$2,071}{\$5,000} = 41.4\%$$

On the basis of this back-end ratio, the Smiths also qualify, since their total monthly expenses are less than 42 percent. Borrowers must qualify on both tests. Some qualify on the first test but not on the second test because they have excessive debts. The second ratio is almost always the more important of the two. Figure 9.2 summarizes the qualifying procedure for conventional loans.

Income
    Allowable Gross Income $5,000

Housing Payment and Expenses

Principal and interest	1,331
Property taxes	260
Homeowner's Insurance	55
Total mortgage payment	$1,646
Long-term debts	425
Total monthly expenses	$2,071

Qualifying Guidelines:

1. $\dfrac{\text{Mortgage payment}}{\text{Gross income}} = \dfrac{\$1,646}{\$5,000} = 32.9\%$ (front-end ratio)

This ratio should not exceed 33%. (under "Perfect" Ratio Requirements)

2. $\dfrac{\text{Total monthly expense}}{\text{Gross income}} = \dfrac{\$2,071}{\$5,000} = 41.4\%$ (back-end ratio)

This ratio should not exceed 42% (under "perfect" ratio requirements)

Figure 9.2 Summary of qualifying procedure for conventional lenders.

9.4 Qualifying Under Government-Backed Loans

Federal Housing Administration (FHA)

The FHA uses the same qualifying procedure as conventional lenders, except that the FHA states that the front-end ratio should not exceed 29 percent, while the back-end ratio—the more important of the two qualifying tests—should not exceed 41 percent, including MMI. The 29/41 ratios are considered "just right" but, as in conventional financing, there is some flexibility allowed.

Department of Veterans Affairs (DVA)

The DVA uses a two-phase qualifying procedure: (1) the **residual income** method and (2) application of qualifying income ratio.

Figure 9.3 outlines the DVA's procedure. The DVA starts with **gross income** and subtracts federal and state income tax and Social Security or retirement payments to arrive at *net take-home pay.*

Phase 1: Residual Income Method

Housing expense consists of principal and interest, taxes, fire insurance, maintenance, and utilities. The DVA estimates for maintenance and utilities vary with the condition, age, and size of the house. To give a rule of thumb would be dangerous because maintenance and utility estimates can vary widely depending on the house and area. Local DVA offices are able to offer guidelines for your area.

To the housing expense, the DVA adds alimony, child support payments, and long-term debts. What does the DVA consider a long-term debt? Any debt that will take six months or more to pay off is a long-term debt. Once again, this is not a hard and fast rule; the DVA tries to be realistic. For example, if an applicant has car payments of $400 a month with a balance of $1,500 and little cash reserve, it would probably count this debt, even though it has less than six months remaining. The DVA considers the first few months of the loan critical. A large payment of $400 a month, lasting for five months, could naturally affect the buyer's ability to make loan payments during the first few months, and therefore the DVA would count it in qualifying.

Another expense item that the DVA includes is called job-related expense. This item mainly refers to babysitting expenses when both husband and wife work and have small children, travel and/or living expenses when employment requires commuting, or those jobs in

Allowable gross income	$5,000
Less: Federal income tax	677
State income tax	172
Social Security or retirement	382
Net take-home pay	$3,769
Housing payment and fixed obligations:	
Principal and interest	$ 1,331
Property taxes	260
Homeowner's insurance	55
Total mortgage payment	$1,646
Maintenance/utilities (@14 cents/sq. ft.)	140
Total housing expense	$1,786
Alimony and child support	0
Long-term debts	$ 425
Job-related expense	0
Total housing and fixed obligations	$2,211
Analysis:	
Net take-home pay	$3,769
Less: Housing and fixed expenses	2,211
Residual income	$1,558

Figure 9.3 Summary of DVA qualifying procedure.

which additional expenses are likely to occur for uniforms, tools, etc. Policemen, firemen, and construction workers, among others, fall into this category. There is no specific rule as to how much you subtract for job-related expenses. Schedule A of the 1040 tax returns generally identify the amount of "unreimbursed business expenses" a borrower has incurred. This is the amount most often shown in the qualifying formula. The babysitting expenses can be mitigated if one parent works at home or a relative is available for child care. Commuting expenses can be reduced if living away from home is with a relative or paid for by the employer. In our example, because the husband is self-employed at home, we have not identified any babysitting costs.

Now that we have determined net take-home pay for the Smiths, along with their total expenses, we're ready to qualify them. The DVA subtracts the total expenses of $2,211 from the net take-home pay of

$3,769, leaving $1,558 as residual income. The next question we must answer is, "Is this residual income enough money to buy food and clothes, and provide for the other needs of the family?" To answer this, we must look at a several significant factors:

1. *Family size.* It is obvious that one would need more money to feed and clothe six children than two children.

2. *Geographic area.* Cost of living varies according to area.

3. *Price of home and neighborhood.* The more expensive the house and neighborhood, the more it costs a family to live.

4. *Borrower's living pattern.* Not all borrowers are created equal. All have their own lifestyle. When considering the question, Is this enough to live on?, we must consider how the particular family lives. An older couple with no children will likely require less income than a large family. To do a proper job of qualifying, we must consider these factors. It is easy to think about, but in practice difficult to apply, because it is not so simple to obtain the facts. However, there are clues that help. Looking at previous housing expenses and how much the borrowers were able to save is a good clue as to how they live. The number of debts and size of each also give a good indication of their lifestyle.

A number of factors affect how much money is needed to support a family. We have listed some basic ones and you can probably think of more. The DVA considers each case to determine how much a prospective home buyer will need. The Department of Labor provides statistics regarding cost of living for various family sizes.

Going back to our sample case, the Smiths have $1,558 left over to support their family. Based on the geographic area, we use guides provided by DVA residual income tables, which vary by region. In California, for example, we have (for 2006):

Family Size	Amount Needed
1	$491
2	823
3	990
4	1,117
5	1,158
6+	Add $80 for each additional family member up to 7

Using the guide, Mr. and Mrs. Smith with their two children need $1,117 a month to qualify. The "amount needed" is of course subject to periodic increases as cost of living increases. They actually have $1,558; therefore they would qualify under the residual income method.

Phase 2: DVA Income Ratio Application

The income ratio is determined by taking the monthly housing expenses—principal, interest, property taxes, insurance, and long-term debts—and dividing this by gross monthly income. If this ratio is 41 percent or less, the borrowers qualify. If the ratio is above 41 percent, then the DVA underwriter must look at other things such as an above-average income under the cash flow approach, a high net worth, or a large down payment. DVA allows 41 percent ratios because it includes items other than those used by conventional lenders.

In the case of the Smith family, we show:

$$\frac{\text{Housing Payment and Long-Term Debt}}{\text{Gross Monthly Income}} = \frac{\$2,211}{\$5,000} = 44.2\%$$

Based on the general guideline of 41 percent or less, the Smiths do not qualify, but via the use of compensating factors they would likely be approved. On the other hand, if we were to add $250 a month for babysitting, this ratio would increase to 49.2% and is pushing the envelope for approval, even with compensating factors.

DVA administrators stress that DVA underwriting standards are guidelines and that they are willing to review individual veteran borrowers who do not automatically qualify, similar to the ***compensating factors*** considered by FHA. Examples of compensating factors include larger than normal down payment, insignificant use of credit cards, no vehicle payments, substantial net worth, and stable work experience and history and sufficient residual income, as there is in this case. DVA uses the tightest qualifying standards in lending due to the lack of initial equity.

Cal-Vet

The qualifying procedure used by Cal-Vet is as follows: From gross income, subtract federal and state income taxes and Social Security to arrive at ***adjusted gross income.*** Housing expense is arrived at by adding principal, interest, taxes, property and disability insurance, maintenance, and utilities. Next, long-term debts, which are any debts that will take longer than one year to pay off, are totaled and subtracted. The *remaining income* is then divided by adjusted gross income to determine the relationship between that and the amount of money left over. This residual should be at least 50 percent of adjusted gross, though under some circumstances it can be less. This is merely a guide, since Cal-Vet looks closely at the balance of funds left over to determine if they are sufficient to support the family.

9.5 What Is Income?

We have learned how a lender determines if a borrower earns enough to qualify for a loan. The next consideration is what income lenders include. There is no question that income from regular employment is included, but do lenders count income from overtime, part-time work, or sales commissions? To be counted as stable, income must normally be earned in the same or similar occupation for at least two years. This section covers how lenders look at a variety of income sources.

FNMA and FHLMC

How do the Federal National Mortgage Association (FNMA) and Federal Home Loan Mortgage Corporation (FHLMC) influence the qualification process? First, they affect the purchasing of qualifying loans. While borrowers do not deal directly with either FNMA or FHLMC, these two agencies vitally affect the process of qualifying loan applicants. This is due to the secondary markets in which these agencies operate. As detailed in Chapter 7, conventional lenders sell loans in the secondary market, where Fannie Mae and Freddie Mac are by far the biggest buyers.

Second, they foster uniformity. Loans sold to either FNMA or FHLMC must comply with the qualifying ratios of the purchasing agency. Consequently there is greater standardization and uniformity in qualifying borrowers if lenders expect to sell any of their loans to either of the "big players." Any conventional loan sold to these agencies, in 2006, cannot exceed $417,000 for a one-unit dwelling, fixed-rate loan. Hence most lenders will limit their loans secured by houses to $417,000. Of course this figure is subject to periodic changes, usually upward as house prices go up.

Commissioned People and Tradespeople

Commissioned people do not earn a set figure each month. Since their income varies over the year, they must be judged on the basis of annualized earnings. Lenders usually look at the earnings over the last two to three years. Some commissioned people incur expenses that are not reimbursed by the employer. These expenses, shown on Schedule A of the 1040 tax returns, must be subtracted from income to arrive at a true income figure. Lenders require income tax returns from commissioned people to verify incomes.

Tradespeople, such as carpenters and painters, are treated basically the same as commissioned salespeople. The lender determines the previous two years' income by means of W-2 forms or tax returns. Hourly rates are not used because employment may not have been regular and full time during the year.

Overtime and Bonus

Lenders are reluctant to include overtime because, in most cases, it is not consistent and dependable. If borrowers can prove that they will continue to work overtime in the future, lenders will consider overtime pay. In other words, the borrower must have had consistent overtime in the past and must have a job that demands overtime. A good example would be a police officer working as a detective, since such work consistently requires overtime due to the nature of the job. Other examples include firefighters, grocery clerks, truck drivers, and phone company and other utility employees.

Bonus income counts only if the lender believes it will continue in the future. A past record of consistent bonuses is the main way to prove it will continue. How many years are required to show that a bonus is consistent? This is a matter of lender policy, though most lenders require at least two years of bonus pay before they include it as income.

Part-Time Work

At one time, earnings from part-time work were not counted by lenders. The Federal Equal Credit Opportunity Act specifically prohibits lenders from discounting income solely because it is part time. For example, if a borrower works only 20 hours a week, the income must be counted if the job is stable.

Spousal/Alimony and Child Support

Income from alimony and child support must be counted by the lender if the borrower can provide a court order and a history of consistent payments. However, as will be demonstrated in Chapter 10, under the Equal Credit Opportunity Act borrowers need not reveal such income and lenders cannot ask about receipt of income from either child support or alimony. However, a lender can ask about *payment* of child support or alimony for long-term debt purposes.

Pensions and Social Security

Income from pensions and Social Security are counted if such sources are expected to continue on a steady basis. Copies of pension plans are required. Because this income may not always be fully taxable, lenders allow the amount to be "grossed up" using a 1.15 to 1.25 percent factor.

Military Personnel

Military personnel receive extra pay for quarters, clothing, and rations in addition to their base pay. When qualifying someone in the military, all of these extras are added to arrive at the true income. In addition, lenders take into account that military personnel receive free medical and other services.

Income from Real Estate

Lenders consider positive cash flow, or spendable income, from real estate as income. Cash flow is gross income less mortgage payments, taxes, and operating expenses. Generally, an investment in a single-family dwelling shows little or negative cash flow. A negative cash flow is regarded as a long-term debt rather than a reduction of income.

When a person wishes to buy and occupy a unit in a two-, three-, or four-unit building, the question that pops up is, Does the income from the other units count? The answer will vary by lender. The typical lender will count the income after subtracting a realistic figure for expenses and vacancy factor. The DVA includes the same income except for one condition: the veteran must have enough cash reserve to be able to absorb from three to six months' payments to cover the likelihood of vacant units. The reason for this is that the DVA has found that most foreclosures on two-to-four-unit buildings occur in the first year.

Self-Employment

A self-employed borrower must supply the lender with a balance sheet and profit and loss statements for the business, usually to the end of the most recent quarter. A balance sheet shows the assets, liabilities, and net worth of the business. Profit and loss statements must be provided for the last two years; some lenders require as many as three years of P&L statements. The borrower's income is based on these statements if it appears that the business will continue to produce the same level of income. Profit and loss statements should be carefully analyzed to arrive at a true net income figure. For example, depreciation on real estate is shown as an expense; however, since it is not a cash expense, it can therefore usually be added back to net income. By the same token, capital gains taxes must be deducted. In addition, copies of income tax returns filed for at least two years are required.

9.6 Co-Borrowing

What effect do multiple borrowers—more than one borrower on a loan—have on an application for a real estate loan? The technical name lenders give a sole borrower is mortgagor. If there is more than one borrower, we have **co-mortgagors** (often husband and wife), sometimes called co-borrowers. Co-mortgagors sign the note and deed of trust and their names go on the title together. It should be noted that **co-signers** are not the same as co-mortgagors: Co-signers sign the note as guarantors but are not on the title, do not sign the trust deed, and therefore are rarely acceptable to real estate lenders. Co-mortgagors help with income qualifying but, contrary to common belief, will not help to cure bad credit.

Lenders include all income and all debts from all parties to qualify for the loan. If one or more of the co-mortgagors is not to occupy the home, then things can get complicated. Some lenders insist that all co-mortgagors occupy the home or they will deny the loan. Other lenders will try to work with the parties by counting some of the non-occupying co-mortgagor's income after deducting the co-mortgagor's own housing expenses and other monthly debts. Some lenders require the nonoccupying co-mortgagor to be a close relative. Fannie Mae and Freddie Mac, however, have dropped the close relative requirement, but insist that the co-mortgagor not be the seller, builder, real estate broker, or any party who has an interest in the sales transaction. In short, the issue of nonoccupying co-mortgagor is fluid and constantly changing and it is difficult to give any definitive guidelines.

9.7 After Income, What Then?

Stability of Income

After a lender has determined whether a borrower earns enough money, the next step is to analyze the stability of that income. To accomplish this, lenders look at such things as:

1. *Length of time on the job*. If the borrower has been on a new job for only one month, is the job secure? Probably not, because the borrower hasn't been on the job long enough. Lenders want borrowers

to have established jobs. How long do you have to be on the job before lenders consider the job stable or "established"? Generally, in the same line of work for about two years, but there are exceptions. For example, consider an engineer who has been on the job for one month, with prior work in another company for five years, also as an engineer. The new job was an advancement and it pays a higher salary. A lender would qualify this engineer because both jobs are in the same line of work and the new job is an advancement.

2. *Type of job.* The type of work a person does also determines the stability of income. A highly skilled individual whose skills are in demand, such as a physician, will not have to worry about a job. The same cannot be said about professional athletes, such as boxers or football players, whose jobs are volatile. Other jobs that are considered relatively stable include civil service positions and tenured teachers. Examples of nonstable jobs include carpenters, painters, roofers, and other construction workers. No one working in the construction industry can be sure of the length of his or her job, since it is so transitory.

   Self-employed borrowers are another group that are carefully scrutinized to determine their stability of income. Lenders look at the length of time they have been in business, the net income, financial condition of the business, and the general prospects for the particular type of business.

3. *Age of the borrower.* Many borrowers ask, "I'm over 50 years old. Do you think I could get a 30-year loan?" Years ago the answer would have been no. Lenders used to have a rule that said the age of the borrower plus the term of the loan could not exceed age 65, the normal retirement age. Lenders were understandably concerned about how the borrower was going to make the payments after retirement. Now lenders are concerned only if the borrower is going to retire in the next few years. If the borrower is going to retire one year from now, for example, the lender wants to know what the borrower's income will be after retirement. If there is sufficient income to make the payments, lenders will approve such loans. It makes no difference if applicants are 55 or 95; if they make enough money to meet loan repayments, they will be approved. Age is no longer a factor.

Borrower's Assets

When analyzing a borrower's capacity to pay, it should be apparent why lenders want to know how much money the borrower earns and the stability of those earnings. What is not so apparent is why lenders analyze borrower assets: because they want to be sure the borrower has enough cash for the down payment and closing costs. If borrowers can't show enough cash, the assumption is that the funds will be sought elsewhere and another debt incurred. This, in turn, can reduce the borrower's ability to make mortgage payments.

Young couples often receive money for a down payment from their parents. If it is a gift and not a loan, no lender objects to it. However, most lenders insist that the gift be verified, usually in writing. This is called a "***gift letter***." Gift giving is restricted in certain programs. For example, under certain loans, including FHA, home buyers have to document the gift with a cancelled check or other evidence showing that the funds came from the parents' account.

The amount and type of assets a borrower has will influence lenders. If the borrower has substantial liquid assets, lenders feel more secure, realizing that, with ample assets, a borrower will continue making the loan payments even if some problems arise. Lenders also give some leeway in qualifying if borrowers have reserves to fall back on. Borrowers with good bank accounts or other assets also demonstrate that they live within their means, are conservative in financial affairs, and have the *ability to accumulate and manage money*.

9.8 **Desire to Pay**

It was stated earlier that there are two major considerations in qualifying. One is the *ability* or capacity of the borrower to pay, which has been discussed. The other is the **desire** (or willingness) **to pay** of the borrower. Does the borrower really have a sincere desire to continue making payments once the loan has been granted? It is difficult to answer that question. When they apply for a loan, borrowers automatically imply that they will repay the loan. But the lender has to have something more tangible than the borrower's *intent*. How does a lender determine a borrower's *desire*? Let's look at some indicators.

Past Payment Record

How a borrower has paid debts in the past is a good indication of what can be expected in the future. If borrowers have paid debts on time in the past, they will likely continue paying on time. On the other hand, if they had problems paying debts in the past, chances are that they will have problems in the future. People develop specific credit patterns. Lenders are interested in the overall pattern and are not concerned about one or two isolated slow payments. Say a borrower has six credit references and five are rated as "paid as agreed" and the other a little slow. Lenders usually ignore the one slow payment because the borrower's overall credit rating is good. The one slow payment is probably an error in rating or may even be a disputed bill. Some buyers are concerned about a problem they may have had with one creditor. They are afraid one bad rating will ruin their chances for a loan. This is not true. Most lenders will accept a valid explanation and be guided by the overall credit history of the borrower.

If the borrower has owned a home before, the lender is particularly interested in the previous payment record. Since the borrower is applying for another home loan, past payment records on a previous mortgage loan are the best indication of what can be expected in the future.

What if the borrower has had a poor credit history? Does it mean the borrower is automatically eliminated from any type of real estate loan? It is certainly a big strike against the borrower. However, it does not mean the borrower will never obtain a loan. If the borrower is able to explain the reason for the poor credit and convince the lender that he or she is now a good risk, the loan will be seriously considered. People get into financial difficulties for reasons beyond their control. Unemployment, sickness, and divorce are the most common reasons. If a borrower had a credit problem in the past because of unemployment, it does not mean the borrower lacks the desire to pay. It just means there was a temporary problem.

People who have had bankruptcies are a special problem. They have had "credit failures." It is possible for them to get another loan, but much more difficult, because bankruptcy is usually regarded as an inability to accumulate and manage money.

In considering those who have had a bankruptcy, lenders want to know the type of bankruptcy. Was it a liquidation (Chapter 7) bankruptcy or a Chapter 13 bankruptcy? Under a Chapter 13, also called the wage-earner's bankruptcy, the individual pays off all creditors in full under a schedule approved by the bankruptcy court. The debtor makes payments to a court-appointed trustee, who, in turn, makes the payments to the creditors over a two- to three-year period. It is obvious that lenders look at someone who opted for a Chapter 13 bankruptcy with more leniency.

Lenders want a complete explanation as to why the bankruptcy took place. Was it due to circumstances beyond the borrower's control? Or was it due to poor financial management? The answer makes a big difference in the lender's decision. Lenders also insist that a certain time period has elapsed since the discharge of the bankruptcy, with most conforming lenders requiring a minimum of three years. Under a Chapter 13 bankruptcy, lenders consider the borrower after all creditors have been paid. In some cases, they may even consider the loan if the borrower has completed most of the payments. Another requirement is that borrowers have established good credit since the bankruptcy. Lenders want evidence that the buyer is paying existing debts on a timely basis. Under a Chapter 13 bankruptcy, payments to the trustee would serve as a credit reference.

Credit Scoring—FICO

Credit "scoring" has become the accepted method of evaluating an applicant's **credit history** for the purpose of determining the probability of repayment of debts. The process is ordinarily identified as FICO, from Fair Isaac Corporation. This type of credit analysis has been in use for many years by users of credit information for purposes other than real estate loans, such as automobile credit purchases.

Scoring ranges from about 300 to about 900, with the lower scores indicating a greater likelihood of default. Below a score of about 620, the applicant-borrower becomes marginal and compensating factors become more important.

Three reporting agencies enter the picture—Equifax, Experian, and TransUnion—and different scores can be disclosed by each of them, indicating differences in attitudes by the reporting companies. Also, various firms that extend credit to consumers may not report to all companies. It is the lender's copy of the report that carries the score, not the applicant-borrower's copy. Borrowers now have the right to see their scores. Under the Federal Fair and Accurate Credit Transaction (FACT) Act, everyone is entitled to a free copy of their credit report once a year, thus helping to keep tabs on credit score and help guard against identity theft.

More than 30 underwriting factors are taken into consideration in arriving at a FICO score. The number of credit accounts are observed. Having either too many accounts, especially if opened in the past 12 months, or too few accounts is not considered "good"—the lender wants to know the ability of the borrower to manage credit payments.

If late payments turn up, such as 30, 60, or 90 days late within the preceding two years, if there are current delinquencies, or if credit has been used to its maximum allowance, scores drop. How long the credit has been established is important, since the lender must be in a position to evaluate its use.

If there are collections, judgments, or write-offs, they must be considered. Of definite concern is bankruptcy, as well as the type of bankruptcy (Chapter 7, Chapter 13) and how much time has lapsed since the filing. An older bankruptcy with clean credit for the past several years is acceptable.

The number of credit inquiries, particularly recently, are taken into consideration in the ratings. Too many unused accounts with zero balances provide opportunities for use, which could be detrimental to the borrower's score.

While FICO scores provide a basis for underwriting, the lender is nonetheless still in the position of decision making and may use compensating factors for loan approval.

Note: As of June 2006, the credit scoring system is in the process of being revised by the three credit agencies, and this may change the credit score numbering system in the future.

Motivation

When examining a borrower's desire to pay, we must also consider the borrower's motivation. Sometimes a strong desire on the part of the borrower to make the payments is one of the most important reasons for approving a loan. Among the things a lender considers when trying to determine motivation are the following:

1. *Down payment.* The amount of down payment heavily influences the borrower's desire to keep up loan payments. If you purchased a house for $300,000 and made a down payment of $100,000, you would do everything possible to maintain the payments. If it became impossible to keep up the payments, you would sell the house. One way or another, you would not let the lender take your house by foreclosure. You would protect your $100,000 investment.

   On the other hand, if you had purchased the same property with little or no down payment, you would not be as motivated to maintain the payments. If you ran into financial problems, it might be easy to talk yourself into letting the lender take back the property. If you have no money invested in the property, you really have nothing to lose except your credit rating. You could easily decide to let the lender foreclose.

   Lenders recognize the importance of the size of the down payment. As the down payment increases, the lender's risk decreases. The size of the down payment is one of the most important factors in determining whether a loan will be approved.

2. *Reason for buying.* When trying to determine the borrower's motivation, lenders also examine the reason for buying. Is the borrower buying the home for *personal* use or is the purchase an *investment* that is going to be rented? If the purchase is for personal use, the borrower is more likely to keep up the payments. If the purchase is an investment, the borrower may not have the same motivation.

9.9 Working with Lenders

By now, you have learned that qualifying a borrower is not a precise mechanical function. A lender does not decide to say yes or no by looking at any one thing. The borrower's income, the stability of that income, and the credit record are all analyzed, and the decision is based on an overall impression of the borrower. There are no hard and fast rules when it comes to qualifying, only guidelines. It is because of this that we find inconsistencies among lenders. More than one person looking at the same loan and using the same standards will come up with different opinions because they are using different judgment criteria. The human element cannot be eliminated—one must be able to recognize and learn how to work with it. Learn the idiosyncrasies of the various lenders. Some are lenient in qualifying buyers, others are just the opposite, so selecting a lender to fit the type of loan being sought is all-important. In short, shop for your loan.

Every lender, if at all possible, would approve every loan submitted because it is more pleasant to approve loans than to reject them. There would be no arguments and no unhappy customers. Lenders prefer to say yes, but borrowers and real estate agents must make it easy for them to say yes.

What are some of the things that can make it easier to obtain a loan?

1. *Possibility.* Don't insult the lender with a loan that can't possibly be approved. For example, if the borrower declared bankruptcy a few months ago, don't try to force the loan through. You know what the answer will be. The lender will be irritated because you are wasting valuable time.

2. *Honesty.* Always be honest with the lender. If the borrower has had credit problems, he or she should level with the lender. If the borrower has a good reason, lenders will listen and try to help. If the borrower tries to hide credit problems, lenders will find out anyway after the credit report comes in.

3. *Cooperation*. Lenders ask for items that are necessary, so cooperate with them. Arguing with a lender as to why documents are needed does not get the loan approved. Different lenders may very well require different documentation.

4. *Lender input*. Do not be insulted if the lender says the borrower is not qualified for the loan. Ask the loan officer what you can do to make the borrower qualified. A good lender may have some helpful suggestions. For example, the loan officer may suggest a co-mortgagor, a larger down payment, or a reduction of long-term debt and may explore other ways of making the loan acceptable.

5. *Government-backed loans*. As with all loan submissions, a loan can be approved or disapproved depending upon how well the information is presented. Most lenders today are FHA "direct endorsement" and DVA "automatic" lenders that speed up the process as compared to when, in the past, loan packages had to be submitted directly to the agencies. It is rare today to have a loan submitted directly to the FHA or the DVA. Sometimes the loan can be approved or disapproved depending on how well the information is presented. Be sure the lender you are working with has had experience processing FHA and DVA loans.

6. *Exceptions*. If the borrower does not qualify under the normal guidelines, be prepared to prove to the lender that an exception should be made. If you can present a convincing argument, the borrower will have a good chance of being approved, but back up your case with written documentation.

Finally, if you are in doubt as to how to proceed with a particular loan, ask yourself this question: "If I were going to use my own money to make this loan, what would my attitude be?" You will be surprised at some of the answers. It will help you in dealing with lenders and understanding them.

For additional information on how lenders view credit and what goes into a credit score, access the website of Fair, Isaac through the link at http://bond.swcollege.com/.

SUMMARY

When qualifying a borrower, lenders try to answer the question "Will the borrower repay the loan on a timely basis?" Lenders qualify borrowers by analyzing their ability or capacity and their desire to pay.

An analysis of ability to pay includes the amount and stability of income; the borrower's income is probably the most important factor in qualifying. Conventional lenders and the FHA use front- and back-end (top and bottom) ratios when they qualify the borrower's income, while the DVA uses cash flow and income ratio methods. Cal-Vet looks for a residual or remaining income—after deducting for all housing debt, nonhousing long-term debt, and disability insurance—that is at least 50 percent or more of adjusted income. The stability of income must also be considered. It is influenced by the length of time on the job and by the type of job.

Lenders measure a borrower's desire to pay partly by past credit performance. They also examine the borrower's motivation to continue making payments; the amount of down payment is the main measuring stick.

One rule of thumb that applies to all lenders is that qualifying a borrower is a matter of applying guidelines with a great deal of judgment.

IMPORTANT TERMS AND CONCEPTS

Ability/capacity to pay	*Front-end ratio (top ratio)*
Adjusted gross income	*Gift letter*
Back-end ratio (bottom ratio)	*Gross income*
Cash flow	*Income ratio*
Co-mortgagor	*Long-term debt*
Compensating factors	*Monthly payments*
Co-signer	*PITI*
Credit history	*Qualifying ratio*
Credit scoring	*Residual income*
Desire to pay	*Stability of income*
Equifax	*Total monthly expense*
Experian	*TransUnion*
FACT	

REVIEWING YOUR UNDERSTANDING

Questions for Discussion

1. What is the difference between "ability to pay" and "desire to pay"?

2. If a lender requires that the monthly payment not exceed 33 percent of the borrower's income, what is the maximum monthly housing payment for a borrower with a $3,600 gross monthly income?

3. With a gross monthly income of $3,000 and long-term debts of $200 per month, will this borrower qualify for a monthly housing payment of $1,000 if the lender uses ratios of 30 percent and 38 percent?

4. List four reasons why a borrower might have the income to qualify for a real estate loan but still be turned down by a lender.

5. How do real estate lenders count commissions? Part-time jobs? Alimony? Income from real estate investments?

6. Why are lenders concerned with a borrower's credit score? Will a past bankruptcy automatically disqualify a borrower from a real estate loan?

Multiple-Choice Questions

1. A monthly loan payment is called PITI. This stands for
   a. principal, interest, taxes, indebtedness.
   b. payments, including timed interest.
   c. past due, insurance, taxes, interest.
   d. principal, interest, taxes, insurance.

2. To arrive at adjusted gross income under Cal-Vet financing, the agency takes the gross income and subtracts
   a. long-term debts, including total housing expense.
   b. long-term debts, excluding housing expense.
   c. all voluntary payroll deductions.
   d. payroll taxes, including Social Security.

3. Given a gross income of $5,000, mortgage payments (PITI) of $1,400, and long-term monthly debts of $350, the monthly payment or front-end ratio is
   a. 15 percent.
   b. 28 percent.
   c. 35 percent.
   d. 41 percent.

4. Referring to Question 3, the back-end ratio is
   a. 35 percent.
   b. 28 percent.
   c. 7 percent.
   d. none of these.

5. Which of the following is considered a negative for credit-scoring purposes?
   a. a score of 800.
   b. an average number of current credit accounts.
   c. no bankruptcy.
   d. a former collection account paid in full.

6. In qualifying a GI loan, the Department of Veterans Affairs deducts income taxes, Social Security, and retirement contributions from allowable gross income. The balance is called
   a. gross effective income.
   b. net effective income.
   c. net take-home pay.
   d. gross spendable income.

7. Which of these is likely to be the most important factor in qualifying a buyer for a loan?
   a. amount of savings.
   b. type of job.
   c. number of dependents.
   d. adequacy and stability of income.

8. You are applying for an FHA loan. Your gross income is $3,200 per month. The total monthly payment is $800. Another $600 is paid out monthly for long-term debts. The ratio of total mortgage payment to gross income is
   a. 32.8 percent.
   b. 25 percent.
   c. 43.8 percent.
   d. none of these.

9. Using the data from Question 8, the total back-end ratio to gross income is
   a. 43.8 percent.
   b. 50 percent.
   c. 53.8 percent.
   d. none of these.

10. In the process of making a loan, the loan officer will correlate the characteristics of the borrower, characteristics of the loan, and the characteristics of the property in making a decision to grant a loan. The most important consideration is
    a. property rental value.
    b. degree of risk.
    c. location of property.
    d. neighborhood.

11. The rules used by conventional lenders to qualify borrower-applicants
    a. are rigid and uniform throughout the industry.
    b. are all different with no two the same.
    c. can be similar, with each lender setting its own flexible policies.
    d. are strictly governed by regulatory bodies.

12. In qualifying borrowers, conventional real estate lenders generally
    a. use ratios that relate monthly payments to income.
    b. will always make loans if the circumstances appear reasonable.
    c. state that a loan is available to borrowers whose monthly payment does not exceed 50 percent of gross income.
    d. apply a "20 percent standard."

13. Income from overtime in regular occupations
    a. will not be considered by most lenders.
    b. is counted if it is stable and consistent.
    c. will be considered by a lender only to offset an equal amount of long-term debt.
    d. must be earned for at least three years before lenders will count it.

14. Income is considered stable by most lenders if
    a. it has been earned regularly for two years.
    b. the applicant has been in the same line of work for several years, even if he or she has been on a new job for one month.
    c. the type of occupation would normally warrant it.
    d. all of the above apply.

15. The total assets of a borrower-applicant
    a. are of little concern to a lender.
    b. can have a beneficial influence on a lender.
    c. are ignored by most lenders, who look only to income.
    d. will not influence a lender unless the borrower qualifies according to its strict standards.

16. FNMA and FHLMC influence the borrower qualification process by
    a. buying qualifying loans.
    b. applying uniform qualifying ratios for all lenders.
    c. both (a) and (b).
    d. neither (a) nor (b).

17. For condominiums, the initials PITIA designate
    a. principal, interest, time, insurance, assessments.
    b. points, inflation, trustor, impounds, assurances.
    c. profits, income, transfers, installments, acceleration.
    d. principal, interest, taxes, insurance, assessments.

18. Each of the following is considered income except
    a. continuing spousal support.
    b. gifts from family members.
    c. positive cash flows from rentals.
    d. self-employment income.

19. The capacity to pay is best defined as the
    a. applicant's total assets.
    b. borrower's willingness to repay loans.
    c. ability to repay debts.
    d. current mortgage activity.

20. Lenders would feel justified in approving a higher loan ratio when there are compensating factors present, such as
    a. exceptional education and training.
    b. large down payment.
    c. substantial net worth.
    d. any of the above.

CHAPTER 10
PROCESSING, CLOSING, AND SERVICING REAL ESTATE LOANS

PREVIEW

This chapter describes how lenders process real estate loans. Section 10.1 starts with the loan application form and proceeds through a typical loan package. Section 10.2 illustrates the loan approval process. Section 10.3 discusses the steps required to close the loan and Sections 10.4 and 10.5 explain loan servicing after the escrow closes.

After completing this chapter, you should be able to:

1. List the items that make up a loan package.
2. Describe the process by which conventional, FHA, and DVA loans are approved.
3. List and explain borrowers' closing costs.
4. Describe the difference between "assuming" a loan and taking the property "subject to" the loan.
5. List rights that prospective borrowers have under the Fair Credit Reporting Act in the event errors are shown in their credit reports.
6. Cite the chief provisions of the Truth-in-Lending Law.

10.1 Processing the Loan

Loan processing starts with the *loan application*. Most lenders use the FNMA/FHLMC standard application form shown as Figure 10.1.

After receiving the application and other requested documents, the lender can make a preliminary determination of the borrower's likelihood of qualifying for a loan. In many cases, the information is either forwarded to an underwriter or submitted to an automated qualifying program to acquire a preapproval. The preapproval identifies the "conditions" required from the borrower before final loan approval.

Armed with the preapproval, the lender starts the loan processing, which includes getting needed information to meet the lender's conditions, if any, ordering the appraisal, and acquiring title and escrow information.

Qualifying the borrower continues as the various exhibits required are received by the lender. Chapter 9 discussed the standards used to qualify a borrower. In this chapter, we will go step by step into how real estate lenders process and close loans.

Even though applications may vary in format and length, they generally ask the same basic questions. The basic items in loan applications include (1) employment, (2) income, (3) assets, (4) debts, and (5) credit history. Many lenders use the FNMA 1003 form even if the loans are not intended to be sold in the secondary market.

Completing Loan Application Forms

The application form provides the lender with the borrower's financial and other information with which to make a loan decision. The completeness and accuracy of the information can affect whether a loan request is approved or rejected.

The lender's loan submission package typically contains two applications, a handwritten one provided by the borrower and a typed application that often includes an expansion of the information originally supplied by the borrower. The typed application is the result of a personal interview and allows the lender and/or mortgage broker to fill in any gaps left by the handwritten application.

With the increase in financial fraud, the importance of the loan application, in the borrower's own handwriting, has taken on greater significance. In the Acknowledgement and Agreement section of the loan application (Figure 10.1, Section IX), the borrower confirms that the information provided is accurate and is warned that deliberate misrepresentation can result in severe punishment.

Uniform Residential Loan Application

This application is designed to be completed by the applicant(s) with the Lender's assistance. Applicants should complete this form as "Borrower" or "Co-Borrower," as applicable. Co-Borrower information must also be provided (and the appropriate box checked) when ☐ the income or assets of a person other than the Borrower (including the Borrower's spouse) will be used as a basis for loan qualification or ☐ the income or assets of the Borrower's spouse or other person who has community property rights pursuant to state law will not be used as a basis for loan qualification, but his or her liabilities must be considered because the spouse or other person has community property rights pursuant to applicable law and Borrower resides in a community property state, the security property is located in a community property state, or the Borrower is relying on other property located in a community property state as a basis for repayment of the loan.

If this is an application for joint credit, Borrower and Co-Borrower each agree that we intend to apply for joint credit (sign below):

Borrower _____ Co-Borrower _____

I. TYPE OF MORTGAGE AND TERMS OF LOAN

Mortgage Applied for:	☐ VA ☐ FHA	☐ Conventional ☐ USDA/Rural Housing Service	☐ Other (explain):	Agency Case Number	Lender Case Number

Amount $	Interest Rate %	No. of Months	Amortization Type:	☐ Fixed Rate ☐ GPM	☐ Other (explain): ☐ ARM (type):

II. PROPERTY INFORMATION AND PURPOSE OF LOAN

Subject Property Address (street, city, state & ZIP)	No. of Units

Legal Description of Subject Property (attach description if necessary)	Year Built

Purpose of Loan ☐ Purchase ☐ Construction ☐ Other (explain): ☐ Refinance ☐ Construction-Permanent | Property will be: ☐ Primary Residence ☐ Secondary Residence ☐ Investment

Complete this line if construction or construction-permanent loan.

Year Lot Acquired	Original Cost $	Amount Existing Liens $	(a) Present Value of Lot $	(b) Cost of Improvements $	Total (a + b) $

Complete this line if this is a refinance loan.

Year Acquired	Original Cost $	Amount Existing Liens $	Purpose of Refinance	Describe Improvements ☐ made ☐ to be made Cost: $

Title will be held in what Name(s)	Manner in which Title will be held	Estate will be held in: ☐ Fee Simple ☐ Leasehold (show expiration date)

Source of Down Payment, Settlement Charges, and/or Subordinate Financing (explain)

III. BORROWER INFORMATION

Borrower	Co-Borrower
Borrower's Name (include Jr. or Sr. if applicable)	Co-Borrower's Name (include Jr. or Sr. if applicable)

Social Security Number	Home Phone (incl. area code)	DOB (mm/dd/yyyy)	Yrs. School	Social Security Number	Home Phone (incl. area code)	DOB (mm/dd/yyyy)	Yrs. School

☐ Married ☐ Separated ☐ Unmarried (include single, divorced, widowed)	Dependents (not listed by Co-Borrower) no. ages	☐ Married ☐ Separated ☐ Unmarried (include single, divorced, widowed)	Dependents (not listed by Borrower) no. ages

Present Address (street, city, state, ZIP) ☐ Own ☐ Rent ___No. Yrs.	Present Address (street, city, state, ZIP) ☐ Own ☐ Rent ___No. Yrs.
Mailing Address, if different from Present Address	Mailing Address, if different from Present Address

If residing at present address for less than two years, complete the following:

Former Address (street, city, state, ZIP) ☐ Own ☐ Rent ___No. Yrs.	Former Address (street, city, state, ZIP) ☐ Own ☐ Rent ___No. Yrs.

IV. EMPLOYMENT INFORMATION

Borrower	Co-Borrower
Name & Address of Employer ☐ Self Employed	Yrs. on this job	Name & Address of Employer ☐ Self Employed	Yrs. on this job
	Yrs. employed in this line of work/profession		Yrs. employed in this line of work/profession
Position/Title/Type of Business	Business Phone (incl. area code)	Position/Title/Type of Business	Business Phone (incl. area code)

If employed in current position for less than two years or if currently employed in more than one position, complete the following:

Figure 10.1 FNMA/FHLMC residential loan application.

IV. EMPLOYMENT INFORMATION (cont'd)

Borrower

Name & Address of Employer	☐ Self Employed	Dates (from – to)
		Monthly Income $

Position/Title/Type of Business	Business Phone (incl. area code)

Name & Address of Employer	☐ Self Employed	Dates (from – to)
		Monthly Income $

Position/Title/Type of Business	Business Phone (incl. area code)

Co-Borrower

Name & Address of Employer	☐ Self Employed	Dates (from – to)
		Monthly Income $

Position/Title/Type of Business	Business Phone (incl. area code)

Name & Address of Employer	☐ Self Employed	Dates (from – to)
		Monthly Income $

Position/Title/Type of Business	Business Phone (incl. area code)

V. MONTHLY INCOME AND COMBINED HOUSING EXPENSE INFORMATION

Gross Monthly Income	Borrower	Co-Borrower	Total	Combined Monthly Housing Expense	Present	Proposed
Base Empl. Income*	$	$	$	Rent	$	
Overtime				First Mortgage (P&I)		$
Bonuses				Other Financing (P&I)		
Commissions				Hazard Insurance		
Dividends/Interest				Real Estate Taxes		
Net Rental Income				Mortgage Insurance		
Other (before completing. see the notice in "describe other income," below)				Homeowner Assn. Dues		
				Other:		
Total	$	$	$	Total	$	$

*   Self Employed Borrower(s) may be required to provide additional documentation such as tax returns and financial statements.

Describe Other Income

Notice: Alimony, child support, or separate maintenance income need not be revealed if the Borrower (B) or Co-Borrower (C) does not choose to have it considered for repaying this loan.

B/C		Monthly Amount
		$

VI. ASSETS AND LIABILITIES

This Statement and any applicable supporting schedules may be completed jointly by both married and unmarried Co-Borrowers if their assets and liabilities are sufficiently joined so that the Statement can be meaningfully and fairly presented on a combined basis; otherwise, separate Statements and Schedules are required. If the Co-Borrower section was completed about a non-applicant spouse or other person, this Statement and supporting schedules must be completed about that spouse or other person also.

Completed ☐ Jointly ☐ Not Jointly

ASSETS Description	Cash or Market Value	Liabilities and Pledged Assets. List the creditor's name, address, and account number for all outstanding debts, including automobile loans, revolving charge accounts, real estate loans, alimony, child support, stock pledges, etc. Use continuation sheet, if necessary. Indicate by (*) those liabilities, which will be satisfied upon sale of real estate owned or upon refinancing of the subject property.		
Cash deposit toward purchase held by:	$			
		LIABILITIES	**Monthly Payment & Months Left to Pay**	**Unpaid Balance**
List checking and savings accounts below		Name and address of Company	$ Payment/Months	$
Name and address of Bank, S&L, or Credit Union				
		Acct. no.		
Acct. no.	$	Name and address of Company	$ Payment/Months	$
Name and address of Bank, S&L, or Credit Union				
		Acct. no.		
Acct. no.	$	Name and address of Company	$ Payment/Months	$
Name and address of Bank, S&L, or Credit Union				
		Acct. no.		

Figure 10.1 FNMA/FHLMC residential loan application (*continued*).

VI. ASSETS AND LIABILITIES (cont'd)

Acct. no.	$	Name and address of Company	$ Payment/Months	$
Name and address of Bank, S&L, or Credit Union				
		Acct. no.		
Acct. no.	$	Name and address of Company	$ Payment/Months	$
Stocks & Bonds (Company name/ number & description)	$			
		Acct. no.		
Life insurance net cash value	$	Name and address of Company	$ Payment/Months	$
Face amount: $				
Subtotal Liquid Assets	$			
Real estate owned (enter market value from schedule of real estate owned)	$			
Vested interest in retirement fund	$			
Net worth of business(es) owned (attach financial statement)	$	Acct. no.		
Automobiles owned (make and year)	$	Alimony/Child Support/Separate Maintenance Payments Owed to:	$	
Other Assets (itemize)	$	Job-Related Expense (child care, union dues, etc.)	$	
		Total Monthly Payments	$	
Total Assets a. $		Net Worth ► $ (a minus b)	**Total Liabilities b.** $	

Schedule of Real Estate Owned (If additional properties are owned, use continuation sheet.)

Property Address (enter S if sold, PS if pending sale or R if rental being held for income) ▼	Type of Property	Present Market Value	Amount of Mortgages & Liens	Gross Rental Income	Mortgage Payments	Insurance, Maintenance, Taxes & Misc.	Net Rental Income
		$	$	$	$	$	$
Totals		$	$	$	$	$	$

List any additional names under which credit has previously been received and indicate appropriate creditor name(s) and account number(s):

Alternate Name	Creditor Name	Account Number

VII. DETAILS OF TRANSACTION

a.	Purchase price	$
b.	Alterations, improvements, repairs	
c.	Land (if acquired separately)	
d.	Refinance (incl. debts to be paid off)	
e.	Estimated prepaid items	
f.	Estimated closing costs	
g.	PMI, MIP, Funding Fee	
h.	Discount (if Borrower will pay)	
i.	Total costs (add items a through h)	

VIII. DECLARATIONS

If you answer "Yes" to any questions a through i, please use continuation sheet for explanation.

	Borrower Yes / No	Co-Borrower Yes / No
a. Are there any outstanding judgments against you?	☐ ☐	☐ ☐
b. Have you been declared bankrupt within the past 7 years?	☐ ☐	☐ ☐
c. Have you had property foreclosed upon or given title or deed in lieu thereof in the last 7 years?	☐ ☐	☐ ☐
d. Are you a party to a lawsuit?	☐ ☐	☐ ☐
e. Have you directly or indirectly been obligated on any loan which resulted in foreclosure, transfer of title in lieu of foreclosure, or judgment?	☐ ☐	☐ ☐

(This would include such loans as home mortgage loans, SBA loans, home improvement loans, educational loans, manufactured (mobile) home loans, any mortgage, financial obligation, bond, or loan guarantee. If "Yes," provide details, including date, name, and address of Lender, FHA or VA case number, if any, and reasons for the action.)

Figure 10.1 FNMA/FHLMC residential loan application (*continued*).

VII. DETAILS OF TRANSACTION	VIII. DECLARATIONS				

VIII. DECLARATIONS

If you answer "Yes" to any questions a through i, please use continuation sheet for explanation.

	Borrower		Co-Borrower	
	Yes	No	Yes	No

j. Subordinate financing

k. Borrower's closing costs paid by Seller

l. Other Credits (explain)

m. Loan amount (exclude PMI, MIP, Funding Fee financed)

n. PMI, MIP, Funding Fee financed

o. Loan amount (add m & n)

p. Cash from/to Borrower (subtract j, k, l & o from i)

f. Are you presently delinquent or in default on any Federal debt or any other loan, mortgage, financial obligation, bond, or loan guarantee? If "Yes," give details as described in the preceding question. ☐ ☐ ☐ ☐

g. Are you obligated to pay alimony, child support, or separate maintenance? ☐ ☐ ☐ ☐

h. Is any part of the down payment borrowed? ☐ ☐ ☐ ☐

i. Are you a co-maker or endorser on a note? ☐ ☐ ☐ ☐

j. Are you a U.S. citizen? ☐ ☐ ☐ ☐

k. Are you a permanent resident alien? ☐ ☐ ☐ ☐

l. Do you intend to occupy the property as your primary residence? If "Yes," complete question m below. ☐ ☐ ☐ ☐

m. Have you had an ownership interest in a property in the last three years? ☐ ☐ ☐ ☐
(1) What type of property did you own—principal residence (PR), second home (SH), or investment property (IP)? _____ _____
(2) How did you hold title to the home—solely by yourself (S), jointly with your spouse (SP), or jointly with another person (O)? _____ _____

IX. ACKNOWLEDGEMENT AND AGREEMENT

Each of the undersigned specifically represents to Lender and to Lender's actual or potential agents, brokers, processors, attorneys, insurers, servicers, successors and assigns and agrees and acknowledges that: (1) the information provided in this application is true and correct as of the date set forth opposite my signature and that any intentional or negligent misrepresentation of this information contained in this application may result in civil liability, including monetary damages, to any person who may suffer any loss due to reliance upon any misrepresentation that I have made on this application, and/or in criminal penalties including, but not limited to, fine or imprisonment or both under the provisions of Title 18, United States Code, Sec. 1001, et seq.; (2) the loan requested pursuant to this application (the "Loan") will be secured by a mortgage or deed of trust on the property described in this application; (3) the property will not be used for any illegal or prohibited purpose or use; (4) all statements made in this application are made for the purpose of obtaining a residential mortgage loan; (5) the property will be occupied as indicated in this application; (6) the Lender, its servicers, successors or assigns may retain the original and/or an electronic record of this application, whether or not the Loan is approved; (7) the Lender and its agents, brokers, insurers, servicers, successors and assigns may continuously rely on the information contained in the application, and I am obligated to amend and/or supplement the information provided in this application if any of the material facts that I have represented herein should change prior to closing of the Loan; (8) in the event that my payments on the Loan become delinquent, the Lender, its servicers, successors or assigns may, in addition to any other rights and remedies that it may have relating to such delinquency, report my name and account information to one or more consumer reporting agencies; (9) ownership of the Loan and/or administration of the Loan account may be transferred with such notice as may be required by law; (10) neither Lender nor its agents, brokers, insurers, servicers, successors or assigns has made any representation or warranty, express or implied, to me regarding the property or the condition or value of the property; and (11) my transmission of this application as an "electronic record" containing my "electronic signature," as those terms are defined in applicable federal and/or state laws (excluding audio and video recordings), or my facsimile transmission of this application containing a facsimile of my signature, shall be as effective, enforceable and valid as if a paper version of this application were delivered containing my original written signature.

Acknowledgement. Each of the undersigned hereby acknowledges that any owner of the Loan, its servicers, successors and assigns, may verify or reverify any information contained in this application or obtain any information or data relating to the Loan, for any legitimate business purpose through any source, including a source named in this application or a consumer reporting agency.

Borrower's Signature X	Date	Co-Borrower's Signature X	Date

X. INFORMATION FOR GOVERNMENT MONITORING PURPOSES

The following information is requested by the Federal Government for certain types of loans related to a dwelling in order to monitor the lender's compliance with equal credit opportunity, fair housing and home mortgage disclosure laws. You are not required to furnish this information, but are encouraged to do so. The law provides that a lender may not discriminate either on the basis of this information, or on whether you choose to furnish it. If you furnish the information, please provide both ethnicity and race. For race, you may check more than one designation. If you do not furnish ethnicity, race, or sex, under Federal regulations, this lender is required to note the information on the basis of visual observation and surname if you have made this application in person. If you do not wish to furnish the information, please check the box below. (Lender must review the above material to assure that the disclosures satisfy all requirements to which the lender is subject under applicable state law for the particular type of loan applied for.)

BORROWER ☐ I do not wish to furnish this information | **CO-BORROWER** ☐ I do not wish to furnish this information

Ethnicity: ☐ Hispanic or Latino ☐ Not Hispanic or Latino | Ethnicity: ☐ Hispanic or Latino ☐ Not Hispanic or Latino

Race: ☐ American Indian or Alaska Native ☐ Asian ☐ Black or African American ☐ Native Hawaiian or Other Pacific Islander ☐ White | Race: ☐ American Indian or Alaska Native ☐ Asian ☐ Black or African American ☐ Native Hawaiian or Other Pacific Islander ☐ White

Sex: ☐ Female ☐ Male | Sex: ☐ Female ☐ Male

To be Completed by Interviewer
This application was taken by:
☐ Face-to-face interview
☐ Mail
☐ Telephone
☐ Internet

Interviewer's Name (print or type)

Interviewer's Signature   Date

Interviewer's Phone Number (incl. area code)

Name and Address of Interviewer's Employer

Freddie Mac Form 65 7/05 | Page 4 of 5 | Fannie Mae Form 1003 7/05

Figure 10.1 FNMA/FHLMC residential loan application (*continued*).

CONTINUATION SHEET/RESIDENTIAL LOAN APPLICATION			
Use this continuation sheet if you need more space to complete the Residential Loan Application. Mark **B** f or Borrower or **C** for Co-Borrower.	Borrower:	Agency Case Number:	
	Co-Borrower:	Lender Case Number:	

I/We fully understand that it is a Federal crime punishable by fine or imprisonment, or both, to knowingly make any false statements concerning any of the above facts as applicable under the provisions of Title 18, United States Code, Section 1001, et seq.

Borrower's Signature	Date	Co-Borrower's Signature	Date
X		X	

Freddie Mac Form 65   7/05   Page 5 of 5   Fannie Mae Form 1003   7/05

Figure 10.1 FNMA/FHLMC residential loan application (*continued*).

If the loan officer or mortgage correspondent's workload allows, there is a number of good reasons why it may be beneficial to have he/she be present as a guide when the borrower completes the loan application.

- This gives the loan person an opportunity to further interview the borrower and perhaps acquire additional information helpful to the borrower not asked for in the application.

  For example, the borrower may be receiving a promotion or an increase in salary in the immediate future. When the loan officer recognizes that this information will help in qualifying the borrower it can be added to the application.

- Many borrowers are applying for a real estate loan for the first time. They are not sure what to expect and have questions regarding the whole process. The loan officer can answer their questions and explain the process to them. If they understand what is involved, the entire transaction will go much more smoothly.

- If during the interview the borrower seems unable to qualify, the loan officer or correspondent may be able to offer alternative loan options with which the borrower may be able to qualify. In some cases, the loan person merely creates a "roadmap" by providing the prospective borrower with a list of what they must do regarding, income, assets, etc., to qualify for a loan.

A prospective borrower usually is provided a basic list of required items the lender will need when the borrower applies for a loan. The list is a reminder of the information a lender will need to make a final loan decision. The list usually includes pay stubs, bank statements, tax returns, W-2 forms, etc. If the borrower is applying for a "stated income" or "no documentation" type of loan, the list of required documents shrinks accordingly.

Equal Credit Opportunity Act (ECOA)

The federal ECOA prohibits discrimination on the basis of race, color, religion, national origin, age, sex, or marital status, or on the grounds of receipt of income from a public assistance program. Since the act includes any person who regularly extends or arranges credit, it clearly applies to real estate lenders.

Some of the basic provisions of the act that affect real estate lenders are these:

1. Lenders cannot ask if the borrower is divorced or widowed. They may ask if the borrower is married, unmarried, or separated. For purposes of the law, unmarried means single, divorced, or widowed.

2. Lenders cannot ask about receiving alimony or child support unless the borrower is first notified that it need not be revealed. However, lenders may ask about obligations to pay alimony or child support.

3. Lenders cannot ask about birth control practices or childbearing intentions or capabilities.

4. Lenders must notify applicants in writing within 30 days as to what action has been taken on their applications. In case of disapproval, the reason must be given.

5. If applicants request, lenders may consider information provided by the borrower explaining the reasons for a bad joint account in the credit report. It should be noted, however, that many lenders do not consider divorce as "beyond the control" of the borrower (unlike a job loss or medical complications), and a bad credit history because of divorce often impacts a loan decision.

Real Estate Settlement Procedures Act (RESPA)

Known as RESPA, this law applies only to first loans on one-to-four-unit residential properties. The main provisions of the act are as follows:

1. A lender must give the borrower a written estimate of the settlement or closing costs. This estimate is called a GFE, or good faith estimate. The estimate does not include reserves collected for taxes, insurance, or prorations. The estimate must be given or mailed to the borrower within three business days of the date of the loan application. One day before settlement, the borrower has the right to inspect an itemized list of the closing costs.

2. Within the same three business days, the borrower must be given the Department of Housing and Urban Development's booklet that explains and gives information on closing costs.

3. Escrow and/or title companies must use a HUD-1 Settlement Sheet.

4. An anti-kickback provision prohibits real estate agents from generating unearned referral fees.

Verifying the Information on the Application

What happens after the loan application is completed? Fully documented loans as well as many other loan options require written verification of employment and checking and savings account data. A credit report is ordered, which itemizes current debts balances and monthly payments. Each of these debts is then rated. Credit reports also disclose recorded information, such as judgments, divorces, and other liens against the borrower. Then, the borrower's credit history is given as a credit score. See Chapter 9, Qualifying the Borrower, for more details.

Because conventional lenders depend more and more on credit scores for their approval decisions, to stay competitive, Fannie Mae, Freddie Mac, FHA, DVA, and Cal-Vet have adopted an "alternative documentation" process for their loan-verification requirements. The most recent three months of bank statements and pay stubs plus the last two years of W-2 forms often are used as sufficient verification, especially for borrowers with high credit scores.

Loan Package

The loan officer or correspondent's next job is to assemble the **loan package**, which consists of all the forms, documents, and reports the lender needs to make a decision on the loan. If the loan officer does not have the authority to make the loan, the package is then given to a loan committee or to an underwriter who represents a lender.

A typical loan package might include: (1) borrower's loan application, (2) appraisal of the property, (3) verification of employment, (4) verification of banks statements, (5) credit report, (6) purchase contracts, (7) escrow instructions and preliminary title report, (8) documentation showing where the funds for the down payment and closing cost are coming from, which is often called "sourcing the funds," and (9) other supporting documents, such as tax returns, W-2 forms, and so on.

Experienced loan officers realize the importance of a loan package. They know that a complete and neat package is more likely to be approved. They also anticipate questions or objections a committee may have and answer them in advance. For example, if the borrower has had a bankruptcy, the loan officer knows that the committee will ask questions such as: Why did the borrower have a bankruptcy? When was it discharged? Has the borrower reestablished credit? In today's market, all unfavorable items on the credit report will need a full explanation before the loan is approved. The loan officer includes this information in the loan package. There may also be additional information regarding the property or borrower that is not covered in the appraisal report or borrower's application. If the loan officer feels the information is pertinent, it is submitted to the committee.

10.2 How Is a Loan Approved?

The loan approval process varies depending upon the lender. Conventional loans made by banks and thrift institutions are approved by authorized individuals or by a loan committee. If the approval is to be made by an individual, he or she will have the authority to approve loans up to a specific dollar amount. Any loan greater than the said dollar amount must be approved by a supervisor or a loan committee. Large banks and thrift institutions may have layers of committees with loan amount limitations at each level.

Conventional loans that are scheduled to be resold to Fannie Mae or Freddie Mac are approved by authorized underwriters. Most underwriters use an automated loan analysis program to determine whether the loan meets Fannie Mae or Freddie Mac standards.

Federal Housing Administration (FHA) and Department of Veterans Affairs (DVA)

Criticism of the old practice of submitting all FHA- and DVA-backed loan packages directly to these agencies led to the adoption of the FHA Direct Endorsement System and the DVA Automatic System. Lenders approved to underwrite loans under these systems are labeled as either **supervised** or **nonsupervised** lenders, with nonsupervised lenders having the most latitude. Today, the majority of FHA- and DVA-backed loans are approved by nonsupervised lenders like mortgage companies.

To be approved as a nonsupervised lender, companies must meet the guidelines set forth by FHA and DVA. For example, a nonsupervised mortgage company may be sponsored by an approved direct endorsement lender, to whom the mortgage company submits the FHA-backed loan for final approval. In this case, FHA requires both the direct endorsement lender and the mortgage company to meet certain net worth requirements and to submit to an annual audit procedure.

Once the mortgage company submits the FHA or DVA package to their sponsoring direct endorsement lender, and said lender approves the package, the loan is automatically approved by FHA or DVA. This "in-house" form of underwriting dramatically reduces the time required for FHA or DVA loan approval and closing.

Fair Credit Reporting Act

The federal Fair Credit Reporting Act affects credit reporting agencies and users of credit information. If a loan is rejected because of information in a credit report, the borrower must be notified and given the name and address of the credit agency. The borrower then has the right to obtain from the agency the following:

1. All the information it has in its file on the borrower.

2. Sources of the information.

3. All the creditors to whom the agency has furnished reports within the last six months.

If an error is found, the credit agency must make the correction. If there is a dispute over any reported credit information, the borrower has the right to submit a Consumer Statement, which is generally limited to 100 words or less, explaining his or her side of the story. The credit agency must include this consumer statement in all subsequent credit inquires.

The reliance upon credit scoring has spawned a process by which, for a fee, consumers can accelerate a positive change in their credit scores by correcting inaccurate information quickly and then have the credit agency recalculate their new credit score to take advantage of more favorable interest rate on their loan. Normally, a correction and recalculation of a credit score could take 60 days or longer. This fee-based special fast-track system might be able to reduce that time to just a day or two.

10.3 Closing the Loan

Once a loan has been approved, the next phase is called closing. Loan closings are usually handled by independent third parties, such as title and escrow companies. All the parties involved in the real estate transaction (buyer, seller, and lender) deliver their instructions, documents, and money to the escrow agent. While a broker may deliver "instructions" to the escrow holder, it should be noted that the broker is not a party and does not directly control the closing. Exceptions arise, of course, when brokers act as principals.

In southern California, it is customary for escrows to be handled by independent escrow companies or the escrow departments of banks and title companies. In northern California, it is more common for escrow departments of title companies to handle the escrow. Some real estate companies, particularly the larger ones, have their own escrow departments. These companies close their own transactions and use the title company only for the title insurance, if approved by the lender to do so.

When all the instructions have been complied with, the escrow is closed. The escrow agent records certain documents such as the grant deed and deed of trust, prepares closing statements, and disburses the money.

Loan Documents for Escrow

The main loan documents prepared by the lender are:

1. Promissory note (Figure 10.2).

2. Deed of trust (Figure 10.3).

3. Truth-in-lending disclosure statement (Figure 10.4).

The promissory note outlines the financial terms of the loan: amount of loan, interest rate, monthly payments, date of first payment, and so on. The promissory note also lists other conditions such as late charges, prepayment privileges and penalties, and acceleration clauses.

A deed of trust is used to secure the repayment of the loan by creating a lien against the property. As explained in an earlier chapter, deeds of trust are used in California instead of mortgages, because of the ease with which a lender can foreclose in case of a borrower's default.

As shown in Figure 10.3, a deed of trust *does not* outline specific financial terms like the promissory note. A deed of trust shows only the loan amount, not the interest rate, monthly payments, or other information. The deed of trust shows that, if the debt it secures is not paid, the property may be sold to satisfy the debt. The deed of trust is recorded, while the promissory note is not. Thus, to maintain confidentiality between the lender and borrower, the deed of trust shows only the amount of the loan, not the repayment terms. In addition, the deed of trust contains many other detailed agreements between the borrower and lender.

Truth-in-Lending Law (Regulation Z)

In 1968, Congress passed the Truth-in-Lending Law, known as TIL, in an effort to create a way for borrowers to compare loan costs from one lender to another as they shop for the best terms. A key feature of TIL is the requirement for lenders to calculate and present to the borrower a statement showing the Annual Percentage Rate (APR). In addition to the interest rate on the loan, the APR takes into account certain fees and other costs incurred to acquire the loan.

NOTE

MIN   100033300091089113

California
[State]

[Date]   [City]

[Property Address]

1. BORROWER'S PROMISE TO PAY

In return for a loan that I have received, I promise to pay U.S. $ (this amount is called "Principal"), plus interest, to the order of the Lender. The Lender is

I will make all payments under this Note in the form of cash, check or money order.

I understand that the Lender may transfer this Note. The Lender or anyone who takes this Note by transfer and who is entitled to receive payments under this Note is called the "Note Holder."

2. INTEREST

Interest will be charged on unpaid principal until the full amount of Principal has been paid. I will pay interest at a yearly rate of   ﹪%.

The interest rate required by this Section 2 is the rate I will pay both before and after any default described in Section 6(B) of this Note.

3. PAYMENTS

(A) Time and Place of Payments

I will pay principal and interest by making a payment every month.

I will make my monthly payment on the   1st   day of each month beginning on   . I will make these payments every month until I have paid all of the principal and interest and any other charges described below that I may owe under this Note. Each monthly payment will be applied as of its scheduled due date and will be applied to interest before Principal. If, on   , I still owe amounts under this Note, I will pay those amounts in full on that date, which is called the "Maturity Date."

I will make my monthly payments at

or at a different place if required by the Note Holder.

(B) Amount of Monthly Payments

My monthly payment will be in the amount of U.S. $

4. BORROWER'S RIGHT TO PREPAY

I have the right to make payments of Principal at any time before they are due. A payment of Principal only is known as a "Prepayment." When I make a Prepayment, I will tell the Note Holder in writing that I am doing so. I may not designate a payment as a Prepayment if I have not made all the monthly payments due under the Note.

I may make a full Prepayment or partial Prepayments without paying a Prepayment charge. The Note Holder will use my Prepayments to reduce the amount of Principal that I owe under this Note. However, the Note Holder may apply my Prepayment to the accrued and unpaid interest on the Prepayment amount, before applying my Prepayment to reduce the Principal amount of the Note. If I make a partial Prepayment, there will be no changes in the due date or in the amount of my monthly payment unless the Note Holder agrees in writing to those changes.

MULTISTATE FIXED RATE NOTE—Single Family—**Fannie Mae/Freddie Mac UNIFORM INSTRUMENT**   Form 3200 1/01

GREATLAND ■

ITEM 1646L1 (0011)   *(Page 1 of 3 pages)*   To Order Call: 1-800-530-9393 ☐ Fax 616-791-1131

MFCD3002   9108911

Figure 10.2 Promissory note (partial).

RECORDING REQUESTED BY

AND WHEN RECORDED MAIL TO

──────────────────────────────────────[Space Above This Line For Recording Data]──────────

DEED OF TRUST

MIN: 100033300091089113

DEFINITIONS

Words used in multiple sections of this document are defined below and other words are defined in Sections 3, 11, 13, 18, 20 and 21. Certain rules regarding the usage of words used in this document are also provided in Section 16.

(A) "Security Instrument" means this document, which is dated   , together with all Riders to this document.

(B) "Borrower" is

Borrower is the trustor under this Security Instrument.

(C) "Lender" is
Lender is a   organized and existing under
the laws of   . Lender's address is

(D) "Trustee" is

(E) "MERS" is Mortgage Electronic Registration Systems, Inc. MERS is a separate corporation that is acting solely as a nominee for Lender and Lender's successors and assigns. **MERS is the beneficiary under this Security Instrument.** MERS is organized and existing under the laws of Delaware, and has an address and telephone number of P.O. Box 2026, Flint, MI 48501-2026, tel. (888) 679-MERS.

(F) "Note" means the promissory note signed by Borrower and dated   The Note
states that Borrower owes Lender
                                          Dollars (U.S. $) plus interest. Borrower has promised
to pay this debt in regular Periodic Payments and to pay the debt in full not later than

(G) "Property" means the property that is described below under the heading "Transfer of Rights in the Property."

CALIFORNIA—Single Family—**Fannie Mae/Freddie Mac UNIFORM INSTRUMENT**   **Form 3005 1/01**
                                                                                                   GREATLAND ■
ITEM 9926L1 (0011)—**MERS**   *(Page 1 of 12 pages)*   To Order Call: 1-800-530-9393 □ Fax 616-791-1131

MFCA3114   _9108911

Figure 10.3 Deed of trust (partial).

TRUTH-IN-LENDING DISCLOSURE STATEMENT
(THIS IS NEITHER A CONTRACT NOR A COMMITMENT TO LEND)

Applicants: Prepared By:

Property Address:

Application No: Date Prepared:

ANNUAL PERCENTAGE RATE	FINANCE CHARGE	AMOUNT FINANCED	TOTAL OF PAYMENTS
The cost of your credit as a yearly rate	The dollar amount the credit will cost you	The amount of credit provided to you or on your behalf	The amount you will have paid after making all payments as scheduled
%	$	$	$

☐ REQUIRED DEPOSIT: The annual percentage rate does not take into account your required deposit
PAYMENTS: Your payment schedule will be:

Number of Payments	Amount of Payments **	When Payments Are Due	Number of Payments	Amount of Payments **	When Payments Are Due	Number of Payments	Amount of Payments **	When Payments Are Due
		Monthly Beginning:			Monthly Beginning:			Monthly Beginning:

☐ DEMAND FEATURE: This obligation has a demand feature.
☐ VARIABLE RATE FEATURE: This loan contains a variable rate feature. A variable rate disclosure has been provided earlier.

CREDIT LIFE/CREDIT DISABILITY: Credit life insurance and credit disability insurance are not required to obtain credit, and will not be provided unless you sign and agree to pay the additional cost.

Type	Premium	Signature	
Credit Life		I want credit life insurance.	Signature:
Credit Disability		I want credit disability insurance.	Signature:
Credit Life and Disability		I want credit life and disability insurance.	Signature:

INSURANCE: The following insurance is required to obtain credit:
☐ Credit life insurance ☐ Credit disability ☐ Property insurance ☐ Flood insurance
You may obtain the insurance from anyone you want that is acceptable to creditor
☐ If you purchase ☐ property ☐ flood insurance from creditor you will pay $ for a one year term.
SECURITY: You are giving a security interest in:
☐ The goods or property being purchased   ☐ Real property you already own.
FILING FEES: $
LATE CHARGE: If a payment is more than   days late, you will be charged   % of the payment
PREPAYMENT: If you pay off early, you
☐ may   ☐ will not   have to pay a penalty.
☐ may   ☐ will not   be entitled to a refund of part of the finance charge.
ASSUMPTION: Someone buying your property
☐ may   ☐ may, subject to conditions   ☐ may not   assume the remainder of your loan on the original terms.
See your contract documents for any additional information about nonpayment, default, any required repayment in full before the scheduled date and prepayment refunds and penalties
☐ * means an estimate   ☐ all dates and numerical disclosures except the late payment disclosures are estimates.

* * NOTE: The Payments shown above include reserve deposits for Mortgage Insurance (if applicable), but exclude Property Taxes and Insurance.

THE UNDERSIGNED ACKNOWLEDGES RECEIVING A COMPLETED COPY OF THIS DISCLOSURE.

_____   _____
(Applicant)   (Date)   (Applicant)   (Date)

_____   _____
(Applicant)   (Date)   (Applicant)   (Date)

_____
(Lender)   (Date)

Calyx Form - til.hp (02/95)

Figure 10.4 Sample truth-in-lending disclosure statement.

The TIL applies whether the loan is for a real estate or personal property. For example, when you borrow to purchase a car, the lender must disclose the APR. Today's use of computers and financial calculators has eliminated the use of old fashion charts and tables to arrive at the APR.

Confusion continues to surround what the APR is and how it is calculated. The APR is usually greater than the interest rate on the promissory note. To understand the APR, let's start with some definitions. A ***prepaid finance charge*** is a fee paid separately to a lender or a fee withheld from the loan proceeds. These prepaid finance charges typically include loan origination fees, prepaid interest, tax service fee, and mortgage insurance, to name a few. The *amount financed* is the loan amount minus the prepaid finance charges. The amount financed is the figure used to calculate the APR. Here is a simple example:

If a borrower applies for a $50,000 loan and the prepaid finance charges total $2,000, the *amount financed* is $48,000 ($50,000 − $2,000). The APR is computed on the $48,000. Now assume the interest rate for the $50,000 loan is 7 percent amortized for 10 years and that this will results in a monthly payment of $580.54.

The APR would be calculated as follows:

Total Payments	$69,665	[$580.54 × 120 months (10 yrs × 12) = $69,664.80 round to $69,665]
Less: Loan Amount	−50,000	
Total Interest	$19,665	(total interest to be paid over the life of the loan)
Plus: Prepaid Finance Charge	+2,000	
Total Finance Charge	$21,665	

Then using a computer program or a programmed financial calculator, the APR would be determined to be 7.928 percent. Compare this with the 7 percent interest rate that appears on the promissory note. The APR is higher because when financing charges are brought into the picture, the cost of money is higher than the stated rate on the note.

The bottom line is that, when shopping a loan, interest rate quotes can be deceiving when closing costs vary from lender to lender, so one can use the APR as a guide as to which loan offer might be best. To trace the keystrokes on a financial calculator to arrive at an APR, see Chapter 13, Basic Mathematics of Real Estate Finance.

In addition to disclosing the APR, TIL requires the lender to disclose other information about the loan, such as the prepayment

Sales Price	$250,000
Loan Amount	$200,000
Loan Origination	$3,000
CLTA Title Policy	1,122
ALTA Title Policy	475
Escrow Fee	450
Credit Report	20
Appraisal Fee	400
Tax Service	75
Notary and Misc. Fees	140
Recording Fees	80
Pest Control Inspection	125
Total Nonrecurring Closing Costs	$5,887
Tax Proration	$275
Hazard Insurance Premium	475
Prepaid Interest	690
Total Recurring Closing Costs	$1,440
Combined Closing Costs	$7,327

Figure 10.5 Sample closing cost.

penalty if any, late charge fees, and, if applicable, the three-day right to cancel on any refinance loan. TIL is regulated by the Federal Reserve under its Regulation Z.

Closing Costs

Calculating closing costs for a borrower is not a simple task. Real estate agents frequently estimate closing costs using simple rules of thumb. Lenders must be more precise by itemizing each cost and then give a good faith estimate of the total.

Figure 10.5 lists the typical closing costs for the sale of a $250,000 studio condo, financed with a $200,000 loan at 7 percent amortized for 30 years. Closing costs may vary by location.

Nonrecurring Closing Costs

The following costs are *one-time charges* that the buyer-borrower usually pays at close of escrow. However, it must be stressed that the payment of closing costs is negotiable between the buyer and seller.

1. *Loan origination fee.* This fee compensates the lender for some of its expenses in originating the loan, preparing documents, and related work. The fee is usually a percentage of the loan.

2. *Title policy.* Title policies are issued by title insurance companies, insuring buyers' and lenders' interests in the property against defects of title. There are two basic types of coverage in California—the California Land Title Association or CLTA, and the American Land Title Association or ALTA. Most lenders require the ALTA policy because it provides additional coverage for the lender. Who pays for the CLTA or standard title policy varies in California. For example, it is customary for the seller to pay in Los Angeles and Orange counties; in Contra Costa and San Francisco counties, it is customary for the buyer to pay. There are other counties, such as Merced and San Joaquin, where the cost is split between buyer and seller. In our example, the buyer is paying for the policy. Buyers normally pay for an ALTA policy. However, it must be stressed that regardless of custom, the issue of who pays can always be negotiated.

3. *Escrow fee.* The escrow fee is charged for handling and supervising the escrow. As with title policies, custom also tends to dictate who pays the escrow fee. The buyer is paying the entire fee in our example, though in reality escrow fees are often split in some fashion between buyer and seller.

4. *Credit report.* The lender obtains a credit report in qualifying a buyer. The cost of the report is usually charged to the buyer.

5. *Appraisal.* The cost of the appraisal varies with the type of loan and property.

6. *Tax service.* This fee is paid to a tax service agency that, for the life of the loan, each year reviews the records of the taxing agencies. If a borrower fails to pay the property taxes, the agency reports this to the lender. If the lender is paying the taxes for the borrower, the agency also obtains the tax bill for the lender.

7. *Recording fees.* These cover the cost of recording the grant deed and deed of trust reconveyance.

8. *Notary fees.* Signatures on documents to be recorded, such as the grant deed, deed of trust, and reconveyances must be notarized.

9. *Pest control inspection fee.* The buyer or seller may pay this charge, depending on local custom. The charge varies from area to area but is always negotiable.

Recurring Closing Costs

The buyer also pays recurring closing costs, which are the expenses that continue during the ownership of the property. In our example in Figure 10.5, the buyer will be paying property tax prorations, hazard insurance premium, and prepaid interest. In other transactions these recurring closing costs could include additional items beyond our example.

1. *Tax proration.* Most sales agreements provide for property tax prorations between the buyer and seller. This includes any prepaid or past due property taxes the seller may have paid or still owes.

2. *Hazard insurance premiums.* Lenders require that the property be covered by insurance. In special flood zones, flood insurance is also required. The buyer pays for the first-year premium at the close of escrow. Our example is a studio condo and part of the insurance for the outside of the building is included in the home-owner association dues. However, insurance is still needed for any interior losses and most condo owners add personal liability coverage.

3. *Prepaid interest.* Depending upon which day escrow closes, the first loan payment may not be due on the first day of the next month, but rather the following month. However, the lender is entitled to interest from the day of funding which is usually the close of escrow. The escrow company collects interest from the buyer on behalf of the lender from the day escrow closes until the day the buyer's loan payments begin to cover the interest. This is called prepaid interest.

10.4 After the Loan: Rights and Responsibilities

Loan Payments

Loan payments are usually due on the first of each month. After the loan is closed, the borrower is notified as to how to make payments. There are basically three methods lenders use to collect payments. One is the *monthly billing system*. Before the first of each month, lenders mail a notice of payment due. Borrowers mail payments with the notice. The second method is the use of *coupons*. Each month, borrowers send in the monthly payment and enclose a coupon furnished by the lender. The third is the automatic monthly withdrawal from the borrower's checking account.

After the first of the year, most lenders give borrowers a yearly statement for the previous year. The statement shows the principal, interest, and taxes and insurance (if included in the payments) that were paid during the year. If taxes and insurance are included in the payment, a reserve analysis is also included. The analysis calculates the amount of tax and insurance reserve that should be in the reserve account.

If there is a shortage in the impound (reserve) account due to a tax or insurance increase, the lender may ask that the shortage be made up immediately. A more common practice is to spread the shortage over the next 12 months along with the required increase for the future. For example, assume a borrower had a shortage of $180 in the reserve account. Rather than demand the entire $180 immediately, the lender would increase the monthly payment by $15, which would make up the shortage in one year. In addition, an adjusted amount would be collected for any shortages expected in the following year. If there is a surplus in the account, the borrower may either apply it to a future mortgage payment, ask for it in cash, or apply it against the principal.

In addition to checking the reserve balances, the lender also analyzes the monthly payment. The payment may be increased or decreased if there has been a change in taxes or insurance premiums.

Late Charges

When borrowers fail to make payments on time, lenders may collect late charges. The amount of the late charge and when it is collected is stated in the promissory note or deed of trust and on the payment coupon. Late charges by type of loan are as follows:

1. *FHA and DVA.* Four percent of the monthly payment if not paid within 15 days of the due date. If the payment, including taxes and insurance, were $1,000 per month, the late charge would be $40.

2. *Cal-Vet.* Payments are late if made after the 10th of the month. The late charge is a flat $4.

3. *Conventional Loans.* Late charges on conventional loans vary. The State of California has a civil code provision that limits late charges on single-family, owner-occupied dwellings to 6 percent of the principal and interest payment, with a $5 minimum. The borrower must be given a minimum of 10 days to make payment, but conventional lenders sometimes charge 5 percent of the monthly payment if not paid within 15 days of the due date.

Prepayment Privileges and Penalties

Most lenders allow borrowers to make extra payments on the principal balance without penalty. This is called a *prepayment privilege*. Typical conventional loans allow 20 percent of the original loan amount as a prepayment privilege per year as set forth in civil code. This 20 percent includes any amounts paid toward principal reduction. For example, if the original loan amount were $100,000, the borrower could make an extra $20,000 payment, that is, 20 percent of $100,000, in any one year without penalty. If the borrower exceeds the privilege, a prepayment penalty of six months' interest on the then remaining balance may be charged. FHA and DVA loans do not permit **prepayment penalties**. However, FHA requires that the interest on a loan be paid for the full month in which it is paid off. Thus, if a loan is paid off on the 5th of the month, the interest must be paid thorough the end of the month. For this reason, when FHA insured loans are to be paid off, especially via a new refinance loan, the refinance is generally scheduled to close near the end of the month.

Cal-Vet does not charge penalties for early repayment. There is no standard prepayment penalty on conventional loans. Effective January 1, 2006, California law (Chap. 531; Financial Code Section 497) prohibits a prepayment penalty on certain owner-occupied dwellings after 36 months. However, recall from Chapter 3, that the time stretches to seven years for loans that come under the Real Property Loan Law. Because of this array of rules and laws, a borrower should check the promissory note and deed of trust to find out what a prepayment penalty, if any, might be.

Finally, in recent times prepayment penalties have virtually disappeared on most conventional loans. However, during times of high turnover due to frequent refinancing, lenders may reinstate prepayment penalties to reduce this "churning."

10.5 Handling Loan Takeovers

Loan Assumptions

Although enforceable due-on-transfer (sale) clauses in most promissory notes prevent the takeover of existing loans by another new owner without the lender's prior permission, a short discussion on loan assumptions is given below.

A real estate loan is *assumed* when the new borrower is approved by the lender and a formal assumption agreement is executed. When a loan is assumed, the original borrower—the seller—can be relieved of responsibility, provided *release of liability* is given. In other words, if the original borrower wants to be relieved of liability, the new borrower must formally assume the loan and the original borrower must obtain a release of liability. Unless there is a complete novation, *both* parties could be liable on a formal assumption. Loans can be formally assumed by applying to the lender.

Subject To's

Where property is purchased "subject to" the existing loan of record, the buyer does not agree to assume primary liability for the debt. Instead, the seller continues on the obligation; that is, although the buyer makes the payments directly to the lender, the seller remains responsible for any deficiency, if a judgment is obtained.

As a practical matter, however, even though the buyer is not obligated to make the payments, the buyer will naturally continue the payments in order to keep the property. This is because the debt is secured by the property and the lender's security is held intact regardless of who makes the payments. Thus, if the buyer fails to make the payments, the lender proceeds against the property through foreclosure. The only time that the distinction between "assumption" and "subject to" becomes important is when the foreclosure results in a deficiency. If a deficiency judgment is obtained, the lender could proceed only against the maker of the note, the seller, if the buyer purchased subject to the existing loan. Had the buyer assumed primary liability for the debt, the buyer could be held liable for the deficiency. As for when a lender may or may not be able to obtain a deficiency judgment, see Chapter 11.

SUMMARY

Loan processing starts with receipt of the loan application, which includes basic information regarding the borrower's employment, income, assets, and debts. The lender usually confirms the information, by obtaining verifications of employment and bank deposit, and checks the borrower's credit. During this time an appraisal is ordered. After a loan package is assembled, the loan is submitted to appropriate individuals or committees for approval.

After the loan is approved, loan documents are prepared by the lender and sent to the escrow agent. Loan documents include a promissory note, deed of trust, and truth-in-lending disclosure statement.

The closing costs paid by the borrower are broken down into nonrecurring and recurring costs. Payments on loans are usually due on the first of the month. If the payments are late, the borrower owes a late charge. If the loan is paid off early, there may be a prepayment penalty. FHA, DVA, and Cal-Vet loans do not have a prepayment penalty, while some conventional loans do. With the lender's permission, some loans may be formally assumed or they may be taken subject to an existing loan.

IMPORTANT TERMS AND CONCEPTS

Annual percentage rate (APR)	*Nonrecurring closing costs*
Closing costs	*Nonsupervised lender*
Credit report	*Prepaid finance charge*
Direct Endorsement (FHA)	*Prepayment penalty*
DVA automatics	*Prepayment privilege*
Equal Credit Opportunity Act (ECOA)	*Real Estate Settlement Procedures Act (RESPA)*
Fair Credit Reporting Act	*Recurring closing costs*
Finance charge	*"Subject to"*
Loan application	*Supervised lender*
Loan assumption	*Truth-in-Lending Law (Regulation Z)*
Loan committee	
Loan origination fee	*Verification of deposit*
Loan package	*Verification of employment*

REVIEWING YOUR UNDERSTANDING

Questions for Discussion

1. Explain why many real estate lenders might qualify the buyer before appraising the property.

2. Briefly explain the purpose of the (a) Equal Credit Opportunity Act, (b) Real Estate Settlement Procedures Act (RESPA), (c) Fair Credit Reporting Act, and (d) Truth-in-Lending Law (Regulation Z).

3. **List five forms, documents, or reports that are contained in a typical loan package.**

4. **Discuss how the procedures for approving a conventional real estate loan may differ from the procedures for approving an FHA-insured loan.**

5. **Define annual percentage rate (APR), prepaid finance charge, and loan origination fee.**

6. **Indicate who in your area customarily pays for the following closing costs: title insurance policy, escrow fee, pest control work, broker's commission, loan origination fee, discount points on an FHA or DVA loan, pest control inspection fee, credit report, appraisal fee, and tax service.**

7. **What is the difference between recurring and nonrecurring closing costs? Give four examples of each.**

8. **What is the difference between assuming a seller's existing loan and purchasing subject to a seller's existing loan?**

Multiple-Choice Questions

1. Which of the following would be the most important information sought by lenders about a potential borrower?
   a. sex of the borrower.
   b. need for a loan.
   c. credit history of the applicant.
   d. racial makeup of the area in which the property is located.

2. Under the Equal Credit Opportunity Act, lenders are required to notify loan applicants on what action has been taken within a reasonable time period not exceeding
   a. two weeks.
   b. 30 days.
   c. three months.
   d. any time mutually agreed to between borrower and lender.

3. Processing an application for a real estate loan may include verification of
   a. employment.
   b. bank deposits.
   c. debts.
   d. all of the above.

4. Under the Fair Credit Reporting Act, an applicant who has been denied credit is entitled to receive which of the following information from the credit reporting agency?
   a. sources of the information
   b. the financial standing of the reporting agency
   c. all of the debtors to whom the agency has furnished reports
   d. only the data that the agency provided the lender that rejected the loan

5. APR as used under Regulation Z stands for
   a. annuity percentage rate.
   b. annual percentage rate.
   c. annual property return.
   d. amortized property return.

6. The last step in originating and processing loans is
   a. formal closing.
   b. qualifying the buyer.
   c. completing the application.
   d. qualifying the property.

7. A federal law that prohibits discrimination in lending solely on the basis of sex or marital status is the
   a. Equality in Sex and Marital Status Act.
   b. Equal Credit Opportunity Act.
   c. Truth-in-Lending Law.
   d. Fair Credit Reporting Act.

8. Property taxes for the fiscal year, July 1 to June 30, are $3,600 and they have not been paid. Escrow closes August 1. The tax proration will be:
   a. credit the seller $300.
   b. debit the seller $3,300.
   c. debit the buyer $3,300.
   d. credit the buyer $300.

9. For a typical home loan, the final approval or rejection rests with the:
   a. real estate broker.
   b. mortgage broker.
   c. underwriter.
   d. escrow officer.

10. Recurring closing costs include
    a. title fee.
    b. property taxes.
    c. appraisal fee.
    d. credit report.

11. Under the Real Estate Settlement Procedures Act, lenders
    a. must comply with all requirements for income properties.
    b. must provide the applicant with a booklet on closing costs.
    c. are required to provide exact closing costs.
    d. may not use their own escrow firms.

12. The loan committee of a conventional home lender
    a. contains at least three members.
    b. might be one individual with authority limited to a specific dollar amount.
    c. typically meets only three days per week.
    d. has only limited authority to approve loans, since final authority for loan approval always rests with the chief managing officer of the lender.

13. In California, once a person has an owner-occupied home, any refinances or junior loans secured by a junior lien
    a. are illegal.
    b. are made only by private lenders.
    c. involve a three-day right of rescission.
    d. are not made by institutional lenders.

14. Nonrecurring closing costs include which of the following items: I. Loan origination fees, II. Escrow fees, III. Hazard insurance fees, IV. Tax reserves, V. Recording fees
    a. I, II, and III only.
    b. II, III, and IV only.
    c. I, II, and IV only.
    d. I, II, and V only.

15. Loan payments, whether required on the first of the month or another date,
    a. may include reserves for taxes and insurance.
    b. are billed by either the monthly billing system, the coupon method, or by automatic deduction from a checking account.
    c. may involve charges for a late payment.
    d. involve all of the above.

16. The APR for a $100,000 loan at 7 percent amortized for 30 years, with no loan fees or financing charges of any sort is:
    a. 8.1%
    b. 7.4%
    c. 7.12%
    d. 7%

17. Under the Truth-in-Lending Law, the initials APR represent
    a. nominal interest rate.
    b. effective interest rate.
    c. stated interest rate.
    d. any of the foregoing.

18. Loan escrows may not close without full compliance with the written instructions of
    a. lender and borrower.
    b. escrow company and borrower.
    c. escrow company and lender.
    d. broker and borrower.

19. RESPA is specifically designed to
    a. reduce settlement costs.
    b. standardize settlement costs.
    c. accomplish both (a) and (b).
    d. accomplish neither (a) nor (b).

20. Assumption of a loan is best illustrated when a
    a. property is sold subject to the loan.
    b. new owner of the property makes payments on a timely basis.
    c. takeover buyer signs a formal assumption and is approved by the lender.
    d. seller agrees to let buyer assume the loan, subject to approval by buyer's agent.

CHAPTER 11
FORECLOSURES AND OTHER LENDING PROBLEMS

PREVIEW

The basic responsibilities of the parties to a real estate loan appear very simple. In exchange for money loaned, borrowers agree to repay the loan according to the terms and conditions stipulated in the promissory note and deed of trust. However, in actual practice there is much more to real estate loans than merely repaying principal and interest.

After completing this chapter, you should be able to:

1. Explain the major provisions outlined in a typical promissory note and deed of trust.

2. Outline the steps in a foreclosure procedure.

3. Demonstrate why lenders in California prefer trust deeds over mortgages as security for their loans.

4. List five ways a borrower and lender can minimize the possibility of a default and foreclosure.

5. Discuss how private and government mortgage insurance has reduced the lender's risk in granting real estate loans.

6. Calculate the mechanics of insurance coverage under PMI for 90 percent and 95 percent loans.

7. Describe the controversial practice known as redlining.

8. Explain the role of the Community Reinvestment Act (CRA).

11.1 Collateral Provisions of Deeds of Trust

Figure 11.1a is an example of the front page of a typical deed of trust, while Figure 11.1b is a list of major items in the complete document, which can run many pages, and contains several provisions designed to reduce the chance of default and foreclosure. The deed of trust defines the rights and duties of the three parties to the loan—the trustor or borrower, trustee or title holder, and the beneficiary or lender. Even if the trustor is current with payments on the promissory note, the beneficiary can still foreclose should the trustor default in the performance of any of the other requirements—the collateral provisions of the trust deed—including the following:

1. *Maintenance of the property.* The typical trust deed requires the trustor to keep the property in good condition, to pay for labor and materials whenever improvements are made, not to lay waste to the property and to comply with local building ordinances and other laws affecting the property—in short, to preserve the value of the property as security for the repayment of the loan.

2. *Hazard insurance.* To protect the security, the trustor agrees to maintain basic fire and windstorm insurance, with a "loss payee" clause in favor of the beneficiary. Under a loss payee provision the lender may use any insurance proceeds to reduce the loan indebtedness, or turn over the funds to the owner to rebuild. When the trustor fails to maintain insurance satisfactory to the beneficiary, the latter may obtain a policy and charge the cost to the trustor. This is usually accomplished by adding the premium cost to the principal, constituting an **advance** to the trustor, thus resulting in a default. Therefore, if a borrower fails to maintain adequate insurance, the lender may accelerate the loan—that is, call the principal immediately due and payable.

3. *Property taxes and other liens.* The trustor agrees to pay for property taxes, assessments, and all prior liens. Unless this is done, the beneficiary's interest can be eliminated by a tax sale. To help guard against this, the beneficiary may pay for these tax liens and then be reimbursed by the borrower. Depending on the lender, such advances may be billed to the trustor directly, with possible foreclosure action in the event of failure to repay, *or* the beneficiary may simply add the advances to the principal indebtedness. The loan is considered in default until the lender is reimbursed.

Order No.
Escrow or Loan No.

RECORDING REQUESTED BY

When Recorded Mail To:

_____

SPACE ABOVE THIS LINE FOR RECORDER'S USE

DEED OF TRUST WITH ASSIGNMENT OF RENTS
(With Acceleration Clause)

This DEED OF TRUST, made _____, between _____ herein called TRUSTOR, whose address is _____, Placer Title Company, a California corporation, herein called TRUSTEE, and _____, herein called BENEFICIARY, WITNESSETH: That Trustor grants to Trustee in Trust, with Power of Sale, that property in the _____ County of _____, State of California, described as:

Together with the rents, issues and profits thereof, subject, however, to the right, power and authority hereinafter given to and conferred upon Beneficiary to collect and apply such rents, issues and profits.

For the Purpose of Securing (1) Payment of the sum of _____ with interest thereon according to the terms of a promissory note or notes of even date herewith made by Trustor, payable to order of Beneficiary and extensions or renewals thereof, and (2) the performance of each agreement of Trustor incorporated by reference or contained herein (3) Payment of additional sums and interest thereon which may hereafter be loaned to Trustor, or his successors or assigns, when evidenced by a promissory note or notes reciting that they are secured by this Deed of Trust.

If the Trustor shall convey or alienate said property or any part thereof or any interest therein or shall be divested of his title in any manner or way, whether voluntary or involuntary any indebtedness or obligation secured hereby, irrespective of the maturity date expressed in any note evidencing the same, at the option of the holder hereof and without demand or notice shall become due and payable immediately.

Signature of Trustor

BY _____   BY _____

BY _____   BY _____

BY _____   BY _____

Dated:
STATE OF CALIFORNIA   )
COUNTY OF _____)

On _____ before me, the undersigned Notary Public in and for said County and State, personally appeared
_____
_____
_____
personally known to me (or proved to me on the basis of satisfactory evidence) to be the person(s) whose name(s) is/are subscribed to the within instrument and acknowledged to me that he/she/they executed the same in his/her/their authorized capacity(ies), and that by his/her/their signature(s) on the instrument the person(s), or the entity upon behalf of which the person(s) acted, executed the instrument.

Witness my hand and official seal.

_____
Notary Public in and for said County and State   (Space above for official notarial area.)

Figure 11.1a Partial deed of trust form.

1. *Document number:* This is assigned to the document by the County Recorder's office. The book and page of the County Recorder's index books where the document is entered are shown adjacent to the document number.

2. *County recorder stamps:* The large stamp reflects the time and date of recording of the document as well as reference to the fee paid for recording. These stamps are placed on the document by the clerk in the Recorder's Office.

3. *Recording requested by:* This identifies the party requesting that the document be recorded and often shows the names of title companies when they submit groups of documents to the county for recording.

4. *When recorded mail to:* After recording, the document will be mailed by the county to the addressee shown in this section. This would be the lender who issued the loan.

5. *Title order no. and escrow no.:* On this line the title company order number will appear along with the customer escrow number if the document was recorded as part of a title order that culminated in the closing of an escrow.

6. *Date of execution:* This should be the date of the signing of the deed of trust by the trustor (borrower) and also can be the date the document is prepared.

7. *Trustor:* The name of the borrower, who is the record owner and identified as the trustor, is shown, as well as the borrower's status of record.

8. *Trustee:* The name of the entity that is being granted the property with legal title to exercise a power of sale if necessary is shown and is referred to as the trustee.

9. *Beneficiary:* The name of the lender is shown and is referred to as the beneficiary. This is the creditor to whom the debt is owing.

10. *Words of conveyance:* These are the words used by which legal title to the property is transferred from the trustor to the trustee with power of sale. On the sample the wording "grants, transfers, and assigns to trustee, in trust, with power of sale" satisfies this need.

11. *Legal description:* This identifies the property in question, which is usually by lot, block, and tract, by metes and bounds, or by government survey.

12. *Amount of indebtedness:* The amount shown in the promissory note.

13. *Signature of the trustor:* The signature of the trustor (borrower) will appear on the line in this section, and the name should be printed or typed beneath the signature.

14. *Acknowledgment:* In this area a formal declaration is personally made before a notary public by the borrower who has executed (signed) the document, that such execution is borrower's act and deed. (This is a requirement before the instrument can be accepted for recording.) The borrower signs before the notary public, who then completes the acknowledgment.

15. *Venue:* This identifies the state and county where the acknowledgment is taken.

16. *Notary seal or stamp:* In this section the official seal of the notary public must be affixed or stamped.

Figure 11.1b Partial deed of trust form (*continued*).

4. *Assignment of rents.* This clause is found in almost every trust deed. It provides that upon default by the trustor, the beneficiary may take possession of the property through a court-appointed trustee or receiver and collect the rents, applying them to the loan and to costs and expenses incurred. When there are sufficient sums collected from tenants in a property, it is possible that by applying them to the delinquent payments during the reinstatement period, default may be avoided.

11.2 Default and Foreclosure

Borrowers default on repayment of loans for a variety of reasons, some because of events beyond their control. Medical expenses, disability, death, and financial reversals such as loss of a job or business probably head the list. Other circumstances include the dissolution of marriage, bankruptcy, the excessive use of credit, and poor budgeting, although these circumstances are not considered beyond the control of the individual. Unless arrangements can be made with the lender to work out a satisfactory schedule for repayment following default, foreclosure is the ultimate price that the delinquent borrower must pay. However, most lenders try to avoid foreclosure wherever possible and use it only as a last resort, since most lenders are in the business of lending money and do not want to become involved in owning and managing real estate.

As noted earlier, a borrower may be in default not only through delinquency on payments of principal and interest, but also when there is a violation of other terms of the trust deed agreement to maintain the property and pay other liens in a timely manner. Regardless of the violation, lenders in California must follow a prescribed procedure in removing the delinquent debtor. Foreclosure may be accomplished through either trustee's sale or judicial sale.

Trustee's Sale

Virtually all trust deeds contain a *power of sale* clause, which empowers the trustee, in the event of default by the trustor, to sell the property at public auction. While the provisions of the power of sale are a matter of contract and may vary from instrument to instrument, there are statutes that specifically regulate foreclosures through a **trustee's sale**, found in California's Civil Code. The statutory requirements are as follows:

1. *Notice of default.* After the beneficiary is reasonably certain that a trustor is unable to make good on delinquent installment payments, the beneficiary physically delivers the note and trust deed to the trustee. The trustee is instructed to record a **Notice of Default** in the county where the property is located. It must be recorded at least three months before a notice of sale can be advertised. An example of such notice is given in Figure 11.2. The notice must contain a correct legal description of the property, name of trustor, nature of the breach, and a statement to the effect that the party executing the notice of default has elected to sell the property in order to satisfy the obligation. While a trustor requests a Notice of Default through the Deed of Trust, under California law *anyone* may request a copy of the notice.

   Within 10 days after filing the Notice of Default, a copy must be sent by registered or certified mail to anyone whose request for notice appears on record. To all others with a recorded interest that may be affected, the time is extended to 30 days. This notice must be sent by the trustee.

   During the three-month period preceding the advertising for sale, the trustor may reinstate the loan by paying all delinquent installments, costs, and trustee's fees. This **right of reinstatement**, or period of reinstatement, continues until five business days before the scheduled sale.

2. *Notice of sale.* After expiration of the reinstatement period, which includes three weeks for advertising the time and place of the trustee's sale, the beneficiary is entitled to the entire unpaid balance of the note, plus costs and trustee's fees. But the trustee must first record a **Notice of Sale**, similar to the sample shown in Figure 11.3. The Notice of Trustee's Sale must be recorded at least two weeks before the sale.

   The notice must contain a correct identification of the property, such as the street address or legal description. It also must be published in a newspaper of general circulation in the county or jurisdiction in which the property is located. The publication must appear at least once a week for three weeks, not more than seven days apart. The notice must also be posted in a public place, such as a courthouse, and in some conspicuous place on the property, such as an attachment to a front door. Notice must be posted on the property no later than *20 days* prior to sale. The sale must be held in a public place, during business hours, on a weekday, Monday through Friday. A copy of the Notice of Sale must also be

RECORDING REQUESTED BY
Serrano Reconveyance Company

AND WHEN RECORDED MAIL TO
NAME Serrano Reconveyance Company
STREET ADDRESS 13640 Roscoe Boulevard
CITY STATE ZIP Panorama City, CA 90051

—————— SPACE ABOVE THIS LINE FOR RECORDER'S USE ——————

NOTICE OF DEFAULT AND ELECTION TO SELL
UNDER DEED OF TRUST

NOTICE IS HEREBY GIVEN:

SERRANO RECONVEYANCE COMPANY , a corporation, is Trustee under a Deed of Trust

dated November 1, 20XX

executed by Mr. & Mrs. John Foresight
as Trustor, to secure obligations

in favor of Serrano Mortgage Company
(Loan # 277529)
as beneficiary

recorded November 10, 20XX as document no. 77-281295
in book T10686 page 822 of Official Records in the office of the
Recorder of Los Angeles County, California, describing land therein as:

Lot 11 of Tract 5852 as per map recorded in Book 61, page 69 of Maps; and that
portion of Montevista, in the City of Los Angeles, County of Los Angeles, as per
Map recorded in Book 6, Page 324 of Miscellaneous Records, all known as 10522
Fernglen Ave, Tujunga
said obligations

including one note for the sum of $ 23,000

That the beneficial interest under such deed and the obligations secured thereby are owned by the undersigned;
That a breach of, and default in, the obligations for which such deed is security has occurred in that payment has
not been made of:

The November 15, 20XX and all subsequent installments are now in default
with interest paid to October 10, 20XX .

That by reason thereof, the undersigned, present beneficiary under such deed, has executed and delivered to said
Trustee a written Declaration of Default and Demand for Sale, and has deposited with said Trustee such deed and
all documents evidencing obligations secured thereby, and has declared and does hereby declare all sums secured
thereby immediately due and payable and has elected and does hereby elect to cause the trust property to be sold
to satisfy the obligations secured thereby.

NOTICE

You may have the right to cure the default described herein and reinstate the mortgage or deed of trust.
Section 2924c of the Civil Code permits certain defaults to be cured upon the payment of the amounts
required by that section without requiring payment of that portion of principal and interest which would not
be due had no default occurred. Where reinstatement is possible, if the default is not cured within three months
following the recording of this notice, the right of reinstatement will terminate and the property may be sold.
To determine if reinstatement is possible and the amount, if any, necessary to cure the default, contact the
beneficiary or mortgagee or their successors in interest, whose name and address as of the date of this notice is

Name Serrano Mortgage Company

Address 3731 Wilshire Blvd, Los Angeles

Dated March 8, 20XX

Serrano Mortgage Company

Penny Pincher, President

Title Order No. _____ T.S. No. 47739

TS-1 A&B(o.s.)

Figure 11.2 Sample notice of default.

Foreclosures

Notice of Trustee's Sale
Under Deed of Trust
TF 47739
Loan No. 277529
57831
BT

Notice is hereby given that SERRANO RECONVEYANCE COMPANY, A California corporation as trustee, or successor trustee, or substituted trustee pursuant to the deed of trust recorded November 10, 20XX in book T10686 page 822 of Official Records in the office of the County Recorder of Los Angeles County, California, and pursuant to the Notice of Default and Election to Sell thereunder recorded March 21, 20XX Instrument No. 77-281295 of said Official Records, will sell on August 16, 20XX at 11:00 A.M., at the Oxford Street entrance to the building located at 3731 Wilshire Boulevard, City of Los Angeles, County of Los Angeles, State of California, at public auction, to the highest bidder for cash (payable at the time of sale in lawful money of the United States) all right, title, and interest conveyed to and now held by it under said deed in the property situated in said County and State described as follows:

PARCEL 1:

Lot 11 of Tract 5852, in the City of Los Angeles, County of Los Angeles, State of California, as per map recorded in Book 61, Page 67 of Maps, in the office of the County Recorder of said County.

PARCEL 2:

That portion of Montevista, in the City of Los Angeles, County of Los Angeles, State of California, as per map recorded in Book 6, Page 324, of Miscellaneous Records, described as follows:

Beginning at Southeasterly corner of Lot 11 of Tract 5852, in the City of Los Angeles, as per map recorded in Book 61 Page 67 of Maps; thence along the Easterly line of said Lot 11, North 0 degrees 01' 40" West 40 feet to the Northeasterly corner of said Lot 11; thence Easterly along the Easterly prolongation of the Northerly line of said Lot 11 to a line that is parallel with and distant 10 feet Easterly, measured at right angles, from the Easterly line of said Tract 5852; thence South 11 degrees 16' 40" East to the Intersection with the Easterly prolongation of the Southerly line of said Lot 11; thence Westerly along the Easterly prolongation of said Southerly line to the point of beginning.

Property Address purportedly known as: 10522 Frengien Av., Tujunga, CA 91042.

Said sale will be made, but without covenant or warranty, express or implied, regarding title, possession or encumbrances, to satisfy the indebtedness secured by said Deed, including the fee and expense of the trustee and of the trusts created by said deed, advances thereunder, with interest as provided therein, and the unpaid principal of the note secured by said deed; to wit: $23,000.00 with interest thereon from November 15, 20XX as provided in said note.

Dated: July 8, 20XX

SERRANO RECONVEYANCE
COMPANY,
as such Trustee
(213) 385-3321
By J.E. Cornwall,
President
Authorized officer

(J85505 Tues. Jul 19, 26, Aug 2)

Figure 11.3 Sample notice of trustee's sale.

mailed to those who had requested a copy of the notice of default.

3. *Final sale.* Any person, including the trustor and beneficiary, but *not* the trustee, may bid on the property through auction. The holder of the debt may offset the amount owed, up to the amount of the debt. Others must pay cash or its equivalent. A trustee's deed, similar to the one illustrated in Figure 11.4, is issued to the highest bidder. Any surplus funds—that is, funds remaining after paying off all costs, fees, and expenses, along with all junior liens in order of their priority—are given to the trustor.

No right of redemption exists after a trustee's sale. The purchaser acquires all rights held by the former owner, becoming the successor in interest, and is entitled to immediate possession, subject to those having rights prior to the time when the trust deed was recorded. (See Figure 11.5.) Lenders in California prefer the use of the Trustee's Sale under a Deed of Trust due to the fact that the procedures involved and the time required, which is approximately four months, are relatively easy to determine, whereas foreclosures under the judicial method and foreclosures involving mortgages entail court actions, with consequent uncertainty as to time. If a trustee's sale is used instead of a judicial foreclosure, the lender cannot sue for a deficiency should one exist.

Judicial Sale

Instead of a trustee's sale, a trust deed may also be foreclosed as a mortgage, that is, through court action. Court foreclosures of trust deeds are not common and usually occur only when the lender seeks a deficiency judgment.

1. *Procedure.* After serving a complaint upon the defaulting debtor, trial is held and a judgment is entered through a decree of foreclosure and order of sale by an officer of the court, such as a sheriff or marshall. Meanwhile, the debtor has the right to reinstate by paying all delinquent installments plus costs and attorney's fees.

2. *Sale.* A notice of the time, place, and purpose of the sale is posted and publicized. The court thereafter conducts a public auction sale. The highest bidder receives a Certificate of Sale.

This conveys title to the property, subject to the debtor's right of redemption for a period of one year after the sale if there is a

RECORDING REQUESTED BY

SERRANO RECONVEYANCE COMPANY

AND WHEN RECORDED MAIL TO

NAME   Lone Successor

ADDRESS   5800 Felton Avenue

CITY & STATE   Van Nuys, CA 19401

If Required Affix Documentary Stamps Here

SPACE ABOVE THIS LINE FOR RECORDER'S USE

Documentary transfer tax $ 31.35

[X] Computed on full value of property conveyed, or

[ ] Computed on full value less liens & encumbrances remaining thereon at time of sale.

Safeco Title Insurance Company

Signature of declarant or agent determining tax - firm name

[ ] Unincorporated area   City of Tujunga

TRUSTEE'S DEED

Executed by Serrano Reconveyance Company, a corporation, as Trustee under the deed of Trust referred to below and herein called "Trustee," to **Lone Successor, a single person**

herein called "Grantee".

The Deed of Trust herein referred to was executed by **John Foresight & Mary Foresight** and recorded on **November 10, 20XX** in book **T10686** page **822**, of Official Records in the office of the Recorder of **Los Angeles** County, California (herein referred to as "said Official Records", "said Recorder" and "said County and State", respectively) and was made for the purpose of securing obligations stated therein and other obligations thereunder.

Default under said Deed of Trust occurred as set forth in a notice of default and election to sell which was recorded in book **162** page **4** of said Official Records, and such default existed at the time of sale. After the lapse of at least 3 months after the recording of said notice of default and election to sell, Trustee gave notice of sale of the property described below, stating the time and place thereof, in the manner and for a time as required by law and by the provisions of said Deed of Trust. All requirements of said Deed of Trust for sale thereunder, all requirements of law regarding the mailing, publication, posting or personal delivery of copies of notice of default or notice of sale, and all other requirements of law relating to the making of said sale and this Deed were complied with.

Trustee, in the exercise of its powers under said Deed of Trust, offered said property for sale at public auction on **August 16, 20XX** at **11:00** A.M. o'clock, the time stated in said notice

and at the place stated in said notice in **the Oxfords St entrance to the building at 3731 Wilshire Blvd. Los Angeles,** in said county and state, and sold said property to grantee for $ **28,500**, subject to all prior liens and encumbrances, said grantee being the highest bidder.

Trustee, in the exercise of its powers under said Deed of Trust, hereby grants to grantee, without any covenant or warranty whatsoever, the property referred to herein, which is located in said County and State and described as follows:

Lot 11 of Tract 5852 as per map recorded in Book 61, page 69 of Maps; and that portion of Montevista, in the City of Los Angeles, County of Los Angeles, as per Map recorded in Book 6, Page 324 of Miscellaneous Records, all known as 10522 Fernglen Ave, Tujunga.

Dated **August 16, 20XX**

STATE OF CALIFORNIA

COUNTY OF _____ } SS.

On _____ before me, the undersigned, a Notary Public in and for said County and State, personally appeared _____ known to me to be the _____ President, and _____ known to me to be Secretary of the corporation that executed the within Instrument, known to me to be the persons who executed the within Instrument on behalf of the corporation therein named, and acknowledged to me that such corporation executed the within instrument pursuant to its by-laws or a resolution of its board of directors.

_____
Signature of Notary

_____
Name (Typed or Printed) of Notary

SECURITY TITLE INSURANCE COMPANY

By _____   *Joe E. Lewis*   Vice President
Joe E. Lewis

By _____   *Minica M Bond*   Assistant Secretary
Minica M Bond

FOR NOTARY SEAL OR STAMP

MAIL TAX
STATEMENTS TO: _____
Name

Title Order No. _____   T. S. No. _____
Address, City & State   Zip

TS-23 (G.S.)

Figure 11.4 Sample trustee's deed for a foreclosure resale.

WHY CALIFORNIA LENDERS PREFER
DEEDS OF TRUST OVER MORTGAGES

DEED OF TRUST	ITEMS OF COMPARISON	MORTGAGE
Trustee's sale, no court action	Foreclosure	Expensive court action required
As little as 111 to 120 days	Time period to foreclosure	Sometimes up to one year
No redemption rights	Redemption rights of the borrower after foreclosure	Right to redeem for up to one year

In short, it is quicker and cheaper to foreclose under a deed of trust than under a mortgage.

Figure 11.5 Deeds of trust versus mortgages.

deficiency. If there is no deficiency, the deed is issued after three months. In addition to payment of the debt, the debtor is ordinarily also required to pay legal interest. If no redemption is made within this time, a deed is issued to the successful bidder.

Note that there is a right of "reinstatement" when a trustee's sale is undertaken. This allows the trustor to pay all delinquencies, including late charges, plus all costs of foreclosure, including trustee's fees, recording charges, publishing costs, etc. The trustor is then in a position to resume scheduled payments under the loan. When a judicial foreclosure is undertaken, there is a right of "redemption." This involves repayment of the debt.

3. *Deficiency judgments.* In the event that the sale does not bring enough funds to satisfy the debt, the creditor may obtain a **deficiency judgment.** However, certain types of loans are not

subject to deficiency judgments under California's "Anti-deficiency Law." Purchase money loans on owner-occupied dwellings up to four units are the exceptions. Thus, when a person borrows money to purchase a home and thereafter loses it through foreclosure action, no deficiency judgment is permitted, except for FHA- and DVA-guaranteed loans. In the case of FHA and DVA loans, federal law supersedes state law, and the FHA and the DVA can and do seek deficiency judgments.

Deed in Lieu of Foreclosure

To avoid the costly and time-consuming process of foreclosure, the lender may accept a voluntary conveyance from the defaulting borrower. Usually this is accomplished by a **Deed in Lieu of Foreclosure**, though it could be by grant or **quitclaim deed**, which should be simultaneously recorded with a deed of reconveyance. One advantage of such a transaction for the borrower is that there won't be a deficiency judgment. The downside is that lenders will not accept such a deed if there are other liens, such as unpaid real estate taxes, because lenders want to take property free and clear of any other claims.

A Deed in Lieu requires cancellation of debt and reconveyance, while a quitclaim deed does not necessarily require this. Moreover, some future creditor may still view a Deed in Lieu of Foreclosure as a repossession and the borrower as a poor credit risk. The stigma is the same whether the loss of property is through a Deed in Lieu of Foreclosure or by foreclosure itself. There is also a serious question regarding liens not eliminated by a quitclaim deed, but this is better left to an attorney.

11.3 Minimizing Loan Defaults

It has been said that a loan that is not good for the lender is not good for the borrower. If the loan is marginal, as when the credit rating is poor, the borrower is more likely to default on payments, with the result that the lender will end up with a sour loan followed by foreclosure and, usually, the lender will take over the property. This section outlines a variety of ways to minimize or mitigate the chance of loss for both borrower and lender.

Impound Accounts

One way to reduce the possibility of default is through the establishment of an **impound account**. Under this concept, the borrower is required to pay, as a condition for receiving the loan, a pro rata portion of the annual property taxes and insurance each month. This effectively forces the debtor to budget each month amounts that would fall due in large sums if paid only once or twice a year. Requiring such payments 12 times a year by having borrowers add one-twelfth of the tax bill and insurance premiums to monthly payments of principal and interest reduces the chance of default. After all, even if the debtor is current on loan payments, the property may go into foreclosure because of default in payments on other property-related debts, in accordance with the terms of the trust deed.

In some areas an impound account is referred to as an **escrow account** or *loan trust fund*. Whatever its designation, it means the same. The lender deposits the tax and insurance portions of the installment payments into an escrow or impound account, remitting payments to the tax collector and insurance company as they fall due. The lender is assured that these bills are paid, while the debtor is relieved of a large obligation falling due in one or two lump sums at a time when it may be inconvenient to pay. Borrowers may establish these accounts and bear the responsibility for proper payments themselves.

Forbearance

By far the most common default on real estate loans is for delinquent payments. When borrowers have legitimate reasons for their inability to pay, lenders will often make special arrangements to help such debtors retain their properties. Any arrangement that effectively delays or forestalls foreclosure action is referred to as **forbearance**. There are various ways in which lenders (through their loan administration efforts) can assist borrowers. These include a variety of moratorium schemes and recastings.

Moratorium

A **moratorium** is a temporary suspension or **waiver** of payments. It acts to delay or defer action for collection of a debt. Four types of moratoria are explained below.

1. *Waiver of principal payments.* One form of moratorium is the suspension of principal payments, allowing delinquent borrowers to regain their financial balance. Only interest is paid in such cases. A variation of this moratorium is skipping the entire monthly payment of Principal and Interest. For instance, if P&I ran $1,200 per month, and the lender permitted up to 10 months suspension, then $12,000 (10 × $1,200) would be added to the principal, which would result in higher payments once resumed.

2. *Deferring of interest.* Another form of moratorium is the suspension of interest payments. Interest is not forgiven but is added to the principal indebtedness, much like loans with negative amortizations. This can offer significant relief to the debtor whose installments are almost all interest—either because it is a relatively high-interest loan or because it is not a seasoned loan, or both.

   In the case of DVA loans, interest that accrues during a period of forbearance becomes a part of the guaranteed indebtedness. Consequently, holders of DVA mortgages can assist veterans through forbearance without incurring loss.

3. *Partial payments.* Lenders may also agree to accept partial payments. Indeed, the DVA encourages holders of GI loans to extend such privileges so that veterans may be given every opportunity to retain their homes while awaiting financial recovery. This may result in negative amortization, but it's a way to preserve one's property from foreclosure. If by contrast payments were made because of special circumstances, such as temporary unemployment or disability, lenders may be persuaded to stop foreclosure proceedings if assurances can be made that an extra, say, $100 per month will be paid to repay the delinquent installments.

4. *Prepayments.* Prepayments credited to principal in the past may be reapplied for the purpose of curing a default or preventing a subsequent default. Similarly, some loans may have been credited with lump-sum payments derived from proceeds of a partial sale of property to highway departments, local municipalities, or private parties.

Recasting

Another form of borrower assistance is through **recasting** or loan modification. It actually involves a change in loan terms. In order to assist a delinquent borrower, the lender may agree to rearrange the loan in some fashion. This can be done at the outset, when the debtor first defaults, or it may be done after a moratorium, in order to minimize the impact of having to repay both current and past installments.

The Department of Housing and Urban Development (HUD) adopted special forbearance regulations aimed at helping financially troubled homeowners save their houses. Under the relaxed rules, forbearance may be granted under any circumstances contributing to a default beyond the homeowner's control. These circumstances may include, for example, an overextension of the homeowner's income due to rising utility costs and inflation. These are three methods of recasting:

1. *Extended term.* If permitted by law or regulations, one way to recast a loan is to extend the original period of repayment, sometimes called *reamortization.* Extending to 30 years an existing loan that has, say, 15 years remaining of an original 25-year term will result in lower monthly payments. Some lenders may extract a higher interest rate for this privilege, but the alternative might be foreclosure. Regulations may, however, prohibit institutional lenders from extending the term while a default exists.

2. *Increase of debt.* Though it's unlikely in situations where borrowers are going under, some lenders may increase the debt when they are satisfied that the debtor's dilemma will be solved, tiding over the debtor whose financial reversals are apparently temporary in nature. Again, the lender may exact a higher interest rate, but the new note can be extended for a longer term that may more than offset the increase in payments due to the higher rate. The proceeds of the new loan might be put in an "assigned" savings account for the borrower, which is then used to make the payments on both the old and new loans.

   Under DVA-backed loans, advances may be made from the assigned account for maintenance, protective repairs, taxes, assessments, and hazard insurance. GI debtors may well save their homes when such funds are advanced.

3. *Reduction of interest.* Still another form of recasting a loan is a reduction of the interest rate, even if the reduction is only temporary. While most uncommon, a lender may be amenable to reducing the interest rate when the market warrants it. For example, an existing 8.75 percent rate might be reduced to 8 percent when the market is at, say, 7.5 percent.

Mortgage Guaranty Insurance

Insurance against loss through foreclosure is likely the best means of protecting the financial interests of lenders. This is accomplished through public and private mortgage insurance plans.

Government-Insured and Guaranteed Loans

With the introduction of Cal-Vet in 1923, the FHA program in 1934, and the DVA program in 1944, many more buyers have been able to enter the housing market. This is because of the willingness on the part of lenders to extend loans with high loan-to-value ratios that are backed by insurance or a government guarantee.

Federal Housing Administration Options

As noted in an earlier chapter, risks to lenders can be eliminated through a federal insurance plan. The FHA is not the lender, but rather the insurer of the loan made by a qualified lender. Both the Private Mortgage Insurance (PMI) and MMI are now automatically discontinued when the loan-to-value reaches 78 percent of the original loan amount via principal pay down. On most FHA loans the typical length of time to reach this 78 percent loan-to-value level is seven to eight years. Under the plan, the lender is assured that in case of foreclosure, the FHA will pay any loss in either cash or government debentures. Or the lender may, with prior FHA approval, assign the defaulted loan directly to the FHA before final foreclosure action in exchange for insurance benefits. Whichever way it acquires the property, the FHA sometimes repairs, refurbishes, and resells the property in order to minimize the losses to the FHA. In most cases, however, the FHA simply sells the property in an "as is" condition.

The cost of the insurance is borne by the borrower. Either the Mortgage Insurance Premium (MIP) is paid upfront in cash or it is financed as part of the loan. The mutual mortgage insurance (MMI) is paid with the monthly payments.

FHA also offers a loan assignment program. For loans more than three months in default, and when the cause is not the fault of the borrower, the loan is assigned to HUD, which will pay off the lender. The homeowners thereafter make payments directly to HUD under a flexible schedule designed to meet their needs. Contact your local FHA office for additional information on this and their preforeclosure program.

Department of Veterans Affairs Options

For qualified veterans, the DVA guarantees lenders that, if the veteran defaults, the DVA will satisfy at least part of the debt. Suppose, for example, that a 100 percent loan is made for the purchase price of $200,000. Assume the property thereafter goes on the auction block under foreclosure action and sells for $170,000. Finally, assume that there is $180,000 owing at the time of the foreclosure. How much will the DVA be liable for? Recall from Chapter 6 that loans in excess of $144,000 have a maximum guarantee of 25 percent of the loan balance.

Multiplying the $180,000 loan balance by 25 percent equals $45,000. Next we compare this figure with the *actual* loss (ignoring costs), which is $180,000 less $170,000, or $10,000. Hence, the DVA's liability to the lender will be limited to $10,000.

Veterans are charged an up-front funding fee for this guarantee. However, should a deficiency arise, the veteran is liable for any claim paid by the DVA, which is said to have the right of *subrogation* for the amount paid.

Suppose a veteran homeowner sells a property secured by a GI loan. How can the veteran be released from liability for any default caused by the new owner? There are two ways to do this: (1) pay off the existing loan in full from the proceeds of the purchaser's new loan, or (2) secure a written release from the Department of Veterans Affairs.

Even though a buyer offers to assume the veteran seller's personal liability for the repayment of the loan, the veteran must still obtain written release from liability on the loan from the DVA. To qualify for a release, four tests must be met:

1. A new purchaser must have requisite entitlement remaining.

2. The loan must not be delinquent.

3. The purchaser transferee must be acceptable to the DVA from an income and credit standpoint.

4. The purchaser assumes the loan and the indemnity obligation signed by the veteran at the time the loan was originally made.

Like the FHA, the DVA offers forbearance for vets in foreclosure. Once the veteran has missed three payments, the lender must notify the DVA and provide a description of what it has done to remedy the default. The DVA provides counseling and mediation services between lender and borrower.

Under the Soldiers and Sailors Civil Relief Act, various forms of relief are provided to active military members who get behind with their mortgage payments. Applicants are encouraged to double check with military lawyers to determine eligibility.

Federal Home Loan Mortgage Corporation (FHLMC)

Guidelines on alternatives to foreclosures give mortgage lenders wide discretion to extend relief to borrowers who encounter hardships, are cooperative, and have proper regard for fulfilling their obligations. Among recommended remedies, Freddie Mac encourages temporary indulgences, allowing borrowers up to three months to cure any delinquency.

California Veterans Farm and Home Purchase Act Assistance

The Cal-Vet plan, as this program is called, contains a life insurance feature that only indirectly benefits the lender, the Department of

Veterans Affairs of the State of California, which holds legal title to the security. The veteran debtor is the party who benefits most from the insurance feature.

Qualified veterans under Cal-Vet financing must purchase life and disability insurance through its home protection plan. The plan insures the debtor's life for the amount of the unpaid loan balance at the time of death. A double indemnity clause is also included, until age 70, up to a maximum of $75,000. The monthly premiums for the home protection plan, including the optional benefits, are based on the age of the insured, varying from $.50 to $.55 per $1,000 of unpaid balance, in addition to a flat monthly charge for a disability benefit. The portion of the life insurance policy covering the remaining loan balance is paid to the California Department of Veterans Affairs.

Permanent and total disability benefits are included for veterans under age 65 and employed full-time, including full-time home-makers. Under the plan, the veteran's full loan payment is paid after the first three months of total disability and payments continue until the contract is paid off or for a maximum of three years, whichever occurs first.

Private Mortgage Insurance

As Chapter 5 discusses, in addition to public insurance, private companies have devised insurance plans to reduce, if not eliminate, the risk of loss on conventional mortgages. Lenders protect themselves by generally requiring PMI coverage on loans in excess of 80 percent Loan-to-Value (LTV). PMI-insured loans can be made up to 97 percent LTV. Private mortgage insurance does not insure the entire loan amount, only the top portion of the loan. Regulations govern how PMI coverage can be discontinued when the lender's equity is no longer endangered.

Although residential properties make up the bulk of private mortgage insurance, coverage is being extended into commercial and industrial loans and into lease guarantee insurance. Special policies are written for five years, with a renewal fee charged at the end of the period if the insurance is extended. There is no reason to believe that this shared-risk concept, under which both an insured lender and a private mortgage insurer assume part of the risk, could not be extended to virtually any type of property and any kind of financing transaction.

Automatic Payment Plans

Another way to reduce the chance of default is through an automatic mortgage pay plan offered by many lenders. Under the plan, a system of preauthorized monthly mortgage payments is established. It relieves the homeowner of the chore of paying each month and protects the debtor against forgetting to make a payment. Borrowers simply authorize their banks to make an automatic monthly deduction from their checking accounts and to forward this amount to the real estate lender.

Consumer Protection Laws and Regulations

Still another way to mitigate or reduce the chance of default is through consumer protection laws and regulations.

Public Regulations

A wide variety of laws and regulations protect real estate buyers in one way or another. Among these is the Truth-in-Lending Law (see Chapter 10). Also called the Consumer Credit Protection Act, this federal law prescribes full disclosure of all borrowing charges. This calculation of the total cost of borrowing and the effective interest is called the APR. The federal government's anticipation is that borrowers can compare APR calculations to obtain the best loan terms when shopping for home financing. With certain kinds of loans, such as junior loans and refinancings, the borrower may rescind or cancel the credit arrangement within three business days without declaring any reason for doing so. This right does not apply in the case of a first trust deed created or assumed for the purpose of financing the purchase of a dwelling in which the borrower expects to reside.

On the state level, an important law designed to protect consumers is the right to cancel home-improvement contracts within three days of the time of their solicitation by a door-to-door salesperson. Even when such a contract is initiated by the homeowner, the truth-in-lending provisions allow cancellation within three business days if financing is involved. Thus, homeowners who change their minds for any reason may cancel during the first three days after signing any contract.

Private Home Warranties

Buyers of new or existing homes can encounter problems with major components of the home, resulting in financial hardship and difficulty in making their mortgage payments. Private industry over the years has offered a variety of home-warranty programs in an effort to mitigate financial burdens at a time when borrowers can least afford such repairs. Most programs protect the new buyer for a specified time period, usually one year after close of escrow. Although warranties can differ, most cover the major home components, including plumbing, electrical system, heating and/or air conditioning, walls, roof, and foundation. Special elements, like swimming pools, can be protected via the payment of additional policy fees. Sellers and real estate licensees most often provide and pay for a home warranty as a way to provide a benefit to the new buyer but also to protect themselves from being negatively impacted by unknown component difficulties after the close of escrow. Buyers also may purchase home warranties but must do so before the close of escrow.

11.4 Other Lending Problems

Usury

The cost of money is always related to the anticipated risk to the lender providing the financing. One way in which lenders may be compensated for any increase in potential loss is to charge higher interest rates. Those borrowers most susceptible to high interest rate loans are those who, for various reasons, have proven to be potential credit risks. However, there are state limitations on the amount of interest that can, regardless of the reason, be charged a borrower. The maximum rate that may be charged on loans made by nonexempt *individuals*, whether or not secured by real estate, is 10 percent, or 5 percent above the Federal Reserve discount rate, whichever is greater. Usury laws do not apply to sellers carrying back under a purchase money transaction.

Regulated institutional lenders in California are not limited in the rate of interest they may charge. The marketplace generally dictates their rates. Effective yields are increased through the use of points or discounts, as illustrated in Chapter 7.

Borrowers who deal with noninstitutional lenders are protected against usurious transactions. These lenders consist of private parties making hard money loans. This protection is reinforced with the disclosure requirements under Regulation Z of the Truth-in-Lending Act. As pointed out in Chapter 10, this federal law requires that borrowers receive a written statement of the total costs involved in any financial transaction. Truth-in-Lending does not prescribe limits on interest rates. But by requiring that the prepaid costs and expenses be translated into an annual percentage rate, it provides one way for borrowers to compare loan costs when shopping for their best loan terms.

Lenders making loans secured by junior trust deeds usually charge the maximum interest rate allowed in an effort to secure the highest yield permitted by law, in order to offset the increased risks associated with their secondary positions.

What does usury have to do with foreclosures and other lending problems? When sellers are dissatisfied with their rate of return dictated by the maximum rate allowed by law, they may seek ways to circumvent the law. One commonly used method is to increase the sales price of the property, which effectively increases the amount to be repaid. This, in turn, could result in a borrower's financial overextension and ultimate default.

Assume, for example, that an owner is selling property for $185,000, and that the buyer is to make a small down payment and take over the existing first trust deed. The seller is to carry back a second mortgage for the difference. The seller could raise the sales price to, say, $188,000, with the extra $3,000 being added to the second lien. Even though the second trust deed is drawn at the maximum interest rate negotiated, the yield has been effectively raised by the additional amount of money included in the junior lien. Sellers carrying back loans—so-called carrybacks—are exempt from usury laws, as are real estate brokers.

The impact of usury statutes on money markets is a controversial subject. Proponents insist that borrowers need protection from unscrupulous lenders. Critics suggest that such limitations can reduce the money supply. Their argument is that by keeping interest rates down, at whatever levels, lenders naturally gravitate to those places where money can be put to more productive use. Thus, a lender from an eastern state with a usury rate of, say, 9 percent, may pour money into California, where there might be a higher usury limit. If California were to lower its usury rate, the flow of funds from other states would decline. The net effect on potential home buyers would be a decrease in mortgage funds and a postponement of purchases.

Redlining

A problem that occasionally resurfaces in real estate lending is redlining, the practice of systematic refusal to lend mortgage money in high-risk areas. These are usually older urban areas containing high minority concentrations, around which lenders in the past placed red lines delineating such neighborhoods as off-limits to mortgage credit. Little if any consideration is given to the creditworthiness of the individual borrower.

By limiting or refusing credit, the lender hopes to reduce its exposure to delinquencies and foreclosures. However, in the process, it has been demonstrated that the withholding of real estate financing has hastened the decay of these neighborhoods. The so-called closed neighborhoods fall prey to speculators and absentee landlords, dubbed "slumlords" in some areas, who, some claim, drain the community, leaving deterioration and destruction in their paths. The few homes that are financed often end up abandoned and foreclosed—thus compounding the problem of redlining. Meanwhile, buyers in these neighborhoods find the money spigots turned off, with no place to turn for help. These buyers may be the very ones who place their savings into local financial institutions and then find themselves unable to borrow from these institutions while their deposits may be used to finance homes outside the redlined areas.

Both the federal and state governments have tried to resolve this dilemma. All federally regulated mortgage lenders are required to disclose publicly just where they make their mortgage loans. Also, the State of California has imposed guidelines relating to fair lending practices that prohibit denying credit or altering the terms of a loan solely because of neighborhood factors. When a person is denied a loan, the lender must notify the applicant, in writing, of the reasons for denial within 30 days of the application.

To help guard against the continued practice of redlining, state-chartered savings banks are required to file periodic reports with the California Department of Financial Institutions. Written details of how and where loans are being made are submitted so lending patterns can be determined. Many items must be included in the report: county and census tract; purpose of the loan and outcome—made, denied, purchased, or sold; amount of loan requested and amount issued; type of property, appraised value, year built, square footage; sales price; interest rate, and whether fixed or variable, discounts, fees charged; existing balance on loans refinanced and how the proceeds were used, such as for repairs or improvements; borrower's and total family income; race or ethnic makeup of the applicant, sex and age of borrower; data on co-borrowers and co-applicants; and information on whether neighborhood factors were considered in underwriting the loan.

Community Reinvestment Act (CRA)

To stop discriminatory practices, including redlining, Congress passed the **Community Reinvestment Act (CRA)**, which requires federally supervised financial institutions to disclose lending data in their lobbies and elsewhere. The Financial Institutions Reform, Recovery and Enforcement Act (FIRREA) requires lenders to report data on the race, gender, income, and census tract of people to whom they make loans. Its stated purpose is "to assist in identifying discriminatory practices and enforcing antidiscrimination statutes." CRA and FIRREA encourage lenders to offer mortgages for low- and moderately priced housing and meet other credit needs for low- and moderate-income families. Lenders are required to make positive efforts to provide loans in areas from which savings are received.

FIRREA requires evaluation reports and CRA ratings of lender practices to be made public for all institutions. In cooperation with other government agencies, it grades each institution on how well it

- Knows the credit needs of its community.
- Informs the community about its credit services.
- Involves its directors in setting up and monitoring CRA programs.
- Participates in government-insured, guaranteed, or subsidized loans.
- Distributes credit applications, approvals, and rejections across geographic areas.
- Offers a range of residential mortgages, housing rehabilitation loans, and small business loans.

All of these criteria are designed to protect consumers against unlawful discrimination. A positive CRA rating is a prerequisite for institutions to open new branches and to engage in expansions, acquisitions, and mergers, since outside third parties can petition agencies to deny these activities to institutions with poor CRA grades.

Home Mortgage Disclosure Act (HMDA)

Mortgage lenders are required to provide an annual report regarding the borrowers who both applied for and acquired loans. Referred to as the HMDA report, the information is obtained via section X of the loan application. This section, entitled Information for Government Monitoring Purposes, seeks voluntary information from borrowers regarding ethnicity, race, and sex. Although the information is voluntary, borrowers are informed that "if you do not furnish ethnicity, race or sex, under federal regulations, this lender is required to note the information on the basis of visual observation and surname." Combating discrimination is critical in every aspect of the lending industry.

Short Sales

This chapter contains the words "lending problems" in its title. Due to a dramatic decline in home values between 1990 and 1996, a significant number of lenders have had to work out what have come to be known as **short sales** (and by some, called *short paybacks* or *short pay-offs*) with sellers who could not sell their homes for prices sufficient to cover even the outstanding loan balances and costs of selling. Rather than taking back properties through foreclosure, lenders compromised the debt, accepting less than what was owed at the time of the sale. Depending on defaulting borrowers' financial condition, the lender may require repayment of a portion of the mortgage shortfall.

Is this phenomenon likely to continue? If markets in the future demonstrate huge resale losses, the answer may be yes. But lenders will more likely protect themselves by immediately selling their trust deed notes in the secondary market, reducing loan-to-value ratios, or undertaking more protective underwriting.

Before undertaking a short sale, whether for yourself or a client, consult with an attorney and accountant experienced in both real estate and income taxation, since loan relief or forgiveness may have income tax consequences.

SUMMARY

A deed of trust securing a promissory note requires more than simply repaying a loan. A default and possible foreclosure may result not only from delinquencies and nonpayment of the loan but also from noncompliance with many other provisions of the trust deed. These include proper maintenance of the property, carrying adequate hazard insurance, paying property taxes and other liens when due, and complying with all local building and safety ordinances.

A foreclosure action through a trustee's sale begins with the filing of a Notice of Default, followed by the publication of a Notice of Sale, and then the actual sale through auction. Liens are paid off in their order of priority, with remaining proceeds, if any, paid to the defaulting trustor. No redemptive rights exist thereafter. Foreclosure through judicial action is much more complicated and time consuming. Up to a one-year redemption period exists in favor of the defaulted trustor following final sale. Lenders therefore mostly resort to a trustee's sale, unless a deficiency judgment is sought, in which case court action is the only remedy.

Defaults can be largely minimized through establishment of an impound account; forbearance proceedings, including moratoriums and modifications or recasting; mortgage insurance, both public and private; automatic payment plans; repayment workouts; temporary indulgences; and an assortment of consumer protection laws and regulations.

IMPORTANT TERMS AND CONCEPTS

Advances	*Moratorium*
Assignment of rents	*Notice of Default*
Automatic payment plan	*Notice of Sale*
Community Reinvestment Act (CRA)	*Quitclaim deed*
Deed in Lieu of Foreclosure	*Recasting*
Deficiency judgment	*Redlining*
Escrow account	*Request for Notice of Default and Notice of Sale*
Extended term	*Right of reinstatement*
Forbearance	*Short sale*
Foreclosure	*Subrogation*
Government mortgage insurance	*Trustee's sale*
Impound account	*Usury*
Judicial sale	*Waiver*
	Warranties (Private Home)

REVIEWING YOUR UNDERSTANDING

Questions for Discussion

1. List four ways in which a borrower can default under the terms of a trust deed.
2. How does an assignment-of-rents clause operate to protect a lender?
3. What is meant by power of sale? Which party benefits from it, the beneficiary or trustor?
4. Contrast a Notice of Default to a Notice of Sale.
5. How does an impound account mitigate against risk of loss?
6. List six ways that a lender's procedures can assist delinquent borrowers.
7. What is redlining? How does it affect lenders? Borrowers? Neighborhoods?

Multiple-Choice Questions

1. Reasons for defaulting on the repayment of a real estate debt are many and varied, including which one of the following?
   a. marriage.
   b. increased earnings.
   c. judicious budgeting.
   d. disability.

2. Following a foreclosure sale, surplus funds remaining after paying off all costs, fees, expenses, and liens are given to the
   a. successful bidder.
   b. trustee.
   c. beneficiary.
   d. trustor.

3. The successful bidder at a judicial sale of real estate property receives a
   a. Trustee's Deed.
   b. Certificate of Sale.
   c. Judicial Deed.
   d. Deed in Lieu of Foreclosure.

4. A temporary suspension or waiver of payments on a debt is termed
   a. forbearance.
   b. forestallment.
   c. wavering.
   d. recasting.

5. The MIP premium on FHA-insured loans
   a. must be paid at the end of the loan.
   b. can be added to the loan.
   c. is optional.
   d. is usually paid by the seller.

6. In the event of nonpayment of property taxes, the beneficiary may pay for the obligation directly, and thereafter
   a. bill the trustor directly.
   b. add the advances to the principal indebtedness.
   c. do either (a) or (b).
   d. do neither (a) nor (b).

7. Which of the following parties is not generally permitted to bid on a property offered at a foreclosure auction?
   a. trustor.
   b. outside party.
   c. beneficiary.
   d. trustee.

8. The right of redemption following a trustee's sale is good for
   a. one year.
   b. 90 days.
   c. three months.
   d. none of the above.

9. Assume that in a declining market, a small condo with an existing $119,000 GI loan sells for only $110,000 at a foreclosure sale. Ignoring foreclosure costs, the DVA will reimburse the foreclosing lender
   a. $9,000.
   b. $21,000.
   c. $27,500.
   d. $30,250.

10. The trustor under a deed of trust became delinquent in his monthly payments, thereafter abandoning the premises and moving to another city. Which of the following actions is *not* part of the foreclosure procedure?
    a. Notify trustor of default.
    b. Issue reconveyance deed.
    c. Publish Notice of Sale.
    d. Record Notice of Sale.

11. If a borrower does not provide a real estate lender with proof of hazard insurance when required, the lender may
    a. purchase insurance coverage and add it to the principal balance of the loan.
    b. purchase insurance coverage and proceed with foreclosure if the borrower does not pay for it.
    c. institute foreclosure proceedings.
    d. do any of the above.

12. A trustee in a deed of trust may issue a trustee's deed upon a foreclosure sale as a result of
    a. violation of the due-on-sale clause.
    b. the power of sale contained in the deed of trust itself.
    c. provisions of the Business and Professions Code.
    d. the applicable sections of the Civil Code.

13. Proper foreclosure procedures include
    a. advertising in a newspaper of general circulation at least once a week for three months.
    b. posting a copy of the Notice of Sale on the property and in a public place.
    c. recording a copy of the newspaper advertisement.
    d. mailing a copy of the notice to the trustee by certified mail.

14. After the issuance of a Trustee's Deed at a foreclosure sale,
    a. all rights formerly held by the trustor are extinguished.
    b. the trustor has a one-year right of redemption.
    c. a successful bidder gets the full fee title, free of restrictions and with priority over the deed of trust foreclosed.
    d. the trustor has a three-month right of reinstatement.

15. Mortgage guaranty insurance, whether undertaken through government-backed or private sources,
    a. is designed to pay off the mortgage balance in the event of the death of a borrower.
    b. protects the lender against loss in the event of foreclosure.
    c. is paid for by the lender, since it is the lender that is protected.
    d. is a one-time charge paid for by borrowers.

16. The Community Reinvestment Act (CRA)
    a. prohibits redlining practices.
    b. requires posting of lending data for federally chartered lenders.
    c. may inhibit lender expansions and mergers.
    d. is involved in each of the above.

17. Recasting a loan may be accomplished by
    I.   extending the term of the loan.
    II. increasing the debt.
    III. reducing the interest rate.
    IV. giving a Deed in Lieu of Foreclosure.
    a. I only.
    b. I and II only.
    c. I, II, and III only.
    d. I, II, III, and IV.

18. A homeowner fails to pay her special bond assessment due to loss of her job. The lender may
    a. pay the overdue tax and bill the homeowner.
    b. pay the overdue tax and add the amount to the loan.
    c. do either (a) or (b).
    d. do neither (a) nor (b).

19. A home with an existing $140,000 DVA loan nets $120,000 at a foreclosure sale. The amount owing at time of sale was $110,000. The borrower-trustor is entitled to
    a. $10,000.
    b. $20,000.
    c. $30,000.
    d. none of the above.

20. Should a borrower fail to maintain satisfactory property insurance, the lender's best cause of action would be to
    a. foreclose without any notice to the borrower.
    b. evict the borrower.
    c. sue the borrower for breach of contract.
    d. purchase a policy and add the premium to the loan.

CASE & POINT

The Decision to Refinance: An Analysis

Assume that you are 10 years from retirement and do not wish to increase the size of your home loan. Here is a method some mortgage brokers use to compare various refinancing options and their costs.

Section A. *Break-even Point*

Assumptions: You have an existing 30-year loan at 8% interest, payable at $1,080 per month. You are offered a new loan to replace the existing balance of $140,000, at 7.25% interest, fixed for 30 years, and $2,950 in closing costs, including a one-point loan origination fee. Monthly payments of principal and interest (P+I) will be $955. At what "point" should you consider whether to refinance, and at what terms?

Step 1 Monthly payment of P&I on existing loan	$1,080
Step 2 Less monthly payment of P&I on new loan	955
Step 3 Monthly savings by refinancing	$ 125
Step 4 Refinancing costs	$2,950
Step 5 Divide step 4 by step 3 {2,950/125}	23.6

Preliminary conclusion: It will take about 24 months to recoup your $2,950 costs of refinancing, without considering income tax consequences and time value of money. Stated differently, you would consider refinancing only if you plan to remain in your home for at least two years.

Now that we have determined the "break-even point" for residency, the next consideration is to compare the new loan with other options, that is, to "shop around" among lenders and mortgage brokers, whether physically or via the Internet (see Addenda at end of Chapter 3). For instance, say you are also offered an alternative $140,000 loan at 7.75%, payable at $1,003 monthly P&I, but with $1,400 less in closing costs, or roughly half those of the lower-interest (7.25%) mortgage. Which is better?

Section B. *Comparing Options*

Step 6 Total refinancing expenses for higher-cost loan	$2,950
Step 7 Less reduction in refinancing expenses for lower-cost loan	1,400
Step 8 Refinancing expenses for lower-cost loan	$1,550
Step 9 Monthly savings changing from existing loan to the higher-cost loan (step 3)	$ 125
Step 10 Monthly savings changing from existing loan to the lower-cost loan (step 1 minus $1,003)	$ 77
Step 11 Divide step 8 by step 10	20

Conclusion: It will take 20 months for the lower-cost loan to reach the break-even point with the higher-cost loan. From a purely financial point of view, you would remain in your home for at least 20 months to come out ahead.

Considering refinancing? We analyzed the decision to refinance in Chapter 10. Here we concentrate on websites to follow through on the many options available, but first, a definition.

The Mortgage Bankers Association defines refinancing as "the process of taking out a new mortgage or deed of trust and using the money to close out, or pay off, your current mortgage." The best sources for home "refis" are mortgage companies, thrift institutions, commercial banks, and credit unions. But suppose you'd like to accomplish this through the Internet? In addition to providing refinancing sources, accessing the Internet also provides a ready source for useful information and answers to questions. Here are some websites from which to obtain this information:

www.mortgage101.com (Calculator computes refinancing payments and financial analysis.)

www.mbaa.org (This is the site for the Mortgage Bankers Association of America.)

www.fanniemae.com (Federal National Mortgage Association offers a calculator to compare loan costs.)

www.bankrate.com (Refinancing information and calculator.)

www.interest.com/refinance (Calculates differences in current loan vs. new loan.)

www.hud.gov (Discusses streamlined refinancing of FHA mortgages and offers list of approved lenders and housing counseling agencies. Link to Federal National Mortgage Association website.)

www.consumersunion.org (Information on refinancing, in English and Spanish, and how to avoid falling prey to home equity fraud.)

www.hsh.com (Site of HSH Inc., a mortgage researcher, that has a refinancing calculator and also sells mortgage refinancing kits.)

www.planetloan.com (Directory of lenders specializing in refinancings.)

www.ftc.gov [General refinancing information under its Consumer Education category. Toll-free (877) 382-4359.]

www.quickenmortgage.com, www.quickloans.com (Mortgage lending geared toward the consumer.)

www.homegain.com

www.ditech.com

www.imoneynet.com (Mortgage Borrowing.)

www.mortgagemag.com

www.lendingtree.com

www.easierhomeloans.com (Home buying essentials: loan application rates, credit considerations.)

www.hrblock.com

www.realestate.com (Loan auctions: borrower posts criteria and lenders bid for the loan.)

www.onerealtorplace.com (National Association of REALTORS.)

www.thinkglink.com (Ilyce Glink, real estate and personal financial reporter.)

Of course, not all of these will answer every question or solve every problem that you as a potential candidate for refinancing may have. Websites will address the issues of up-front fees and costs, interest rates, and repayment differentials. But before deciding, additional factors that should be taken into account include the need for liquidity; impact on cash flow, including paying down credit card debt from the proceeds; federal, state, and local income tax brackets; effect on retirement funding, including time left before retiring; educational and other funding requirements; alternative investment opportunities, or what economists refer to as opportunity costs; and estate needs and other criteria that are best solved by a competent financial planner. Other questions that ought to be considered are: Should I refinance with a 15-year or 30-year loan? Should I take the longest possible loan but make additional payments from time to time? Should I opt for a fixed or variable rate? Even the condition of one's health may play a role in the decision-making process. For example, if you refinanced for a much higher loan than the existing one, the higher monthly payments could ultimately jeopardize your fiscal health should high uninsured medical expenses cut into ability to meet the ongoing, fixed obligations.

Some on-line lenders even offer rebates in one form or another. Example: www.pricelinemortgage.com boasts "Check around for the lowest rate you can find. If we can't beat or match it, we'll pay you $300." Then there's Virtumundo, Inc, which, through its website, www.virtumundo.com, states that it is a "direct marketing company that specializes in providing demographically targeted solutions for advertisers, both online and in traditional media." In checking that site, you may find a lender, New Century Mortgage Corporation, offering on-line applications to prequalify prospective borrowers. Finally, there are the financial planners who are getting into the mortgage business, adding still another tool to their arsenals: originating mortgages and other loans for their clients. As the magazine *Investment Advisor* reports, planners can access the website www.verticallend.com to sign up for that site's training from a designated loan specialist. Subscribers log on to Vertical Lend's password-protected site, click on the residential mortgage section, and fill out an express application to get the loan started. Each financial professional is assigned a loan specialist who provides back-office support and acts as a business partner when performing loan originations. The loan specialist retrieves the application, runs a credit check, examines debt ratios, and then shops the loan for the best rate. Welcome to the world of the Internet!

CHAPTER 12
CONSTRUCTION LOANS

PREVIEW

This chapter covers the broad field of financing construction projects. Topics in this chapter include sources and types of construction loans, loan costs, the construction loan process, and mechanic's liens.

After completing this chapter, you should be able to:

1. List five types of construction lenders.

2. List and define at least six technical words and terms that are common to the field of construction lending.

3. Explain borrowers' costs under a construction loan.

4. List the stages followed in processing a construction loan.

5. Discuss the supporting documentation used in connection with construction financing.

6. Outline the steps to take in filing mechanic's liens.

7. Cite three California laws that deal with assessments for the cost of construction of public improvements.

12.1 Nature of Construction Loans

Construction financing is the providing of funds to pay for labor and materials that go into the erection of a building. The funds may come from two sources: (1) a general line of personal credit that a borrower has with financial institutions, materials suppliers, or subcontractors, and (2) a construction or building loan that is evidenced by a promissory note and secured by a trust deed. The first involves the use of bank and commercial unsecured credit and is not classified as real estate credit. The second, the construction loan, is the subject of this chapter.

A *construction loan* is a short-term, interim, or temporary loan for building purposes, as contrasted to permanent or long-term financing on already existing buildings. A typical construction loan for a single-family residence is usually for a term of 9 to 12 months and for a major project, such as an apartment house, a term of 18 months to two years may be normal. Apartment house construction loans generally allow sufficient time for completion and partial rental before full loan payments begin. Permanent loans on existing structures are written for longer terms, typically 15 to 30 years. When used in conjunction with a construction loan, a permanent loan is called a **take-out loan**. It is not unusual for a borrower to obtain a short-term construction loan from one lender, then, when the project is completed, obtain a permanent or take-out loan from another lender to pay off the amount owed on the construction loan. Commercial banks favor interim construction loans (particularly where take-outs have been provided), while savings banks prefer combination loans.

A construction loan is made for a specific dollar amount agreed upon before work begins. Construction funds are not paid to the borrower in a lump sum, but advanced in stages as construction progresses. The permanent loan, in contrast, is placed after construction is completed and is paid over the loan term.

The construction loan is usually evidenced by a promissory note and secured by a deed of trust on the property under construction. The principal sum of the construction loan is nonamortized, though interest payments are periodically required from the borrower, but only on the money advanced.

Sources of Funds

Construction loans are made primarily by local financial institutions, mainly banks and credit unions.

The extent to which lenders are active in the construction loan market in a given area depends on several factors. Some lenders as a matter of policy do not make construction loans, whereas others may be in and out of the market as economic conditions change. Still others may make construction loans on a regular basis.

Kinds of Loans

There are two basic kinds of construction loans. The first is one that combines a construction loan with a permanent take-out mortgage, called a **combination loan** (sometimes mistakenly called a *package*). These construction-permanent combination loans involve only one loan closing. The second type is the interim, short-term, straight construction loan, which is independent of the permanent loan, though the lender does anticipate that the proceeds of a permanent loan from some source will pay off the construction loan.

Construction-Permanent Combination

Both the construction loan and the permanent loan originate in advance of construction and are secured under one instrument. The construction money is disbursed in installments as construction progresses. The permanent loan begins according to the terms on the note at a predetermined time, designed to coincide with completion of construction. Two variations are common. In the first one, the lender approves the ultimate borrower on the permanent mortgage, has the borrower sign the loan instruments, and makes advances as construction proceeds. Interest-only payments are made on money as it is advanced during construction. This is frequently done in the financing of single-family homes built for an owner under contract with a builder for a custom home.

The second variation is also used in cases of single dwellings. Here the lender commits itself in advance of construction to make both the construction loan and permanent loan but retains the right to approve the ultimate borrower, who is perhaps not yet known. The legal instruments are prepared so that the permanent loan can be assumed by the ultimate borrower. This kind of arrangement is in contrast with large-scale projects where lenders provide builders with construction money, perhaps a conventional blanket construction mortgage on an entire tract of land or subdivision, and the builders refer home buyers to the lender for permanent financing. The buyers, however, have no obligation to place their loan through that particular lender.

The combination loan has potential advantages for both builder and ultimate buyer. Presumably there will be fewer expenses for the lender and these reductions or savings benefit the builder and buyer.

Short-Term Construction Loans

The interim, short-term, straight construction loan and the take-out loan often involve two lenders and two sets of loan instruments compared with the single lender and instrument under the combination loan. The **short-term construction loan** can be made by a lender other than the lender making the permanent loan. The construction lender may require a commitment from the permanent take-out lender, or the construction loan may be made to the builder without any commitment from a final take-out lender. The loan is for a short term—say, one year—at which time it is due and payable. It is up to the borrower-builder to provide a take-out buyer or to obtain permanent financing.

Loan Costs

The costs of a construction loan to the borrower consist of several items. Lenders may charge a flat fee, usually a percentage of the amount of the loan (such as 1, 2, or 3 percent) at the time the loan originates. These fees increase the effective rate of return on the loan to the lender, though a portion of the fee is used to cover the cost of originating the loan.

Charges may be made to cover the necessary items of expense in the origination and underwriting of the loan. Typical borrower's items would be charges for the appraisal report, credit report, survey, title insurance, legal fees, accrued interest, escrows, and premiums for hazard insurance and performance bond if required. Recall that these are similar to the nonrecurring costs discussed in Chapter 10 under closing costs for home loans. Sometimes lenders charge a flat fee, expressed as so many points (typically two to three), to cover all these items, or charge them in addition to their required points.

Construction loans, including combination loans, almost always involve higher fees than purchase money loans. This is due to higher overhead costs to the lender, such as on-site inspections, progress payments, and checking for mechanic's liens, and because of the higher risks involved. This is especially true if the home or project is being built "on spec" meaning that there is no predetermined buyer or tenant.

12.2 Evaluation and Lending Process

Lender Considerations for a Construction Loan

Before committing themselves to financing a construction project, construction lenders consider several factors.

Plans and Specifications

The construction lender will require a set of plans sufficiently detailed to determine room or space size, appropriateness of design features, proper use of lot topography, layout, and competitive amenities. The materials used in the project—and listed in the specifications (specs)—are viewed as to their durability, soundness, and appeal. A soil report is also required in some cases.

Cost Breakdown

On improvement projects, competitive bids may be required. Evaluation of costs is of great concern to both construction lenders and title insurers who underwrite policies insuring the lender's priority position. This is especially true when construction costs are surging. Cost breakdowns list the cost to the builder of each component of construction.

Construction lenders differentiate between hard costs and soft costs. **Hard costs** are those for which the builder must write a check, while **soft costs** include such noncash items as profit, overhead, and supervision. Some commercial lenders limit their construction loan offerings to the amount of the hard cost.

Construction Contract

The contract between the builder and owner should spell out in detail the segments of construction and performance standards for which the contractor will be responsible, the costs for such construction, the method of funding and disbursement schedule, and other provisions.

Source of Repayment

Loan repayment may take on many forms. The developer may request a *combination loan*, where the construction loan is combined with the permanent loan, using only one lender.

When government-insured or -guaranteed loans are used, commitments from the applicable agency are required in addition to a commitment to finance the ultimate purchaser's loan by an approved permanent lender. In the case of income property, the permanent loan to be funded in the future is obtained prior to arrangement for construction financing. A definite commitment for future permanent financing is termed a *take-out commitment*.

Financial Data

Supporting data will be required from the builder, owner, commercial tenants, and others who may have a financial interest in the project.

Lenders also require a narrative history of the builder's past experience, as well as a credit report furnished by a local Industry Credit Bureau (ICB). Other important aspects of the project—such as tract and condominium private deed restrictions, data from an economic and environmental point of view, rental and expense trends, lease provisions for income-producing properties, projected resale prices, and so on—would also have to be analyzed.

A financial analysis of the borrowers is essential in order to assess their capacity to repay the loan. How much do the borrowers now have available to put into the project? How much income will the borrowers have from other sources in the future if there are problems? Borrowers must be able to carry the financial load ahead of draws. What has been the experience with respect to similar projects in the past?

Lending and Disbursement Procedures

There are many variables in financing, and no two lenders have the same standards for making construction loans. There are, however, certain basic steps in the construction lending process that apply to most real estate lenders. These include:

1. Loan application with necessary accompanying data and documents, including plans and specifications, estimated costs for the proposed project, construction contract, credit data, and a financial statement of the borrower and builder.

2. Appraisal of the site and proposed construction, with value determined from plans and specs, based on current market conditions.

3. Title examination, preparation of documents and legal instruments needed to secure the loan, and issuance of the commitment to make the loan.

4. Disbursement system for releasing money as construction progresses according to a predetermined schedule. The payout of loan funds as construction progresses is one of the major distinguishing characteristics of a construction loan. This requires establishment of a LIP (loans in progress) account. Payout schedules are ordinarily incorporated into a *building loan agreement* between lender and borrower, an example of which is found in Figure 12.1. A building loan agreement is a very important document (the heart of a construction loan) that distinguishes a construction loan from other loans. It embodies the whole agreement between lender and borrower, and, if appropriate, a builder.

5. Escrow and settlement procedure.

Building Loan Agreement and Assignment of Account

This Agreement is executed for the purpose of obtaining a building loan from EASTERN NATIONAL BANK, and as a part of the loan transaction, which loan is evidenced by a Note of the undersigned for $ 500,000 of even date herewith, in favor of Bank, and is secured, among other things, by a Trust Deed affecting real property in the County of **Los Angeles**, State of California, described as:

```
Portion of Lot 10, Tract 10907, as shown on map recorded in Book 195, pages 1 and 2
of Maps, in the office of the county recorder.

Otherwise known as 13515 Addison Street, Sherman Oaks, California.
```

Upon recordation of the Trust Deed, the proceeds of the loan are to be placed by the Bank, together with the sum of $ 100,000 deposited by the undersigned, in special non-interest bearing Accounts with the Bank. Such deposit of the loan proceeds shall be deemed full consideration for the Note. Each of the undersigned hereby irrevocably assigns to the Bank as security for the obligations secured by the Trust Deed, all right, title and interest of the undersigned in said Accounts and all moneys to be placed therein. It is agreed that any funds deposited by the undersigned shall be disbursed in accordance with the terms of this Agreement prior to disbursement of the proceeds of the loan. By its acceptance of this Agreement the Bank agrees to use the moneys in said Accounts in accordance with the terms hereof.

The undersigned, jointly and severally, further agree as follows:

1. To commence construction of the improvements to be constructed on the property within 15 days after written notice has been given the undersigned by the Bank that it has received a satisfactory Policy of Title Insurance insuring that the Trust Deed is a first lien on the property. Should work of any character be commenced on, or any materials be delivered upon or to the real property or in connection with said improvement prior to receipt of said written notice from the Bank, the Bank at its sole option, may apply the funds in said Accounts to the indebtedness secured by the Trust Deed and to pay expenses incurred in connection with the transaction.

2. Construction shall be in accordance with plans and specifications approved by the Bank, and without change or alteration, except with the written consent of the Bank, and said construction shall be completed within **six** months from date hereof. All of the materials, equipment and every part of the improvement shall be paid for in full and become a part of the real property.

3. The terms of the Note notwithstanding, to pay to Bank on the first day of each calendar month interest at the rate of 10.00% per annum on loan funds advanced, from the date of the respective advances to **December 21,** 20XX, 20___; thereafter, interest on the entire principal amount of the Note shall be payable at the rate, at the time and in accordance with the terms stated in said Note. If such interest is not paid, the Bank may, at its option, pay the same to itself from the Accounts.

4. Subject to the provisions of this Agreement the proceeds of said Accounts are to be disbursed by the Bank as follows:
   A. To pay all costs and demands in connection with the closing of the loan transaction.
   B. To pay the sum of $ 500,000 in the proportions set out below to provide funds for the construction of the improvements, to any of the undersigned, or at the option of the Bank, to contractors, material-men and laborers, or any of them, and at such time as the construction, in accordance with the plans and specifications, has reached the following stages:

```
    1.  22% ($110,000) when foundation is complete, all ground mechanical systems
                       are in place, sub flooer installed, and all rough lumber is
                       on the site.
    2.  21% ($105,000) when framing is complete, roof on, and all mechanical systems
                       are roughed-in complete.
    3.  12% ($ 60,000) when interior drywall is complete, two coats on exterior
                       and/or wood siding on and primed, including priming of all
                       wood sash, door frames, etc., which contact drywall.
    4.  15% ($ 75,000) when sash and doors, cabinets and finish lumber are installed,
                       flooring set (except hardwood finish, linoleum, or carpet).
    5.  20% ($100,000) when all improvements are complete (including flat concrete
                       work, driveway and grading, plus removal of all debris), Bank
                       has approved final inspection and a valid Notice of Completion
                       has been recorded.
    6.  10% ($ 50,000) when the title company which issued the title policy insuring
                       the lien of the Trust Deed will issue an endorsement or policy
                       of title insurance with mechanics' lien coverage; and gives
                       its written permission  to release funds retained pursuant to
                       an indemnity agreement, if any.
```

Figure 12.1 Sample building loan agreement (partial).

6. Loan servicing system to assure loan repayment during the life of the loan.

As mentioned above, the loan's ***payout schedule***, proceeding as construction progresses rather than in a lump sum, is a major distinguishing feature of a construction loan. These payments are referred to by a variety of names: vouchers, *disbursements*, payouts, draws, *progress payments*, and advances. There are many types of payment systems but, regardless of the method used, the objective is to protect the lender in four matters:

1. The value of the work in place and materials delivered, plus the lot, will equal or exceed the total amount paid out.

2. Waivers of liens (debts owed to subcontractors, laborers, and material suppliers) will be obtained for each item of material work covered by the draw so as to avoid mechanic's liens.

3. The borrower and the lender will jointly authorize all draws.

4. There will always be sufficient funds in the possession of the lender to complete construction of the property.

Under some circumstances, a lot advance—an amount *included* in construction funds—may be made, so that a builder-borrower has funds sufficient to pay off any remaining balance on the vacant land being improved. Disbursement of funds can be made by a variety of methods: *draw system*, with payments made in stages as construction progresses; percentage of progress, involving incremental disbursement of construction completed based on 90 percent of work in place or delivered to the job on a monthly basis, with the remaining 10 percent retained for completion at the expiration of the mechanic's lien period; a *voucher system*, when money is disbursed on presentation of receipted bills by licensed building contractors, subcontractors, and material suppliers with appropriate lien waivers and releases; and through the use of a so-called *builder's control service*, an outside third party that acts as an intermediary in the control and disbursement of funds.

A typical example of how the draw system operates is illustrated in Figure 12.2.

There are many variations in the amount and number of *advances* based on the percentage of construction completed at any given time. The five-draw plan shown in Figure 12.2, for instance, could be rearranged into three advances, or seven advances, and so on. Whatever system is used, the lender inspects the work at regular intervals before, during, and upon completion of construction. The purpose of these compliance or progress inspections is to make certain that the builder has followed the terms of the construction loan agreement and other documents; that construction is proceeding according to the plans, specifications, time schedules, and estimated costs; that a

Five-Draw Release Payments for a Construction Loan

Draw One—20% of loan amount upon completion of foundation, rough plumbing, and subfloor.

Draw Two—30% of loan amount upon completion of framing, roof, windows, and doors.

Draw Three—20% of loan amount upon completion of exterior and interior walls. Includes plumbing, wiring, and ducting.

Draw Four—20% of loan amount upon completion of finished floors, cabinets, trim, and all remaining aspects of construction. Notice of completion is recorded.

Draw Five—Final 10% of loan amount is released after the filing period for mechanic's lien has expired, or after issuance of a lien-free endorsement to the lender's ALTA title insurance policy. This is referred to as **holdback**.

Figure 12.2 Example of a draw system for a construction loan.

claimed stage of construction is actually in place; that there will be no disbursement of funds ahead of actual construction; and that the receipted bills for construction are verified.

Regardless of number of advances, the final draw is normally issued *jointly* to borrower and builder, so that the check cannot be cashed until the parties have all endorsed it and differences, if any, have been ironed out.

12.3 Take-Out or Permanent Loans

As noted earlier, some construction lenders, as a prerequisite to making a construction loan, insist that the borrower have a firm take-out commitment from an approved permanent lender. A take-out commitment is an agreement between the borrower and the permanent lender. It is essentially a promise by the permanent lender that, under stipulated conditions, it will issue a permanent loan upon satisfactory completion of the construction.

Take-out commitments vary depending on the credentials of the borrower, market conditions, property types, and policies of the lender. Certain provisions, however, are found in many take-out or permanent loan commitments, and they are an integral part of the terminology and practice of residential, commercial, and industrial construction financing.

It should be noted that the construction/permanent financing models of the past are being modified by some lenders, particularly in the secondary market. For instance, Fannie Mae has its HomeStyle Construction-to-Permanent Mortgage (HCPM), under which borrowers may finance the construction and permanent mortgage under one package, from qualified lenders. This eliminates a second closing after the construction is complete and, thereby, reduces paperwork. Borrowers receive an "as completed" appraisal on which the loan will be determined. HCPM loans are thereafter sold to FNMA. Interest rates can be locked in for both the construction and postconstruction phases, with interest paid monthly on the amount drawn during the construction phase, based on a series of draws similar to those shown in Figure 12.2.

Subordination Clauses

A **subordination clause** is an agreement to reduce the priority of an existing recorded loan to a new loan to be recorded in the future. For example, a developer purchases vacant land by putting some money down and the seller carries the rest of the purchase price as first deed of trust. The developer then locates construction funds to develop the property but construction lenders usually insist they be the first deed of trust. Under a subordination clause, the seller carry lender agrees to temporarily remove the loan from the public records to allow the construction loan to record, then the seller rerecords his/her loan as a second deed of trust.

The provisions of sections 2953.1 through 2953.5 of the Civil Code require that deeds of trust containing subordination clauses, and separate subordination agreements, contain specified warning language. State judicial decisions require that a subordination clause or agreement be certain in its terms, and unless the maximum amount, maximum rate of interest, and terms of repayment of the loan secured by the future deed of trust are specified, the subordination clause or agreement will not be enforceable. Moreover, recent decisions clearly indicate that a subordination clause or agreement will not be enforceable unless it is fair and equitable to the beneficiary. An example of a subordination agreement is given in Figure 12.3.

Partial Release Clauses

Also common to construction lending is the **partial release clause**. This provision is used with a trust deed placed on more than one parcel of property, termed a **blanket trust deed**, such as in the development of a subdivision. As each individual lot is sold, it is released from the blanket loan, the balance of which is correspondingly, but not necessarily proportionately, reduced. The release is accomplished when the lender issues a **partial reconveyance deed** on the individual lot being sold. Without a partial release clause, the trustor has no automatic right to receive a partial release.

The beneficiary (lender) requests the trustee to execute and record a partial reconveyance deed describing the portion of the property released from the blanket trust deed. The promissory note is usually endorsed to show that a partial release was given. When a series of such partial releases is contemplated, the deed of trust will usually provide that the trustee may receive the released proceeds for the beneficiary and give the partial reconveyance deeds without further demand or request from the beneficiary.

A partial release clause must be carefully examined with respect to such matters as these:

- Whether or not a trustor in default is entitled to partial releases

- Restrictions on the selection of portions of the property to be released

- The precise amount of the **lot release provision** and the method of computing the release price; payments for each release must be provided for in the agreement

- Whether the release prices merely reduce the amount of the secured obligation or apply to past, current, and future installments due on the obligation

Rental Achievement Clauses

When the construction of commercial (and sometimes industrial) property is being financed, a **rental achievement clause** is common.

RECORDING REQUESTED BY

55555

WHEN RECORDED MAIL TO

LAST SAVINGS and LOAN ASSOCIATION

1700 Broadway

Oakland, California

SPACE ABOVE THIS LINE FOR RECORDER'S USE

JOHN DOE and MARY DOE

SUBORDINATION AGREEMENT

THIS AGREEMENT, made this **15** day of **November**, 20XX by **JOHN DOE and MARY DOE**

owner of the land hereinafter described and hereinafter referred to as Owner, and **JOHN SMITH and MARY SMITH** present owner and holder of the deed of trust and note first hereinafter described and hereinafter referred to as Beneficiary,

WITNESSETH

THAT WHEREAS, **JOHN DOE and MARY DOE** did on **August 15, 20XX** execute a deed of trust to **Title Insurance and Trust Company**, as trustee, covering:

Full Legal Description

to secure a note in the sum of $ **155,000.00** dated **August 14, 20XX** in favor of **JOHN SMITH and MARY SMITH** which deed of trust was recorded **August 16, 20XX**, in book/reel **1763** page/ image **183** of Official Records of said County, and

WHEREAS, Owner has executed, or is about to execute loan instructions and a building loan agreement together with a deed of trust and note in the sum of $ **155,000** dated **November 15, 20XX** favor of LAST SAVINGS AND LOAN ASSOCIATION hereinafter referred to as Lender, payable with interest and upon the terms and conditions described therein which deed of trust is to be recorded contemporaneously herewith, and

WHEREAS, it is a condition precedent to obtaining said loan that said deed of trust, last above mentioned, shall be and remain a lien or charge upon the land hereinbefore described, prior and superior to the lien or charge of the deed of trust, first above mentioned;

WHEREAS, Lender is willing to make said loan provided the deed of trust to secure the same is a lien or charge upon the above-described property prior and superior to the lien or charge of the deed of trust owned by Beneficiary, and provided that Beneficiary will specifically and unconditionally subordinate the lien or charge of his deed of trust above described to the lien or charge of the deed of trust of Lender.

NOW, THEREFORE, in consideration of the premises and other valuable consideration, receipt of which is hereby acknowledged, and in order to induce LAST SAVINGS AND LOAN ASSOCIATION, to make the loan above referred to, it is hereby declared, understood and agreed as follows:

(1) That said deed of trust securing said note in favor of LAST SAVINGS AND LOAN ASSOCIATION and any renewals or extensions of said deed of trust and the note secured thereby, shall be and remain at all times a lien or charge on the property herein described, prior and superior to the lien or charge of the deed of trust first above mentioned.

(2) That Lender would not make its loan above described without this Subordination Agreement.

Figure 12.3 Sample subordination agreement (partial).

The granting of a construction loan for rental properties is usually contingent on the developer-borrower's ability to prelease a stated amount of space in the building. The developer usually provides a certified rent roll indicating who the tenants will be, the space to be leased, length of the leases, and the annual rents to be paid. The loan servicing agents then recertify that the developer's certified statements have been verified.

The rental achievement condition in the commitment for commercial property is of prime concern to construction lenders. Lenders do not want to finance construction projects and then discover that tenants are lacking for the rental space. Consequently, lenders are hesitant to advance any construction loan until the rental requirements of the take-out or permanent lender have been satisfied. It is typical for the permanent lender, in deference to the construction lender's concern, to provide that a certain portion of the loan be disbursed without any rental requirement and the balance when rentals reach a stipulated level. The amount of the construction loan may be set at the lower amount, called the *floor loan*, at least until the necessary rentals have been achieved. Additional sums are then disbursed later as the rental schedule submitted with the loan application is met; however, this must be done within a specified time, usually one or two years after the closing of the floor loan.

There can be a gap between the higher amount that the permanent lender will commit to if all rentals are achieved, and the lower floor amount it will loan if the rental roll is not achieved as planned. The gap is usually 15 to 20 percent of the larger amount. The developer would like to obtain the full amount of the loan, that is, the full rental achievement commitment, in order to generate as much leverage as possible. Yet, the construction lender will usually commit itself only for the floor amount.

The construction lender may be willing, however, to commit for the full or larger amount if another lender will "stand by" or commit itself to provide the gap financing. The *gap commitment* guarantees that the borrower will have the difference between the floor loan and the upper level of the permanent loan if the rental achievement for the larger amount is not reached. A fee is charged for the gap commitment and the interest rate is often higher because the loan, if made, would be a second mortgage. The developer, however, does not expect to actually have to draw the funds from the gap commitment (and the gap lender does not expect it either).

Mechanic's Liens and Their Impact on Construction Loans

All construction lenders are wary about the possibility of mechanic's liens, that is, creation of liens against real estate by those improving it. Mechanic's liens can arise if a builder does not complete the project or if the job is completed and the builder fails to pay material suppliers and subcontractors and workers. The probability of a lien by one or more subcontractors and material suppliers is ever present, possibly jeopardizing the construction lender's priority position. This applies to all forms of real estate construction, including home improvement loans. An example of a mechanic's lien is given in Figure 12.4.

Mechanic's lien rights are protected by the state constitution and are granted to contractors, subcontractors, laborers, and material suppliers who have contributed to or worked on the property and have not been paid for their services. The law requires that in addition to a contract to do the work, a *pre-lien notice* in the form of a notice of intent to lien, if provider is not paid, must be filed with the owner and construction lender's office within 20 days of commencement of each particular segment of work. The period for filing a lien varies from as few as 30 days to not more than 90 days after completion of a building or other work of improvement.

Notice of Completion

If a **Notice of Completion** (see Figure 12.5) is filed by the owner (not the contractor) within 10 days after the job is substantially completed, the *original contractor* has 60 days in which to file a lien, while all other parties have 30 days. If no notice of completion is recorded, or if a notice of completion is faulty in any respect, all parties have 90 days from the date of **substantial completion**. To protect themselves, as well as the builder and lender, against mechanic's liens, owners can purchase **completion bonds**—extremely rare with home construction loans, but required for Cal-Vet construction loans, and always required for government construction jobs—usually costing 1.5 percent of hard costs.

Should a job not be completed due to acts of God, strikes, impossibility of performance, disagreements, work stoppage, or for any other reason, then a **Notice of Cessation of Labor** or **Notice of Abandonment** may be filed. These have time limits similar to those of a completion notice.

If any work of improvement started prior to recording the construction loan, a mechanic's lien may take priority over other liens that were placed on the property after the job was started. This is

RECORDING REQUESTED BY
CHARLES L. LOAFER
WHEN RECORDED MAIL TO

1436

Name Charles L. Loafer
Street Address 2432 Mountain Ave
City & State Willow Springs, Calif.

Recorded in Official
Records of Oakdale
County, Calif.

May 23, 20xx at 1:00p.m.

FEE
$3.00
A

GEORGE L. FISH, County
Recorder

(SPACE ABOVE THIS LINE FOR RECORDER'S USE)

MECHANIC'S LIEN

NOTICE IS HEREBY GIVEN that: Pursuant to the provisions of the California Civil Code
Charles L. Loafer

hereafter referred to as "Claimant" (whether singular or plural), claims a lien upon the real property and buildings, improvements or structures thereon, described in Paragraph Five (5) below, and states the following:

(1) That demand of Claimant after deducting all just credits and offsets, is $3,800

together with interest thereon at the rate of 5 % per annum from April 1 20xx

(2) That the name of the owner(s) or reputed owner(s) of said property, is (are)
James M. Broke and Joanne S. Broke
(name, or state "unknown")

(3) That Claimant did from March 25 20xx, until March 28 ,20xx

perform labor and/or supply materials as follows: Replacement of front main line, meter to
(general statement of kind of work done or materials furnished, or both)

house. Replaced all valves and reconnected to sprinkler system
with all valves up by porch, on a time and material basis.
Material $800, sales tax $70, labor $2,900. Permit $30.

for the construction, alteration or repair of said buildings, improvements or structures, which labor, or materials, or both of them, were in fact used in the construction, alteration or repair of said buildings, improvements or structures, the location of which is set forth in Paragraph Five (5) below.

(4) Claimant furnished work and materials under contract with, or at the request of,
James M. Broke and Joanne S. Broke

(5) That the property upon which said lien is sought to be charged is situated in the City of Harrisport ,

County of Oakdale , State of California, commonly known as

20436 S. Grand, Harrisport, California
(street address)

and more particularly described as Lot 306, tract 1415 as per map recorded in book
563 pages 21 to 25 inclusive of maps, in the office of the county
recorder of said county. (legal description)

DATED: This 22nd day of May 20xx

Firm Name Loafer Plumbing Service
By Charles L. Loafer

(Verification for Individual Claim)

STATE OF CALIFORNIA,
County of Oakdale } ss.

Charles L. Loafer ,
being first duly sworn, deposes and says: That____ he is the
_____ Claimant
named in the foregoing claim of lien, that____ he has read the
same and knows the contents thereof, and that the statements therein
contained are true; and that it contains, among other things, a
correct statement of his demand, after deducting all just
credits and offsets. May
Dated: this 22nd day of 20xx, at Willow Springs,
(City & State) Calif.

Charles L. Loafer
(Signature of affiant)

Subscribed and sworn to before me

May 22 20xx

John Fairchild John Fairchild
Notary Public in and for said State.

OFFICIAL SEAL
JOHN FAIRCHILD
NOTARY PUBLIC — CALIFORNIA
PRINCIPAL OFFICE IN
LOS ANGELES COUNTY
My Commission Expires Nov. 9,

(Verification for other than individual Claim)

STATE OF CALIFORNIA,
County of_____ } ss.

_____
being first duly sworn, deposes and says: That_____
the Claimant herein, is a ¹_____
that affiant is ²_____

and for that reason he makes his affidavit on behalf of said ³
that he has read the same and knows the contents thereof, and that
the statements therein contained are true; and that it contains,
among other things, a correct statement of the demand of Claimant,
after deducting all just credits and offsets.
Dated: this____ day of 20____, at
(City & State)

_____
(Signature of affiant)

Subscribed and sworn to before me

_____19

_____
Notary Public in and for said State.

MECHANIC'S LIEN—1024

8 pt. type or larger

Figure 12.4 Sample mechanic's lien.

RECORDING REQUESTED BY

SAFECO TITLE INSURANCE COMPANY

AND WHEN RECORDED MAIL TO

NAME   Alfred S. Busybody

ADDRESS   14602 Victory Blvd.

CITY & STATE   Van Nuys, CA 91401

SPACE ABOVE THIS LINE FOR RECORDER'S USE

Notice of Completion
Individual
Before using this form, refer to recommended procedure stated on reverse side of this form

NOTICE IS HEREBY GIVEN THAT:

1. The undersigned is owner of the interest or estate stated below in the property hereinafter described.
2. The full name of the undersigned is.... **Alfred S. Busybody**
3. The full address of the undersigned is.. **14602 Victory Blvd, Van Nuys, CA 91401**
4. The nature of the title of the undersigned is: In fee **"Lessee"**
   (If other than fee, strike "In fee" and insert, for example, "purchaser under contract of purchase," or "lessee".)
5. The full names and full addresses of all persons, if any, who hold title with the undersigned as joint tenants or as tenants in common are:

NAMES	ADDRESSES
Alfred S. Busybody	14602 Victory Blvd., Van Nuys, CA

6. A work of improvement on the property hereinafter described was completed on.... **May 1,** 20XX
7. The name of the original contractor, if any, for such work of improvement was.................... **Cave-in Construction Company, Inc.**
   (If no contractor for work of improvement as a whole, insert "none".)
8. The full name(s) and address(es) of the transferor(s) of the undersigned is (are):

NAME(S)	ADDRESS(ES)
N O N E	

(Complete where undersigned is successor to owner who caused improvement to be constructed)

9. The property on which said work of improvement was completed is in the city of.... **Van Nuys**
   ...., county of.. **Los Angeles** ...., state of California, and is described as follows:
   Lot 7, Tract 13075, as per map recorded in Book 326, pages 10 to 15 inclusive of maps, in the office of the county recorder of said county.

10. The street address of said property is.... **14602 Victory Blvd., Van Nuys, CA**

(If no street address has been officially assigned, insert "none".)

Signature of owner named in paragraph 2 } *Alfred S Busybody*
Alfred S. Busybody

Dated.. **June 2,** 20XX

Verification for individual owners

STATE OF CALIFORNIA,

County of.. **Los Angeles** } SS.

The undersigned, being duly sworn, says: That   he is the owner of the aforesaid interest or estate in the property described in the foregoing notice; that   he has read the same, and knows the contents thereof, and that the facts stated therein are true.
Signature of owner named in paragraph 2....................

SUBSCRIBED AND SWORN TO before me on.. **June 2,** 20XX

Robert J Bond

Robert J. Bond

FOR NOTARY SEAL OR STAMP

OFFICIAL SEAL
ROBERT J. BOND
NOTARY PUBLIC - CALIFORNIA
LOS ANGELES COUNTY
My comm. expires JAN 31, 20XX

Title Order No. **7062351**   Escrow No. **1616-22**

511 Van Nuys Blvd., #12, Van Nuys, CA 91401

Figure 12.5 Sample notice of completion.

referred to as the ***doctrine of relation back***, and the financial interests of all others furnishing labor or materials are perceived to have begun from this initial date even though they came on the scene subsequent to the creation of the trust deed securing the construction loan or other liens. For this reason lenders and others making construction loans carefully check to determine that no construction work has been started prior to the recordation of a loan; or lenders may require indemnity of an ALTA title policy protecting them against loss from mechanic's liens.

What constitutes "start of construction"? It could be delivering material, clearing the lot, setting grade stakes, grading, ditching, placing chemical toilets on the lot, setting power poles, setting location markers, marking chalk lines, clearing trees, and so on.

Anyone filing a mechanic's lien must institute a suit to foreclose the lien within 90 days after recording the lien. The suit is similar to a mortgage foreclosure, resulting in a court-ordered sale in order to satisfy the claims. In the event of insufficient funds following the sale, the court may award a deficiency judgment against the debtor for the balance. If no suit is filed, a mechanic's lien expires after 90 days.

Notice of Nonresponsibility

Sometimes a lien is filed against property whose owner did not contract for the improvement, as when a tenant negotiates a contract for major repairs or alterations to a leasehold interest. To protect themselves, the owners may repudiate responsibility and liability by recording a Notice of Nonresponsibility within 10 days of the time they acquired knowledge. A sample is shown as Figure 12.6. A copy of the notice must be posted on the property. The contractor would then have to look to the contract for remedy—that is, sue the contracting party for collection of money due.

Release of mechanic's Liens

A mechanic's lien may be discharged by the running of the statute of limitations after 90 days if no foreclosure action is commenced; by written release, through the recording of a ***Release of Mechanic's Lien*** (illustrated in Figure 12.7); by the issuance of a bond to release the lien; by satisfaction of the judgment lien against the debtor; or by dismissal of the action when the court is convinced that a valid claim is not sustainable.

RECORDING REQUESTED BY

ALBERT E. CAUTIOUS
WHEN RECORDED MAIL TO

21536

Recorded in Official Records
of Oakdale County, Calif.

January 17, 20XX at 10:00a.m.

GEORGE L. FISH, County
Recorder

FEE
$3.00
D

Name
Street
Address
City &
State

Albert E. Cautious
7503 S. Juniper Street
Hawthorne, Calif.

———— (SPACE ABOVE THIS LINE FOR RECORDER'S USE) ————

NOTICE
NON-RESPONSIBILITY

TO ALL WHOM IT MAY CONCERN: NOTICE IS HEREBY GIVEN:

(1) That ___I___ to wit, __Albert E. Cautious__
   (I—we)   (Insert name or names)

(am—are)

the __Fee Owner__
   (Insert herein the nature of title or interest)

of certain property located in the City of __Hawthorne__
County of __Oakdale__ , State of California, and more particularly described as:
Lot__11__ in Block __--__ of Tract No. __27735__
                                                                    as
per map__ recorded in Book __6317__ Page __33__ of
Records of __Oakdale__ County, State of California.

(2) That __I__ have obtained knowledge that __Construction of a Swimming__
   (I—we)   (Insert brief description of improvement, alteration or repair)
__Pool__
                                                                    is
                                                                    (is—are)
__Being Done__ on said property.
   (in the course of construction—are being made)

(3) That ten (10) days have not elapsed since __I__ obtained this knowledge.
                                                (I—we)
(4) That __I__ will not be responsible for the __Construction__
   (I—we)   (erection, alteration or repair)
of said __Swimming Pool__
         (building—improvement)
or for the material or labor used or to be used thereon, or which has been performed, furnished or used in
any manner or way upon said land, or upon the __Swimming Pool__
                                                 (building—improvement)
thereon, or addition thereto, or which may hereafter be
performed, furnished, or used upon said land, or upon the __Swimming Pool__
                                                            (building—improvement)
thereon, or addition thereto, or for the services of any architect.

(5) That _____
              (Insert name or names)   (is—are)
the purchaser__ of said property under a contract of purchase.
(6) That the street address of said property is __7503 S. Juniper St__ , City of
__Hawthorne__ , California, and that __Peter I. Sneak__
                                      (Insert name or names)
__is__ the lessee__ of said property.
(is—are)
Dated __January 13, 20XX__

Albert E. Cautious
Albert E. Cautious

STATE OF CALIFORNIA,
                                          } ss.
County of __Oakdale__

__Albert E. Cautious__ , being first duly sworn, deposes and says: That the above and within
notice is a true and correct copy of a notice posted in a conspicuous place on Lot__ 11__ in Block __--__
of Tract No. __27735__ in the City of __Hawthorne__
County of __Oakdale__ State of California on the __13th__ day of __January__
20XX by __Albert E. Cautious__ and that the facts stated therein are true of __his__ own knowledge,
and that __he is making this affidavit for and on behalf of the person__ for whose protection said notice was given.

Subscribed and sworn to before me this __16th__ day of __January__ 20XX

OFFICIAL SEAL
ARNOLD T. CHECKER
NOTARY PUBLIC — CALIFORNIA
PRINCIPAL OFFICE IN
LOS ANGELES COUNTY
My Commission Expires Nov. 9, 20XX

Arnold T. Checker
Notary Public in and for said County and State.

Title Order No _____   Escrow or Loan No _____

NOTICE—NON-RESPONSIBILITY
WOLCOTTS FORM 1166—REVISED

most usual problems to the field indicated. Before you sign, read it, fill in all blanks,
your transaction. Consult a lawyer if you doubt the form's fitness for your purpose.

Figure 12.6 Sample notice of nonresponsibility.

RECORDING REQUESTED BY

JAMES M. BROKE & JAONNE S. BROKE

AND WHEN RECORDED MAIL TO

NAME James M & Jaonne S Broke
ADDRESS 20536 S Grand Ave.
CITY & STATE Harrisport, California

—— SPACE ABOVE THIS LINE FOR RECORDER'S USE ——

Release of Mechanic's Lien

That Notice of Mechanics Lien executed by <u>Charles L. Loafer</u>

————————————, naming as obligors (including the owners or reputed owners) ————

<u>James M Broke and Jaonne S Broke</u>

Recorded <u>May 23, 20XX</u> ————————, as Instrument No. <u>1436</u>

in Book <u>5883</u>, Page <u>25</u>, Official Records of the County of <u>Oakdale</u>

State of California, upon that Real Property in said County and State described as:

Lot 306, Tract 1415 as per map recorded in Book 563, pages 21 to 25 inclusive of maps, in the office of the county recorder of said county.

Is hereby released, the claim having been fully paid and discharged.

Dated <u>August 14, 20XX</u>

STATE OF CALIFORNIA
COUNTY OF } SS.

On <u>August 14, 20XX</u>
before me, the undersigned, a Notary Public in and for said County and State, personally appeared

<u>Charles L. Loafer</u>

known to me to be the person(s) whose name(s) is (are) subscribed to the within instrument and acknowledged that <u>he</u> executed the same.

Robert J. Bond
Robert J. Bond

Loafer Plumbing Service

By: *Charles L. Loafer*

FOR NOTARY SEAL OR STAMP

OFFICIAL SEAL
ROBERT J. BOND
NOTARY PUBLIC - CALIFORNIA
LOS ANGELES COUNTY
My comm. expires JAN 31.
6511 Von Nuys Blvd, #12, Van Nuys CA 91401

Title Order No. ———— Escrow No. ————

Figure 12.7 Sample release of mechanic's lien.

12.4 Public Construction

Often property owners are assessed for public construction projects that are proposed to improve the general health and welfare of the community. At the same time such public projects increase the value of properties of the affected owners in theory if not also in practice.

Assessment liens are imposed upon properties benefiting from capital projects that are classified as off-site improvements, such as street widening and installation of curbs, gutters, sidewalks, storm drains, sewers, and street lights. A number of state laws allow for the imposition of an assessment tax on the benefited properties, which share in the costs on a proportioned basis. The property owners may either pay the assessment in full within 30 days after completion—defined as final inspection and approval of the job by the applicable local regulatory agency—or pay the lien in installments over a period not to exceed 15 years through an assessment bond.

There are four significant state laws or improvement acts, as they are called, that provide for the construction and financing of capital improvements for which the property owner is assessed in whole or in part:

1. *Vrooman Street Act*. This law confers authority on city councils to grade and finish streets, construct sewers, and perform other improvements within municipalities or counties and to issue bonds secured and redeemed by tax levies. It also provides for the acquisition of public utilities by the local governing body.

2. *Street Improvement Act of 1911*. This law, with its amendments, provides that bonds may be issued by the municipality ordering the improvements and that the assessments may be paid in equal installments during the term of the bonds. The installments may be paid with property taxes over a 15-year period, but can be paid off at any time. The assessee must pay a share of the project within 30 days of its completion or bonds will be issued at an interest rate determined by the issuing local legislative body. The bonds will remain as liens against the property until paid in full.

3. *Improvement Bond Act of 1915*. This law, also as amended, provides for the issuance of series bonds for subdivision street improvements, including the construction of sewers. The cost of the redemption of the bonds issued and the interest thereon, usually 6 percent, is assessed in a proportioned manner against the owners of property directly affected.

4. *Mello-Roos Community Facilities Act.* This law arose as a result of Proposition 13, which restricts taxing districts from raising property taxes above 1 percent to 1.5 percent of assessed value. To finance public improvements for housing developments, a "Mello-Roos tax district" may be formed by local governments, under the terms of which the developer may impose the bonds and then market the properties, subject to individual lot assessments. Each purchaser of a home in such districts is assessed a pro rata share of the costs to put in freeway access routes and build and maintain roads, sewers, community centers, and even schools that serve the housing project.

SUMMARY

Construction loans are short-term or interim loans. Combination loans, combine the short-term interim loan with the permanent or take-out loan.

Construction lenders look for many things before finally committing themselves to fund a construction project. These include evaluation of the plans and specifications, detailed breakdown of the costs involved, analysis of the building contract, source of repayment, and supporting financial data required on the owner, builder, and others who may have a financial interest in the project.

A construction loan contract may contain a variety of provisions that protect the lender and borrower, including a subordination clause, partial release clause, rental achievement clause, and others.

Mechanic's liens protect those who improve real property by means of their labor, skills, services, and materials furnished for the job. Construction lenders must be on guard to see that their security is not impaired because of faulty construction, noncompliance with the building loan agreement, start of work before the construction trust deed is recorded, and other construction problems.

IMPORTANT TERMS AND CONCEPTS

Advances	*Notice of Cessation of Labor*
Assessment lien	*Notice of Completion*
Blanket trust deed	*Partial reconveyance deed*
Builder's control service	*Partial release clause*
Building loan agreement	*Payout schedule*
Combination loan	*Performance bond (see Completion bond)*
Completion bond	*Progress payments*
Conditional commitment	*Release of mechanic's lien*
Disbursements	*Rental achievement clause*
Doctrine of relation back	*Short-term construction loan*
Draw system	*Soft costs*
Floor loan	*Street Improvement Act of 1911*
Gap commitment	*Subordination clause*
Hard costs	*Substantial completion*
Holdback	*Take-out commitment*
Improvement Bond Act of 1915	*Take-out loan*
Lot release provision	*Voucher system*
Mechanic's lien	*Vrooman Street Act*
Mello-Roos Community Facilities Act	
Notice of Abandonment	

REVIEWING YOUR UNDERSTANDING

Questions for Discussion

1. How do construction loans differ from take-out loans?
2. What is meant by progress payments?
3. List several methods of disbursing funds for construction projects.

4. What is a subordination clause? How does such a clause protect the construction lender?

5. Differentiate between a partial release clause and a rental achievement clause. For whose benefit are these provisions set up?

Multiple-Choice Questions

1. A lien filed by contractors due to the failure of an obligated party to pay for work of improvement is a
   a. contractor's lien.
   b. subordination lien.
   c. mechanic's lien.
   d. superior lien.

2. The payoff of a construction loan is normally accomplished through
   a. a take-out loan.
   b. cash flow generated from an income property.
   c. sale of the completed project.
   d. bonded indebtedness.

3. In a five-draw construction loan payment schedule, mechanic's liens are considered in (hint: see Figure 12.2)
   a. draw 4.
   b. draw 5.
   c. draw 1.
   d. draw 2.

4. The system of disbursements of construction funds upon presentation of receipted bills by contractors is called a
   a. percentage of progress.
   b. voucher.
   c. stage of completion.
   d. proof of billings.

5. An agreement between borrower and permanent lender relative to future delivery of a take-out loan upon completion is called a
   a. construction contract.
   b. building loan agreement.
   c. take-out commitment.
   d. tri-party agreement.

6. A contract between borrower, contractor, and lender establishing the obligations and duties of each party during the period of construction is a
    a. construction contract.
    b. building loan agreement.
    c. take-out commitment.
    d. bilateral agreement.

7. A construction loan may lose first-lien position to mechanic's lien claimants by
    a. commencement of work prior to recording of a construction loan.
    b. commencement of work prior to recording of a combination loan.
    c. either (a) or (b).
    d. neither (a) nor (b).

8. The largest number and volume of interim construction loans are generally made by
    a. local institutions.
    b. credit unions.
    c. real estate investment trusts.
    d. casualty insurance companies.

9. The document that is filed by the owner after a project is substantially completed is a
    a. Notice of Cessation of Labor.
    b. Mechanic's Lien.
    c. Notice of Nonresponsibility.
    d. Notice of Completion.

10. When a mechanic's lien is filed against a property, the threat of loss of title rests with the:
    a. lender.
    b. contractor.
    c. owner.
    d. subcontractor.

11. The costs of a construction loan to a borrower are greater than a regular purchase money loan because
    a. costs and interest rates are increasing daily.
    b. the lender knows that construction costs are constantly going up.
    c. the lender knows that values will have risen by the time the project is completed.
    d. the lender has more overhead and greater risks.

12. In California, construction loans cannot be made
    a. unless a take-out loan has been committed by a responsible lender.
    b. for less than one year.
    c. except on an owner-occupied basis.
    d. none of the above is correct.

13. The amount of a construction loan
    a. is paid out in a lump sum upon completion of construction.
    b. normally is paid out in various stages.
    c. must be disbursed in no fewer than five draws.
    d. generally begins to be amortized as soon as the first disbursement is made.

14. A subordination clause in a deed of trust is most likely to be found in the case of
    a. a package deed of trust.
    b. a combination loan.
    c. a regular deed of trust.
    d. land loans.

15. If a developer has signed a deed of trust covering all the lots in a subdivision, he or she will find that partial releases
    a. cannot be required unless provided for specifically in the deed of trust.
    b. can always be obtained, even if not specifically provided for, upon payment of a pro rata amount of the principal balance due.
    c. can be obtained only if a subordination agreement is incorporated in the deed of trust.
    d. cannot be obtained until at least 50 percent of the lots in a subdivision are sold.

16. Which document separates a regular real estate loan from a construction loan?
    a. building loan agreement.
    b. promissory note.
    c. appraisal report.
    d. credit report.

17. Which of the following is a direct result of Proposition 13?
    a. Mechanic's Lien Law.
    b. Improvement Bond Act of 1915.
    c. Street Improvement Act of 1911.
    d. Mello-Roos Community Facilities Act.

18. A partial release clause is usually used in connection with a
    a. combination loan.
    b. blanket loan.
    c. floor loan.
    d. standby loan.

19. Major alterations to a rental house were contracted for by the tenants. To disavow themselves from possible mechanic's liens against their property, the owners should file and post a
    a. Rental Achievement Clause.
    b. Notice of Completion.
    c. Notice of Nonresponsibility.
    d. Release of Mechanic's Lien.

20. Another name for an interim loan is
    a. nonamortized loan.
    b. progress loan.
    c. take-out loan.
    d. short-term loan.

CHAPTER 13
BASIC MATHEMATICS OF REAL ESTATE FINANCE

PREVIEW

A basic understanding of the mathematics of real estate finance is vital to the practitioner, consumer, and investor. Words are hardly enough. Understanding numbers—figures—is essential to close any real estate transaction.

After completing this chapter, you should be able to:

1. Differentiate between a straight note (interest only) and an amortized note.

2. Explain how financial calculators and computers are used to determine monthly payments, principal and interest allocation, balloon payments, price and yields on notes, plus a variety of other real estate calculations.

3. Discuss how biweekly loan payments differ from traditional monthly payments.

4. Understand what inputs are used to calculate the Annual Percentage Rate (APR) for a real estate loan.

13.1 Review of the Basic Components of a Real Estate Loan

1. *Interest is the charge or price, expressed as dollars, paid for the use of money.* From a lender's point of view, a borrower can be viewed as a tenant, renting money for an agreed period of time, returning the rented funds with an additional charge for their use. The "interest rent" may be paid either at the end of the period—the maturity date—or, more commonly, at periodic intervals, such as monthly payments.

2. *Principal is the amount of money borrowed.* It is the initial amount that appears on the promissory note.

3. *Rate is the percentage of interest charged on the principal* and is usually expressed as an annual rate.

4. *Time (or term) denotes the length of the loan and the frequency of payments.* The term is usually expressed as years, with the payment due monthly. Occasionally, payments are due annually, semi-annually, or quarterly.

Review of Promissory Notes

Straight Note (Interest Only Payments)

The **straight note** usually calls for "interest only" payments, with the entire principal due in a lump sum at a future date. The interest is usually paid monthly but some notes may call for other payment intervals such as quarterly or annually.

Example: Assume a $100,000 straight note at 8 percent interest per annum, payable monthly, all due in five years. What is the monthly interest payment?

Solution: $100,000 principal × 8% = $8,000 interest for the year ÷ 12 months = $666.67 per month, with the entire $100,000 principal due and payable at the end of five years.

Amortized Loan

An **amortized loan** calls for installment payments that include both principal and interest. Two main types are these:

1. *Installment Note—Fully Amortized.* This is the most common note found in real estate financing transactions. Each installment remains constant, with interest computed on the unpaid balance of the note, which is defined as simple interest. Hence, every payment represents a decreasing amount applicable to the interest and a corresponding increase in the principal portion. Since the installments continue in equal amounts until the entire obligation is repaid, this type is referred to as a fully amortized note.

2. *Installment Note—Partially Amortized with a Balloon Payment.* This note calls for payments of interest and principal, but not enough principal to competely pay off the loan by the due date, The payments remain constant until a stated date, at which time the outstanding balance, called a balloon payment, is due. As described in Chapter 1, a **balloon payment** is defined as any payment at least twice the size of the normal payments.

Why Amortized Loans Are Used

Prior to the Great Depression of the 1930s, many real estate loans made no provision for the reduction of the principal through periodic payments. In those days, if a person borrowed $10,000 at, say, 8 percent interest, the buyer was expected to pay only the annual interest of $800, in monthly installments, without reducing the principal. Then at some time in the future, the entire principal of $10,000 would become due and payable. During the Great Depression people lost their jobs and could not make the monthly interest payments or pay the principal loan amount when it came due. This resulted in massive foreclosures and the weakness of this "interest only" payment plan became evident. Then lending reforms, led by several government agencies, resulted in the current practice of monthly payments that include principal reduction.

How to Compute Amortized Loan Payments

To determine the required payments on a loan, one can use an amortization book or, preferably, use a financial calculator. The ***amortization book*** contains tables that show the amounts needed to pay off (a) varying amounts of loans, (b) at specified rates of interest, and (c) for specified periods (or terms). A sample page from an amortization book is shown in Table 13.1.

To use Table 13.1 to find monthly payments at 12 percent interest, merely locate the amount of the loan, then the term or number of

Table 13.1 Monthly loan amortization payments at 12 percent.

Amount	TERM (YEARS)							
	3	5	10	15	20	25	30	40
80,000	2657.17	1779.56	1147.85	960.18	880.90	842.60	822.90	806.80
81,000	2690.38	1801.80	1162.19	972.18	891.91	853.13	833.19	816.89
82,000	2723.61	1824.04	1176.54	984.18	902.92	863.66	843.47	826.97
83,000	2756.82	1846.29	1190.89	996.19	913.93	874.19	853.76	827.06
84,000	2790.05	1868.53	1205.24	1008.19	924.94	884.73	864.05	847.14
85,000	2823.22	1890.78	1219.59	1020.19	935.95	895.26	874.33	857.23
86,000	2856.44	1913.02	1233.94	1032.19	946.96	905.79	884.62	867.31
87,000	2889.65	1935.27	1248.28	1044.20	957.98	916.32	894.90	877.40
88,000	2922.88	1957.51	1262.63	1056.20	968.99	926.86	905.19	887.48
89,000	2956.10	1979.76	1276.98	1068.20	980.00	937.39	915.48	897.57
90,000	2989.29	2002.00	1291.33	1080.20	991.01	947.92	925.76	907.65
91,000	3022.42	2024.24	1305.68	1092.20	1002.02	958.45	936.05	917.74
92,000	3055.69	2046.49	1320.02	1104.21	1013.03	968.99	946.34	927.82
93,000	3088.89	2068.73	1334.37	1116.21	1024.04	979.52	956.62	937.91
94,000	3122.09	2090.98	1348.72	1128.21	1035.05	990.05	966.91	947.99
95,000	3155.36	2113.22	1363.07	1140.21	1046.06	1000.58	977.19	958.08
96,000	3188.55	2135.47	1377.42	1152.22	1057.08	1011.12	987.48	968.16
97,000	3221.75	2157.71	1391.76	1164.22	1068.09	1021.65	997.77	978.25
98,000	3255.00	2179.96	1406.11	1176.22	1079.10	1032.18	1008.05	988.33
99,000	3288.22	2202.20	1420.46	1188.22	1090.11	1042.71	1018.34	998.42
100,000	3321.43	2224.44	1434.81	1200.22	1101.12	1053.25	1028.62	1008.50

years of the loan. At the point of intersection the monthly payment is given. For example, an $80,000 loan at 12 percent for 30 years will require an $822.90 monthly payment. What will be the payments for a $100,000 loan at 12 percent payable for 20 years?

Another type of amortization table is shown in Table 13.2. This table shows the amount of payment per $1,000 of loan amount at interest rates from 6 percent to 20 percent, and repayment terms from 3 to 40 years.

To use Table 13.2, assume a $100,000 loan to be repaid in 30 years, in equal monthly installments, including interest of 8 percent per annum. What is the monthly payment?

First locate 30 in the number of years column in Table 13.2. Then look across, to the entry under the column headed 8 percent. Here we find the number 7.34. This means that the monthly payment, including

Table 13.2 Monthly payments needed to amortize a $1,000 loan at various interest rates.

Term (Years)	RATE OF INTEREST (%)									
	6	7	8	9	10	11	12	14	15	20
3	30.42	30.88	31.34	31.80	32.27	32.74	33.22	34.18	34.67	37.17
5	19.34	19.81	20.28	20.76	21.25	21.75	22.25	22.76	23.79	26.50
6	16.58	17.05	17.54	18.03	18.53	19.04	19.56	20.08	21.15	23.96
7	14.61	15.10	15.59	16.09	16.61	17.13	17.66	18.75	19.30	22.21
8	13.15	13.64	14.14	14.66	15.18	15.71	16.26	17.38	17.95	20.96
9	12.01	12.51	13.02	13.55	14.08	14.63	15.19	16.34	16.93	20.03
10	11.11	11.62	12.14	12.67	13.22	13.78	14.35	15.53	16.14	19.33
15	8.44	8.99	9.56	10.15	10.75	11.37	12.01	13.32	14.00	17.57
20	7.17	7.76	8.37	9.00	9.66	10.33	11.02	12.44	13.17	16.99
25	6.45	7.07	7.72	8.40	9.09	9.81	10.54	12.04	12.81	16.79
30	6.00	6.66	7.34	8.05	8.78	9.53	10.29	11.07	12.65	16.72
35	5.71	6.39	7.11	7.84	8.60	9.37	10.16	11.76	12.57	16.69
40	5.51	6.22	6.96	7.72	8.50	9.29	10.09	11.72	12.54	16.68

principal and interest, is $7.34 for each $1,000 of loan amount. Multiplying 7.34 by 100, since we are looking for a monthly payment for a $100,000 loan, results in $734 (rounded to the nearest dollar). It should be understood that this table shows the payments based on so much per thousand, though realistically the figures would typically be rounded to the nearest penny only after carrying them out to at least six places. The actual payment, using a financial calculator, is $733.76 per month.

13.2 The Real World of Financial Calculators and Computers

The computation of loan payments, interest rates, principal and interest allocations, discount yields, remaining balances, balloon payments, and many other mathematical real estate problems are no longer solved by using complicated tables; instead professionals use *financial calculators* and computers. Although surrounded by a world of computers, both desk and laptop, a real estate professional in the field frequently still needs the convenience of a financial calculator. The ability to use a financial calculator and quickly compute loan payments, qualifying ratios, and other numbers is essential in today's competitive real estate market.

Financial calculators should not be confused with the simple four-function calculators sold at variety stores. Nor should they be confused with scientific calculators. Financial calculators are preprogrammed to handle the time value of money and therefore can compute most real estate finance and investment problems without the need for amortization tables. In addition, you do not need to memorize complicated formulas, as financial calculators are programmed to handle all the mathematics internally.

There are many varieties of handheld financial calculators on the market today. Common models are put out by Texas Instruments, Hewlett-Packard, Calculating Financial Industries, and numerous others. It would be impractical to discuss and illustrate applications for each of these models, so we have chosen the Texas Instruments BA Real Estate model to illustrate typical keystokes to solve real estate financial calculations. This financial calculator is specifically designed for real estate computations, so the keys have symbols that are familiar to the industry. At the end of this chapter you will find a Case & Point section where we also illustrate keystrokes using the classic Hewlett-Packard Model 12C.

13.3 Illustrated Use of Texas Instruments BA Real Estate Calculator

All financial calculators have five special keys that deal with the time value of money (TVM). On the Texas Instruments BA Real Estate Calculator, the five financial keys (indicated by vertical lines) are as follows:

|TERM| This refers to the length of time. The period could be years, months, or days. For a loan, here is where you enter the number of payments per period.

|I%| This refers to the interest rate. Here you enter the interest per period, be it annual, monthly, or daily interest.

|LOAN| Here is where you enter the loan amount.

|PMT| This is the key you push to solve for payment, be it annual, monthly, or daily payment.

|FV| This stands for future value. This key is used when you wish to find a financial answer that lies in the future, such as a future balloon payment.

For all real estate loan problems you are given three elements to enter into three of these keys, then you push a fourth key to obtain your answer. Usually one key—the fifth—is not needed. Your job is to figure the three elements you know and enter them, then from the two remaining keys, select the one that will calculate the information you would like. For example, a real estate loan payment has four elements: term (number of payments), interest rate, loan amount, and payment. If you enter any three elements, the TI BA Real Estate calculator solves for the fourth unknown element. *The order in which you enter the known information does not matter.*

Loan Payments

The TI BA Real Estate calculator can compute any type of loan payment. It does not matter if the payment is annual, semiannual, quarterly, monthly, biweekly, weekly, or daily. The thing to remember is that all of the financial keys must be in the same time frame!

Example: On a $100,000 loan at 10 percent for 30 years, what is the monthly payment?

	push on/c button
	push on/c button
100,000	push |LOAN|
10	push |I%|
30	push |TERM|
	push |CPT| (CPT stands for compute)
	push |PMT| −877.57

Notice the minus sign in front of the answer, −877.57. The TI BA Real Estate calculator reads cash flows—it pretends to be your checkbook! The minus sign tells you that it will cost you −877.57 in monthly payments for 30 years to pay off the $100,000 loan at 10 percent per year. *You can enter any element in any order.* You do not need to first put in loan amount, then interest, then payments. Any order is acceptable to all financial calculators.

Caution: A financial calculator should be cleared between each calculation to assure that no leftover numbers remain in the financial keys to distort the correct answer in your next calculation. Make sure that FV (future value) is always shown as 0.00 (zero) when entering computations.

Making Larger Loan Payments

How fast will a loan be paid off if larger monthly payments are made?

Example: Using the same figures as above

100,000	push |LOAN|	
10	push |I%|	
30	push |TERM|	
	push |CPT|	
	push |PMT|	−877.57

Note that a 100,000 loan at 10 percent for 30 years will have a −877.57 monthly loan payment. This means that it will take $877.57 per month for 360 months (30 years × 12 per year) to pay off this loan. If the borrower paid $900 per month, how long would it take to pay off this loan?

Solution: Merely input the $900 per month and solve for TERM

900 [+/−] |PMT| |CPT| |TERM| 26.14 years

Note: the payment must be entered as a negative [+/−] Display will show PMT = −900.00

If the borrower paid $1,000 per month, how long would it take to pay off this loan?

1,000 [+/−] |PMT| |CPT| |TERM| 17.99 years

The lesson here is that a borrower can make larger payments and greatly reduce the total amount of interest paid and the length of time it takes to pay off a loan.

Interest and Principal Allocation

Many times a person wishes to know how much of a payment is interest and how much is principal. Or after a series of payments, how much interest and principal comprise each payment and the remaining balance. The TI BA Real Estate calculator easily does this using the |AMORT| key (amortization).

Example: Assume a $100,000 loan at 10 percent for 30 years. What is the monthly payment? What is the remaining loan balance? How much of the first payment is principal? Interest?

1. First solve for the monthly payment and you should get −877.57
2. Then push |AMORT| and P1 = 1.00 shows (P1 means 1st period)
3. Then push |=| and P2 = 1.00 shows (P2 means 2nd period)
4. Then push |=| BAL = 99,955.76 (this is the new balance)
5. Then push |=| PRN = −44.24 (this is the principal paid)
6. Then push |=| INT = −833.33 (this is the interest paid)

Principal and Interest Allocation for 12 Months

Example: Using the TI BA Real Estate Model, assume a $100,000 loan at 10 percent for 30 years. What is the monthly payment? What is the remaining loan balance after 12 payments? What is the principal paid for 12 months? What is the interest paid after making 12 monthly payments?

1. First solve for the monthly payments, which should be −877.57
2. Then: |AMORT| and P1 = 1.00 (P1 means 1st period)
3. Then: |=| and P2 = 1.00
4. Then enter 12 and push |=| (this indicates there are 12 payments)

    BALANCE = 99,444.14 shows on display screen (balance after 12 payments)
5. Then: |=| PRINCIPAL = −555.86 (principal paid after 12 payments)
6. Then: |=| INTEREST = −9,974.98 (interest paid after 12 payments)

This calculation is handy for estimating interest for annual income tax deductions.

Balloon Payments

Balloon payments are also called remaining loan balance and outstanding loan balance. To solve for the balance on a loan after a series of payments, all four parts of a loan must be in the calculator:

|TERM | |I%| |LOAN| and the payment in the |PMT| key.

If the payment is missing, you first must solve for payment; then the balloon payment can be found by correctly using the |FV| future value key.

Example: Use the TI BA Real Estate Model for a $100,000 loan at 10 percent amortized for 30 years, but due in five years. What will be the balance after five years?

Solution: First solve for the unknown monthly payment and you should get −877.57. Then solve for the loan balance in five years as follows:

N

5 × 12 |=| 60 |2nd| |TERM| |CPT| |FV| −96,574.32
(balance after five years of 60 payments)

What will be the balance after 10 years? Just key :

N

10 × 12 |=| 120 |2nd| |TERM| |CPT| |FV| −90,938.02
(balance after 10 years)

Once you get a balloon payoff, you can solve for any time period just by keying in the new year. You do not need to solve again for loan payment! *Note:* The remaining loan balances above assume that the borrower has already made the last monthly payment. If this is not the case, then the last monthly payment must be added to the balance to get the total balloon pay-off. This type of calculation is handy for estimating how much you will still owe after a series of payments.

More Complicated Calculations

(*Note to readers:* This section is optional and can be skipped by moving to the biweekly payment section.) The foregoing examples are typical real estate calculations that can be done with most financial calculators. In addition, a few financial calculators with special real estate keys can also do the following.

Calculating Loan Payments that Include PITI (Principal, Interest, Taxes, and Insurance)

Example: A buyer is interested in a home that is listed for $500,000. An 80 percent loan of $400,000 at 7.5 percent for 30 years is available to qualified buyers. What would be the monthly PITI required to buy this home?

Solution: First key in the typical property tax and insurance percentage for the area. Let's say property taxes in a high-cost area run 1.5

percent of the purchase price and high-quality personal liability and homeowners insurance is .5 percent of the purchase price.
The keystrokes using the TI BA Real Estate Model are:

TAX%

1. 1.5 |2nd| |RCL| shows TX% = 1.50 (this enters property taxes)

INS%

2. .5 |2nd| |STO| shows IS% = 0.50 (this enters insurance)
3. 500,000 |PRICE| shows PRC = 500,000 (this enters price)
4. 30 |TERM| shows TRM = 30.00 (this enters 30-year loan term)
5. 7.5 |I%| shows I% = 8.50 (this enters the interest rate)
6. 400,000 |LOAN| shows LN = 400,000 (this enters the loan amount)
7. |CPT| |PMT| −2,796.86 (this is the principal and interest payment)
8. |CPT| |PITI| −3,630.19 (this is the PITI payment)

(*Note:* It is important that the price be included, as property taxes and insurance are based on price and not loan amount. Also, property taxes may run as low as 1.15 percent and insurance .3 percent of the purchase price in some areas of California.)

Calculating Monthly Income Needed to Qualify for a Loan

Example: A buyer is interested in a home that is listed for $500,000. An 80 percent loan at 7.5 percent for 30 years is available if the buyers have the 20 percent down payment. The buyers have monthly long-term debts of $500. What would be the monthly income required to buy this home?

Solution: First key in the typical property tax and insurance percentage for the area (property taxes usually run 1.25 percent and insurance .3 percent of the purchase price).

TAX%

1. 1.25 |2nd| |RCL| TX% = 1.25 (this enters taxes)

INS%

2. .3 |2nd| |STO| IS% = 0.30 (this enters insurance)

Then key in typical loan qualifying ratios used by lenders, such as 28 percent for total monthly housing expense and 36 percent for total monthly housing and debt expense.

3.   INC%   DEBT%

   28 |2nd| |000| shows IN% = 28.00; 36 |2nd| |→| shows DB% = 36.00

4.   30 |TERM| (this enters the term of the loan)

5.   7.5 | I%| (this enters the interest rate of the loan)

6.   Start qualification by pressing |QUAL INC| (shows PRC = 0.00)

7.   500,000 |=| (this enters price)

8.   20 |=| (this enters down payment percentage)

9.   500 |=| (this enters monthly debts) shows LN = 400,000 (this is the loan amount)

10. |=| PMT = −2,796.86 (this is the monthly principal and interest payment)

11. |=| PITI = −3,442.69 (this is the PITI payment)

12. |=| QI = 12,295.32 (monthly income needed to qualify)

Note: These standards are flexible.

Calculating What a Buyer Can Afford to Borrow and the Price Range of Homes

Rather than looking at a home and then computing what income is needed to qualify as in the previous example, here we know the buyers' income and debts and we are trying to figure out what price range of homes, given current loan terms, the buyers are qualified to purchase.

Example: The buyers have combined monthly income of $8,000 and monthly debts of $400. Assume an 80 percent loan at 7.5 percent for 30 years is available if the buyers have the 20 percent down payment. What loan amount and price range of homes do the buyers appear to qualify for?

Solution: First key in the typical property tax and insurance percentage for the area (property taxes usually run 1.25 percent and insurance .3 percent of the purchase price).

TAX%

1. 1.25 |2nd| |RCL| TX% = 1.25 (this enters property taxes)

INS%

2. .3 |2nd| |STO| IS% = 0.30 (this enters insurance)

Then key in typical loan qualifying ratios used by lenders, such as 28 percent for total monthly housing expense and 36 percent for total monthly housing and debt expense.

INC%   DEBT%

3. 28 |2nd| |000| shows IN% = 28.00; 36 |2nd| |→| shows DB% = 36.00

4. 30 |TERM| (this enters the term of the loan)

5. 7.5 |I%| (this enters the interest rate of the loan)

6. Start qualification by pressing |QUAL LA| (shows INC = 0.00)

7. 8,000 |=| (this enters monthly income)

8. 400 |=| (this enters monthly debts)

9. 20 |=| (this enters % down) shows PITI = −2,240.00 (PITI payment)

10. |=| PMT = −1,819.79 (this is the monthly principal and interest payment)

11. |=| QLA = 260,261.49 (this is the qualified loan amount)

12. |=| QPR = 325,326.86 (this is the qualified price range)

13. |=| DN$ = 65,065.37 (this is the down payment needed)

This is a handy series of keystrokes to estimate what price range of homes to show buyers, and what will be the loan amount, monthly payment, and down payment requirements.

Finding Price or Yields When Buying Existing Notes and Deeds of Trust

Some people prefer to invest in notes and deeds of trust secured by real estate rather than purchase the real estate itself. They are attracted by the rates of return and do not wish to deal with the problems of being a landlord. Financial calculators make it easy to compute price and *yields* when negotiating for the purchase of notes and deeds of trust.

Finding the Price of a Note
When You Know the Desired Yield

Example: A $79,000 note at 8.5 percent is amortized for 30 years, but due in seven years. An investor wishes buy this note at a price that will yield 18 percent. What price should the investor pay?

Solution: First solve for loan payment.

1. 79,000 |LOAN| 8.5 |I%| 30 |TERM| |CPT| |PMT| −607.44

Then solve for balloon payment.

$$N$$

2. 7 × 12 |=| 84 |2nd| |TERM| |CPT| |FV| −73,532.45

Then solve for the price of the note.

3. 18 |I%| |CPT| |LOAN| 49,955.09

Calculating the Yield When You
Know the Discount Price of the Note

Example: A $79,000 note at 8.5 percent is amortized for 30 years, but due in seven years. An investor can buy this note for $49,955.09. What will be the investor's yield?

Solution First solve for the loan payment.

1. 79,000 |LOAN| 8.5 |I%| 30 |TERM| |CPT| |PMT| −607.44

Then solve for the balloon payment.

$$N$$

2. 7 × 12 |=| 84 |2nd| |TERM| |CPT| |FV| −73.532.45

Then solve for the yield.

3. 49,955.09 |LOAN| |CPT| |I%| 18

Biweekly Loan Payments

Occasionally, some real estate borrowers are given the option of making biweekly instead of monthly loan payments. Biweekly means a payment every two weeks (26 payments per year), instead of once a month (12 payments per year). Many times this better matches the borrower's paycheck (paid on the job every two weeks). In short, a biweekly program takes a monthly payment, then divides it in half, and this amount is paid 26 times per year.

A payment every two weeks is equal to approximately 13 monthly payments per year instead of the usual 12 monthly payments. Making biweekly loan payments can save on interest paid and reduce the time it takes to pay off a loan.

The TI BA Real Estate and some other financial calculators are pre-set to easily compute biweekly payments.

Example: Using the TI BA Real Estate Model, for a $100,000 loan at 10 percent for 30 years, what are the biweekly payments?

Solution:

	CLR TVM
	CLR TVM
|2nd|	|FV| (to clear the calculator)
100,000	|LOAN|
10	|I%|
30	|TERM|
|CPT|	|BI-WKLY| −438.79 (biweekly payment)

Then push \|=\| N = 541.38 (number of payments to pay off the loan)

again push \|=\| YRS = 20.77 (number of years to pay off the loan)

again push \|=\| SAV = 78,378 (dollars saved in interest compared with paying under a monthly payment plan)

This illustrates the savings under a biweekly payment system as compared with the normal monthly payment program.

13.4 Annual Percentage Rates

Under the federal Truth-in-Lending Law, most commercial lenders must disclose the total cost of real estate financing. The disclosure is in the form of total interest paid and the annual percentage rate (APR).

Disclosure of Total Interest Paid

Assume a $100,000 loan at 8 percent interest for 30 years with a monthly payment of $733.76.

The total interest on the actual loan, excluding any financing fees, would be calculated as follows:

Total scheduled to be paid over 30 years
($733.76 × 360 months) $264,155.25

Less: Original loan amount   −100,000.00

Total interest paid over scheduled life
of the loan $164,155.25

Disclosure of Annual Percentage Rate

When there are charges other than interest, some of these charges must be considered in determining the annual percentage rate (APR). On real estate loans the additional financial charges, other than the interest rate on the face of the note, include loan fees and certain other miscellaneous finance fees. The APR calculation must take into consideration loan fees and these other miscellaneous finance fees, as well as the note's interest rate.

Once again the advent of financial calculators has helped the process of computing annual percentage rates on real estate loans.

Example: Assume a $100,000 loan at 8 percent interest for 30 years, and the lender charges 1.5 points, plus $1,000 in other financing fees covered by the Truth-In-Lending Law. What is the APR?

Solution:

First clear the calculator by 2nd |FV|

Enter 30 |TERM|

Then 100,000 |LOAN|

Then push |APR| and calculator shows I% (it is asking for the interest rate)

Then 8 |=| and calculator shows PTS = 0.00 (it is asking the points)

Then 1.5 |=| and calculator shows FEE = 0.00 (it is asking for the other fees)

Then 1,000 |=| and calculator shows APR = 8.27

What this means is that a $100,000 loan at 8 percent for 30 years is costing you not 8 percent, but rather 8.27 percent when the points and other financing fees are taken into consideration. Federal regulations require lenders to give the APR quote so borrowers can compare the true cost of money when various lenders charge different interest rates and add or subtract various other "hidden" financing fees. The APR must be quoted within .125 percent, that is, no more than 1/8 percent above or 1/8 percent below the actual rate. If APR sounds difficult, welcome to the club!

SUMMARY

Real estate mathematics is used to clearly communicate the cost of a loan. Real estate promissory notes come in a variety of forms, and the interest and principal calculations depend on the specific type of note used. The two basic types are: (1) the *straight note*, which is payable interest only and, upon the due date, the entire original principal is due and payable, and (2) the *amortized loan*, which contains payments of both principal and interest. The amortized loan can be either fully or partially amortized. If partially amortized, a balloon payment will be owed on the due date. Financial calculators and computers have simplified all real estate lending arithmetic. In addition to calculating loan payments, principal and interest allocation, and balloon payments, financial calculators and computers can calculate price and yields on notes, biweekly payments, annual percentage rates (APR), and much more.

IMPORTANT TERMS AND CONCEPTS

Amortization tables	*Financial calculator*
Amortized loan	*Partial amortization*
Balloon payments	*Straight (or interest only) note*
Biweekly loan payments	*Yield*

REVIEWING YOUR UNDERSTANDING

Questions for Discussion

1. **If a borrower consistently makes larger payments than required, what impact will this have on a real estate loan?**

2. **Explain how a biweekly loan payment differs from a traditional monthly payment. What impact will a biweekly payment have on the length of the loan?**

Multiple-Choice Questions

1. A partially amortized note will *always* contain
   a. an adjustable interest rate.
   b. a balloon payment.
   c. a level payment for the entire life of the loan.
   d. an alienation clause.

2. A $200,000 straight note at 8 percent interest, payable monthly, will have what size payment?
   a. $1,333.33.
   b. $1,467.53.
   c. $1,274.17.
   d. $1,194.86.

3. You borrow $40,000 secured by a second loan against your home payable at $322 per month, including interest at 9 percent per annum. The first month's interest will be
   a. $322.00.
   b. $300.00.
   c. $36.00.
   d. $289.80.

4. Using the data from Question 3, the unpaid balance remaining at the end of the first month's payment is (in round numbers)
   a. $39,678.
   b. $39,710.
   c. $39,964.
   d. $39,978.

5. Using Table 13.1, a $95,000 loan at 12 percent amortized for 30 years will have a monthly payment of
   a. $950.00.
   b. $977.19.
   c. $990.05.
   d. 1,000.58.

6. Using Table 13.2, a $500,000 loan at 7 percent amortized for 25 years will have what monthly payment?
   a. $2,916.67.
   b. $3,016.43.
   c. $3,535.00.
   d. $3,619.25.

7. The FV key on a financial calculator stands for
   a. forbearance value.
   b. future value.
   c. financial value.
   d. frequence variable.

8. In financial terms, TVM stands for
   a. time variable math.
   b. twice valued multiple.
   c. time value of money.
   d. tomorrow's value of money.

9. On a fixed-rate amortized loan, if a borrower makes larger than required payments,
   a. the total interest paid will increase.
   b. the nominal interest rate will decline.
   c. the balloon payment will increase.
   d. the term of the loan will be reduced.

10. On a fixed-rate amortized loan, if a borrower makes larger than required payments,
    a. the total interest paid will decline.
    b. the income tax deductions for interest will increase.
    c. the owner's equity will decrease.
    d. the lender will foreclose.

11. Under an amortized loan, a balloon payment is defined as any payment
    a. more than twice the size of a regular payment.
    b. under a fully amortized loan.
    c. paid in advance of the due date.
    d. past due.

12. A PITI loan payment includes
    a. prepayment, interest, taxes, and insurance.
    b. principal, interest, taxes, and insurance.
    c. partial amortization, interest, taxes, and insurance.
    d. principal, interest, and taxable income.

13. When a fixed-rate loan is fully amortized, the amount allocated each month to principal
    a. decreases.
    b. increases.
    c. stays constant.
    d. decreases in the early years and increases in the later years.

14. In many ways, interest is to principal as
    a. rent is to land.
    b. capital is to money.
    c. profit is to risk.
    d. yield is to rate of return.

15. When notes and deeds of trust are sold, they are most often purchased at a
    a. discount.
    b. face amount.
    c. par amount.
    d. usury value.

16. The number of biweekly payments in one year is
    a. 26.
    b. 52.
    c. 24.
    d. 13.

17. Biweekly loan payments
    a. increase the amount of interest paid.
    b. are monthly payments divided in half and paid every two weeks.
    c. are illegal in California.
    d. are commonly used on FHA-backed loans.

18. APR stands for
    a. annual percentage rate.
    b. annual prime rate.
    c. amortized packaged rate.
    d. amortized percentage rate.

19. The purpose for requiring lenders to quote their financing terms using APR is to
    a. confuse the general public.
    b. allow borrowers to compare the true cost of money.
    c. increase the lender's yield.
    d. generate fees to support government housing programs.

20. Which of the following is true?
    a. APR and the interest rate on the note are always the same.
    b. The higher the loan fee, the lower the APR.
    c. APR is designed to discover the financial impact of certain specific fees.
    d. APR must be quoted as a dollar amount instead of as a percentage.

CASE & POINT

Using the HP-12C to Simplify Real Estate Math

Functions of the Keys

Notice that the plural is used: since most of the 39 keys in the HP-12C have more than one use, let's briefly acquaint ourselves with the functions most often encountered in real estate problems. We'll expand on their meanings through a series of notes located throughout the manual.

|ON| This is both the on and off key. The calculator has built-in memory, so it will retain information for as long as you wish. If you enter the number 12, that number reappears on your screen even if you don't turn it back to ON until next year (or next century, if your battery doesn't sour).

|ENTER| Enters numbers into the calculator, which automatically appear on the display screen, for doing calculations.

The Financial Keys

In the top row of your HP-12C are the five financial keys that we will be using most of the time: |n| |i| |PV| |PMT| |FV|. A brief description of what the letters generally mean is as follows:

|n|	|i|	|PV|	|PMT|	|FV|
(number of payments)	(rate per period)	(amount of loan)	(amount of payments)	(remaining balance)

◄──────────── DATA keys and QUESTION keys ────────────►

The arrows indicate that these five keys in essence are data and questions keys. Why? Because we enter given data (the *known*) into four of the keys and compute for the fifth key (or *cell*), the unknown. So if you know how long a loan is to run (n), its interest rate (i), the amount of loan (PV), and amortization provision (FV)—balloon vs. no balloon—you push the |PMT| button to determine the amount of payments. The |n| may represent the number of monthly payments, quarterly payments, semiannual payments, annual payments, or any other periods. The |i| is always the rate of interest or yield per period. The three remaining keys, |PV|, |PMT|, and |FV| are always expressed in monetary terms, though the monetary symbols, such as the $ or pound sign, never show up on the screen.

Adapted with permission from "The HP=12C in Action!" by Robert J. Bond, Financial Publishing House, Williamsburg, VA, 1997.

To summarize the financial keys:

|n|	Registers the number of periods, or term.
|i|	Registers the interest rate per period.
|PV|	Registers the Present Value, or *initial cash flow*, of a *loan or amount of investment*.
|PMT|	Registers payments for money paid out or received.
|FV|	Registers the Future Value, or *final cash flow*, of a *loan or investment*.

Let's now examine some less frequently used but equally important keys to help round out our knowledge of the keyboard:

|f|	Gold-colored key to the right of |ON|, used to answer questions for the 16 keys where the gold appears at the top.
|g|	Blue-colored key to the right of |f|, used to answer questions for the 30 keys where the blue appears at the bottom.
|CHS|	Changes a number from positive to negative (Change Sign) or from negative to positive.
|%|	Computes the ratio, or percentage (%).
|R/S|	Runs and Stops programs, similar to a full-fledged computer.
|SST|	Single step in a series of steps used when the calculator is in the program mode.
|R↓|	Rolls down data stored within the calculator.
|X ≷ Y|	Exchanges stored data, in its so-called X and Y registers.
|CLX|	Clears the data displayed in the X register.
|1/x|	Reciprocal key, used to change whole or mixed numbers to fractions, or fractions to whole numbers.
|△%|	Calculates % of difference between two numbers (stored in the calculator's X and Y registers).
|%T|	Calculates % that one number represents of the total.
|STO|	Stores numbers in each of the cells labeled 1 through 9 for later use through recall (RCL).
|RCL|	Recalls stored numbers by pressing RCL and the numerical cell (0 through 9) into which the data was stored.

0, 1, 2, 3, 4, 5, 6, 7, 8, 9

+ − × ÷   Keys on right side of calculator. Used for calculating the numerical or arithmetic functions: addition, subtraction, multiplication, division. When |STO| key is pressed at the same time as one of the cells, data can be stored in that cell.

Lesson 1: How Do I Calculate Trust Deed or Mortgage Payments?

Data

1st Trust Deed	$100,000
Interest Rate	10%
Term	30 years
Balloon Payments	none

Question
How much are the monthly payments?

Solution

Key	Screen
1. 30 |g| |12×|	360
2. 10 |g| |12÷|	0.83
3. 100000 |PV|	100,000
4. 0 |FV|	0.00
5. |PMT|	?

Notes
In step 1 we enter the number of years, 30, followed by the blue-colored |g| key that converts 30 years into months. (The blue key is described in the footnote at the end of this exercise on the next page.) In step 2 the annual interest rate of 10 percent is automatically converted into the monthly rate by using the blue key. Enter the loan amount into the PV cell for step 3. The number 0 is entered for step 4 to reflect that there is no balloon payment, which means that the loan is fully amortized with equal monthly installments for the full term. In step 5 the negative

figure showing on your screen reflects money *paid out*. You would read the monthly payments as shown in the answer below.

Answer
$877.57

Self-Help
To help you master certain financial calculations, throughout this Case & Point we offer a series of test questions. See how well you understand the calculation of mortgage payments by doing the self-test questions that follow. After you finish, compare your answers with the correct ones given at the end of the test.

TEST YOURSELF

Self-Test 1

Trust deed: $200,000

Interest rate: 10 percent

Term: 30 years

Question: How much are the yearly payments?

Self-Test 2

Trust deed: $200,000

Interest rate: 10 percent

Term: 15 years

Question: How much are the monthly payments?

Note: Concerning the gold and blue keys:

To the right of the |ON| button at the lowest rung of keys are the prefix keys, which are secondary to the primary keys that you have been dealing with up to this point.

The |f| key is colored gold and the |g| key is colored blue. These have no meanings per se, but they offer a second and third level of calculations, so that each of the keys in the top three rows to the left of the |ENTER| key, including the enter key itself, can perform three separate functions. Thus if you wanted to calculate the amortization of a mortgage loan, you would press the gold |f| key before pressing the |AMORT| that shows up above the |n| key. This will be demonstrated in a later lesson, so don't be concerned at this stage. All you need to know now is that the HP-12C is a very versatile instrument, allowing you to perform zillions of calculations, combinations, and permutations, offering added meanings when the two specially colored keys are used in conjunction with most of the other keys.

|f|, the gold key, is used for solving problems *above* the key.

Example.   The |AMORT| above the |n| key computes loan payments attributable to principal reduction, called amortization, as well as remaining balances.

|g|, the blue key, is used for solving problems *below* the key.

Example. The |12×| below the |n| key is used to convert the number of years into months.

Self-Test 3

Trust deed: $100,000

Interest rate: 5 percent

Term: 30 years

Question: How much are the monthly payments?

Self-Test 4

Trust deed: $100,000

Interest rate: 10 percent

Term: 30 years

Question: How much are the yearly payments?

Note: When calculating annually, do not convert years into months, and do not convert annual interest into monthly interest.

Answers

Self-Test 1: $1,755.14

Self-Test 2: $2,149.21

Self-Test 3: $536.82

Self-Test 4: $10,607.93

Lesson 2: How Do I Calculate Mortgage Interest Rates?

Data

1st Trust Deed	$100,000
Monthly Payments	$877.57
Term	30 years

Question

What is the interest rate?

Solution

Key	Screen
1. 30 |g| |12×|	360
2. 100000 |PV|	100,000
3. 0 |FV|	0.00
4. 877.57 |CHS| |PMT|	−877.57

5. |i| ?

6. 12 |×| ?

Notes

In step 6 we are converting the monthly interest rate to an *annual* rate by simply multiplying the step 5 result by 12, the number of months in a year. There is another way to calculate step 6. In our model we entered the digits 12 followed by the multiplier sign, ×. You could instead simply take the answer to step 5 and enter the blue key |g|, then press the |12×| key.

Answer

0.83% monthly interest rate (step 5), or annual rate of 10.00% (step 6).

TEST YOURSELF

Self-Test 1

  Trust deed: $200,000

  Term: 30 years

  Monthly payments: $1,755.14

  Questions: Monthly interest rate? Annual rate?

Self-Test 2

  Trust deed: $200,000

  Term: 15 years

  Monthly payments: $2,149.21

  Questions: Monthly interest rate? Annual rate?

Self-Test 3

  Trust deed: $100,000

  Term: 30 years

  Monthly payments: $536.82

  Questions: Monthly interest rate? Annual rate?

Self-Test 4

  Trust deed: $100,000

  Term: 30 years

  Annual payments: $10,607.93

  Question: Interest rate?

  Careful: This asks you for *annual* interest rate, so do not convert annual payments to monthly payments. Thus you'll have the annual rate instantly calculated when you hit the |I| button.

Answers

> *Self-Test 1:* 0.83 percent monthly interest rate, or 10 percent annual rate
>
> *Self-Test 2:* 0.83 percent monthly interest rate, or 10 percent annual rate
>
> *Self-Test 3:* 0.42 percent monthly interest rate, or 5 percent annual rate
>
> *Self-Test 4:* 10 percent annual rate. (The loan is paid once annually, so no need to convert to monthly.)

Lesson 3: How Do I Calculate Annual Percentage Rates (APR), Adjusted for a One-Time Loan Fee?

The calculation for APR is very similar to deriving the nominal, or stated, rate that was performed in the previous lesson. What is the difference? In computing an APR, loan costs, including "prepaid interest," must be deducted from the face amount of the loan.

What constitutes prepaid interest? It includes the familiar "points" paid by the borrower; origination fee; pro rata interest, since there usually are interest charges accumulated from COE to date of the initial mortgage payment; first year's mortgage insurance premium (MIP); and a few smaller items. Prepaid interest does *not* include one-time fees paid for an appraisal, credit report, title insurance, and other forms of insurance and costs that are independent of the loan, such as a homeowners policy or homeowners association (HOA) fees.

In the comprehensive example, we'll assume the same facts as before, except that the borrowers are charged $5,000 loan costs.

Data

1st Trust Deed	$100,000
Prepaid Interest/Loan Costs	$5,000
Nominal Interest Rate	10%
Term	30 years

Question

What is the annual percentage rate (APR)?

Solution

Key	Screen
1. 30 |g| |12×|	360
2. 10 |g| |12÷|	0.83

3. 100000 |PV|	100,000
4. 0 |FV|	0.00
5. |PMT|	−877.57
6. |RCL| |PV| 5000 |−| |PV|	95,000
7. |i|	?
8. 12|×| {or |g| |12×|}	?

Note

In step 8 we convert the monthly rate to an *annual* rate by multiplying step 7 result by 12, the number of months in a year. Step 8 could also be computed by pressing the blue \|g\| button followed by \|12×\|.

Answer

0.89 percent monthly rate (step 7), or 10.62 percent annual (step 8)

Bottom Line: With interest prepayments the effective rate, or APR, increased by .62 percent when compared to the nominal rate. This is equivalent to an increase of 62 "basis points," with each basis point the same as $1/100$th of a percent.

TEST YOURSELF

Data

1st Trust Deed	$150,000
Prepaid Interest/Loan Costs	$7,000
Nominal Interest Rate	10%
Term	30 years

Question

What is the annual percentage rate (APR)?

Answer

0.88 percent monthly, or 10.58 percent APR

Lesson 4: How Do I Calculate Annual Percentage Rates (APR), Adjusted for Points, Fees, and Balloon Payment?

The calculation for APR after adjusting for points and fees is very similar to that of the APR adjusted for a flat charge, with one variation. In the problem that follows we add in a balloon payment.

In the comprehensive example, we'll assume the same facts as before, except that the borrowers are charged two points plus $500 to obtain the loan, and assume a five-year due date with a balloon payment for the remaining balance at the end of five years.

Data

1st Trust Deed	$100,000
Prepaid Interest/Loan Costs	2 points + $500
Nominal Interest Rate	10%
Amortization Term, Due in 5 years	30 years
Monthly Payment	$877.57

Question

What is the annual percentage rate (APR)?

Solution

Key	Screen
1. 10 |g| |12÷|	0.83
2. 100000 |PV|	100,000
3. 877.57 |CHS| |PMT|	−877.57
4. 5 |g| |n|	60
5. |FV|	−96,574.44
6. |RCL| |PV| 2 |%| |−| 500 |−|	97,500
7. |PV|	97,500
8. |i|	0.89
9. 12 |×|	10.66

Notes

Step 5 represents the balloon payment. Step 6 represents the net amount that the borrower actually received after deducting the points (2) plus dollar amount ($500). In step 9 we are converting the monthly rate to an *annual* rate by multiplying step 8 result by 12.

Answer

0.89 percent monthly (step 8), or 10.656 annually (step 9), rounded to 10.66 percent.

Bottom Line: With interest prepayments of two points plus $500, the effective rate, or APR, increased by .66 percent when compared to the nominal rate. This is equivalent to an increase of 66 "basis points," with each basis point the same as $^1/_{100}$th of a percent.

TEST YOURSELF

Data

1st Trust Deed	$120,000
Prepaid Interest/Loan Costs	1 point + $750
Nominal Interest Rate	10%
Amortization Term, Due in 5 years	30 years
Monthly Payment	$1,053.09

Question
What is the APR?

Answer
0.87 percent monthly interest rate, or 10.42 percent annual rate, is the APR.

Lesson 5: How Do I Calculate which Loan Is Better Based upon Costs and Holding Period?

Data

	Option A	Option B
Original 1st Trust Deed	$100,000	$100,000
Interest Rate	11%	10%
Term	360 months	360 months
Loan Fees	None	3 points + $300
Expected Holding Period	30 years	3 years

Question
Which is better, Option A, the "no-cost loan," or Option B, which costs 3 points plus $300 in loan fees, based upon the holding period or occupancy?

Solution for Option A

Key	Screen
1. 30 |g| |12×|	360
2. 11 |g| |12÷|	0.92
3. 100000 |PV|	100,000

4. 0 |FV|	0.00
5. |PMT|	−952.32
6. |i|	0.92
7. 12 |×|	11.00

Answer

0.92 percent per month (step 6), or 11 percent per annum (step 7)

Note

The 11 percent APR is the same as the nominal rate given in the data. This is because there are no loan costs. Let's see how this compares to Option B.

Solution for Option B

Key	Screen
1. 30 |g| |12×|	360
2. 10 |g| |12÷|	0.83
3. 100000 |PV|	100,000
4. 0 |FV|	0.00
5. |PMT|	−877.57
6. |RCL| |PV|	100,000
7. 3 |%| |−| 300 |−|	96,700
8. |PV|	96,700
9. |i|	0.87
10. 12 |×|	10.40

Answer

0.87 percent per month (step 9), or 10.40 percent APR annually (step 10).

Notes

The 10.40 percent APR is higher than the nominal rate of 10 percent because there is $3,300 in loan costs, calculated in step 7, and this results in only $96,700 in net loan proceeds to the borrower. Step 8 is necessary in order to lock the $96,700 into the calculator's memory.

On the surface it appears as if Option B is the better choice because its APR is 10.40 percent, in contrast to the 11 percent APR in Option A. But remember, we need to deal with the holding period, which will have an impact on the real cost of the loan to us, beyond the required APR disclosure. So let's continue with additional steps needed to compute the APR adjusted for the holding period, when the loan is to be paid off.

Key	Screen
11. 100000 |PV|	100,000
12. 10 |g| |12÷|	0.83
13. 36 |n|	36
14. |FV|	−98,151.65
15. |RCL| |PV| 3 |%| |−| 300 |−|	96,700
16. |PV|	96,700
17. |i|	0.94
18. 12 |×|	11.31

Note

It is necessary to reenter the original loan amount, $100,000, in step 11 because that's the amount the borrowers will repay to the lender, and not the $96,700 that they actually received after discounting by the loan fees of $3,300. For the same reason we restore the nominal interest rate, 10 percent, in step 12. In step 13 we enter the period that the borrowers expect to stay with the loan, 3 years or 36 months. Step 14 displays the loan balance at the end of the 3-year period. Step 15 calculates the net proceeds, while step 16 locks the figure into the memory. Step 17 recomputes the true rate based upon the 3-year holding period, and not the original 30 years.

Bottom Line

Though the APR in Option B, the 10 percent loan, was still lower (10.4 percent) than the 11 percent loan in Option A, it is higher when adjusted for the holding period. The APR for Option B rises to 11.31 percent in 3 years because of the much shorter period for recovery of the one-time upfront fees. (Recall the *time value of money* concept.)

Lesson 6: How Do I Calculate Blended Interest Rates?

Data

1st Trust Deed	$100,000
Interest Rate on 1st TD	10%
Second Trust Deed	$25,000
Interest Rate on 2nd TD	12%
Term of Each Loan, Payable Monthly	30 years

Question
What is the blended or composite interest rate?

Solution

Key	Screen
1. 100000 |STO| |0|	100,000
2. 10 |%|	10,000
3. 25000 |STO| |+| |0| 12 |%|	3,000
4. |x ≥ y| |R↓| |+|	13,000
5. |RCL| |0|	125,000
6. |÷|	?

Answer
0.10, or 10 percent. (If you want to expand the rate to three decimal places, enter |f| 3, and your screen will show 0.104, or 10.4 percent.

Notes
Step 1 stores the existing first loan balance for later recall. Step 2 shows the first year's interest on that loan, step 3 stores the $25,000 second loan, then adds this amount to the stored first loan and computes the first year's interest on the second loan. Step 4 combines total interest, adding up steps 2 and 3. Step 5 recalls the total amount of loans ($125,000) and divides this into the total interest of $13,000 (step 4) to answer the question asked in step 6 (10%).

TEST YOURSELF

Self-Test 1

Data

1st Trust Deed	$100,000
Interest Rate on 1st TD	8%
Second Trust Deed	$20,000
Interest Rate on 2nd TD	10%
Term of Each Loan	30 years

Question
What is the blended or composite interest rate?

Answer
0.0833, or 8⅓ percent

Self-Test 2

Data

1st Trust Deed	$150,000
Interest Rate on 1st TD	9%
Second Trust Deed	$50,000
Interest Rate on 2nd TD	10%
Term of Each Loan	30 years

Question

What is the blended or composite interest rate?

Answer

0.0925, or 9.25 percent

Lesson 7: How Do I Calculate the Remaining Term of a Loan?

Data

Original 1st Trust Deed	$100,000
Current Balance	$90,000
Interest Rate	10%
Monthly Payments	$877.57

Question

How many monthly payments are required to pay off the loan if it is fully amortized, that is, if there is no balloon payment?

Solution

Key	Screen
1. 10 |g| |12÷|	0.83
2. 90000 |PV|	90,000
3. 877.57 |CHS| |PMT|	−877.57
4. 0 |FV|	0.00
5. |n|	?
6. |12| |÷|	?

Answer

233 months, computed in step 5. Step 6 converts this to number of years, 19.42, to pay off the loan.

Notes

The calculator will round up to the next whole number. For example, if the exact number of monthly payments was 232.8, the HP-12C will show 233. Thus the final payment will be slightly lower. To compute the exact amount of the last installment, press the following keys:

|RCL| |PMT| |+|

This displays $858.15 as the final payment.

TEST YOURSELF

Self-Test 1

   Trust deed: $200,000

   Interest rate: 10 percent

   Monthly payments: $1,755.14

   Question: What is the term of the loan?

Self-Test 2

   Trust deed: $200,000

   Interest rate: 10 percent

   Monthly payments: $2,149.21

   Question: What is the term of the loan?

Self-Test 3

   Trust deed: $100,000

   Interest rate: 5 percent

   Monthly payments: $536.82

   Question: What is the term of the loan?

Self-Test 4

   Trust deed: $100,000

   Interest rate: 10 percent

   Annual payments: $10,607.92

   Question: What is the term of the loan?

Answers

   Self-Test 1: 360 months, or 30 years

   Self-Test 2: 180 months, or 15 years

   Self-Test 3: 360 months, or 30 years

   Self-Test 4: 30 years

(*Note:* Since payments are made only once a year, and not monthly, Self-Test 4 asks us to compute number of *years* only.)

Lesson 8: How Do I Calculate the Original Amount of a Trust Deed Loan?

Data

Interest Rate	10%
Term	30 years
Monthly Payment	$877.57
Age of Loan	10 years

Questions

1. What was the original loan amount?

2. What will be its value 10 years from now?

Solution

Key	Screen
1. 30 |g| |12×|	360
2. 10 |g| |12÷|	0.83
3. 877.57 |CHS| |PMT|	−877.57
4. 0 |FV|	0
5. |PV|	?
6. 240 |n|	?
7. |PV|	?

Answer for Step 5
$100,000.00

Answer for Step 7
$90,938.00

Notes
Step 5 calculated the original loan amount. In step 6, simply change the number entered in step 1 (360 months) to reflect that the loan has been in existence for 10 years, or 120 months, so there are 240 months remaining. Enter 240 into \|n\|, then press \|PV\|. The identical answer can be derived by taking the 120 months for which the loan has been paid, and entering that number into \|n\|, then pressing \|FV\|.

Deleting Pennies: To delete the pennies column just press the gold key |f|, then enter |0| to the right of the ENTER button. Your answers then would be rounded to 100,000 without the decimal point and two zeros that follow the decimal symbol in step 5, and 90,938 without the 2 cents that follow in step 6. Incidentally, the $877.57 monthly payment from the DATA is already rounded to the nearest penny, so we do not need to press |g| |RND|.

TEST YOURSELF

Self-Test 1

   Interest rate: 10 percent

   Term: 30 years

   Monthly payments: $1,755.14

   Question: What was the original loan amount?

Self-Test 2

   Interest rate: 10 percent

   Term: 15 years

   Monthly payments: $2,149.21

   Question: What was the original loan amount?

Self-Test 3

   Interest rate: 5 percent

   Term: 30 years

   Monthly payments: $536.82

   Question: What was the original loan amount?

Self-Test 4

   Interest rate: 10 percent

   Term: 30 years

   Annual payments: $10,607.92

   Question: What was the original loan amount?

Answers
(*Note:* Enter |f| |0| to delete the pennies.)

   Self-Test 1: 200,000

   Self-Test 2: 200,000

   Self-Test 3: 100,000

   Self-Test 4: 100,000

(*Note:* For Self-Test 4, you don't need to convert to monthly payments as required in the first three tests, since the loan is being repaid on an *annual*, not monthly, basis.)

Lesson 9: How Do I Determine the Unpaid Balance on a Loan?

Data

1st Trust Deed	$100,000
Interest Rate	10%
Term	30 years

Question

What is the unpaid balance after 5 years?

Solution

Key	Screen
1. 30 |g| |12×|	360
2. 10 |g| |12÷|	0.83
3. 100000 |PV|	100,000
4. 0 |FV|	0.00
5. |PMT|	−877.57
6. |F| |RND| |PMT|	−877.57
7. 5 |g| |12×|	60.00
8. |FV|	?

Answer

$96,574.44

Notes

Step 6 is not absolutely necessary. It simply rounds off the monthly payments to the *nearest penny*. Remember, the calculator has a continuous memory, hence it carries the theoretical payment to fractions of a cent. But since the lowest currency in the U.S. dollar is a penny, it is impossible to pay in smaller denominations, i.e., $877.5715701 if carried to the seventh decimal place. All the digits following $877.57 are adjusted up or down (depending on the precise language in the promissory note) in the final monthly installment. Since there are digits that follow the .57, you'd have a larger final installment 360 months from now. If on the other hand the note called for monthly payments of $877.58, your final payment would be *less* than $877.58.

For those of you who appreciate precision, without step 6 the unpaid balance at the end of 5 years would amount to $96,574.32, or a decrease of 12 cents.

TEST YOURSELF

Self-Test 1

Data

1st Trust Deed	$120,000
Interest Rate	10%
Term, Payable Monthly	30 years

Questions

1. What is the unpaid balance after 3 years?

2. What is the unpaid balance after 5 years?

Answers

1. $117,781.98 after 3 years ($117,781.80 if payments of $1053.09 are rounded via |f| |RND|).

2. $115,888.18 after 5 years ($115,888.87 if payments are rounded).

Self-Test 2

Data

1st Trust Deed	$150,000
Interest Rate	10%
Term, Payable Monthly	30 years

Questions

1. What is the unpaid balance after 3 years?

2. What is the unpaid balance after 5 years?

Answers

1. $147,227.47 after 3 years ($147,227.36 if payments of $1316.36 are rounded via |f| |RND|).

2. $144,861.48 after 5 years ($144,861.28 if payments are rounded).

Lesson 10: How Do I Calculate the Number of Payments under a Balloon Loan?

Data

Original 1st Trust Deed	$100,000
Current Balance	$90,000
Interest Rate	10%
Monthly Payments	$877.57
Term	360 months
Balloon, End of Term	$10,000

Question

How many payments are required to pay off the loan if, in addition to periodic monthly payments, there is a balloon payment of $10,000 at the end of the term, payable with the final installment?

Solution

Key	Screen
1. 10 |g| |12÷|	0.83
2. 90000 |PV|	90,000
3. 877.75 |CHS| |PMT|	−877.57
4. 10000 |CHS| |FV|	−10,000
5. |n|	?
6. |12| |÷|	?

Answer

221 months (step 5), or 18.42 years (step 6).

Note

The calculator will round off to the next whole number. For example, if the exact number of monthly payments was 220.8, the HP-12C will show 221. Thus the final payment will be slightly lower. To compute the exact last installment, press the following three keys:
\|RCL\| \|PMT\| \|+\|
This will display $859.15 as the final payment.

TEST YOURSELF

Self-Test 1

　Trust deed: $200,000

　Interest rate: 10 percent

　Monthly payments: $1,755.14

　Balloon: $50,000

　Question: What is the term of the loan?

Self-Test 2

　Trust deed: $200,000

　Interest rate: 10 percent

　Monthly payments: $2,149.21

　Balloon: $25,000

　Question: What is the term of the loan?

Self-Test 3

　Trust deed: $100,000

　Interest rate: 5 percent

　Monthly payments: $536.82

　Balloon: $10,000

　Question: What is the term of the loan?

Self-Test 4

　Trust deed: $100,000

　Interest rate: 10 percent

　Annual payments: $10,607.92

　Balloon, end of term: $20,000

　Question: What is the term of the loan?

Answers

　Self-Test 1: 328 months, or 27$\frac{1}{3}$ years

　Self-Test 2: 168 months, or 14 years

　Self-Test 3: 341 months, or 28.42 years

　Self-Test 4: 28 years

　(*Note:* Self-Test 4 asks us to compute number of *years*, since payments are made only once a year, not monthly.)

Lesson 11: How Do I Calculate Interest and Principal Components of a Loan?

Data

Trust Deed Loan	$100,000
Interest Rate	10%
Term, Payable Monthly, Fully Amortized	30 years

Questions

1. How much are the monthly payments at 10 percent?

2. Of the monthly payments, how much represents interest and how much represents principal during each of the first five years?

Solution

Key		Screen
1a.	30 |g| |12×|	360
1b.	10 |g| |12÷|	0.83
1c.	100000 |PV|	100,000
1d.	0 |FV|	0.00
1e.	|PMT|	−877.57
2a.	12 |f| |AMORT|	−9,974.98
2b.	|x ≥ y|	−555.86
3a.	12 |f| |AMORT|	−9,916.77
3b.	|x ≥ y|	−614.07
4a.	12 |f| |AMORT|	−9,852.46
4b.	|x ≥ y|	−678.38
5a.	12 |f| |AMORT|	−9,781.44
5b.	|x ≥ y|	−749.40
6a.	12 |f| |AMORT|	−9,702.96
6b.	|x ≥ y|	−827.88

Answer 1

$877.57 monthly payments (from step 1e)

Notes

Steps 1a through 1e calculate the monthly payments for the 30-year loan. Steps 2a and 2b compute the (decreasing) interest and (increasing) principal portions of the first year's payments. Steps 3a and 3b compute the interest and principal portions of the second year's payments. Steps 4a and 4b compute the interest and principal portions of the third year's payments. Steps 5a and 5b compute the interest and principal portions of the fourth year's payments. Steps 6a and 6b compute the interest and principal portions of the fifth year's payments. We can summarize these in simpler tabular form as follows:

Answer 2

Year	Interest	Principal
1	$9,974.98	$555.86
2	9,916.77	614.07
3	9,852.46	678.38
4	9,781.44	749.40
5	9,702.96	827.88

TEST YOURSELF

Data

Trust Deed Loan	$100,000
Interest Rate	12%
Term, Payable Monthly, Fully Amortized	30 years

Questions

1. How much are the monthly payments at 12 percent?

2. Of the monthly payments, how much represents interest and how much represents principal during each of the first two years?

Answer

1. $1,028.61

2.

Year	Interest	Principal
1	$11,980.47	$362.85
2	11,934.45	408.87

Lesson 12: How Do I Calculate Negative Amortization?

Data

1st Trust Deed	$100,000
Interest Rate	9% the first year, 10% thereafter
Term, Payable Monthly	30 years

Question

What will the loan balance be at the end of the first year?

Solution

Key	Screen
1. 30 |g| |12×|	360
2. 9 |g| |12÷|	0.75
3. 100000 |PV|	100,000
4. 0 |FV|	0.00
5. |PMT|	−804.62
6. 10 |g| |12÷|	0.83
7. 12 |n|	12.00
8. |FV|	?

Answer

$100,360.77

Notes

Step 6 shows the new interest rate, 10 percent, converted into a monthly rate. Observe also that the $100,361 (enter \|f\| \|0\| to get rid of the pennies) balance is larger than the loan originally secured, $100,000. That's because you paid less than the 10 percent contract interest rate during the first year, resulting in *negative amortization*.

TEST YOURSELF

Self-Test 1

Data

1st Trust Deed	$120,000
Interest Rate:	9%, but at only 8% the first year
Term, Payable Monthly	30 years

Question
What will be the loan balance at the end of the first year?

Answer
$120,243.68

Self-Test 2
Data

1st Trust Deed	$150,000
Interest Rate	5% the first year, 10% thereafter
Term, Payable Monthly	30 years

Question
What will be the remaining balance at the end of the first year?

Answer
$155,588.76

Lesson 13: How Do I Calculate How Much Price and Loan Buyers Can Afford?

Data

Interest Rate	10%
Term, Payable Monthly	30 years
Down Payment	$25,000
Monthly Payments, *including* PITI (Principal, Interest, Taxes, Insurance)	$1,000
Percentage Attributable to Taxes & Insurance	4%

Questions

1. How much loan can buyer-borrower afford?

2. How much property can buyer-borrower afford?

Solution

Key	Screen
1. 30 |g| |12×|	360
2. 10 |g| |12÷|	0.83
3. 1000 |CHS| |ENTER|	−1,000
4. 4 |%| |−| |PMT|	−960
5. |PV|	?
6. 25000 |+|	?

Answer to Question 1
Buyer can afford a loan of $109,392.79 (step 5), rounded to $109,400.

Answer to Question 2
Buyer can afford a property for $134,392.79 (step 6), rounded to $134,400.

Notes
Step 3 shows the monthly PITI of $1,000, but in step 4 we deduct the 4 percent attributable to property taxes and insurance, which shows the net amount going for debt service (principal and interest) of $960. Step 5 calculates amount of loan ($109,400) which buyer-borrower can support for the $960 that goes for the monthly payment of P&I. Step 6 adds the down payment ($25,000) to the loan amount to arrive at the maximum purchase price ($134,400).

TEST YOURSELF

Data

Interest Rate	10%
Term, Payable Monthly for	30 years
Down Payment	$40,000
Monthly Payments, *including* PITI (Principal, Interest, Taxes, Insurance)	$2,000
Percentage Attributable to Taxes & Insurance	4%

Questions

1. How much loan can borrowers afford?

2. How much property can borrowers afford?

Answers

1. $218,785.57, rounded to $218,800.

2. $258,785.57, rounded to $258,800.

Lesson 14: How Do I Calculate Payments for Adjustable Rate Mortgages (ARM)?

The calculation for adjustable rate mortgage payments, or ARMs for short, differs from fixed rate mortgages (FRMs) due to the fluctuations in payments whenever rates go up or down under an ARM loan. Thus we must adjust the payments as interest rates on the loan are adjusted under the terms of the mortgage instrument.

In the example that follows, we'll assume that the borrower starts out with a 7 percent ARM rate, and that the rate can go up or down as much as 1 percent per year, called an *annual cap*, subject further to a 5-point lifetime cap.

Data

1st Trust Deed	$100,000
Beginning ARM Interest Rate	7%
Assumed 2nd Year Interest Rate	8%
Assumed 3rd Year Interest Rate	7.5%
Amortization Term	30 years

Questions

1. What are the monthly payments during the first year at 7 percent?

2. What are the monthly payments during the second year at 8 percent?

3. What are the monthly payments during the third year at 7.5 percent?

Solution

Key	Screen
1. 30 |g| |n|	360.00
2. 7 |g| |12÷|	0.58
3. 100000 |P|	100,000
4. 0 |FV|	0
5. |PMT|	−665.30
6. 12 |f| |AMORT|	−6,967.81
7. |RCL| |n| 24 |−| |n|	348
8. 8 |g| |12÷|	0.67
9. |PMT|	−732.43
10. 12 |f| |AMORT|	−7,886.06
11. |RCL| |n| 24 |−| |n|	336
12. 7.5 |g| |12÷|	0.63
13. |PMT|	−699.19

Answers

Year 1 monthly payments (step 5)	$665.30
Year 2 monthly payments (step 9)	$732.43
Year 3 monthly payments (step 13)	$699.19

Notes

Steps 1 through 5 represent the monthly payments during year 1. Step 6 computes the amount of first-year payments that apply to principal reduction. Step 7 gives us the number of months remaining after one year. Step 8 calculates monthly interest rate for the second year. Step 9 reflects monthly payments for year 2. Step 10 computes the amount of second-year payments that apply to interest. Step 11 calculates the number of months remaining after two years. Step 12 calculates monthly interest rate for the third year. Step 13 shows monthly payments for year 3.

TEST YOURSELF

Data

1st Trust Deed	$120,000
Beginning ARM Interest Rate	6%
Assumed 2nd Year Interest Rate	7%
Assumed 3rd Year Interest Rate	8%
Amortization Term	30 years

Questions

1. What are the monthly payments during the first year at 6 percent?

2. What are the monthly payments during the second year at 7 percent?

3. What are the monthly payments during the third year at 8 percent?

Answers

1. $719.46

2. $796.65

3. $875.37

CHAPTER 14
CREATIVE FINANCING APPROACHES

PREVIEW

The term *creative financing* has been coined to designate approaches to financing real property in ways that are not normally found through traditional sources. Many of these involve people-to-people financing, or OWC (owner will carry), some of which are explained here. The various techniques are limited only by one's imagination and knowledge.

In this chapter we examine some creative methods used to solve both the difficult and not so difficult situations in which borrowers find themselves when they seek a real estate loan in a tight money market. These are not to be confused with the alternative mortgage instruments, or AMIs, discussed in Chapter 4. While AMIs are potentially very creative, they are variations on the basic fixed rate, fixed term, level payment, fully amortized loan that has been part of the permanent financing scene since 1934.

After completing this chapter, you should be able to:

1. Differentiate between traditional and creative financing techniques.

2. Identify at least five ways in which real estate can be financed through ways other than the traditional methods.

3. Contrast the all-inclusive trust deed to the installment Contract of Sale, citing at least three differences.

4. Apply the formula to calculate blended interest rates.

5. **Name the instruments required to close a sale using the creative techniques presented in this chapter.**

6. **List at least six items that must be disclosed under the Creative Financing Disclosure Act.**

14.1 Secondary Financing Techniques

Second Trust Deeds Carried by the Seller

Second trust deeds are sometimes referred to as *gap loans* carried back by sellers, who in effect help to finance a portion of the selling price. The amount so financed represents a part of the seller's equity, measured by the difference between the amount of down payment plus loan amount and the sale price. The loan amount may be either a new loan commitment or an existing loan that the purchaser agrees to take over, whether under an *assumption agreement* or a *subject to* clause. The difference between the down payment plus loan amount and the sale price leaves a gap that is filled by the seller *carrying back paper*—the note secured by the second trust deed. Like first mortgages and trust deeds, seller carrybacks are referred to as purchase money mortgages because the seller carrying back makes the purchase possible.

Example: Assume that a property sells for $300,000 with a $30,000 down payment and that an institutional lender has made a first trust deed commitment of $240,000 for 30 years at 6.5 percent interest per annum. The seller agrees to carry back the $30,000 balance in the form of a purchase money note with a second deed of trust. Terms of the second loan call for a straight, interest only note at a 1 percent per month rate of payoff, with 7 percent interest per annum, all due and payable in four years. Ignoring closing costs, the buyer's position will appear as follows:

Sale price	$300,000
Cash down payment	−30,000
Balance needed to finance	$270,000
First trust deed	−240,000
Purchase money second (gap loan)	$ 30,000
Monthly payments at 1% payoff (1% × 30,000)	$ 300
Lump sum payment, end of 4 years	$ 30,000

The balance due at the end of four years, referred to as a *lump sum payment*, is $30,000 on a $30,000 second loan. In the event the buyer-borrower is unable to meet the lump sum payment, there are several options. He or she (1) may renegotiate the note, if the beneficiary is willing to extend the term of the note; (2) secure a new loan from outside sources in order to pay off the debt; (3) refinance the entire loan. The last alternative assumes, however, that enough equity has been built up during the four years to provide the borrower with funds from a new first trust deed loan that will be sufficient to pay off the balance on the existing first—$228,143—plus the $30,000 due on the second. Thus, a net of $258,143 is needed, after points and other charges are paid from the loan proceeds. Since only $41,857 (or 15 percent of the combined loans) has been repaid on the principal on the two loans, this alternative provides a viable solution only when either the property has substantially increased in value or a higher percentage of loan-to-value ratio is obtainable, or a combination of both.

There are risks involved in carrying back junior trust deeds. Figure 14.1 suggests ways in which sellers can minimize risks to themselves.

PROTECTION DEVICES FOR SELLERS WHO CARRY BACK SECOND DEEDS OF TRUST

1. Insert an alienation (due-on-sale) clause in the promissory note and deed of trust as a condition for granting the extension of credit.

2. File a request for copy of notice of default and sale on the existing first deed of trust.

3. Add the name of the beneficiary (seller) on the new buyers' fire insurance policy as second loss payee.

4. At the time of the sale ask the title company to issue a joint protection title insurance policy coinsuring both the new buyer and the beneficial interest of the seller.

Figure 14.1 Protection devices for sellers.

Collateralizing Junior Loans

Using the previous example, what if the owner does not wish to carry a second trust deed? One solution to this problem is to obtain a collateralized loan using a seller-carried note and second *deed of trust* as an asset. **Collateralization** is a process by which a note and deed of trust are pledged as collateral for a loan, usually through private parties, mortgage brokers, and commercial banks, for a percentage of the face value of said note, at a discounted value.

To illustrate its application, assume the same data as under the credit extension loan above. Also assume a value of one-half of the face amount of the note at a cost of ten points, payable interest only at 7 percent per annum on the note carried back by the seller, with 10 percent payable on the collateralized note. The selling beneficiary's position will appear as follows:

Second loan carried by seller		$30,000
Collateral loan (50% from another lender)		−15,000
Deferred portion		$15,000
Interest seller is to receive on $30,000 second deed of trust at 7%, for 4 years		$ 8,400
Less: Interest paid on $15,000 collateral loan at 10% for 4 years	$6,000	
Less: Discount fee of 10 points (fee to lender for granting collateral loan)	1,500	7,500
Net interest income over interest expense		$ 900
Final installment (lump sum) *receivable* at end of 4 years		$30,000
Final installment (lump sum) *repayable* at end of 4 years		15,000
Net payable to seller-borrower		$15,000

This technique is an alternative for the seller who wishes to retain an interest in the second trust deed but who also needs cash. In this example, the seller received use of $15,000 from the investor.

Collateralizing an existing note and second trust deed may or may not be advantageous, depending on the relationship between the terms and payout on the second loan owned by the seller and the terms and payout on the collateral loan. Collateralizing the note and deed of trust provides a means by which the borrower can obtain immediate cash for $13,500 ($15,000 loan less $1,500 discount fee) and still keep control over an investment yielding 7 percent per year. The seller-borrower will receive interest income of $8,400 over the four-year period, or $2,100 annually, against a yearly payment of $1,500 in interest charges, netting $600 per year (plus the $1,500 discount fee). Then, at maturity, the seller-borrower will receive a lump sum of $30,000 from the purchaser of the property and pay out $15,000 on the collateralized note for net cash proceeds of $15,000.

Advantages of collateralizing to the seller-borrower include retention of the benefits of the original note; avoidance of loss through discounting of the note; and avoidance of additional debt—that is, the cash flow from seller's carryback note may more than offset the payments on the collateral note, as is true in the example above. (Offsetting these would be the interest plus points paid and the time value of money.)

As mentioned, such loans usually are obtainable through mortgage brokers, commercial banks, newspaper ads, and private parties. To save extra title insurance and escrow expenses, it would be more practical to arrange such a transaction during the sale escrow.

Seller Sells the Second Loan

Another solution is for the seller or real estate agent to arrange to sell the note and second trust deed that was carried back as part of the purchase price—in other words, to sell the junior lien. This will generate instant cash for the seller. However, selling junior liens almost always involves selling at a discount. This is particularly true in the case of a newly issued note, since there is no history of payments to establish any past record. Other factors that determine the amount of discount include interest rate, location and appraised value of the property, loan-to-value ratio, type and terms of the note, and the desired yield of the investor.

The amount of discount on the sale of a second note and trust deed depends on many variables (as explained in Chapter 3). Assuming the discount to be 25 percent and given the same facts outlined earlier, the application of discounting would appear as follows:

Face value, second trust deed note	$30,000
Less: 25% discount	7,500
Cash proceeds to seller	$22,500

The sale of notes secured by trust deeds is accomplished through the simple act of an assignment executed by the selling beneficiary, called the *assignor*, in favor of the purchaser, called the *assignee*. To

LTIC-CAL T-400

RECORDING REQUESTED BY

SAFETY TITLE INSURANCE CO.

AND WHEN RECORDED MAIL TO

NAME ⌐ U. R. Gogetter

ADDRESS   5800 Think St.
           Moon City, CA 90020
CITY &
STATE └

Title Order No. 3691215 ⋯ Escrow No. ⋯⋯⋯⋯

─────── **SPACE ABOVE THIS LINE FOR RECORDER'S USE** ───────

Assignment of Deed of Trust

THIS FORM WAS FURNISHED BY LAWYERS TITLE INSURANCE CORPORATION

FOR VALUE RECEIVED, the undersigned hereby grants, assigns and transfers to   U.R. Gogetter,
an unmarried man

all beneficial interest under that certain Deed of Trust dated   June 2, 20XX   ,

executed by   I. M. Tyred, a widower   , Trustor,

to   Docurich Escrow Company   , Trustee,

and recorded as Instrument No.   3691215   on   June 22, 20XX   in book 1850   ,

page   9   , of Official Records in the County Recorder's office of   Lost Angels   County,

California, describing land therein as: Lot 16, Blueview Tract, as per map recorded in
Book 66, page 99, of Maps in the office of the County Recorder of said County.

TOGETHER with the note or notes therein described or referred to, the money due and to become due thereon
with interest, and all rights accrued or to accrue under said Deed of Trust.

Dated   August 14, 20XX   *Igot Stuck*

STATE OF CALIFORNIA
COUNTY OF   Lost Angels   } SS.
On   August 14, 20XX   before me,
the undersigned, a Notary Public in and for said County and
State, personally appeared   Igot Stuck

known to me to be the person(s) whose name(s) is (are)
subscribed to the within instrument and acknowledged that
    he   executed the same.

Knote Airy
Knote Airy

Name (Typed or Printed)
Notary Public in and for said County and State.   (This area for official notarial seal)

Figure 14.2 Sample assignment of deed of trust.

protect the interest of the new holder of the note, the assignment form should be recorded. An illustration of a completed assignment of deed of trust form is shown in Figure 14.2. *Special note:* If the note is to be discounted and sold in the same escrow in which it is created, it must first be offered to the buyer-borrower on the same terms. If the buyer-borrower refuses the offer, written evidence should be maintained in the escrow files and the broker's files, since the California Department of Real Estate may investigate and the broker may be subject to license revocation for not making the offer to the buyer-borrower.

If the note is sold *after* the escrow closes, this offer does not have to be made to the buyer-borrower.

Investors—buyers of seconds—can be found through escrow companies; loan brokers; holders of maturing junior trust deed loans, as disclosed by reconveyance deeds recorded at the County Hall of Records; classified ads; and, in the case of licensees, their own client files, particularly those disclosing previous sellers who carried back paper for part or all of the purchase price. One such purchaser accessible on the World Wide Web is Private Mortgage Investment Services, Inc., whose website is linked from http://bond.swcollege.com/. Sellers are cautioned, of course, to look into a variety of criteria, and not just the amount of discount offered, before entering any transaction with any investor or investor entity.

Broker Participation

Another creative approach to solving real estate finance problems is to have the broker become a lender for part of the equity. Whatever the scheme, the broker effectively becomes a partner with the seller in the secondary loan by breaking down the note into two component parts. The seller is named the beneficiary but assigns part or all of the note to the broker as commission through a collateral agreement such as shown in Figure 14.3. As with the previous secondary loan variations, this plan is utilized when the seller of property needs more cash than is generated through a down payment that is less than the seller's equity after allowance for the senior security. Under the plan, the note and second trust deed are assigned to the real estate agent. *Caveat:* Since you are taking on a partner, that person's attitudes must be considered in any action taken regarding the collateral.

> **Example:** Assume the sale of a home for $300,000 with a $240,000 first loan commitment. Assume further that the buyer has limited resources, say, 10 percent down payment, or $30,000.

INSTALLMENT NOTE--COLLATERAL SECURITY

$ 18,000   Utopia   , California, _____ July 6 _____, 20xx

In installments as herein stated, for value received,_____

Igot Stuck, Sellers   promise to pay to

    Mrs. Broker and Mr. Salesman _____

_____ , or order, at

Utopia, California

the principal sum of ___Eighteen thousand ($18,000) and no/100_____ DOLLARS,

with interest from date endorsed hereon _____ on unpaid principal at the

rate of Twelve (12%) _____ per cent per annum; principal and interest payable in installments of

    Two hundred seventy ($270) and no/100 _____ Dollars

or more on the same _____ day of each calendar _____ month, beginning

on the first (1st) _____ day of September _____ , 20xx , and continuing

until August 1, 20xx , at which time the entire unpaid balance of

principal and interest shall become due and payable.

and continuing until said principal and interest have been paid.
Should any installment of principal or interest not be so paid, then the whole sum of principal and interest shall immediately become due and payable at the option of the holder hereof; principal and interest payable only in lawful money of the United States. Should this note not be paid according to the terms hereof and suit be filed or an attorney employed or expenses incurred to compel payment of this note, or any portion hereof, I agree to pay a reasonable sum in in addition to attorney's fees. The makers and endorsers of this note hereby waive diligence, demand, presentment for payment, notice of non-payment, protest and notice of protest.

                                        /s/ Mr. Igot Stuck

                                        /s/ Mrs. Igot Stuck

As collateral security for the payment of this note and interest as stated therein and expenses which may accrue thereon
we _____ have deposited with Mrs. Broker _____ , the

following personal property of which we are _____ sole owner s , to-wit: _____

1. Note executed by Mr. & Mrs. Buyer, dated July 4, 20xx

2. Deed of Trust securing said Note, recorded July 5, 20xx

3. Duly executed Assignment of Trust Deed and Note by Mr. & Mrs. Stuck,
   recorded August 19, 20xx

And should the said note or any part thereof, or the interest, or the interest that may grow thereon, remain due and unpaid
_____according to the tenor of said note,____we____hereby irrevocably authorize and empower said

Mrs Broker and Mr Salesman _____ , their heirs, executors, administrators or assigns,

to sell and dispose of the above mentioned personal property, or any part thereof, at public or private sale, without any previous

notice to us _____ of any such sale, and from the proceeds arising therefrom to pay the

principal and interest and all charges that shall then be due, and the costs of sale, and the balance, if any, to pay over to

____our_____ or _____ representatives upon demand.   In case of

deterioration of any of the above securities, or fall in the market value of the same we_____
bereby promise__ and agree__ on demand to reduce the amount of said debt, or to increase the security in proportion to
such deterioration or decrease of value, in default of which this note is to be considered due under the above stipulation.   On
the payment of this note and interest according to the terms of the same, and all charges, this agreement is to be void, and the

above named securities to be returned to us .

Presentment, protest and notice of protest are hereby waived.

Dated August 19, _____ 20xx   /s/ Mr. Igot Stuck

                                        /s/ Mrs. Igot Stuck

NOTE—COLLATERAL SECURITY—INSTALLMENT—WOLCOTTS FORM 1428

Figure 14.3 Sample installment note.

The commission rate is 6 percent, and the seller agrees to carry back a second loan if enough cash can be generated so that the seller can in turn purchase another home. Suppose that the seller needs the cash and cannot afford to carry back the four-year note to maturity, yet the seller does not like the idea of collateralizing or selling at discount. The real estate agent can provide the solution by participating in the second trust deed loan, as follows:

Sales price		$300,000
Cash down payment		−30,000
Balance needed to finance		$270,000
First trust deed loan		−240,000
Junior financing for the balance	$30,000	
Broker's share at 6% of sales price	−18,000	
Seller's share for balance	$12,000	
Combined purchase money second trust deed		$ 30,000

The mechanics of this transaction are as follows: A promissory note and trust deed are executed by the buyer of the property in favor of the seller for the full amount of the second deed of trust, $30,000. Then an instrument similar to the installment note, the collateral security form in Figure 14.3, is executed by the sellers to the broker for the amount of commission, $18,000 in this case. The collateral agreement is in effect an assignment of the seller's note and trust deed for the portion representing the broker's interest. It states in so many words that for value received, the seller promises to pay to the broker the agreed amount at so much per month, including interest at so much per annum, and that, in case of default, the broker would have a right to foreclose through either public or private sale of the collateral, the secured promissory note. When more than one licensee is taking part or all of the commission through this mechanism, like a selling salesperson and employing broker, both may be shown under the payee provision of the collateral note for the amount or percentage representing their respective commission interests.

Combination or "Split" Junior Liens

As a compromise to carrying back paper that the seller is unwilling to sell or collateralize, and when the broker is not willing to take a junior lien for all or part of the commission, the seller might be amenable to taking back a concurrent second and third trust deed, both carrying a 12 percent yield. The purchase money loan is "split". Instead of one large second, the seller might agree to two smaller junior liens. Using the sales price and terms outlined in the original example, with a 10 percent down payment and assumed 70/30 split junior lien, the position of the junior trust deeds would appear as follows:

Sales price	$300,000
Cash down payment	−30,000
Balance needed to finance	$270,000
First trust deed	−240,000
Junior financing	$ 30,000
Second trust deed carried by seller	−21,000
Third trust deed carried by seller	$ 9,000

While both loans contain exactly the same terms, the advantage of such an arrangement is that it is easier to market a second of a smaller size, thus providing the seller with some immediate cash relief. Yet the seller is able to retain a relatively safe interest in the property at an attractive rate of return. The $30,000 junior financing may be divided into any portions that will allow the greatest flexibility to the seller. It may be a $21,000 second and $9,000 third as just illustrated, or a $15,000 second and $15,000 third, and so on. The buyers costs are not substantially increased, since split loans require only two extra documents, one extra recording fee, and one extra reconveyance fee. Payoff terms can be adjusted to increase yield on the second or third that is to be sold.

14.2 All-Inclusive Trust Deed (AITD)

Definition

An all-inclusive trust deed, for reasons that will soon become clear, is also referred to as a **wrap-around** or overriding trust deed. It may also be mistakenly referred to as a *blanket trust deed*, since it includes more than one trust deed loan within the framework of the instrument. A blanket trust deed encumbers more than one property, while an all-inclusive trust deed usually covers just one property. An *all-inclusive trust deed* is always a *junior* deed of trust, often a purchase money loan, given back to the seller that includes in its scope the amount of the first encumbrance as well as any secondary liens. It normally contains a provision that the seller will pay off the senior loan or loans from monies the seller is to receive from the buyer. It is subject to, yet includes, encumbrances to which it is subordinate.

Since the concept essentially involves the seller as lender, it is most often used when money is tight or unavailable. Care and discretion must be exercised in its adoption, particularly when a real estate agent recommends its use, because all too often there is an existing loan on the property that is to remain on record.

An example of an all-inclusive deed of trust is shown in Figure 14.4. The instrument could be used on virtually any type of property where circumstances are appropriate. Brokers should not attempt to draft such trust deeds but should have them prepared by the parties' legal counsel and approved by the title company that is to insure them.

Uses for All-Inclusive Trust Deeds

The **all-inclusive trust deed** is used under a variety of circumstances. Some sellers will use it in lieu of an installment sales type contract, the so-called land contract. It may also be used where there exists a loan with a lock-in clause (not to be confused with "lock-in-rate") that provides that the existing loan cannot be paid off before a certain date. A third use is when an owner is anxious to sell and a prospective purchaser will buy only under an all-inclusive device that incorporates features favorable to the buyer such as income tax benefits. Sellers may also offer this type of instrument when they have overpriced the property. Low down payments may also tempt owners to sell this way.

Another type of transaction calling for a wrap-around is when there is a low-interest loan that the seller would prefer to keep, particularly when a buyer's credit is marginal, so that in the event of foreclosure by the selling beneficiary, the underlying low-cost loan is retained. When the seller is firm on price but not on terms, again its use may be justified.

Another circumstance is when a prospective buyer cannot qualify for required financing under a normal sale. When a seller would need to carry back a substantial junior loan, the all-inclusive may be more satisfactory. In cases involving heavy and burdensome prepayment penalties, buyers and sellers may resort to the all-inclusive trust deed. In still another situation, an owner may need cash but the beneficiary under the existing trust deed will not commit itself to additional advances, forcing the seller to retain the prior lien or liens using an all-inclusive. Finally, when a severe money crunch hits the mortgage

ALL INCLUSIVE PURCHASE MONEY PROMISSORY NOTE SECURED BY
ALL-INCLUSIVE PURCHASE MONEY DEED OF TRUST
(INSTALLMENT NOTE, INTEREST INCLUDED)

$ __500,000__   __Van Nuys__ , California, __April 15__ 20**XX**

In installments as herein stated, for value received, I/We ("Maker") promise to pay to __James W. Johnson__

("Payee") or order, at __6515-6517 Van Nuys Blvd, Van Nuys, CA__

the principal sum of __Five hundred thousand and no/100__ _____ DOLLARS, with interest

from __date hereof__ _____ on unpaid principal at the rate of

__twelve (12%)__ per cent per annum; principal and interest payable in installments of __$5143.00__

or more on the __first (1st)__ day of each __calendar__ month, beginning

on the __first (1st)__ day of __June__ 20**XX** , and continuing until said p̶r̶i̶n̶c̶i̶p̶a̶l̶ a̶n̶d̶

i̶n̶t̶e̶r̶e̶s̶t̶ h̶a̶v̶e̶ b̶e̶e̶n̶ p̶a̶i̶d̶/ June 1, 20**XX**, when the unpaid balance shall be due and payable.

Each installment shall be applied first on the interest then due and the remainder on principal; and interest shall thereupon cease upon the principal so credited.

The total principal amount of this Note includes the unpaid principal balance of the promissory note(s) ("Underlying Note(s)") secured by Deed(s) of Trust, more particularly described as follows:

1. (A) PROMISSORY NOTE:
   Maker: __Newstate S & L and Allstate Mortgage Ltd.__
   Payee: _____
   Original Amount: __$300,000__
   Date: _____

   (B) DEED OF TRUST:
   Beneficiary: _____
   Original Amount: _____
   Recordation Date: _____
   Document No. _____ Book _____ Page _____
   Place of Recordation: _____ , County, California

2. (A) PROMISSORY NOTE:
   Maker: _____
   Payee: _____
   Original Amount: _____
   Date: _____

   (B) DEED OF TRUST:
   Beneficiary: _____
   Original Amount: _____
   Recordation Date: _____
   Document No. _____ Book _____ Page _____
   Place of Recordation: _____ , County, California

By Payee's acceptance of this Note, Payee covenants and agrees that, provided Maker is not delinquent or in default under the terms of this Note, Payee shall pay all installments of principal and interest which shall hereafter become due pursuant to the provisions of the Underlying Note(s) as and when the same become due and payable. In the event Maker shall be delinquent or in default under the terms of this Note, Payee shall not be obligated to make any payments required by the terms of the Underlying Note(s) until such delinquency or default is cured. In the event Payee fails to timely pay any installment of principal or interest on the Underlying Note(s) at the time when Maker is not delinquent or in default hereunder, Maker may, at Maker's option, make such payments directly to the holder of such Underlying Note(s), in which event Maker shall be entitled to a credit against the next installment(s) of principal and interest due under the terms of this Note equal to the amount so paid and including, without limitation, any penalty, charges and expenses paid by Maker to the holder of the Underlying Note(s) on account of Payee failing to make such payment. The obligations of Payee hereunder shall terminate upon the earliest of (i) foreclosure of the lien of the All-Inclusive Purchase Money Deed of Trust securing this Note, or (ii) cancellation of this Note and reconveyance of the All-Inclusive Purchase Money Deed of Trust securing same.

Should Maker be delinquent or in default under the terms of this Note, and Payee consequently incurs any penalties, charges or other expenses on account of the Underlying Note(s) during the period of such delinquency or default, the amount of such penalties, charges and expenses shall be immediately added to the principal amount of this Note and shall be immediately payable by Maker to Payee.

Notwithstanding anything to the contrary herein contained, the right of Maker to prepay all or any portion of the principal of this Note is limited to the same extent as any limitation exists in the right to prepay the principal of the Underlying Note(s). If any prepayments of principal of this Note shall, by reason of the application of any portion thereof by Payee to the prepayment of principal of the Underlying Note(s), constitute such prepayment for which the holders of the Underlying Note(s) are entitled to receive a prepayment penalty or consideration, the amount of such prepayment penalty or consideration shall be paid by Maker to Payee upon demand, and any such amount shall not reduce the unpaid principal balance of this Note.

At any time when the total of the unpaid principal balance of this Note, accrued interest thereon, all other sums due pursuant to the terms hereof, and all sums advanced by Payee pursuant to the terms of the All-Inclusive Purchase Money Deed of Trust securing this Note, is equal to or less than the unpaid balance of principal and interest then due under the terms of the Underlying Note(s), Payee, at his option, shall cancel this Note and deliver same to Maker and execute a request for full reconveyance of the Deed of Trust securing this Note.

Should default be made by Maker in payment of any installments of principal, interest, or any other sums due hereunder, the whole sum of principal, interest and all other sums due from Maker hereunder, after first deducting therefrom all sums then due under the terms of the Underlying Note(s), shall become immediately due at the option of the holder of this Note. Principal, interest and all other sums due hereunder payable in lawful money of the United States. If action be instituted of this Note, I/we promise to pay such sums as the Court may fix as attorney's fees. This Note is secured by an ALL-INCLUSIVE PURCHASE MONEY DEED OF TRUST to Lawyers Title Insurance Corporation, a Virginia corporation, as Trustee.

_____ _Jack B. Quick_ Jack B. Quick
(Maker)   (Maker)

The undersigned hereby accept(s) the foregoing All-Inclusive Purchase Money Promissory Note and agree(s) to perform each and all of the terms thereof on the part of Payee to be performed.
Executed as of the date and place first above written.

_____   _____
(Payee)   (Payee)

(THIS NOTE IS FOR USE ONLY IN PURCHASE MONEY TRANSACTIONS. IT IS RECOMMENDED THAT, PRIOR TO THE EXECUTION OF THIS NOTE, THE PARTIES CONSULT WITH THEIR ATTORNEYS WITH RESPECT THERETO.)

061-4-284-0000
FORM T394

THIS FORM FURNISHED BY LAWYERS TITLE INSURANCE CORPORATION

Figure 14.4 Sample all-inclusive deed of trust.

market, this device takes on added significance. After all, it is especially during periods of tight money that most creative financing techniques appear on the market.

Although we have advanced a dozen reasons for using the all-inclusive deed of trust, sellers and buyers may, of course, be motivated by a combination of two or more of these. Remember, an AITD cannot be used to get around an otherwise enforceable **due-on-sale clause** The loan must be assumable. Lenders can discover a concealed AITD when the homeowners insurance policy is endorsed.

Comprehensive Application of All-Inclusive Trust Deed

As an example of an all-inclusive trust deed, assume that a property is to sell for $600,000 and that it has an existing first trust deed loan of $236,000 payable at $2,360 per month, including interest at 8 percent per annum; and a second loan of $64,000 payable at $640 per month, including 10 percent annual interest. Deducting the $300,000 in loans from the $600,000 sale price leaves an equity of $300,000. Suppose the parties agree to a one-sixth down payment, or $100,000. The balance of the purchase price, $200,000 is the remaining seller's equity that could be financed by carrying back either a third trust deed or an all-inclusive trust deed. Since a substantial third would be involved—representing one-third of the sales price—such a step may not be advised. A better resolution may lie, therefore, with the wraparound, if the existing loan(s) is assumable and/or the lenders agree to waive their due-on-sale rights. Schematically, the transaction would appear as follows:

SALE PRICE: $600,000			
$100,000	$500,000 All-inclusive trust deed, $5,143 per month at 12%		
Down payment (Buyer's equity)	$236,000 First loan payable $2,360 per month at 8% annual interest	$64,000 Second loan payable $640 per month at 10% annual interest	$200,000 Seller's remaining equity

In the illustration, the seller's remaining equity is $200,000 and it is added to the existing liens under the banner of an all-inclusive trust deed, payable at $5,143 per month including interest of 12 percent per annum.

Characteristics and Limitations

The all-inclusive trust deed is characterized by a number of features. First, it can increase the seller's rate of return above what the rate would be under a traditional carryback loan. Second, it is a purchase money transaction, subject to but still including encumbrances to which it is subordinate. The buyer becomes a trustor-grantee, while the seller becomes a beneficiary-grantor. By virtue of its purchase money character, the transaction is subject to California's antideficiency statutes if it is a one-to-four-unit owner-occupied residential property, so that the buyer-trustor is held harmless in the event of a deficiency on the promissory note should foreclosure occur.

Legal title is actually conveyed, usually by grant deed, and may be insured by a policy of title insurance. Finally, in the event of default and foreclosure, the seller-beneficiary follows the same procedures that would apply in the foreclosure of any trust deed. However, the action is filed only against the seller's equity, representing the difference between the underlying liens and the overriding obligation—$200,000 in the preceding illustration. Again, the AITD is useful only if existing loans are assumable, or if the due-on-sale clause is waived by the prior lender.

Types of AITDs

The AITD may be one of two types:

1. *Equity payoff.* This takes place when the buyer, who is the trustor on the AITD, with the permission of the lender, takes over the prior loans after the seller's equity has been paid off. A deed of reconveyance is issued by the seller-beneficiary of the AITD. In the preceding example, once the buyer has paid off the difference between the $500,000 AITD and the $236,000 first trust deed plus the remaining due under the $64,000 second, the buyer steps into the shoes of the seller and makes payments on the prior notes directly to the beneficiaries of these senior liens.

2. *Full payoff.* Here the buyer-trustor is obligated to the seller until the entire balance of the AITD is paid off. Thus the seller-beneficiary continues to pick up the override, the difference between the 12 percent paid the seller and the lower rates due on the underlying notes (8 percent on the first, 10 percent on the second).

Benefits to Seller

There are a number of advantages to the seller in using the all-inclusive to solve financing problems. It may be the only practical way to dispose of a property when there is a lock-in clause. Furthermore, a broader market is created for the property when a seller is willing to carry back substantially all of the paper. A carryback by a seller does not incur loan fees and a variety of other financing charges. This attracts buyers and thereby increases the demand for the seller's property.

Moreover, the all-inclusive device affords flexibility so that the seller may be able to obtain a higher price due to the built-in financing terms. In effect the seller has manufactured money by deferring the recapture of the seller's equity through this method. The seller retains the favorable terms of the existing loans in the event the seller is forced to repossess the property through foreclosure. During the holding period, the seller is able to increase the net yield on the overall trust deed. Recall that sellers' carryback purchase money mortgages and trust deeds are not subject to any interest rate limitations. Using the data from our previous example, if a simple interest rate were applied to each of the loans, the yield to the investor on the all-inclusive trust deed (AITD) would be almost 17.4 percent, computed as follows:

Interest income:	12% of $500,000 on AITD		$60,000
Interest expense:	8% of $236,000 on existing first deed	$18,880	
	10% of $64,000 on existing second deed	6,400	25,280
Net interest income over interest expense:			$34,720

$$\text{Yield} = \frac{\text{Seller's net interest income}}{\text{Seller's equity}} = \frac{\$34,720}{\$200,000} = 17.4\%$$

The effective yield is significantly greater than the 12 percent stated on the AITD note because the seller will collect 12 percent while paying out only 8 percent and 10 percent on the existing notes, thereby earning an additional 4 percent on the first, and 2 percent on the second trust deed. The extra $34,720 interest received is equivalent to another 5.4 percent return on the $200,000 remaining equity. That is,

$$\frac{(4\% \times \$236,000) + (2\% \times \$64,000)}{\$200,000} = 5.4\%$$

Adding this to the 12 percent buyer's contract rate produces a 17.4 percent effective rate to the seller. It should be noted that calculations using the foregoing formula are only approximations. They show the yield on a first-year basis only and not over the life of the loan. Furthermore, they do not take into account other variables, including special features of the note, such as term, balloon payments, or variable rates; nor do they take into account income tax consequences and time value of money. Use the formula judiciously.

Another benefit might ensue in the event the seller-beneficiary had to cash out the all-inclusive note secured by a trust deed. A lower discount is commanded when a high effective yield is obtained. Even without a discount, when the purchaser could assume the underlying liens, in the previous example the yield would be 17.4 percent.

A significant advantage to the seller is that this device makes the seller aware immediately of any buyer's default, in contrast to taking back a junior deed of trust accompanied by the recording of a request for notice: months may pass before a senior lienholder files a notice of default should the trustor-buyer default in a prior loan, so that if the seller—junior lienholder's own loan payments are current such default would be unnoticed. When compared to a land contract of sale, the all-inclusive trust deed may again be superior, because in case of foreclosure a trustee's sale is speedier, surer, and absolute, while foreclosure under a land contract requires court action to become effective.

Finally, income tax advantages to the seller may be enhanced. For example, in a straight sale with conventional forms of financing, the entire gain is recognized in the year of sale. In contrast, in the all-inclusive trust deed, the seller may declare only the actual receipts received each year on a prorated basis over the term of the AITD note. This is because an AITD, since it is payable over more than one calendar year, is by its very nature an installment sale as defined in the Internal Revenue Code, Section 453.

Benefits to Buyer

The all-inclusive trust deed also offers many advantages to buyers. They may be able to acquire properties for which they may not otherwise qualify—for example, the purchaser who is retired and, although having substantial resources, has relatively little if any dependable income. When financing can be obtained, the buyer may acquire a larger property for the same low down payment, utilizing the principle of leverage. Moreover, one monthly payment will be required instead of a series of payments that would ensue when the buyer assumes the prior liens and executes another junior secured note in favor of the seller. Costs are reduced on appraisal fees, loan points, loan escrow fee, and other charges.

Greater flexibility may also be offered in the structure of the loan. When the seller is cooperative, the purchaser might be able to tailor the spendable income to his or her particular needs, such as through a lower *debt service* stretched over a longer period of time, and thus afford to pay more for the property by bargaining for better terms. There are no restrictions on lending, unlike institutional financing. Thus extra-long terms can be negotiated, with no points and no pre-payment penalties as part of the bargain. And if the purchaser should pay more for the property, the basis will be thereby increased, with a subsequent lower capital gain (or larger write-off in the event of a qualified sale at a loss).

Finally, when contrasted with a purchase under a land contract, the buyer gets a grant deed, or ownership in fee, up front, as opposed to a land contract, which gives *legal* title at the end of the contract, though it is also an *insurable* title.

Another advantage to *both* buyer and seller is that since the buyer will not ordinarily incur loan fees and a variety of financing charges, properly structured, this feature should attract more buyers and increase the demand for the seller's property.

Some Pitfalls of All-Inclusive Trust Deeds

Just as there are benefits to both buyers and sellers who structure the AITD correctly, precautions must be taken since this vehicle is not a cure-all for most housing transactions.

Precautions for Sellers

Of course, both parties should take steps to guard against certain pitfalls that may arise in connection with the use of the wrap-around trust deed. For example, an impound account might be set up to cover taxes, insurance, and balloon payments on the prior liens. The seller might also have the installment payments on the wrap-around loan fall due at least a week before payments on the senior loan are due. This way the seller will be using the buyer's money to make the payments on any senior loan.

A limit, if not an outright prohibition, might be imposed on further use of another all-inclusive trust deed upon resale by inserting a due-on-sale clause in the AITD. Similarly, the seller should reserve the right to have the buyer refinance the property. The seller may wish to have the buyer refinance when the money market is more favorable, or when the lock-in period has expired, or when balloon payments are due on the senior debt. The seller should also make provision for the time when the purchaser may need to assume the existing loans (as discussed above, under Types of AITDs), should such loans outlive the all-inclusive trust deed.

Finally, when income-producing property is involved, the seller should reserve the right to approve all leases that might impair the value of the all-inclusive trust deed. A shrewd buyer might, for example, lease the premises with substantial prepaid rents paid to the buyer, intending to "milk" the property, then walk away from it, leaving the seller stuck with the legal problems of dealing with the prepaid rents for each of the lessees, in addition to having to deal with the remaining lease terms, which may be economically unfavorable to the seller who must now step in to protect remaining interests. By reserving the right to pre-screen all leases, the seller is protected against such problems in the AITD, since all subsequent leases are to be subordinated to the seller's superior interest as the beneficiary under the all-inclusive trust deed. (It should be noted that leases with priority over the underlying deed of trust are extremely rare.)

Precautions for Buyers

Precautions should also be taken by the buyer, of course. The all-inclusive agreement should provide machinery to protect the buyer in case the seller defaults on the loan being wrapped.

The buyer might, for example, insert the right to make payments on the seller's underlying liens, and credit such payments toward the all-inclusive trust deed. Payments might be made to a bank collection department, escrow, trust, or directly to the holder of the included encumbrances, stipulating that they be used in turn to reduce existing liens. The costs of setting up such machinery should be stipulated. If payments on the all-inclusive trust deed are not sufficient to cover existing liens, provision should be made for seller's payment of any differences, such as through a bond. Further, the buyer might reserve the right to pay off part or all of the senior debts, assuming or retiring some or all of them.

All buyers should record a *request for notice of default and notice of sale* on the seller's senior liens to make sure they keep abreast of the status of these loans. If a notice of default is recorded, buyers will automatically receive notice.

Procedures in Setting Up an All-Inclusive Trust Deed

The procedures required in negotiating for and creating an all-inclusive trust deed might follow these broad steps:

1. Examine existing trust deeds to determine whether there is an enforceable due-on-sale, alienation, or acceleration clause. If any exist, provision should be made either to pay off the loans or renegotiate them.

2. Outstanding balances, periodic payments, and balloon provisions should be ascertained so that a realistic payment schedule can be set up on the all-inclusive. For example, the new loan schedule may call for a longer or shorter period for payment, depending on the particular requirements of the respective parties. The all-inclusive trust deed is of course recorded as a junior lien, subject to the existing liens. The purchaser may later, with the lender's permission, take over the senior loans, whereupon the seller would need to obtain a reconveyance of the all-inclusive trust deed as a fully discharged instrument.

   A realistic payment schedule should be constructed to cover (a) periodic installments, (b) outstanding balances, (c) partial balloons on existing loans, and (d) any variations in payments, such as for adjustable or variable rates.

3. Decide who is to collect and disburse payments on the all-inclusive trust deed and who is to pay the cost of setting up and administering the collection process. If the payments under the AITD are not sufficient to cover the senior loans, a system should be set up to see that the additional amounts are paid. Similarly, if there is an impound account for taxes, insurance, or other matters in the underlying note, it would be prudent to incorporate an impound in the AITD note as well.

4. Spell out the conditions giving rise to default and what foreclosure procedure is to be followed. These are similar to those found in the standard trust deed, except that only the seller's remaining equity is affected.

5. Have the necessary agreements and documents drawn up, using essential phraseology to gain acceptance by title companies for insurance purposes. A joint protection policy of title insurance, insuring both the interests of the buyer as owner and the interests of the seller as lender and as to priority of lien, should be obtained.

6. Determine property insurance coverage so all parties are amply protected.

14.3 Installment Sales Contract

The *installment sales contract*, more popularly called a conditional sales contract, or *land contract of sale* is another vehicle that can be used to solve real estate financing problems. Unlike the all-inclusive deed of trust, however, the fee title remains with the seller-vendor until the terms and conditions of the contract are fulfilled. This is an important distinction for a number of reasons, among which is that the use of the all-inclusive deed of trust permits a private sale of the property by the trustee in the event of default, eliminating the problems of a time-consuming and cumbersome judicial foreclosure. In contrast, the usual land contract may not contain a power of sale provision, so that a lawsuit is necessary for an effective foreclosure by the vendor. However, it may be noted that almost all title companies have produced contract forms that incorporate a power of sale provision. Figure 14.5 is an example of one furnished by an early pioneer in this field, Stewart-West Coast Title Company.

Example: To illustrate the math involved in the sale of real property through a land contract, suppose a vacant lot sold for $100,000 and has an existing assumable 10 percent first trust deed loan of $60,000. The buyer is to make a down payment of 10 percent, or $10,000, and has agreed to execute an installment contract secured by the property for the balance of the purchase price. The contract is to be repaid at $966, rounded to the next dollar, per month, based on a *30-year amortization* schedule including interest of 13 percent per annum, all due and payable in 15 years. Note that under such schedule the payments are reduced from the $1,138.72 that would be payable under 15-year amortization.

Sales price	$100,000
Down payment at 10%	−10,000
Balance payable $996 monthly at 13%	$ 90,000

The seller continues to make payments on the $60,000 first trust deed, at the more favorable 10 percent interest rate. Instead of a second trust deed of $30,000 ($90,000 less $60,000) at, say, 10 percent, the seller will receive more on a 13 percent loan on the entire unpaid balance of $90,000—meanwhile continuing with a 10 percent interest rate on the existing $60,000, yielding a differential of 3 percent on the full $60,000.

RECORDING REQUESTED BY

AND WHEN RECORDED MAIL TO

Name   James Oliva

Street Address

City & State

————————SPACE ABOVE THIS LINE FOR RECORDER'S USE————————

FORM 1   **LONG FORM SECURITY (INSTALLMENT) LAND CONTRACT WITH POWER OF SALE**

THIS AGREEMENT, made and entered into this   **20th**   day of   **May**   , 20XX , by and between   **JAMES OLIVA, a married man and MICHAEL OLIVA, a married man,**   (Vendor's name), **each as to an undivided one-half interest**

whose address is

(hereinafter sometimes referred to as "Vendor"), and   **WILLIAM FERRELL and SHARON FERRELL**

husband and wife, and RONALD SACHS and

CAROL SACHS, husband and wife, all as joint tenants (hereinafter sometimes referred to as "Vendee"); and **STEWART-WEST COAST TITLE CO.** (hereinafter sometimes referred to as "Trustee.")

W I T N E S S E T H :

WHEREAS, Vendor is now the owner of certain real property situated in the County of

State of California, commonly known as   **8527 Sunshine Ln, Panorama City, CA**

(property street address), and described as follows:

Lot 62 of Tract No. 15479, as per map recorded in Book 336, Pages 44,45, and 46 in the office of the County Recorder of said County.

WHEREAS, Vendor has agreed to sell, and Vendee has agreed to buy said real property on the terms and conditions hereinafter set forth;

WHEREAS, Vendor shall retain legal title as a security interest in said real property until the payment of the balance of the purchase price has been paid by Vendee to Vendor as set forth below.

NOW, THEREFORE, THE PARTIES HERETO DO HEREBY AGREE AS FOLLOWS:

PURCHASE PRICE

1. Vendor agrees to sell, and Vendee agrees to buy all of the aforedescribed real property for the sum of

(Total purchase price) ($_____),

lawful money of the United States, as hereinafter more fully set forth.

REQUEST FOR NOTICE OF DEFAULT

2. In accordance with Section 2924b, Civil Code, request is hereby made by the undersigned Vendor and Vendee that a copy of any Notice of Default and a copy of any Notice of Sale under Deed of Trust recorded_____ in Book_____, Page_____, Official Records of _____ County, California, as affecting above described property, executed by _____as Trustor in which_____ is named as beneficiary, and_____as Trustee, be mailed to Vendor and Vendee at address in paragraph 3 below.

NOTICES AND REQUEST FOR NOTICE

3. Notices required or permitted under this agreement shall be binding if delivered personally to party sought to be served or if mailed by registered or certified mail, postage prepaid in the United States mail to the following:

Vendor: _____

_____

_____   Trustee: Stewart-West Coast Title Co.

Vendee: _____   2675 West Olympic Boulevard

_____   Los Angeles, California 90006

Vendor and Vendee hereby request that notice of default and notice of sale hereunder be mailed to them at the above address.

PAYMENT OF PURCHASE PRICE

4. Vendee shall pay said purchase price of $_____ as follows:

(a) Vendee shall pay to Vendor the sum of $_____ (Down Payment) as and for a down payment.

(b) Vendee shall take subject to and pay the balance due on that certain note secured by a first trust deed on the above mentioned real property, the principal balance of which is $_____, together with interest thereon at the rate of ____ percent per annum, payable in installments of

$_____, (monthly payments amount; add "or more" if applicable) per month on the ____ day of each and every month with the whole of the then outstanding balance thereof due on the ____ day of 19____. Each such payment includes payment of the following items under the terms of said note and trust deed:

(1) Principal and interest;

(2) Impounds for taxes;   (Strike out

(3) Impounds for fire insurance;   inapplicable items.)

(4) Impounds for

Payments shall be made by Vendee directly to beneficiary of said first trust deed at the following address:

_____

_____

(If a second trust deed exists, complete (c) below)

(c) Vendee shall take subject to and pay the balance due on that certain note secured by a second trust deed on the above mentioned real property, principal balance of which is $_____ together with interest thereon at the rate of ____ percent per annum, payable in installments of $_____ (monthly payment amount; add "or more"

Figure 14.5 Sample land contract (partial).

Like any seller carryback, including the AITD, the installment contract of sale offers a significant income tax benefit to sellers, the ability to prorate capital gains over the life of the note. Check with a tax consultant for further details. Incidentally, a land contract can be used for *any* type of real estate, including vacant land.

14.4 Lender Participations

A *participation* is the sharing of an interest in the property by a lender. When money is tight or available only at high interest rates or both, the lender will insist on a higher yield to itself to compensate for the greater risk involved. Without this, the lender may not be motivated to commit funds. This is especially true of large projects, for which an equity participation provides a means by which substantial investment capital could be raised.

Participation can be created in a variety of ways and may be classified according to the following categories:

1. *Lender participation in the revenue of the project*. For example, if a project costs $1 million to develop, in order to maximize leverage and yield on return, the developer will want to obtain the largest possible loan. But lenders may not be content with a fixed rate of return. One alternative would be to offer a "piece of the action" through a participation in the income. This may be either a percentage of gross revenue or a percentage of net revenue. Since there may be a minimum amount, or floor, the excess income is referred to as overage. For instance, an institutional lender might finance 75 percent of the project at 10 percent interest per annum, payable over 25 years, with the provision that the lender is to also receive 20 percent of net income before depreciation and income taxes. If net income amounted to $50,000, the lender would receive $10,000 in addition to the 10 percent on the $750,000 loan—an effective yield of approximately 11.33 percent. Of course, to make the venture attractive to the developer, the overall yield will need to equal or exceed 11.33 percent per annum return.

2. *Equity participation*. In the previous example, instead of a percentage of profits, the lender may insist on a certain percentage of the property. If 20 percent were agreed upon, the lender would have a direct title interest in 20 percent of the equity in the real property (or stock or other ownership interest) as a condition for making the loan. Assuming again a $250,000 equity in

the development, after a $750,000 commitment on a $1 million project, the lender would thus have a $50,000 ownership interest (20 percent × $250,000), or 5 percent of the entire property. The lender would thus be entitled to 5 percent of all income, in addition to all of the other benefits of ownership, such as depreciation writeoff and capital gain. Of course, the lender would also be burdened by 5 percent of all expenses and costs of operation, just as with any real property ownership.

3. *Fees and discounts*. The lender could also increase the loan yield by charging a fixed interest rate but, in addition, requiring a one-time fee or points as a condition of making the loan. In effect, the loan is discounted by the amount of points charged at the front, much as government-backed loans are when the buyer or seller is charged a loan commitment fee.

4. *Profit participation*. Instead of sharing in the income, the lender may opt for a participation in the profits of a venture. Thus, when a lender believes that a project is expected to increase in value, it may prefer to share in capital gains at time of sale or exchange, rather than in the income during the holding period. For example, if the parties agreed to a 25 percent participation, and the $1 million development were subsequently sold for a net of $1.4 million, the lender would be entitled to 25 percent of the $400,000 gain, or $100,000.

5. *Multiple lenders*. This involves the purchase of a portion of loans made by other lenders. It is similar to the concept of reinsurance, when two or more insurance companies participate in a high-risk project. Similarly, in mortgage lending, large loans may be underwritten by more than one lender. Such schemes are common in corporate loans for large capital projects.

14.5 Sale-Leaseback

The *sale-leaseback* is also referred to as a purchase and lease-back, a purchase-lease, a sale-lease, a lease-purchase, and so on. But whatever its designation, it is characterized by a sale of one's property to another party, usually a large financial institution, which, in turn, leases it back to the seller. The property could consist of land only (*ground lease*), improvements only, or both land and improvements. This technique is a popular financing vehicle among strongly rated companies with excellent credit. Although it can be used with the sale and purchase of homes, our primary focus in this section is on nonresidential transactions.

Procedure

The mechanics of a sale-leaseback encompass four essential steps: (1) Investors buy property that they desire. This may be improved or unimproved. (2) If unimproved, the investor develops the land to its specifications. A large grocery chain, for example, may wish to build a 50,000-square-foot grocery store on a parcel of land it now owns. (3) The owner sells the land or improvements to a major investor, such as a life insurance company, pension fund, trust, or even a nonprofit association. (4) The investor-purchaser leases the property back to the seller at an agreed rent under a long-term lease.

The seller becomes the lessee, and the buyer becomes the lessor. No specific form is used. An offer to purchase is a contract that describes the terms and conditions; after acceptance, it is followed by a mutually acceptable lease agreement between the parties to the transaction.

Advantages to Seller

Among the possible advantages and benefits to the seller-lessee are the following:

- Lease payments are fully tax deductible for business and investment properties. This includes rents paid on both land and improvements, which in most instances will result in a greater write-off than interest payments on a loan or depreciation on just the value of the improvements.

- Rent may be lower than loan payments. During an inflationary period, a fixed rental schedule favors the lessee. Furthermore, the lease term can be made longer than the loan term—leases may run for as long as 99 years in some cases.

- Improvements made by the lessee can be deducted through depreciation write-off.

- When only the land is sold and leased back, not only are the ground rent payments deductible but depreciation on the improvements is deductible as well.

- Capital that would otherwise be tied up in equity is freed for other uses. To the extent that funds are raised through outright sale, maximum financing is achieved. More capital can normally be raised in this way than by borrowing.

- Since long-term leases are not ordinarily shown as a long-term liability, the balance sheet of the seller-lessee will appear stronger, thereby enhancing the credit position of the lessee.

- By selling the development at a profit, the lessee is able to obtain cash today but repay with constantly inflating dollars. Additionally, the time value of money, due to the return on invested capital, works to the lessee's advantage.

- The owner may structure the sale so as to provide a buy-back privilege through a repurchase option.

Disadvantages to Seller

Obviously the seller may find some drawbacks to a sale and lease-back arrangement, including the following:

- The seller-lessee is committed to a lease contract that may run for a considerable length of time.

- Any increase in the value of the property will not accrue to the lessee's benefit.

- Fixed rental schedules may prove cumbersome, if not fatal, in times of economic distress. Even in normal times, the rents may be higher than payments on a fully amortizing loan.

- The expiration of the lease period may come at an inopportune time, with either no provision for renewal, or renewal only at excessively high rents. This might occur, for example, after the seller-lessee, who is using the property, has developed the business to a very successful level that may be due in large measure to the specific location of the property.

- When land only is sold and leased back, the costs to the seller-lessee of constructing improvements may absorb the bulk of the capital generated from the sale of the land.

Advantages to Buyer

Among the possible benefits or advantages to the buyer-lessor are the following:

- The sale-leaseback may return a higher yield than is available through a trust deed investment. Furthermore, there are none of the risks of a premature payoff that are associated with early retirement of a secured debt either through sale or refinancing of property. Hence, the investor-lessor will not need to be concerned with seeking alternative good-quality investments when suddenly confronted with a large amount of cash. (This is one of the reasons that lenders charge prepayment penalties on premature loan payoffs.) Also, the lessor has better control of the property through ownership than is gained through a security interest in a deed of trust.

- Any increase in value through appreciation will accrue to the lessor-owner.

- In the event of the lessee's default, the lessor may proceed against other assets of the lessee. When the lessee has a high credit rating, these assets may be substantial.

- Lease payments may be sufficiently large to recover the original investment several times over, in the case of long-term leases, and still leave the lessor with the fee title to the property. Moreover, by continued leasing, regardless of how long the leasehold period may extend, a capital gains tax is avoided.

- Depending on the arrangement, the lease could specify that the lessee is to pay for all repairs, maintenance, insurance, utilities, taxes, and operating expenses, so that the lessor is left with a carefree investment (such an arrangement is termed a ***triple net lease***, or net-net-net.)

- A buyer in a poor cash position may be able to resell yet retain the same lessor interests through a second sale-leaseback arrangement.

Disadvantages to Buyer

- Lease payments to lessor, including the first month's payment, and perhaps the last two months' payments, are fully taxable as ordinary income, after deducting lessor-incurred operating expenses.

- Unless carefully structured, the leasehold term may, in a time of inflation, favor the lessee, whose contractual rents in time may be less than the economic rent. A shrewd lessor will guard against such a prospect by inserting a clause that would tie the rents to an index, such as the Consumer Price Index (CPI) or the Producer's Price Index (PPI), a wholesale price index.

- If the lessee defaults, the buyer will have to operate the property. This may occur at an economically depressed time and could lead to disastrous consequences for the buyer.

- When only a ground lease is involved, the buyer-lessor will not be entitled to the benefits of depreciation deductions when the land is subsequently improved by the lessee.

- Capital that could otherwise be used in the buyer-lessor's business is tied up in equity.

- In the event of insolvency of the seller-lessee, the buyer-lessor's rights are restricted to those of a lessor only, and not to those of a secured creditor, for the balance owed on account of the purchase price.

- Though the lessee may be strong at the execution of the lease, the lessee may turn sour at a later date. If the lessee improves the property in a special way and then files for bankruptcy, the lessor may be left with a special-purpose development that is unsaleable and unleaseable.

- In times of inflation, the lessor is paid rents with constantly deteriorating dollars.

- When a repurchase option (which can be tied to an index) is inserted in the contract, the lessee may be allowed to profit at the expense of the lessor should the agreed repurchase price be significantly less than the value existing at the time the repurchase option is exercised.

14.6 Open-End Trust Deed

In some deeds of trust, no provision is made for the borrower to secure additional funds. Thus, in order to obtain additional money to finance repairs or improvements, a borrower would need to refinance the property or seek other sources of funds. This could prove very expensive, not only because of the prepayment penalties and other costs incurred in such a transaction, but because of the added burden incurred when market rates are higher than the interest rate currently being paid on the note. Homeowners are particularly vulnerable, since dwellings cannot generate revenue as is the case with income-producing properties. Secondary financing may not be the answer because it is unavailable or very expensive.

The solution is to find a loan at the very outset that will include an open-end clause, permitting a borrower, at the lender's option, to add to the loan amount at periodic intervals. In addition to reborrowing the amount repaid through amortization, the debtor could in some cases arrange to have the loan increased to reflect the appreciated value of the property. Such arrangements are more readily realized during times when demand for funds is sluggish, while the supply is abundant.

Under the open-end mortgage or trust deed, the new loan is added to the old one. Monthly payments can be increased to absorb the differential, or the term for repayment can be extended so that the combined loan will be amortized through monthly installments. Such clauses are permitted in government-backed as well as conventional loans. The procedure is to fill out an application, sign a new note, and record a notice of additional advance. The new note is still secured by the original deed of trust. The original note continues to carry the original interest rate and terms, while the new note can carry *any* interest rate and terms agreed by the parties. These do not merge into one debt. Moreover, the notice of additional advance does not have to be recorded to be valid, but it should be recorded to avoid possible situations where priority could be disturbed. This procedure dates back to the days when institutional lenders could not legally make loans secured by second deeds of trust unless they also held the first. It should be noted that since most lenders can now legally make second mortgages, the need for an open-end clause is less frequent.

14.7 Commercial Loan

A nonmortgage way of financing real estate is through a loan from a commercial bank. Since these are unsecured, they are usually of short duration, seldom extending beyond three years, and are ordinarily limited to borrowers of substance. And because there will be no real property collateral, reliance is placed on the credit of the borrower or other security. The amount and terms of the loan are based on the income and credit standing of the borrower, along with the condition of the money market. However, proceeds from a straight bank loan of this type can be used to purchase real estate or to finance home improvements.

If the prospective borrower is interested only in financing home improvements, a home improvement loan or installment purchase contract may be more advisable. This is ordinarily a secured transaction, in the nature of a secondary loan at relatively high interest, and repayable in periodic installments, usually monthly.

A third use for commercial loans is in the area of equity buying. Investors who specialize in purchasing at foreclosure and other forms of involuntary sales are required to pay all cash. After the property has been successfully acquired, repaired, and marketed, proceeds from the resale can in turn be used to pay off the commercial loan.

14.8 Stock Equity/Pledged Asset Loans

A *stock equity* loan, another type of personal loan, is obtainable most commonly through a securities brokerage firm or commercial bank. Securities owned by the borrower, including those bought on margin—that is, with funds borrowed from the brokerage firm—are pledged as collateral. These include common and preferred stock, bonds, and debentures. One Wall Street firm did about half of its $10 billion in annual client home loans with pledged asset mortgages. Like the straight bank loan, the proceeds from the note can be used to purchase real estate, to finance desired improvements, or for further investment. Like the commercial loan, after the property's value is enhanced as a consequence of installing improvements, the appreciated value of the property will likely justify a significantly larger mortgage thereafter—in time to pay off the short-term note at maturity.

14.9 Blended-Rate Loans

A s an alternative to all-inclusive or other forms of seller carryback, the buyer-borrower may consider approaching a lender for a **blended-rate loan**, also called blended-yield. Under this plan the buyer would not take over an existing low-interest-rate loan, because it may have too low a balance. Instead, a new loan for a higher amount is negotiated with the existing lender, providing an interest rate that is based upon a weighted average of the relatively low existing rate and the relatively high rate charged on the added funds needed to complete the purchase of a property.

The central idea is to combine the low existing contract rate and the high new market rate into a blended rate that accomplishes two objectives: (1) increases the loan amount and (2) blends the two interest rates into one single rate that is higher than the existing rate but lower than the market rate. Such an approach is especially important if the existing loan is callable, that is, if the alienation clause is enforceable.

The method for determining the blended yield, or weighted average between the old and new interest rates, is as follows:

$$\text{Blended yield} = \frac{\begin{array}{c}(\text{Existing rate} \times \text{Existing loan balance})\\ +(\text{Market rate} \times \text{Net new money})\end{array}}{\text{Total financing}}$$

In the numerator we have what is essentially the total annualized interest cost. In the denominator, total financing consists of both the old loan and the amount added thereto, so we could call this combined figure the new loan amount. An example will help to clarify.

Example: Assume that interest rates skyrocket during a credit crunch and you are buying a $225,000 property that has an existing loan of $80,000 at 10 percent. You need a total of $180,000, however, after the 20 percent ($45,000) down payment. Assume that the existing lender is charging 15 percent for new loans. What will be the probable charge under a blended rate?

$$\text{Blended yield} = \frac{(10\% \times \$80,000) + (15\% \times \$100,000)}{\$180,000}$$

$$\text{Blended yield} = \frac{\$8,000 + \$15,000}{\$180,000}$$

$$\text{Blended yield} = 12.78\%$$

The 12.78 percent rate, which may be rounded up to $12\frac{7}{8}$ (12.875) percent by the lender, is higher than the 10 percent on the existing loan, but lower than the 15 percent market rate.

For those conversant with the financial calculator, blended-rate problems are readily solved by following the steps outlined in the Case & Point section in Chapter 13. Check the figures from this example using your HP-12C to see if you come up with the same result, 12.78 percent.

Benefits of the Blended Rate

• Buyers receive a below-market rate.

• The borrower qualifies more easily, since the loan is based upon a lower rate.

• Cash proceeds are greater, so that the seller is not required to carry back as much paper.

Table 14.1 Blended yield with seller carryback of junior trust deed.

	Loan Amount	×	Interest Rate	=	Annualized Interest Cost
Existing loan balance	$ 80,000		10%		$ 8,000
Net new money	70,000		15		10,500
Second trust deed	30,000		12		3,600
Totals	$180,000				$22,100

$$\text{Blended yield} = \frac{\$\ 22{,}100}{\$180{,}000} = 12.28\%$$

- The lender has an opportunity to increase its effective yield on old low-rate loan balances. Indeed, the blended rate need not necessarily be a fixed rate but can be a variable or adjustable blended rate.

- The blended-yield loan can be made even more creative through seller participation when financing is tight. Referring to the previous example, suppose the existing lender is willing to offer total financing of only $150,000, and not $180,000, and that the seller is willing to accept a note secured by a second trust deed for the balance of $30,000 at 12 percent per annum. What is the effective or blended rate? Table 14.1 summarizes the data and provides the answer.

The blended rate for the three separate rates is 12.28 percent, or 0.5 percent less than the blended rate of 12.78 percent in the previous case, where the seller did not participate in the financing.

14.10 Creative Financing Disclosure Act

For the protection of both sellers and buyers when sellers are to carry back loans in the sale of properties of from one to four dwelling units, certain disclosures must be made. These usually involve small investors or individuals dealing with private homes, who are less likely to understand the obligations and difficulties involved with creative financing. The law requires that arrangers of credit, usually real estate brokers involved in the sale of the property, must disclose the following items for the benefit of the buyer-borrower:

1. Description of the terms of the loan taken back by the seller.

2. Description of any other financing on the property.

3. A warning that if refinancing of the seller's existing loan is required because of negative amortization, such financing might be difficult or impossible to obtain.

4. If an AITD is involved, information about who is responsible for potential problems with senior trust deeds.

5. Terms of any balloon payments involved in the transaction.

The law also requires disclosures by agents for the seller's benefit, including:

6. Credit information about the buyer, including occupation, employment, income, debts, and the like. In the alternative, a written statement may be made that no representation as to the creditworthiness of the buyer is being made by the credit arranger.

7. Warnings to the seller about antideficiency limitations available to the seller in case of the buyer's default, if applicable.

Additional provisions of the law include requirements for balloon payments. Holders of such loans on one-to-four-unit dwellings must give written notices to the debtor not less than 90 days nor more than 150 days before the balloon payment is due, with date due, amount, and a description of the rights of the borrower to refinance the balloon. Failure to provide the notice does not excuse the liability, but the holder cannot collect the payment until 90 days after proper notice is made. See Figure 14.6 for the creative financing disclosure form most commonly used in California.

14.11 Imputed Interest

On certain income and investment property sales, when the seller carries a loan for $4,217,500 (subject, of course, to increase periodically) or less, the IRS says the seller must carry at 9% interest or the *applicable federal rate (AFR)* whichever is lower. If the seller carry loan exceeds $4,217,500, then the minimum rate must be the AFR. The AFR is the rate on federal securities with similar lengths as the seller carry loan. Why is the IRS concerned with the interest rate on these seller carry loans? The IRS is afraid that a seller who carries at a very low interest rate will be able to increase the sales price. The increase in sales price would be taxed a low capital

SELLER FINANCING ADDENDUM AND DISCLOSURE
(California Civil Code §§2956-2967)
(C.A.R. Form SFA, Revised 10/02)

This is an addendum to the ☐ Residential Purchase Agreement, ☐ Counter Offer, or ☐ Other _____
_____, ("Agreement"), dated _____,
On property known as _____ ("Property"),
between _____ ("Buyer"),
and _____ ("Seller").
Seller agrees to extend credit to Buyer as follows:
1. **PRINCIPAL; INTEREST; PAYMENT; MATURITY TERMS:** ☐ Principal amount $ _____, interest at _____%
    per annum, payable at approximately $ _____ per ☐ month, ☐ year, or ☐ other _____,
    remaining principal balance due in _____ years.
2. **LOAN APPLICATION; CREDIT REPORT:** Within **5 (or** ☐ _____**) Days** After Acceptance: **(a)** Buyer shall provide Seller a completed
    loan application on a form acceptable to Seller (such as a FNMA/FHLMC Uniform Residential Loan Application for residential one to four
    unit properties); and **(b)** Buyer authorizes Seller and/or Agent to obtain, at Buyer's expense, a copy of Buyer's credit report. Buyer shall
    provide any supporting documentation reasonably requested by Seller. Seller, after first giving Buyer a Notice to Buyer to Perform, may
    cancel this Agreement in writing and authorize return of Buyer's deposit if Buyer fails to provide such documents within that time, or if
    Seller disapproves any above item within **5 (or** ☐ _____**) Days** After receipt of each item.
3. **CREDIT DOCUMENTS:** This extension of credit by Seller will be evidenced by: ☐ Note and deed of trust; ☐ All-inclusive
    note and deed of trust; ☐ Installment land sale contract; ☐ Lease/option (when parties intend transfer of equitable title);
    OR ☐ Other (specify) _____
    **THE FOLLOWING TERMS APPLY ONLY IF CHECKED. SELLER IS ADVISED TO READ ALL TERMS, EVEN THOSE NOT
    CHECKED, TO UNDERSTAND WHAT IS OR IS NOT INCLUDED, AND, IF NOT INCLUDED, THE CONSEQUENCES THEREOF.**
4. ☐ **LATE CHARGE:** If any payment is not made within ____ **Days** After it is due, a late charge of either $ _____,
    or ____% of the installment due, may be charged to Buyer. **NOTE:** On single family residences that Buyer intends to occupy,
    California Civil Code §2954.4(a) limits the late charge to no more than 6% of the total installment payment due and requires a
    grace period of no less than 10 days.
5. ☐ **BALLOON PAYMENT:** The extension of credit will provide for a balloon payment, in the amount of $ _____,
    plus any accrued interest, which is due on_____ (date).
6. ☐ **PREPAYMENT:** If all or part of this extension of credit is paid early, Seller may charge a prepayment penalty as follows (if
    applicable): _____. Caution: California Civil Code
    §2954.9 contains limitations on prepayment penalties for residential one-to-four unit properties.
7. ☐ **DUE ON SALE:** If any interest in the Property is sold or otherwise transferred, Seller has the option to require immediate
    payment of the entire unpaid principal balance, plus any accrued interest.
8.* ☐ **REQUEST FOR COPY OF NOTICE OF DEFAULT:** A request for a copy of Notice of Default as defined in California Civil
    Code §2924b will be recorded. **If Not,** Seller is advised to consider recording a Request for Notice of Default.
9.* ☐ **REQUEST FOR NOTICE OF DELINQUENCY:** A request for Notice of Delinquency, as defined in California Civil Code §2924e,
    to be signed and paid for by Buyer, will be made to senior lienholders. **If not,** Seller is advised to consider making a Request for
    Notice of Delinquency. Seller is advised to check with senior lienholders to verify whether they will honor this request.
10.* ☐ **TAX SERVICE:**
    A. If property taxes on the Property become delinquent, tax service will be arranged to report to Seller. **If not,** Seller is
    advised to consider retaining a tax service, or to otherwise determine that property taxes are paid.
    B. ☐ Buyer, ☐ Seller, shall be responsible for the initial and continued retention of, and payment for, such tax service.
11. ☐ **TITLE INSURANCE:** Title insurance coverage will be provided to **both** Seller and Buyer, insuring their respective interests
    in the Property. **If not,** Buyer and Seller are advised to consider securing such title insurance coverage.
12. ☐ **HAZARD INSURANCE:**
    A. The parties' escrow holder or insurance carrier will be directed to include a loss payee endorsement, adding Seller to
    the Property insurance policy. **If not,** Seller is advised to secure such an endorsement, or acquire a separate
    insurance policy.
    B. Property insurance **does not** include earthquake or flood insurance coverage, unless checked:
    ☐ Earthquake insurance will be obtained; ☐ Flood insurance will be obtained.
13. ☐ **PROCEEDS TO BUYER:** Buyer will receive cash proceeds at the close of the sale transaction. The amount received will be
    approximately $_____, from _____(indicate source of
    proceeds). Buyer represents that the purpose of such disbursement is as follows:_____.
14. ☐ **NEGATIVE AMORTIZATION; DEFERRED INTEREST:** Negative amortization results when Buyer's periodic payments are
    less than the amount of interest earned on the obligation. Deferred interest also results when the obligation does not
    require periodic payments for a period of time. In either case, interest is not payable as it accrues. This accrued interest
    will have to be paid by Buyer at a later time, and may result in Buyer owing more on the obligation than at its origination.
    The credit being extended to Buyer by Seller will provide for negative amortization or deferred interest as indicated below.
    (Check A, B, or C. CHECK ONE ONLY.)
    ☐ **A.** All negative amortization or deferred interest shall be added to the principal _____
    (e.g., annually, monthly, etc.), and thereafter shall bear interest at the rate specified in the credit documents (compound interest);
    OR ☐ **B.** All deferred interest shall be due and payable, along with principal, at maturity;
    OR ☐ **C.** Other _____.

*(For Paragraphs 8-10) In order to receive timely and continued notification, Seller is advised to record appropriate notices and/or to
notify appropriate parties of any change in Seller's address.

SFA REVISED 10/02 (PAGE 1 OF 3) Print Date

Buyer's Initials (_____)(_____)
Seller's Initials (_____)(_____)

Reviewed by _____ Date _____

EQUAL HOUSING
OPPORTUNITY

SELLER FINANCING ADDENDUM AND DISCLOSURE (SFA PAGE 1 OF 3)

Figure 14.6 Sample seller financing disclosure statement.

Property Address: _____   Date: _____

15. ☐ **ALL-INCLUSIVE DEED OF TRUST; INSTALLMENT LAND SALE CONTRACT:** This transaction involves the use of an all-inclusive (or wraparound) deed of trust or an installment land sale contract. That deed of trust or contract shall provide as follows:
   A. In the event of an acceleration of any senior encumbrance, the responsibility for payment, or for legal defense is: _____ _____ ; OR ☐ **Is not** specified in the credit or security documents.
   B. In the event of the prepayment of a senior encumbrance, the responsibilities and rights of Buyer and Seller regarding refinancing, prepayment penalties, and any prepayment discounts are: _____ ; OR ☐ **Are not** specified in the documents evidencing credit.
   C. Buyer will make periodic payments to _____ (Seller, collection agent, or any neutral third party), who will be responsible for disbursing payments to the payee(s) on the senior encumbrance(s) and to Seller. **NOTE:** The Parties are advised to designate a neutral third party for these purposes.

16. ☐ **TAX IDENTIFICATION NUMBERS:** Buyer and Seller shall each provide to each other their Social Security Numbers or Taxpayer Identification Numbers.

17. ☐ **OTHER CREDIT TERMS** _____ _____

18. ☐ **RECORDING:** The documents evidencing credit (paragraph 3) will be recorded with the county recorder where the Property is located. **If not**, Buyer and Seller are advised that their respective interests in the Property may be jeopardized by intervening liens, judgments, encumbrances, or subsequent transfers.

19. ☐ **JUNIOR FINANCING:** There will be additional financing, secured by the Property, junior to this Seller financing. Explain: _____

20. **SENIOR LOANS AND ENCUMBRANCES:** The following information is provided on loans and/or encumbrances that will be **senior** to Seller financing. **NOTE:** The following are estimates, unless otherwise marked with an asterisk (*). If checked: ☐ A separate sheet with information on additional senior loans/encumbrances is attached

	1st	2nd
A. Original Balance	$_____	$_____
B. Current Balance	$_____	$_____
C. Periodic Payment (e.g. $100/month)	$_____	$_____/_____
Including Impounds of:		$_____/_____
D. Interest Rate (per annum)	_____%	_____%
E. Fixed or Variable Rate:	_____	_____
If Variable Rate: Lifetime Cap (Ceiling)	_____	_____
Indicator (Underlying Index)	_____	_____
Margins	_____	_____
F. Maturity Date	_____	_____
G. Amount of Balloon Payment	$_____	$_____
H. Date Balloon Payment Due	_____	_____
I. Potential for Negative Amortization? (Yes, No, or Unknown)	_____	_____
J. Due on Sale? (Yes, No, or Unknown)	_____	_____
K. Pre-payment penalty? (Yes, No, or Unknown)	_____	_____
L. Are payments current? (Yes, No, or Unknown)	_____	_____

21. **BUYER'S CREDITWORTHINESS:** (CHECK EITHER A OR B. Do not check both.) In addition to the loan application, credit report and other information requested under paragraph 2:
   A. ☐ No other disclosure concerning Buyer's creditworthiness has been made to Seller;
   OR **B.** ☐ The following representations concerning Buyer's creditworthiness are made by Buyer(s) to Seller:

Borrower	**Co-Borrower**
1. Occupation _____	1. Occupation _____
2. Employer _____	2. Employer _____
3. Length of Employment _____	3. Length of Employment _____
4. Monthly Gross Income _____	4. Monthly Gross Income _____
5. Other _____	5. Other _____

22. **ADDED, DELETED OR SUBSTITUTED BUYERS:** The addition, deletion or substitution of any person or entity under this Agreement or to title prior to close of escrow shall require Seller's written consent. Seller may grant or withhold consent in Seller's sole discretion. Any additional or substituted person or entity shall, if requested by Seller, submit to Seller the same documentation as required for the original named Buyer. Seller and/or Brokers may obtain a credit report, at Buyer's expense, on any such person or entity.

Buyer's Initials (_____)(_____)
Seller's Initials (_____)(_____)

| Reviewed by _____ Date _____ |

SELLER FINANCING ADDENDUM AND DISCLOSURE (SFA PAGE 2 OF 3)

Figure 14.6 Sample seller financing disclosure statement *(continued)*.

Property Address: _____ Date: _____

23. CAUTION:

   A. If the Seller financing requires a balloon payment, Seller shall give Buyer written notice, according to the terms of Civil Code §2966, at least 90 and not more than 150 days before the balloon payment is due if the transaction is for the purchase of a dwelling for not more than four families.

   B. If **any** obligation secured by the Property calls for a balloon payment, Seller and Buyer are aware that refinancing of the balloon payment at maturity may be difficult or impossible, depending on conditions in the conventional mortgage marketplace at that time. There are no assurances that new financing or a loan extension will be available when the balloon prepayment, or any prepayment, is due.

   C. If **any** of the existing or proposed loans or extensions of credit would require refinancing as a result of a lack of full amortization, such refinancing might be difficult or impossible in the conventional mortgage marketplace.

   D. In the event of default by Buyer: (1) Seller may have to reinstate and/or make monthly payments on any and all senior encumbrances (including real property taxes) in order to protect Seller's secured interest; (2) Seller's rights are generally limited to foreclosure on the Property, pursuant to California Code of Civil Procedure §580b; and (3) the Property may lack sufficient equity to protect Seller's interests if the Property decreases in value.

If this three-page Addendum and Disclosure is used in a transaction for the purchase of a dwelling for not more than four families, it shall be prepared by an Arranger of Credit as defined in California Civil Code §2957(a). (The Arranger of Credit is usually the agent who obtained the offer.)

_____
Arranger of Credit - (Print Firm Name)   By _____ Date _____

Address _____ City _____ State _____ Zip _____

Phone _____ Fax _____

BUYER AND SELLER ACKNOWLEDGE AND AGREE THAT BROKERS: (A) WILL NOT PROVIDE LEGAL OR TAX ADVICE; (B) WILL NOT PROVIDE OTHER ADVICE OR INFORMATION THAT EXCEEDS THE KNOWLEDGE, EDUCATION AND EXPERIENCE REQUIRED TO OBTAIN A REAL ESTATE LICENSE; OR (C) HAVE NOT AND WILL NOT VERIFY ANY INFORMATION PROVIDED BY EITHER BUYER OR SELLER. BUYER AND SELLER AGREE THAT THEY WILL SEEK LEGAL, TAX AND OTHER DESIRED ASSISTANCE FROM APPROPRIATE PROFESSIONALS. BUYER AND SELLER ACKNOWLEDGE THAT THE INFORMATION EACH HAS PROVIDED TO THE ARRANGER OF CREDIT FOR INCLUSION IN THIS DISCLOSURE FORM IS ACCURATE. BUYER AND SELLER FURTHER ACKNOWLEDGE THAT EACH HAS RECEIVED A COMPLETED COPY OF THIS DISCLOSURE FORM.

Buyer _____ Date _____
            (signature)

Address _____ City _____ State _____ Zip _____

Phone _____ Fax _____ E-mail _____

Buyer _____ Date _____
            (signature)

Address _____ City _____ State _____ Zip _____

Phone _____ Fax _____ E-mail _____

Seller _____ Date _____
            (signature)

Address _____ City _____ State _____ Zip _____

Phone _____ Fax _____ E-mail _____

Seller _____ Date _____
            (signature)

Address _____ City _____ State _____ Zip _____

Phone _____ Fax _____ E-mail _____

THIS FORM HAS BEEN APPROVED BY THE CALIFORNIA ASSOCIATION OF REALTORS® (C.A.R.). NO REPRESENTATION IS MADE AS TO THE LEGAL VALIDITY OR ADEQUACY OF ANY PROVISION IN ANY SPECIFIC TRANSACTION. A REAL ESTATE BROKER IS THE PERSON QUALIFIED TO ADVISE ON REAL ESTATE TRANSACTIONS. IF YOU DESIRE LEGAL OR TAX ADVICE, CONSULT AN APPROPRIATE PROFESSIONAL.

This form is available for use by the entire real estate industry. It is not intended to identify the user as a REALTOR®. REALTOR® is a registered collective membership mark which may be used only by members of the NATIONAL ASSOCIATION OF REALTORS® who subscribe to its Code of Ethics.

SURE TRAC
The System for Success®

Published and Distributed by:
REAL ESTATE BUSINESS SERVICES, INC.
a subsidiary of the California Association of REALTORS®
525 South Virgil Avenue, Los Angeles, California 90020

Reviewed by _____ Date _____

EQUAL HOUSING OPPORTUNITY

SFA REVISED 10/02 (PAGE 3 OF 3)

SELLER FINANCING ADDENDUM AND DISCLOSURE (SFA PAGE 3 OF 3)

Figure 14.6 Sample seller financing disclosure statement *(continued)*.

gain tax rate, rather than the higher ordinary rate that applies to interest income. This imputed interest rule is complicated and information can be found in IRS Publication 537, www.irs.gov. **Special note:** This imputed interest provision *does not* apply to seller carryback loans in which buyers use the property as their principal residence.

The whole idea of imputed interest rates is to prevent sellers from converting interest income on deferred payments from ordinary income tax rates to the lower capital gains tax rate by making interest a part of the purchase price without specifying it as interest. Thus, if a seller carryback fails to specify any interest, or provides for an unreasonably low rate, the IRS may step in and read into the agreement its own interpretation of what it should be, thereby restructuring the transaction in a way that converts some of the capital gain into ordinary income.

SUMMARY

Secondary financing techniques include notes secured by second trust deeds carried back by sellers, representing the gap between sales price and liens now on the property or to be placed thereon. Collateralizing junior loans is a method by which existing loans are pledged as security for a loan without giving up legal title to the junior trust deed. Brokers may resort to a variety of techniques to put together transactions when the money market is tight.

All-inclusive deeds of trust are used in a variety of ways. They may be used in lieu of land contracts or when a lock-in clause is enforceable by a beneficiary. Low down payments, especially with an overpriced listing, make the all-inclusive trust deed a mutually attractive vehicle. Care must be exercised to structure the all-inclusive trust deed properly, including minimum interest rates that must be charged under the imputed interest rules, so as to protect both seller and buyer.

Lenders may increase their yields through participations or "equity kickers." They can participate in the revenue of a project, take a percentage of the equity, charge fees or discounts, or participate in the profit.

Sale-leaseback, open-end trust deeds, stock equity, and commercial loans are further examples of financing that can be effected through other than traditional approaches. Indeed, financing schemes are limited only by the knowledge, creativity, and ingenuity of the people involved.

IMPORTANT TERMS AND CONCEPTS

All-inclusive trust deed (AITD)

Applicable Federal Rate (AFR)

Blended-rate loan

Broker participation

Collateralization

Commercial loan

Creative Financing Disclosure Act

Due-on-sale clause

Imputed interest

Installment sales contract

Open-end trust deed

Participation

Purchase money

Sale-leaseback

Seller carryback

Split junior loan

Stock equity

Triple net lease

Wrap-around

REVIEWING YOUR UNDERSTANDING

Questions for Discussion

1. How does collateralization of a junior loan provide for retention of the legal title by the junior holder?

2. In what ways may a broker use junior liens to put together a real estate transaction when money is "tight"?

3. Describe five ways in which an all-inclusive trust deed can be more effectively used instead of the traditional junior trust deed transaction.

4. List three ways in which lenders may increase their yields through participations.

5. State the basic purpose of the Creative Financing Disclosure Act. Do you think this law is accomplishing what it was intended to accomplish?

Multiple-Choice Questions

1. Jayne Buyer is unable to meet a balloon payment on a junior lien now that it came due. Among her remedies might be to
   a. renegotiate the junior loan.
   b. secure a new loan from outside sources.
   c. refinance the entire loan.
   d. seek out any of the foregoing remedies.

2. A purchase money junior lien, given back to a seller, that includes the amount of the first encumbrance as well as any secondary liens, is called
   a. a hold-harmful lien.
   b. a wrap-around loan.
   c. a due-on-encumbrance lien.
   d. an overextension loan.

3. Retention of legal title by the seller in the financing of property is accomplished through the use of which one of the following instruments?
   a. all-inclusive trust deed.
   b. mortgage instrument.
   c. installment land contract.
   d. exchange agreement.

4. Assume a property is to sell for $160,000. It has an existing first loan of $78,000 and a second lien of $20,000. If a purchaser pays 15 percent as a down payment and an all-inclusive deed of trust is to be used to finance the transaction, the seller's remaining equity at close of escrow will amount to
   a. $38,000.
   b. $58,000.
   c. $62,000.
   d. $116,000.

5. A lender holding a junior trust deed, who wants to be informed when defaults and foreclosures occur on senior liens, should record:
   a. Assignment of Note and Trust Deed.
   b. Request for Notice of Default and Notice of Sale.
   c. Disclosure Statement.
   d. Collateral Security Agreement.

6. A variation of the secondary financing approach to solving real estate finance problems, wherein a junior trust deed is assigned to the licensee for part or all of his commission, is referred to as
   a. a broker participation loan.
   b. an assignment loan.
   c. a split junior lien.
   d. an open-end trust lien.

7. An all-inclusive trust deed is characterized by which one of the following statements?
   a. The seller-trustor under the existing liens becomes the beneficiary under the all-inclusive deed of trust.
   b. It is a senior encumbrance that includes all of the underlying liens.
   c. Legal title is retained until the terms and conditions of the lien are satisfied.
   d. Title insurance is not issued at the time of the sale.

8. Under the Creative Financing Disclosure Act, the written disclosure is prepared by the
   a. buyer.
   b. seller.
   c. insurer.
   d. agent.

9. Lenders may take participation interests in a property on which They are making a loan in a variety of ways. Which of the following would be the *least likely* method of participating in a lending transaction?
   a. a one-time initial points charge.
   b. open-end provisions.
   c. participation in the equity.
   d. revenue sharing.

10. Creative financing refers to techniques that are
    a. insured or guaranteed.
    b. used by institutional lenders to avoid banking regulations.
    c. legally used to finance a property in a nontraditional manner.
    d. commonly used on most home loans.

11. If you collateralize a note secured by a second deed of trust, it means that
    a. the note and deed of trust is sold at a discount.
    b. a third party lends money using the note and second deed of trust as security.
    c. the beneficiary's interest therein has been fully transferred.
    d. an additional junior lien has been created on the security property.

12. An all-inclusive trust deed (AITD) cannot be used to
    a. increase the seller's yield.
    b. lower the buyer's closing costs.
    c. help generate a higher sales price.
    d. avoid an enforceable due-on-sale clause.

13. A disadvantage found in a sale-leaseback transaction is that
    a. the seller-lessee can take full tax deduction for lease payments.
    b. the buyer-lessor gets a steady tenant.
    c. the seller-lessee can write off depreciation on improvements he or she adds.
    d. payments to buyer-lessor are taxed as ordinary income.

14. A $100,000 loan at 10 percent interest with payments of $800 per month appears to be
    a. fully amortized.
    b. partially amortized.
    c. negatively amortized.
    d. fundamentally sound.

15. Assume a new loan amount of $180,000 under a blended-rate arrangement. The existing loan has an $80,000 balance at 10 percent interest per annum. The rate the lender seeks for new loans is 15 percent. The blended rate will compute at
    a. 10.722 percent.
    b. 13.33 percent.
    c. 12.5 percent.
    d. 12.778 percent.

16. Legal title is transferred to the buyer by a deed when the property is financed by using
    a. an installment sales contract.
    b. an all-inclusive trust deed.
    c. a land contract.
    d. an agreement of sale contract.

17. You sold your home for $300,000. The buyers pay 15 percent down and secure a first trust deed for 80 percent of the purchase price. The amount needed to fill in the gap will be
    a. $30,000.
    b. $45,000.
    c. $22,500.
    d. $15,000.

18. Under the Creative Financing Disclosure Act, the agent must disclose the drawbacks of creative financing to
    a. all subagents to a transaction.
    b. buyers only.
    c. sellers only.
    d. both buyers and sellers.

19. The imputed interest rules found in the Internal Revenue Code apply to
    a. certain seller carryback loans.
    b. assumptions of existing loans.
    c. loans at 10 percent or greater interest rate.
    d. new loans granted by institutional lenders.

20. A creative financing scheme is best illustrated by
    a. seller carrying back a first trust deed loan for 25 percent of the sale price.
    b. seller carrying back under an all-inclusive trust deed.
    c. buyer paying 10 percent down, obtaining the balance through a PMI loan.
    d. buyer paying 50 percent down and getting a private hard-money loan for the balance.

CHAPTER 15
FINANCING SMALL INVESTMENT PROPERTIES

PREVIEW

"What you owe today you are worth tomorrow!" This statement was made some years ago by a prominent Chicago real estate economist who advocated the purchase of investment real estate with as little cash down payment as possible and with maximum financing. The buyer could then either exchange upward or refinance and buy other properties with maximum financing until the buyer owed the amount of money he or she eventually wanted to be worth. At that point the buyer could halt buying and simply continue managing the existing property until the loans were paid off. The buyer would then be worth what he or she owed, and probably a lot more as inflation raised the real estate prices.

In this chapter we examine the financing characteristics of different residential investment properties—single-family dwellings, two-to-four-unit dwellings, and large apartment houses—and stress the advantages and disadvantages of each type of investment. Finally, we introduce the financing of commercial and industrial properties.

After completing this chapter, you should be able to:

1. Describe financing alternatives for residential income, commercial, and industrial properties.

2. List and briefly explain advantages and disadvantages to investing in each of the categories of investment property.

3. Calculate and apply "break-even analysis" to income-producing properties.

4. Discuss how financing conditions affect prices of income-producing properties.

5. Compute debt-coverage ratios.

15.1 The Single-Family House as Income Property

Key Characteristics

There is usually a large supply of single-family properties on the market from which to make a selection. The management of a single-family home is easier than practically any other type of residential property. A single-family house generally has an active resale market, thus offering a high degree of liquidity for investors; single-unit dwellings can be sold outright or exchanged tax deferred for other like-kind property. Like-kind property refers to the nature or character of the property. Another way to describe eligible exchange property are the words "real for real," meaning that real property must be exchanged for other qualified real property and cannot be exchanged for personal property. Under this definition, a rental home can be exchanged for another rental home, multiple units, apartment complex, commercial property, or unimproved property (land).

Kinds of Financing Available for Nonowner-Occupied Single-Family Dwellings

A nonowner-occupied conventional loan of 75 percent of the lower of appraised value or the purchase price is the most often available loan from the majority of lending institutions. Fannie Mae and Freddie Mac now make financing available up to the 90 percent Loan-to-Value level. Few borrowers can meet the qualifying criteria to borrow to this level because the result is nearly always a considerable negative cash flow. FNMA/FHLMC now require a borrower to have at least one year's experience as a landlord to be eligible for nonowner financing. Lenders are not likely to count 100 percent of economic rents to offset debt service, usually factoring in no more than 75 percent of rents to make note payments.

Complete seller financing is also possible. Many owners have had homes for years and own them free and clear. Rather than sell for cash, some may sell on an installment sale plan, charging the buyer an interest rate that generates a monthly cash flow.

Interest Rate and Other Loan Terms for Rental Houses

Conventional lenders generally ask for 0.25 to 0.5 percent more interest on a rental home than if the same home were owner occupied. Of all residential rental properties, the single-family home commands the lowest interest rate and the best overall terms.

Conventional lenders may ask for the same loan fee or points from buyers as in the case of an owner-occupied home, but in many cases they may ask for a higher loan fee.

Term of loan, late charges, and other provisions are generally the same as on owner-occupied, single-family homes. Although fixed rate financing is available, many lenders prefer to make adjustable rate loans, which are fully indexed with the first payment—no "teaser" rates. As a rule, many lenders offer only adjustable rate loans, which are fully indexed with the first payment—no "teaser" rates.

With respect to prepayment penalties, California law limits these for owner-occupied, single-family homes to the first three years (seven years for loans covered under the Mortgage Loan Broker Law). The prepayment requirements can differ if the rental property loan is made by a niche lender.

Advantages of the Single-Family Home as an Investment Vehicle

1. A large selection of properties is usually available.

2. Management is easier than on other types of income properties.

3. The investment is more liquid than other forms of real property.

4. Tenants usually pay for all utilities and do the gardening and minor repairs, in contrast to larger properties where these services are furnished by outside employees.

5. The ratio of improvements to overall investment may be high, giving a greater **depreciation** write-off, generally from 70 percent to 80 percent. This gives a greater tax shelter to the investor, since improvements are depreciable while investments in raw land are nondepreciable.

6. Many tenants rent unfurnished homes, eliminating the relatively high maintenance cost of furniture. Also, tenants usually remain longer in single-family homes than in apartments.

7. "Passive loss" rules apply to rental houses, allowing investors to deduct up to $25,000 of losses against certain other taxable income, such as wages, salary, interest, dividends, etc.

8. Few people build single-family homes for investment, so there is little danger of glutting the market with competitive rentals. Thus vacancy factors in single-family homes are lower than in any other type of residential investment.

9. Home prices have risen more quickly and at a greater rate in inflationary years than any other class of investment property, thereby giving investors a good hedge against inflation.

10. A recent survey shows that half of all baby boomers—those born between 1946 and 1964—intend to buy a home for retirement, including income-producing second homes.

11. A single-family dwelling that is a rented can be exchanged for other rental property of equal or greater value under section 1031 of the Internal Revenue Code.

Disadvantages of the Single-Family Home as an Investment Vehicle

1. *Cash flow.* Due to higher prices, level rents, and possibly higher interest rates, it is almost a certainty that the house will generate a negative cash flow, that is, the income will be less than the outgo, even after allowance for tax shelter. The lender will require the investor to have the economic resources with which to meet the qualifying ratios and accommodate the negative cash flow.

2. *Footage.* Homes tend to have more square footage than apartments; the larger the unit, the less the rent per square foot in comparison with compact rentals and those with higher densities.

3. *Vacancy.* When a home is vacant, 100 percent of the rent is lost until it is rerented. Stated differently, since only one tenant is living in the house at any given time, the vacancy factor will be either 0 percent or 100 percent.

4. *Management.* In many cases the investor must personally manage the property because there is no resident manager, but professional management firms will now more often agree to take on single

family homes for management. The fee for such management can be substantial in comparison with the rental income acquired, and owners may prefer to find their own tenants, show property, and take time from personal activities. Some owners are not temperamentally fit to handle calls from tenants, especially when complaints are made in the middle of the night because the sewer stops up or just as the owner sits down for dinner.

5. *Repairs.* If the owner cannot do minor repair work, the cost of hiring plumbing, electrical, mechanical, and other contractors is becoming greater. One repair can take a full month's rent and more.

6. *Economy of operations.* As an investor acquires more houses, in scattered locations, more money and time are required for travel and other expenses than if the units were all under one roof, as in an apartment house.

7. *Tax deductions.* Tax benefits are increasingly subject to the whims of Congress, as demonstrated by the severity of the 1986 Tax Reform Act, especially in the passive loss rules. And even as we go to print, Congress and the President are considering a sweeping overhaul of the tax code.

15.2 The Two-to-Four-Unit Residential Property

Key Characteristics

In many areas two- and three-unit properties are becoming increasingly scarce, with fourplexes in slightly greater supply. Management of the units by new or inexperienced investors is still relatively simple. This type of property is in great demand by investors and will usually resell quickly, thus giving good liquidity. As demonstrated throughout the text, many laws that apply to protect investors in residential buildings of up to four units don't apply to five or more units, such as prepayment privileges and penalties, provision for late charges, disclosures, and other consumer protection laws.

Kinds of Financing Available on Two-to-Four-Unit Dwellings

Conventional loans of up to 75 percent of value are usually available from most lenders. Some may allow 15 percent down and permit the borrower to obtain a second loan for the balance. However, rarely will institutional lenders finance this way if there is a large negative cash flow. As with a single dwelling converted to a rental, lenders are not likely to count all of economic rents to offset monthly payments.

Seller financing for the first loan is generally not possible, since few have free and clear properties. However, many sellers will carry second loans behind new first loans.

Interest Rates and Other Terms on Two-to-Four-Unit Properties

Conventional lenders generally ask from 0.5 percent to 1 percent higher interest than on owner-occupied single-unit dwellings. Borrower loan fees sometimes run higher than on owner-occupied houses. For two-to-four-unit properties, prepayment penalty provisions usually call for six months' unearned interest, with a 20 percent payoff allowable in any one calendar year without penalty.

Advantages of Two-to-Four-Unit Dwellings as Investment Vehicles

Two-to-four-unit properties can be found in most communities. The owner can manage the property without the need for a resident manager. Tenants often pay their own utilities, maintain the garden, and do minor repairs. Units can be rented without furnishings. Three- and four-unit properties may have appliances, carpets, and drapes. If the owner desires to delegate some of the management duties, such as gardening, sweeping, and laundry room cleanup, one of the tenants may often do such work for a nominal fee, saving the owner time and expense. This party may also show vacant units to prospective tenants.

For tenants, two-to-four-unit properties are very popular and will often rent while large multiunit apartment complexes remain vacant. Two-to-four-unit properties offer more privacy, with fewer people above or below a tenant's own apartment. These units can obtain good loan-to-value ratios from conventional lenders, offering greater **leverage** and requiring less cash. Generally there is a high ratio of improvements to overall investment, ranging from 70 percent to 80 percent of building to total value, offering a maximum depreciation basis and tax shelter.

Disadvantages of Two-to-Four-Unit Dwellings as Investment Vehicles

As land and building costs increase, there are fewer duplexes, triplexes, and fourplexes being built, and it is becoming more expensive to purchase existing units at a realistic price. Many inexperienced investors are bidding prices up, and the yield to the investor will not always be sufficient to meet operating costs and debt service, requiring owners to "feed the property" because of negative cash flow.

In most newer two-to-four-unit properties, appliances, carpets, and drapes are included, and reserves should be put aside for repairs and replacements. However, many owners fail to set aside reserves or to recognize such operating expenses, thus resulting in massive capital outlays at inconvenient times when these furnishings are needed. In newer properties, the owner must also generally pay the water, outside lights, and laundry room utilities, thereby creating more expense than in single-unit investments where the tenant pays all. Generally, repair costs are higher than for single-unit homes. At certain times, when there is a high vacancy factor or a rise in uncollectible rents, owners are forced to keep rents lower than the break-even point, in order to compete with other units on the market. In some areas, rental income has lagged behind the inflation of operating costs, resulting in a smaller net cash flow to the owner. Owners should keep rents advancing at the same rate of increase as their taxes and other operating costs. Many inexperienced owners apparently either do not realize this or are reluctant to upset their tenants with rent increases.

15.3 Apartment House Investments: 5 to 24 Units

Depending on local market conditions, a well-located apartment property may be difficult to find at a fair market price, or conversely, there may be overbuilding resulting in large vacancies and below-market prices.

When the supply is greater than the demand, it is easy to obtain an apartment house at an extremely fair price, often at less than current construction costs. However, owners must be able to withstand temporary financial losses because of excessive vacancies.

In time, recurring tight money cycles, together with mounting costs of new construction, often lead to a complete halt in construction. Assuming an increase in demand with a fixed supply, vacancy rates begin to decline. This tends to stabilize the rental market and raise rents, and marginal owners move from a negative cash flow to a breakeven or positive cash flow position. As yields from apartment buildings rise, owners may become satisfied to the point that they will not sell except at premium prices. At such times, many buyers come into the market and bid against each other to buy desirable apartment houses in prime locations. Even less-desirable buildings begin to disappear from the market. If this condition is accompanied by a recurring cycle of good financing, it brings even more buyers into the market. Buyers must compete with each other and pay a higher price than the net operating income can justify. This, in turn, may lead to rent increases. Since this takes time, the buyer must have capital backing and must "feed the property" until rents can be increased to reflect fair market values.

Environmental factors are making apartments more expensive to build. New energy requirements, insulation, and reduced land density in new city and county general plans all reflect higher prices for new apartments.

Kinds of Financing Available for 5 to 24 Units

Most apartment houses are financed by conventional loans, which are generally available, except in a tight money market, at from 60 percent to 75 percent of property value. Often the loan ratio is reduced from 75 percent to 60 percent or less as the size of the building increases. In the final analysis, LTV (loan-to-value) ratios are governed by the property's cash flow and the income "break-even" point.

As a rule, conventional lenders require at least 15 percent down, even if the seller is carrying back a second loan. Interest rates range from 0.5 to 2 percent higher, and loan fees are higher than for single units. The loan can be amortized for 30 years, but may have a shorter term, say 15 to 25 years.

Lenders generally are also concerned about credit requirements. Borrowers must have good financial statements and stable income independent of the property, although the latter is used in evaluating the merits of the loan. Lenders examine operational costs of the property and add these to **debt service** (monthly payments). If income from the property will not fully support these items after allowing for a reasonable vacancy factor, the loan may be declined, even if the borrower has good credit and good personal income. In short, institutional lenders are more concerned about the ability of this kind of property to carry itself.

Lenders are extremely concerned about location. If location is marginal, a smaller loan will be offered, with a higher interest rate and a shorter term. Regardless of the sale price of the building, lenders make their own evaluation of properties and base their loan-to-value ratios on their appraisal. For example, if present rents from the apartment are abnormally high, lenders may use the average loan market rents (economic rents) for similar units in the area as being a realistic long-run trend. If the apartment house is furnished, lenders deduct all of the rental income attributable to furniture and use **capitalized income stream** from the unfurnished unit to determine the loan value. Thus a $5 million furnished building may be valued at $4,500,000 on an unfurnished basis, resulting in a smaller overall loan and a greater down payment.

When money becomes tight, lenders often make apartment loans only to exceptionally qualified borrowers. Even those who do qualify may have to pay excessive interest rates, and perhaps even points, to obtain any type of loan. When conventional loans are unavailable, many of the creative financing techniques discussed in Chapter 14 can be used, either on an interim basis until conventional financing is again available or on a permanent basis.

Advantages of Investing in 5 to 24 Units

There is a constant demand for housing, regardless of the ups and downs of the business cycle, since housing is a basic need. Therefore, apartment investments tend to be safer than other real estate for the average investor. (However, it might be asked just how many "average investors" can afford to buy apartment houses.)

Management is concentrated in one location rather than diffused over a wide area for the same number of small units. A relatively inexperienced investor can acquire an apartment house and with some personal effort learn the business of apartment house management. The owner can hire a resident manager to handle the day-to-day work of managing the property, such as showing units, maintaining grounds, and collecting rent. The owner can then supervise the property overall and set up management policies. In California, apartment complexes of 16 units or more must have a resident manager, unless the owner resides on the premises.

The cost of operation is usually less per unit than in scattered properties. For instance, the cost of a new, inexpensive roof on a 1,200-square-foot rental house might run up to $5,000. This is the cost per unit. The cost of reroofing a three-story apartment house containing 24 units might be $24,000, but the cost per unit is only $1,000 because the one roof covers three stories.

In recent years, as building costs have increased, and as land for development has become more scarce due to governmental and environmental controls, fewer apartment houses have been built. Existing buildings are becoming more valuable because of the decreasing rate of new construction. Owners then are able to increase rents at a reasonable rate to offset mounting operational costs, thereby sustaining a fair yield on investment.

Large apartment complexes can provide excellent tax shelter, since typically 80 percent of the value is in improvements that can be depreciated. Personal property (such as carpets, drapes, appliances, or furnishings) may be written off (deducted) on a 200 percent declining balance, typically ranging from five to seven years. An existing residential building can be written off over 27.5 years straight line. (These, of course, are subject to change as tax laws change.)

Continuing inflation and a shortage of new apartment construction tend to build equity through appreciation in addition to equity acquired by principal reduction (loan amortization). This tends to protect the investment against inflation and may provide an income for retirement years.

Disadvantages of Investing in 5 to 24 Units

Inexperienced investors often do not realize the true expenses of owning an apartment house, gloss over maintenance costs, do not set aside reserves for carpet and appliance replacements, and can wind up with a negative cash flow. Unless investor capital can be added to meet the cash outflow, the investor can wind up having to sell the building at a sacrifice price, especially at times when financing has become more difficult.

Changing neighborhood patterns and encroachments of heavy business or industrial buildings may cause building values to decrease. There are high crime areas where apartment buildings are selling for less than they did 10 years before, despite the inflation factor, because tenants are unwilling to rent in these areas. Decreasing rents, high vacancies, bad debts, and difficulty of financing may make a sale of the building almost impossible.

New consumer laws pertaining to owner-tenant relationships can lead to rent-collection problems and increasing legal fees. The cost of evicting tenants for nonpayment of rent, when they exercise their legal rights to defend against such an action, can run as high as $1,000 or more, including attorney fees, legal papers, and other eviction costs. This is in addition to lost rent and any refurbishing costs if a tenant has damaged an apartment.

As apartment vacancy factors go down and there is an insufficient supply of housing for the people of this state, local jurisdictions may try to pass **rent control** laws that limit the amount of rental increases. Such laws tend to decrease the yield from an apartment, since allowable rental increases might lag behind operating costs. Investment capital would flow to other uncontrolled types of investments or to states with no rent control, making it difficult to sell an apartment house.

Many owners do not have the temperament to deal with problems of management or with the multiplicity of tenant requests for services. Patience, tolerance, and the ability to deal with people tactfully are absolutely vital to operate apartment buildings successfully. Finally, since tenants might not have the pride of ownership or the stability of a long-term lease, damage to the property is far more likely than for single dwellings.

15.4 Break-Even Analysis

Both lenders and investors are interested in the viability of investments based upon financing considerations. One tool to help assess cash flow and the profitability of an investment property is ***break-even analysis***. Figure 15.1 shows the number of apartment units (though the process can apply to any property, both real and personal) that would need to be rented in an apartment project to break even—that is, the point at which the revenue exactly equals the outgo.

In the example below, let's assume a 30-unit apartment house, at $600 monthly rental each. Fixed outlays for taxes, insurance, debt service, licenses, and so on equal $8,000 per month. Variable costs, including management, maintenance, repairs, and utilities, are estimated at $100 per month per apartment. We must then ask ourselves, given the amount of rent per unit, the fixed expenses that continue regardless of the number of units rented, and the variable expenses

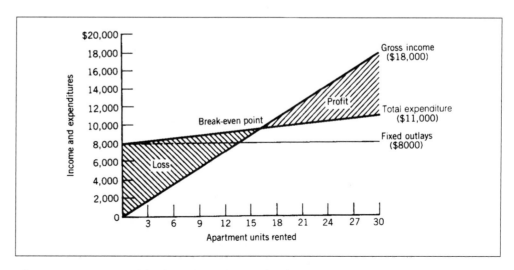

Figure 15.1 Monthly break-even analysis.

that are tied to the number of units actually rented, at what point does income equal the costs and expenses?

The vertical bar represents the dollar amount of income and expenses. The horizontal bar represents the number of apartment units rented. Since the fixed expenses are $8,000, a straight horizontal line is drawn at the $8,000 level to represent fixed outlay. Then, as each unit is rented, $100 of variable expenses is added, thus adding to the $8,000 figure. We simultaneously plot the income figures at increments of $600 for each unit rented. Finally, where the total expenses equal gross income, we arrive at the break-even point. In the example this is at 16 units. At this point the income totals $9,600 and the expenses, including debt service (loan payments), equal $9,600. This is arrived at by charting the fixed expenses at $8,000, and superimposing thereon $100 per unit, cumulatively, for each rented unit. Since we know that each rented unit is $600 per month, we simply add $600 for each additional unit, cumulatively for all 30 units as if each were occupied. Where the two lines intersect, presto!—our break-even point.

Why such a fuss over break-even analysis? It is simply because as a condition for prudent lending and investing, both sides (the lender and investor) need to know exactly what the risks (and rewards) are, and at which point. The prudent lender is cognizant of the level below which the property is not carrying itself, and therefore increasing the risk of delinquency and foreclosure; the prudent investor is aware of the level above which the property is profitable, or above which he or she need not feed the property from outside income. As shown in Figure 15.1, the area below the break-even point is labeled the loss zone, where there is a negative cash flow; that is, expenses exceed revenues. In contrast, the area above the break-even point is labeled the profit zone, where there is **positive cash flow**; that is, revenues exceed expenses.

The number of units rented and plotted on the horizontal axis could just as conveniently be labeled occupancy-vacancy ratio, expressed as percentages. Thus, the break-even point would be 16/30, or 53.3 percent, so that 16 of the 30 units, or just over 53 percent of the total number of available units, would need to be rented out to break even.

It should be emphasized that the analysis shown for apartment units holds true for any type of occupancy-vacancy ratios. Thus, the analyses have equal application to commercial properties as well. It is not uncommon for lenders on commercial properties, for instance, to hold back a portion of the projected loan until a minimum percentage agreed upon by lender and borrower is reached in the rentals. The minimum is called the floor amount, and could be 70 percent of the total loan amount.

15.5 Financing Starts with the Listing

Why Sell Your Apartment House?

Reasons for selling one's apartment house are many and varied. The reasons given by the owner for selling may not be the real reasons. The agent must explore in depth to find the real reason why the owner is selling.

The agent should ask if the city has issued an order for improvements on the building. An owner frequently wishes to sell to avoid spending money to comply with the requirements of city building inspections. Or the owner may want to sell because the area's property values may be decreasing and the owner wants to sell now before the property value shrinks more. Or the owner is in an area that has just passed a rent control ordinance or is considering controls (see Figure 15.2). Frequently the amounts allowed for rental increases bear little resemblance to the actual costs of operating the apartment complex; the potential inability to increase rents due to rent control ordinances tends to discourage development, ownership, and operation of apartment investments.

The owner may have a high turnover of tenants or poor rent collection. An agent must know the real reasons for selling in order to give the owner adequate financing advice. The key is knowing what questions to ask. It is axiomatic that answers are easy, but questions are hard.

Obtain Financing Information on the Building

The agent should find out the name of the lender, address, phone number, loan number, and correct balance due on the loan. If the owner does not know the exact balance, the agent should be authorized in writing to request that the lender supply this information.

If there is more than one loan, the agent should find out similar information for each loan. Ask the owners for a copy of their note and deed of trust for each loan. Read each note thoroughly. Determine the monthly payments to the last penny, interest rate, and due dates. Check for prepayment penalties. Is there a time limit on such penalties? Determine whether there is an effective due-on-sale clause or acceleration clause on the notes, along with any other clauses that

RENT CONTROLS—DO THEY MAKE SENSE?

LANDLORD   TENANT

Rent control is a controversial topic, with emotions and misconceptions running rampant on both sides of the issue.

From a purely economic point of view, rent controls make little sense. The issue has been repeatedly studied by both liberal and conservative economists, and most agree that rent controls do not solve housing problems. Rents are high because demand for apartment housing is high and supply is inadequate. The solution is to either decrease demand for rental units, increase the supply, or a combination of both.

Rent controls do neither. Rent controls artificially depress rent levels, which in turn stimulates demand instead of reducing demand. Rent controls reduce returns and yields on apartment investments, thereby discouraging the construction of new units or the conversion of large homes into apartments. In short, rent controls tend to perpetuate the ill they are supposed to cure!

Figure 15.2 The argument against rent controls.

may affect the property. Determine whether the loan is held by an institutional investor or by a private party, and whether the loan was taken back by the sellers at the time they purchased the property. If the loan is to be assumed, the buyer should also consider any assumption fees.

Plan for Probable Financing of Sale

The agent should check with the existing lenders on all loans. Even if the loans have an enforceable due-on-sale clause, ask lenders if they will allow the loans to be assumed. If so, how much will be the increase in interest or payments? Is the lender willing to increase the loan to a new buyer? If a new loan is made to a buyer, will the lender waive the prepayment penalty for the benefit of the seller? If not, how much will the lender charge? Will the lender split the prepayment penalty, that is, waive at least a portion of the penalty?

Determine what special terms the new loan will contain with respect to the interest rate, term of the loan, prepayment penalty, acceleration clause, loan fee, and other requirements. What down payment will be required? Will the lender allow a second loan? Will the new lender require an impound account for taxes or will this be waived? If a new first loan can be obtained for a higher amount than the present one, ascertain how much the holder of the second loan will require for a complete payoff. Will the second loan holder take some payoff and leave a portion of the loan on the property, to follow the lien of the new first loan?

After the foregoing information is obtained, the agent should hold another conference with the sellers. If the sellers do not need cash, will they carry back a second loan behind a new first loan? If there is an existing first loan with no due-on-sale clause, determine whether the sellers will take back an all-inclusive deed of trust, "wrapping around" the existing loan, and thereby eliminating the need for a new first loan and saving the buyer loan fees. If so, discuss the possibility of a 30-year amortization, but set up a due date of five or 10 years in order to enable the sellers to reevaluate their investments periodically.

If the current financing market is poor, perhaps the owner can carry back a first loan or an all-inclusive loan with a provision that whenever the finance market improves, the owner can present the buyer with new financing at rates not in excess of the current rate being paid. The buyer may then be obligated to take out such new loan and pay off to the owner all or a portion of the seller carryback loan. This gives the buyer time to obtain conventional financing when the market is stronger and allows the seller to sell the building at a time when poor financing is available to the buyers.

How Market Financing Conditions Affect Property Prices

When interest rates go up, the net income after interest expenses decrease, unless the rents can be raised or the expenses lowered. Since rents and expenses cannot always be easily changed, the net result of an increase in interest rates may be to decrease yields. Since apartment investments are competing in the marketplace with other investments, an increase in the interest rate results in a lower market value for the apartment house. Conversely, when interest rates decrease, yields are increased, tending to raise the value of a property.

As a rule of thumb, the property's capitalization rate (cap rate) is computed by dividing the net operating income by the sale price or value of the property. If the capitalization rate of the building is 10 percent and the buyer must pay 12 percent interest, the buyer is losing 2 percent on every borrowed dollar. This has the effect of reducing the yield to a much lower amount, resulting in negative leverage. If the cap rate is 12 percent and the interest rate is 10 percent, the investor has positive leverage, and the yield will be increased by the use of borrowed funds.

In difficult financing markets, existing low-interest assumable loans should be preserved if at all possible. There may be such loans, including insurance company loans, private loans, FHA loans, and so on. The balances on these loans may be low if they have been in existence for many years, so the sellers may have a large equity. If the buyers put down only 15 or 20 percent, the sellers may have to carry an excessively large second loan, and if they need cash, over and above the down payment, they cannot sell such a loan because of its size. In such event, the agent can structure the sale so that the sellers' remaining equity could be split. For example, if the equity were $150,000, it could be split into a $50,000 second loan and $100,000 third loan. The sellers could then sell the second loan at the prevailing discount, receive some cash, and hold a $100,000 third loan until its due date or until the refinance clause can be invoked.

Economic Principles versus Tax Shelter

A property should be priced so that the apartment house is a good investment for the buyers based upon economic principles and not just on **tax shelter**. If the property shows a return on investment based only upon its tax shelter, it may not be a good investment for the buyer because tax laws may be changed to eliminate certain tax shelter items; the depreciation shrinks each year so that the tax shelter decreases; and if the buyer later sells the property, there will invariably be recapture of some of the depreciation as taxable gain.

The agent must explain to the sellers that investors expect a realistic rate of yield and since an apartment house requires more management and work than other types of investment, this additional work and risk must be taken into account in the form of a greater yield on the investment.

If a property is listed at a correct price and if the owner has been informed of prevailing market conditions and will assist with some kind of financing to help the sale, the agent will have a highly marketable apartment complex. The buyer will then have a reasonable chance to have a successful investment. This can create good will for all and will build the reputation of the agent for integrity and honesty, without which no one can really succeed in the real estate brokerage business.

15.6 Introduction to Commercial and Industrial Properties

Financing requirements for commercial and industrial properties are more strict than for residential property unless the tenant is a major corporation with good credit standing.

In shopping centers, a new freeway may alter travel patterns, encouraging the construction of competing centers, with resultant losses to older centers. Before illustrating the financing of a commercial property, it may be of interest to observe that many lenders prefer multipurpose office buildings and multipurpose retail buildings as security for loans. Special purpose facilities, such as bowling alleys, theaters, handball courts, restaurants, and so on generally are not considered attractive security for real estate loans.

Commercial Properties

Commercial properties consist of the following:

- Neighborhood stores, including old "strip stores," that is, stores running parallel to and fronting the street—"along the strip"

- Free-standing commercial buildings, either single purpose or multipurpose

- Neighborhood convenience centers, including clusters of stores around a minimarket, usually with some off-street parking

- Community shopping centers, consisting of a larger group of stores surrounding a major supermarket

- Department stores

- Service stations

- Garage buildings

- Franchise outlets
- Fast-food chain stores, either in a free-standing building or as part of a center, including automotive franchise buildings
- Motels, hotels, mobile-home parks
- Office buildings, including ground floor and multistory, such as medical-dental buildings
- Rest homes and convalescent hospitals
- Special-purpose buildings, such as built-to-order drive-in banks

Industrial Properties

Industrial properties can be classified into three categories:

1. *Small industrial properties*. These are free-standing single buildings in industrially zoned areas of a city. Such buildings may be from 10,000 to 100,000 square feet, often divided into many small individual units that can be rented to many different tenants. They may or may not have rail facilities.

2. *Larger industrial properties*. These are large industrial buildings leased to one tenant on a long-term lease.

3. *Industrial parks*. These are planned parks where developers can buy land and develop individual buildings to the specifications of the master plan. They usually have landscaped areas surrounding the buildings.

Office Parks

An **office park** is an area for which a master plan of development is adopted and in which all buildings are designed for office occupancy. There are off-street parking areas and often landscaping to give a park-like setting. In many areas, the master plan of such a park allows restaurants and shops to be located in certain areas to serve the persons working in the office park. Hotels and motels may also be situated within the area to allow conferences. Examples of this type of development can frequently be found around airports and freeway interchanges.

Advantages of Investing in a Commercial or Industrial Property

If the property has a long-term lease with a strong tenant, there is a high likelihood of steady income. When compared with residential income properties, commercial and industrial ownership offers the advantage of greater stability of lessees as well as potentially low vacancy factors. Sometimes the lessee will need to make major capital improvements to the property to make it suitable for its business.

Most commercial leases contain either a cost-of-living increase clause or a **percentage lease** in the case of retail establishments. This allows an owner to realize increased rents as operating costs mount. If the property is in a prime commercial location, the successful operation of the business tenant will result in a high percentage of the gross, thereby giving overall rent of more than just minimum base rent.

The growth of the city creates greater demand for commercial properties, giving the owner increased rents. There is little risk of rent control, unlike apartment properties. Business tenants are easier to deal with than tenants of apartment houses. Finally, lease insurance is available to protect both landlord and tenant in case of business interruption due to specified hazards outlined in the insurance policy, such as the destruction of part or all of the premises through fire, windstorm, earthquake, and the like.

Disadvantages of Investing in a Commercial or Industrial Property

A leased commercial or industrial property with a strong tenant is a good investment. Those that are available often sell at a high price, which results in a lower yield than the interest required on the purchase loan. In periods of overbuilding, the market is flooded with unused commercial space. This results in lower rents and poor investment returns.

Investments in older types of commercial buildings, such as older "Main Street" stores, can be a greater risk, because tenants may move to newer centers, and as they are created the resulting vacancies may take a long time to fill. Succeeding businesses may be of lower quality and not able to pay as high a rent. Changing neighborhood patterns may result in an entire commercial area becoming less desirable, with entire blocks of stores remaining vacant and subject to vandalism.

Some tenants may have long-term leases with fixed rental rates, thereby freezing the owners into fixed income while taxes and other expenses rise.

City requirements often force owners to add expensive improvements to safeguard the safety of occupants. For instance, a hotel may have to install new fire doors, outside fire escapes, or different elevators to conform to fire, safety, and disability requirements. This can require owners to spend a substantial amount of capital.

15.7 Debt Coverage Ratio

After carefully analyzing the borrower's qualifications, income property appraisal, and cash flow forecast, the loan underwriter frequently does a debt coverage ratio analysis. The property's annual *net operating income (NOI)* is divided by the property's annual debt service to compute the debt coverage ratio (DCR).

$$\text{Debt coverage ratio} = \frac{\text{Annual net operating income}}{\text{Annual debt service}}$$

Annual net operating income is the annual estimated rents less vacancies and operating expenses; annual debt service is the required monthly loan payments $\times$ 12 months which is labeled "loan constant."

Example: On a small income property, the figures might be as follows:

Gross rent estimate	$100,000
Less vacancy (10%)	−10,000
Gross operating income	$ 90,000
Less operating expenses (taxes, insurance, repairs, management, etc.)	−30,000
Net operating income	$ 60,000

The potential borrower has applied for a $500,000 loan at 9 percent amortized for 30 years with payments of $4,023 per month; multiplied by 12 this equals $48,276 annual debt service.

$$\text{Debt coverage ratio} = \frac{\$60,000}{\$48,276} = 1.24$$

The loan underwriter would then compare this DCR with the company policy guidelines to determine if the property's net income justifies the loan. If the DCR is acceptable and the borrower's qualifications and the appraisal are cleared, then the income property loan is approved. If the DCR is too low, the loan may be denied until either the net operating income is increased or the annual debt service is reduced (or both) to bring the DCR into line.

A lender's debt coverage ratio requirements will vary by property types, market conditions, and portfolio requirements. A call to your local loan representative can give you the current requirements. In today's real estate market, most lenders want a DCR of 1.1 or better.

Few if any lenders will accept a debt coverage ratio that breaks even or is negative, where income will not cover loan payments.

The main line of defense for an income property lender is the amount of net operating income (gross annual rents less vacancies and operating expenses). Income property lenders know that the money for the loan payments comes from the net income of the property. If the property has a negative cash flow, net income will not cover the loan payments.

From this discussion, you can see why income property lenders place such importance on a property's net operating income and debt coverage ratios. However, it must be understood that an excellent net operating income and debt coverage ratio will not guarantee an approved loan if the borrower has questionable qualifications and the property appraisal is too low! Income property lenders insist upon good borrowers and adequate appraisals, but tremendous emphasis is placed on the property's net operating income.

SUMMARY

Houses that are converted to rentals are not usually financed under the same terms as owner-occupied. Some speculators simply buy for short-term gain, renting out the house until an opportunity for a favorable resale arises. In cases where they believe that a house is being purchased by a speculator, lenders have been known to (1) reduce the loan-to-value ratio, (2) increase the interest rate, (3) adjust loan fees (points) upward, or, in extreme cases, (4) refuse the loan altogether.

Apartment houses and two-to-four-unit buildings are generally financed for from 60 percent to 75 percent of the lender's appraised value. For "oversold" properties where the rental income does not cover all expenses and loan payments, often the lender's estimate of value will be below the actual sales price. Lenders reason that a project must be economically sound. Negative cash flows invite problems that may lead to subsequent delinquencies and defaults.

Interest rates for apartments are higher than for single dwellings because of the higher risks involved. More favorable terms can be negotiated if the property and the borrower's credit are both sound.

Financing of commercial and industrial properties requires specialized knowledge of market conditions, management, quality and quantity of tenants, and other factors. There is no uniform lending pattern, though institutional lenders tend to shy away from loan-to-value ratios exceeding 75 percent. The key for commercial and industrial properties is an adequate debt coverage ratio (DCR).

IMPORTANT TERMS AND CONCEPTS

Break-even analysis	*Net operating income (NOI)*
Capitalized income stream	*Office parks*
Debt coverage ratio (DCR)	*Passive loss*
Debt service	*Percentage lease*
Depreciation	*Positive cash flow*
Leverage	*Rent control*
Like-kind	*Tax shelters*
Negative cash flow	

REVIEWING YOUR UNDERSTANDING

Questions for Discussion

1. List two advantages and two disadvantages of investing in
   a. apartment houses.
   b. commercial properties.
   c. industrial properties.

2. Discuss the risks involved in overfinancing or overleveraging, that is, too much borrowing against a property.

3. From a marketing viewpoint, why is it important to determine the motivation of owners who desire to sell their properties?

4. What is meant by the expression "feeding the property"?

Multiple-Choice Questions

1. The main advantage of a single-family rental, as compared to other real estate investments, is its
   a. liquidity.
   b. higher interest rates.
   c. fewer choices.
   d. difficulty of management.

2. Which of the following statements concerning the financing of large apartment projects is correct?
   a. The larger the size of a building, the lower the loan-to-value ratio.
   b. Loan fees for large complexes are usually lower than for single dwellings.
   c. Loan terms seldom exceed 15 years.
   d. Lenders ignore debt service in assessing the loan collateral.

3. If an owner is required to "feed the property" to meet operating costs and debt service, it is always due to
   a. positive cash flow.
   b. negative cash flow.
   c. excellent management.
   d. excess depreciation write-off.

4. Most apartment properties are financed by
   a. private loans.
   b. government loans.
   c. conventional loans.
   d. foreign loans.

5. The ability to assume an existing loan is determined by the
   a. method of taking title to the property.
   b. existence of a due-on-sale clause.
   c. amount of taxes.
   d. title insurance required by the lender.

6. Buying real estate with little down payment and with maximum financing is called
   a. equity buying.
   b. leverage.
   c. progression.
   d. regression.

7. The California Civil Code limits prepayment penalties on certain types of real estate loans to the first three years. Which of the following transactions qualifies for the limitation?
   a. owner-occupied single-family residence.
   b. a house purchased for rental.
   c. houses purchased on speculation.
   d. a vacant lot.

8. "Break-even analysis" refers to
   a. debt coverage ratio.
   b. use of very low leverage.
   c. positive cash flow.
   d. the point at which income equals outgo.

9. If the yield on a property is 9 percent, but the buyer must pay 11 percent interest, the net effect is termed
   a. negative leverage.
   b. positive leverage.
   c. neutral leverage.
   d. trading on the equity.

10. Which of the following properties are most likely to be subject to rent control ordinances?
    a. commercial.
    b. industrial.
    c. parking lots.
    d. apartments.

11. Buyers of nonowner-occupied single-family rentals
    a. are generally charged more interest than for owner-occupied homes.
    b. will never pay a higher loan origination fee than on an owner-occupied home.
    c. cannot be required to pay a prepayment penalty for an early payoff.
    d. are considered safer than equally qualified owners who occupy the premises.

12. The financing of a nonowner-occupied duplex generally means that
    a. lenders will never loan more than 70 percent of value.
    b. interest rates are higher than on owner-occupied single-family dwellings.
    c. new loans are not available.
    d. rental management is not required.

13. With respect to apartment complexes, the experienced investor knows that
    a. a resident manager or owner is required by California law for 16 or more units.
    b. management of apartment units is scattered, rather than concentrated.
    c. the cost of operation per unit is greater for apartment units than in scattered properties.
    d. none of the above are true.

14. While the issue of rent controls is a controversial one, we find that
    a. the imposition of rent controls actually enhances rental income.
    b. yields on apartment houses increase under rent controls.
    c. rent controls discourage construction of apartment houses, leading to diminished supply and greater demand.
    d. rent controls tend to increase the capitalized value of apartment houses.

15. Special-purpose properties, such as restaurants, franchise fast-food outlets, and the like,
    a. are usually considered the best security by most lenders.
    b. are considered too risky by most lenders as security for loans.
    c. normally command lower interest rates than most other commercial properties because of their history of financial success.
    d. are favored by lenders because of their relatively easy conversion to other uses.

16. Which of the following statements concerning the financing of large apartment projects is true?
    a. Lenders usually don't bother with the borrower's credit for income-producing properties.
    b. In general, the larger the size of the project, the lower the loan-to-value ratio.
    c. Lenders usually ignore debt service in qualifying the loan.
    d. Loan fees are lower than for smaller properties.

17. Operating expenses for an apartment complex include
    a. interest payments.
    b. principal payments.
    c. depreciation write-offs.
    d. management fees.

18. Investors in two to four rental units find that
    a. lenders qualify both the borrower and the property.
    b. loan assumptions are commonplace.
    c. no secondary financing is permitted if there is negative cash flow.
    d. government-backed financing is in abundance.

19. From a real estate agent's perspective, thoughts about financing should always begin with the
    a. offer.
    b. acceptance.
    c. listing.
    d. appraisal.

20. Investing in commercial property
    a. requires less down payment than apartment projects.
    b. requires a debt coverage ratio of less than 1.
    c. may involve the use of percentage leases.
    d. is less sophisticated than investing in rental homes.

ANSWERS TO MULTIPLE-CHOICE QUESTIONS

Chapter 1

1. b	2. c	3. a	4. c	5. d
6. d	7. b	8. a	9. d	10. d
11. c	12. a	13. b	14. a	15. c
16. b	17. b	18. b	19. d	20. d

Chapter 2

1. a	2. d	3. b	4. c	5. b
6. d	7. d	8. c	9. a	10. c
11. a	12. c	13. b	14. b	15. c
16. a	17. d	18. a	19. d	20. d

Chapter 3

1. b	2. d	3. c	4. b	5. d
6. b	7. a	8. c	9. b	10. b
11. d	12. b	13. d	14. a	15. c
16. a	17. a	18. d	19. b	20. b

Chapter 4

1. d	2. d	3. a	4. b	5. c
6. c	7. d	8. c	9. b	10. d
11. d	12. d	13. c	14. b	15. a
16. a	17. c	18. d	19. b	20. a

Chapter 5

1. c	2. a	3. a	4. a	5. b
6. c	7. d	8. a	9. b	10. a
11. c	12. c	13. c	14. b	15. b
16. c	17. b	18. b	19. c	20. c

Chapter 6

1. a	2. d	3. c	4. b	5. d
6. c	7. b	8. d	9. b	10. b
11. a	12. c	13. d	14. d	15. a
16. a	17. b	18. b	19. b	20. d

Chapter 7

1. b	2. c	3. b	4. c	5. b
6. b	7. b	8. d	9. a	10. d
11. b	12. b	13. d	14. c	15. b
16. d	17. b	18. b	19. b	20. a

Chapter 8

1. b	2. b	3. a	4. c	5. d
6. a	7. d	8. a	9. a	10. a
11. a	12. b	13. d	14. d	15. c
16. b	17. c	18. b	19. a	20. c

Chapter 9

1. d	2. d	3. b	4. a	5. d
6. c	7. d	8. b	9. a	10. b
11. c	12. a	13. b	14. d	15. b
16. c	17. d	18. b	19. c	20. d

Chapter 10

1. c	2. b	3. d	4. a	5. b
6. a	7. b	8. d	9. c	10. b
11. b	12. b	13. c	14. d	15. d
16. d	17. b	18. a	19. d	20. c

Chapter 11

1. d	2. d	3. b	4. a	5. b
6. c	7. d	8. d	9. a	10. b
11. d	12. b	13. b	14. a	15. b
16. d	17. c	18. c	19. a	20. d

Chapter 12

1. c	2. a	3. b	4. b	5. c
6. b	7. c	8. a	9. d	10. c
11. d	12. d	13. b	14. d	15. a
16. a	17. d	18. b	19. c	20. d

Chapter 13

1. b	2. a	3. b	4. d	5. b
6. c	7. b	8. c	9. d	10. a
11. a	12. b	13. b	14. a	15. a
16. a	17. b	18. a	19. b	20. c

Chapter 14

1. d	2. b	3. c	4. a	5. b
6. a	7. a	8. d	9. b	10. c
11. b	12. d	13. d	14. c	15. d
16. b	17. d	18. d	19. a	20. b

Chapter 15

1. a	2. a	3. b	4. c	5. b
6. b	7. a	8. d	9. a	10. d
11. a	12. b	13. a	14. c	15. b
16. b	17. d	18. a	19. c	20. c

APPENDIX A

Introduction to Internet Searching for Home Loans

Fannie Mae info on what to consider when buying, refinancing, or making home improvements: www.homepath.com. To learn mortgage lingo: www.loanlibrary.com. The Mortgage Bankers Association of America offers mortgage planning tools via www.mbaa.org. Then there's the Mortgage 101 that furnishes interactive tools on a range of mortgage topics: www.mortgage101.com. "The Mortgage Expert" contains mortgage rate updates through its www.mortgageexpert.com website. First American Real Estate Services furnishes detailed information on mortgages and loans from public records at www.firstamres.com. "Mortgage Market Commentary" is a helpful column at www.inman.com. Creative Real Estate Online, through its www.creonline.com, provides real estate financing discussions by people who e-mail to that site with their questions and concerns. The Center for Responsible Lending deals with predatory lending via www.responsiblelending.org. A directory of mortgage brokers is available from www.reals.com. Additionally, many real estate firms offer financing information through their websites; see www.century21.com and www.remax.com for examples.

There are also on-line mortgage bankers and brokers such as www.eloan.com, www.lendingtree.com, www.mortgage.com, and www.loansdirect.com. And how about an Internet bank? I-Bank was started as a division of a traditional bank, designed for those not needing traditional banking services, including those dissatisfied with having to maintain minimum balances—view more details at its site, www.nationalinterbank.com. A competitor is www.bankone.com, though it may require a minimum balance to avoid fees.

There are numerous residential lenders on the Internet, which make shopping for a mortgage less tedious. Let's look at a few of these. Virtually all of them provide a method for applying via the Internet, simplifying the cumbersome process. "E-Lenders" include: www.theloanpage.com, which offers free quotes for refinancing loans, second mortgages, consolidation loans, and home improvement loans. Countrywide Financial at www.countrywide.com advertises "home loan consultation at no cost or obligation. We offer a wide range of home loan products, commonsense lending decisions, reduced paperwork options, and more—even if your credit history is less-than-perfect. We welcome the opportunity to serve your home financing needs!" Ameriquest, www.ameriquestmortgage.com, offers "Home Equity Loans for homeowners without perfect credit." Another source for a variety of home loans is www.quickenloans.com. A link to financial products and services, including mortgages, is at www.forbes.com. "Check around for the lowest rate you can find. If we can't beat or match it, we'll pay you $300" is the boast at www.pricelinemortgage.com. Still another lender offering its services on the Web is www.championmortgage.com. Other websites include Wells Fargo at www.wellsfargo.com/mortgage and SmartMoney is at www.smartmoney.com.

Finally, DiTech advertises extensively on TV for its services and has a wide assortment of websites. Newsletter@ditech.com states, in one of its messages:

> Don't let your credit-card bills or other debts compromise your financial well-being. Being a homeowner allows you the opportunity to increase the power of your monthly debt payments through better credit management. . . . Aside from the monthly savings, think of the convenience of having only one monthly payment to worry about rather than writing many checks to each one of your credit card companies each and every month! . . . DiTech also offers useful loan tools to help you make decisions about mortgage loan needs.

For seniors seeking to convert the equity in their homes into income, the following websites are available: www.fanniemae.com, www.hud.gov, www.reverse.org, and www.aarp.org. Related discussions of Web applications are in Chapter 7.

Additional websites: www.LendingTree.com. www.MortgageProfessor.com offers Option ARM variations by professor of finance at the

University of Pennsylvania. www.Kiplinger.com provides calculators to see how loans compare and to plan ahead for various scenarios. See www.aarp.org/money/revmort/ for reverse mortgages.

FICO, aka Your Credit Profile

Fair, Isaac (FICO) is the leading producer of software for home and consumer lenders. The creditworthiness of virtually every applicant for a real estate loan (along with credit cards, insurance, etc.) is largely predicated on what Fair Isaac produces in its scoring process, which had been held secret until 2001, when a California court decision gave consumers the right to see their scores on-line. Congress is considering mandating disclosure for the rest of the country. Fair Isaac, designer of the scoring/rating system, is releasing its scores on-line, at www.myfico.com. Equifax, a major credit reporting agency, is also offering credit scoring at www.equifax.com—and www.TransUnion.com and www.Experian.com are the two other national credit reporting agencies. Each of them, for a fee, provides a report detailing which of the 33 possible built-in criteria most influenced it. Additional helpful information from Fair Isaac on credit scoring can be retrieved through www.fairisaac.com.

On-line lender E-Loan offered consumer credit scores for free before running into industry opposition. Check their latest policies, including fees, if any, on their website, www.eloan.com.

Another player in the business of credit scoring is iPlace. The firm enables consumers to directly access their credit scores, which, until recently, were a closely guarded secret made available only to lenders and not to consumers themselves. Access the www.orbimage.com/partn/place.html site for more information.

Finally, www.IngDirect.com is heavily involved in financial services, linking its "Orange Savings Account" to customer's checking account. Its site offers a section on how to get a free credit report and what to look for in spotting ID theft.

Securing Credit on the Internet

We'll discuss credit scoring in Chapter 9, but meanwhile let's jump in and briefly introduce credit bureaus. We have learned that while there are many credit reporting bureaus or agencies, the three major ones are TransUnion Credit Services (www.transunion.com), Equifax Credit Services (www.equifax.com), and

Experian Credit Services (www.experian.com)—collectively, TEE. How do they influence the mortgage business? In short, they report debt histories of borrower-debtors to creditors and others having an interest in the credit-granting process. What TEE reports to lenders can make or break the consummation of mortgage transactions, since real estate lenders subscribe to firms that convert credit and debt histories into credit scores. A number of firms, such as the Credit Monitoring Service, offer a Three Bureau Online Credit Report, many on a limited free trial basis, typically for 30 days, after which a periodic fee kicks in. Getting reports from all three bureaus, delivered almost instantaneously online, should not only provide a comprehensive profile of where you stand but will also typically show differences between the three, allowing you to communicate with each to correct the errors and inconsistencies.

California requires lenders to provide borrowers their credit scores. As explained in Chapter 9, "credit score" or "risk score" is a measure of a loan applicant's creditworthiness that is determined by comparing the applicant's credit record with millions of others. The scores, which range from 300 to 900, were developed by Fair Isaac and Co. (FICO), located in San Rafael. They are available for a modest price on several websites, including www.myfico.com, www.equifax.com, and others. The higher the score, the better, with scores above 700 considered very good. It's estimated, for instance, that the delinquency rate for scores above 750 is 2 percent, while for scores of 630 it is 31 percent. Another firm, E-Loan, offers an alternative score on its website, www.eloan.com. Other sources of credit reporting include the website www.freecreditreport.com, available on-line from Experian. Also, both www.qspace.com and www.worthknowing.com attempt to analyze and quantify one's credit standing, though neither is as popular as the FICO scoring system.

There are many sources of credit assistance on the Internet. To cite just a few, there's the popular Consumer Credit Counseling Services, a nonprofit that states on-line: "Free help to reduce your debt, lower finance charges, end credit harassment." Another, www.moneynest.com, advertises that "MoneyNest.com is a free mortgage and debt management search-service which lets you shop 100s of lenders for the best rates conveniently and securely without sales pressure. Get your free mortgage quote, get a free-debt relief quote."

Ameriquest Mortgage advertises:

Getting the money you need to pay off high-interest debts and credit cards may be just a call or a click away. For more than 20 years, homeowners have been turning to *Ameriquest Mortgage* to get money for debt consolidation, home improvements and to give their families the things they need. To learn more, click on www. ameriquestmortgage.com.

The Internet provides a welcome anonymity for many borrowers. Unfortunately, it also has a certain amount of unaccountability that accompanies the acquisition of mortgage loans. The process today may be best suited for those who possess some financial moxie.

Using the Internet as a Useful Tool

To conclude our discussion, here's a plethora of websites providing information in the field of real estate financing:

www.mortgageinfocenter.com (Mortgage strategies)

www.imoneynet.com, www.bankrate.com (Rating rates)

www.iloans.com (Amortization schedules, closing costs)

www.amo-mortgage.com (Refi, debt consolidation, Mortgage University)

www.homepath.com, www.fanniemaefoundation.org (Fannie Mae)

www.countrywide.com (Countrywide)

www.eloan.com (Listing of more than 60 lenders)

www.thirdage.com (Links)

www.mortgagecalc.com (Affordability)

www.mortgage101.com (Downloadable forms, etc.)

www.seniorsites.com (Nonprofit housing for seniors)

www.inman.com (Inman News Features)

www.reprofile.com (Stewart Title)

www.tnlg.com (Kevin Hawkins R.E. Resources)

www.kiplinger.com (Buying/Selling home)

www.recyber.com (R.E. Cyberspace Society)

www.quickenmortgage.com, www.mortgage.quicken.com (Mortgage lending geared toward the consumer)

www.homegain.com (Home Gain)

www.ditech.com (DiTech)

www.imoneynet.com (Mortgage Borrowing)

www.hsh.com,

www.mortgagemag.com, www.lendingtree.com

www.mortgage101.com (Step-by-step guides)

www.easierhomeloans.com (Home buying essentials: loan application, rates, credit considerations)

www.hud.gov

www.hrblock.com

www.realestate.com [Loan auctions (Borrower posts criteria and lenders bid for the loan)]

www.onerealtorplace.com (Media and consumers)

www.thinkglink.com (Ilyce Glink, real estate and personal financial reporter)

www.howtorentbyowner.com—Evaluates different types of vacation properties and weighs pros and cons of each, determining how much rent to charge to break even

As noted in Chapter 11, some on-line lenders even offer rebates in one form or another. Example: www.pricelinemortgage.com boasts "Check around for the lowest rate you can find. If we can't beat or match it, we'll pay you $300." Then there's Virtumundo, Inc., which through its website, www.virtumundo.com, states that it is a "direct marketing company that specializes in providing demographically targeted solutions for advertisers, both online and in traditional media." In checking that site, you may find a lender, New Century Mortgage Corporation, offering on-line application for prequalify prospective borrowers. Finally, there's the financial planners who are getting into the mortgage business, adding still another tool to their arsenals: originating mortgages and other loans for their clients. As the magazine *Investment Advisor* reports, planners can access www.verticallend.com to sign up for that website's training from a designated loan specialist. Subscribers log on to Vertical Lend's password-protected site, click on the residential mortgage section, and fill out an express application to get the loan started. Each financial professional is assigned a loan specialist who provides back-office support and acts as a business partner when performing loan originations. The loan specialist retrieves the application, runs a credit check, examines debt ratios, and then shops the loan for the best rate. Welcome to the world of the Internet!

GLOSSARY

Many of the entries below correspond to end-of-chapter Important Terms and Concepts. For these entries, numbers are given in parentheses to indicate the pages on which the term is defined or discussed. Entries without page references are included to define global concepts related to the field of real estate finance.

A

Ability/Capacity to Pay (213) The position of a borrower relative to repaying a loan, based on income and other assets.

Acceleration Clause Clause in trust deed or mortgage giving a lender the right to all sums owing to be immediately due and payable upon the happening of a certain event, such as a loan default.

Accrued Depreciation The difference between the cost of replacement of a building new, as of the date of the appraisal, and the present appraised value. Depreciation that has accumulated over a period of time.

Adjustable Rate Mortgage (ARM) (80) A loan pegged to an index; as the index goes up or down, the borrower's interest rate follows according to contractual limits, spelled out in the note and trust deed.

Adjusted Cost Basis The income tax cost basis of property with certain additions, such as the cost of improvements, and certain subtractions, such as depreciation in value.

Adjusted Gross Income (221) Gross income less federal and state income taxes and Social Security.

Adjustment Interval The time between changes in the interest rate or monthly payments for an ARM, typically six months to one year.

Adjustments (191) As part of an appraisal, the subtractions from the replacement cost of a property to allow for any loss in value due to age, condition, and other factors; also the additions to and subtractions from the values of comparable properties.

Advances (268, 308) Money advanced by the beneficiary under a trust deed to pay real estate taxes or other items to protect the lender's interest under the trust deed. Also refers to additional funds loaned under an open-end trust deed or mortgage. Also, periodic payments to the builder as construction progresses.

Alienation Clause (403) A special type of acceleration clause that gives the lender the right to demand payment of the entire loan balance upon a sale or transfer of title. Also known as a due-on-sale clause.

All-Inclusive Trust Deed (AITD) (384) A deed of trust that includes the amount due under a senior trust deed or deeds on the same property. Also known as a wrap-around.

Alternative Mortgage Instruments (79) Nonstandardized financing loans.

Amortization Tables (332) A table that shows amounts needed to pay off different loan amounts at specified interest rates for specified terms.

Amortized Loan (19, 328) A loan that is completely paid off, interest and principal, by a series of regular payments that are equal or nearly equal. Also called a level-payment loan.

Annual Percentage Rate (APR) (157, 251) Under the Truth-in-Lending Law, the APR is used to disclose the total cost of a loan to a borrower and is converted to the so-called effective rate.

Annuity A series of equal or nearly equal payments to be made over a period of time. The installment payments due to a landlord under a lease or installment payments due to a lender are examples of annuities.

Antideficiency Legislation Legislation that prohibits a lender from obtaining a judgment for money against a defaulting borrower under a note and deed of trust when the value of property foreclosed upon is not adequate to satisfy the debt. See *Deficiency Judgment*.

Applicable Federal Rate (406) The rate used for imputed interest in a seller-financed transaction, equal to the rate on federal securities with a similar term.

Appraisal An estimate or opinion of value.

Assessment Lien (320) A lien against property for public construction projects that benefit the property, such as street improvements or sewers.

Assignment of Deed of Trust An instrument that transfers the security interest under a deed of trust from one lender to another.

Assignment of Rents Clause (271) A clause in a trust deed that gives the beneficiary the right under limited circumstances to collect rents of the property if the borrower defaults.

Assumption Fee A lender's charge for changing and processing records for a new owner who is assuming an existing loan.

Assumption of Deed of Trust or Mortgage Taking over responsibility and liability for the payment of the existing deed of trust loan from the seller.

Automatic Payment Plan (284) A plan whereby the borrower authorizes deduction of monthly payments from a checking account rather than sending payments.

B

Back-End Ratio (Bottom Ratio) (216) A ratio representing the sum of the borrower's mortgage payment and long-term debts, divided by gross income.

Balloon Payment (19, 56, 92, 329) One installment payment on an amortized note that is at least double the amount of a regular installment. Frequently this is a final payment on the due date.

Basis Property owner's "book value" for income tax purposes. Original cost plus capital improvements less depreciation.

Beneficiary (21) A lender under a note secured by a deed of trust.

Biweekly Loan Payments (96, 340) Real estate loan payments made every two weeks. A monthly payment is divided by two and paid 26 times per year.

Blanket Trust Deed (311) A single trust deed covering more than one parcel of real estate.

Blended-Rate Loan (403) An interest rate that is less than market rate, but greater than the existing contract rate. Sometimes offered as an alternative to a new buyer who wishes to assume an existing loan and needs additional funds.

Break-even Analysis (427) Calculation of the point where the income and expenses for a proposed project would be equal.

Bridge Loan (36) A loan that bridges the gap between two other loans, usually for a short term. See Swing Loan.

Broker Participation (381) A plan in which part of a seller's interest in a trust deed is assigned to the real estate broker to pay the commission on the sale, making the broker a partner with the seller on the loan.

Broker's Loan Statement A statement signed and received by the borrower at the time of a loan transaction, indicating the costs and deductions, including commissions, of a loan negotiated by a real estate licensee.

Builder's Control Service (308) An outside third party that acts as an intermediary in the control and disbursement of funds to the builder in a building project.

Building Loan Agreement (306) A document that contains the agreement between the lender, builder, and borrower concerning a construction project, including the schedule of disbursements to the builder.

Buy-down Loan (113) The purchase of a reduced interest rate, usually by home builders, allowing the borrower to qualify at a lower income level.

C

Cal-Vet Loans (143) Loans made to eligible veterans by the Department of Veterans Affairs of the State of California for the purchase of real estate, utilizing a contract of sale.

Cap (84) Upper limit on adjustable or variable interest rate loans on a periodic basis during life of loan.

Capital Gains Gains on the sale of property, as qualified by statute.

Capitalization (194) In appraising, a method used to determine value of a property by dividing annual net operating income by a desirable capitalization rate.

Capitalization Rate (195) The rate that is believed to represent the proper relationship between the value of the real property and the net operating income generated from the property.

Capitalized Income Stream (425) Valuation approach to income-producing property measured by converting the income into a single present value.

Cash Equivalency Price in terms of cash vs other assets, such as trust deed, stocks, and bonds that may be worth less than their face amount.

Cash Flow (5) The pattern of income and expenditures, which affects investment properties.

Certificate of Eligibility (139) A certificate issued by the Department of Veterans Affairs that shows the amount of the veteran's entitlement.

Certificate of Reasonable Value (CRV) (141, 178) A document issued by the Department of Veterans Affairs that shows the appraised value of the property.

Certified Appraisal Report (201) A written communication of an analysis, opinion, or conclusion relating to the value of real property certified according to state and federal requirements.

Closing Costs (256) Costs paid by the borrower when borrowing for the purchase of a property. Costs paid by buyers and sellers on the sale of a property.

Cost of Funds Index (COFI) Adjustable-rate mortgage with rate that adjusts based on cost of funds index, after the 11th District Cost of Funds.

Collateralization (378) The hypothecating of property, as security for a loan.

Collateralized Mortgage Obligation (CMO) (166) A security issued by FNMA that is designed to limit the investor's risk that borrowers will prepay the loans early.

Combination Loan (303) One loan combining a construction loan and permanent take-out loan after construction is completed.

Commercial Bank (35) A financial institution chartered by a state or the federal government to receive, lend, and safeguard money and other items of value.

Commercial Loan (402) Non-mortgage method of financing real estate through a personal loan from a commercial bank.

Commitment Agreement by a lender to lend mortgage money at a future date, subject to compliance with stated conditions.

Community Home Buyer's Program (115) An FNMA/FHLMC program for purchasers with lower incomes that features 97 percent financing, with reduced closing costs and cash reserve requirements.

Community Reinvestment Act (288) Federal law requiring financial institutions to lend in communities served, including low- and moderate-income areas, consistent with considerations of safety and soundness.

Co-mortgagor (225) A person who signs a note and deed of trust in addition to the primary borrower to give extra security to the loan. The co-mortgagor is jointly liable for the repayment of the loan, and is in title to the real estate.

Comparables (192) Recently sold properties near the property being appraised and similar to it.

Comparative Market Analysis (199) An opinion on a property's value prepared by a real estate licensee rather than a certified appraiser.

Compensating Factors (221) Positive factors that are considered by lenders to approve loans to otherwise marginal borrowers.

Completion Bond (314) A bond that the owners of a project can purchase to protect themselves, builders, and lenders from mechanic's liens.

Computerized Loan Originations (CLO) (69) Accessing lender loan programs via computer.

Conditional Commitment (131, 177) The FHA appraisal, issued by an independent fee appraiser on the property, that includes any conditions such as repairs the FHA will require before insuring a loan.

Conditional Sale Contract (394) A contract for the sale and purchase of property stating that delivery and possession is to be given to the buyer-vendee, but that legal title is to remain with the seller-vendor until the conditions of the contract have been fulfilled.

Condominium (197) A form of ownership in which separate units of three-dimensional airspace are owned by individual owners. The individual owners also jointly own an undivided interest in the common areas such as hallways, swimming pools, and land. Sometimes referred to as a vertical subdivision.

Conduit Purchase of loans from mortgage bankers and commercial banks, then collateralizing them with mortgage-backed securities.

Conforming Loan (167) Maximum loan amount purchased by FNMA and FHLMC.

Constant Debt service payments as a percentage of the original loan amount.

Construction Loan Loan made for the construction of improvements. Usually funds are disbursed at periodic intervals as the work progresses.

Contract of Sale See *Conditional Sale Contract.*

Conventional Loan (106) Any loan that is not insured or guaranteed or made by a government agency.

Convertible Rate Loan (90) A loan that starts out as an adjustable rate loan, then, at the option of the borrower during a designated period, can be converted to a fixed rate loan.

Co-Op (200) Similar to a long-term lease, but with right to sole and exclusive possession of the unit for an indefinite period.

Correspondent (40, 57) An abbreviated term meaning mortgage loan correspondent. Applies when a mortgage company originates a loan for an investor.

Co-signer (225) One who signs a note as guarantor but whose name is not on the title to the property.

Cost Approach (190) A method in which the value of a property is derived by estimating the replacement cost of the improvements, then deducting the estimated depreciation, then adding the market value of the land.

Cost of Funds Costs incurred by lenders to obtain capital.

Creative Financing Any financing out of the ordinary, such as seller carry-backs and wraparounds.

Creative Financing Disclosure Act (405) California law that requires disclosure of specified terms to the buyer-borrower in a seller carryback financing situation covering one to four dwelling units.

Credit History (229) Summary of applicant's credit accounts that includes repayments, past

due accounts, judgments and foreclosures.

Credit Life Insurance (121) A form of declining term life insurance that will pay all or part of the mortgage if the borrower dies.

Credit Report (257) Credit history of a person or business issued by a company in the credit reporting business, used to help determine creditworthiness.

Credit Scoring (229) A method of evaluating an applicant's credit history for the purpose of determining the probability of repayment of debts. Also called "FICO" score.

Credit Unions (57) Cooperative organizations of members of particular groups who agree to save money and make loans to members.

D

Debenture Bonds issued without security, backed only by the credit standing and earning capacity of the issuer.

Debt Coverage Ratio (DCR) (436) Net operating income divided by annual debt service. Used by lenders when analyzing income property loans.

Debt Service (194, 424) Another term for the principal and interest payments on a loan. Widely used for commercial and industrial properties.

Debt-to-Income Ratio Borrowers' monthly payment obligations as a percentage of their income.

Deed in Lieu of Foreclosure (278) A voluntary conveyance to the lender from the defaulting borrower that avoids the foreclosure process.

Deed of Reconveyance Upon the repayment of a promissory note secured by a trust deed, trustee transfers legal title back to the trustor (borrower), thereby releasing the lien.

Deed of Trust (18) Instrument by which title to real estate is transferred to a third-party trustee as security for repayment of a real estate loan. Used in California instead of a mortgage.

Default Failure to fulfill a duty or promise. Failure to make the payments on a real estate loan.

Deferred Interest See *Negative Amortization*.

Deficiency Judgment (277) A judgment given when the security pledged for a loan does not satisfy the debt upon foreclosure. Certain conditions must be met.

Delinquency Failure to make timely payments on loans.

Demand Deposit Checking account or transaction deposit withdrawable upon demand, as opposed to time deposit.

Department of Veterans Affairs (DVA) Federal government agency that guarantees approved lenders against foreclosure loss on loans made to eligible veterans.

Deposit Receipt A form used to accept earnest money to bind an offer for the purchase of real property. When accepted by the seller, it creates a sale contract.

Depreciation (419) A loss of value in real property brought about by age, physical deterioration, or functional or economic obsolescence. Broadly, a loss in value from any cause. Also called "write-off."

Desire to Pay (227) The predisposition of a borrower to repay a loan, suggested by prior credit history, size of down payment, and reason for buying.

Desktop Originator (FNMA) (69) A program of the Federal National Mortgage Association that allows loan agents to take applications and prequalify borrowers immediately.

Development Loans Loans that finance the acquisition of land and the installation, prior to building, of utilities, sewage systems, roads, and so on. Sometimes called a "Land Loan."

Direct Endorsement (249) An automatic approval that is available on FHA loans using an in-house underwriter.

Direct Private Lender (54) Individual who invests directly in loans without going through an intermediary and expects to receive higher interest rate yields.

Disbursements (308) Periodic payments as construction progresses.

Discount (156) An amount deducted in advance from the loan before the borrower is given the money. Also referred to as *Points*. In secondary market sales, a discount is the difference between the sale price and the principal balance on the note. Contrast *Premium*.

Discount Rate (9) The interest rate that the Federal Reserve Bank charges local member banks for funds they borrow.

Discount Tables Tables used by lenders and investors to show how much a given value is, called the discounted value, based upon various interest rates and terms of maturity.

Discrimination by Effect (117) Lending practices that have a discriminatory effect against protected groups, unless required to achieve a legitimate business purpose.

Disintermediation (3) Relatively sudden outflow of funds from a financial intermediary when depositors can obtain higher returns elsewhere.

Doctrine of Relation Back (317) The principle that if work on a project begins before the trust deed is recorded, all who furnish labor or materials thereafter may file mechanics' liens that have precedence over the trust deed.

Down Payment The difference between the sale price of the property and the loan amount.

Draws (308) Periodic payments to the builder as construction proceeds.

Due-on-Sale Clause (387) Clause in a trust deed that allows lenders to demand immediate payment of the loan balance if borrower sells or transfers an interest in the property.

DVA Department of Veterans Affairs, a federal agency (not Cal-Vet). Formerly VA.

DVA Automatics (249) Approvals of DVA loans by certain lenders qualified to use in-house underwriters.

DVA-Guaranteed Loan (136) A loan for veterans under which the Department of Veterans Affairs guarantees to reimburse the lender a specified maximum amount in case of foreclosure.

___

E

___

Earnest Money Money paid with an offer to purchase, given to bind a sale.

Easy Money (10) Loose money policy of the Federal Reserve Board, indicating increased availability of money in circulation.

Economic Life The period during which an improvement on a parcel of land can be used for any beneficial purpose.

Economic Obsolescence (189) A loss in property value caused by forces outside the property, such as adverse zoning or neighborhood nuisances.

Effective Age The age assigned to the improvements by the appraiser, not necessarily the chronological age.

Effective Interest Rate (157) The percentage of interest actually being paid by the borrower for the use of the money, including certain expenses for obtaining the loan. See *Annual Percentage Rate (APR)*.

Endowment Funds (67) The invested funds that are received as gifts by institutions such as colleges and charities.

Entitlement (139) The maximum amount that the DVA will pay if the lender suffers a loss on a DVA loan.

Equal Credit Opportunity Act (ECOA) (246) Federal law prohibiting discrimination in the extension of credit.

Equity The interest or value that an owner has in real estate over and above liens against the property. The difference between market value and the existing indebtedness.

Equity Financing Lender finances high-ratio loan in exchange for a percentage of ownership and the right to share in the property's cash flow.

Equity Participation (41) When a lender receives partial ownership interest in the project in order to increase its return on the loan.

Escalation Clause Refers to rent increases or decreases tied to an appropriate index.

Escrow A neutral depository, where a third party carries out instructions for the lender, buyer, and seller and is responsible for handling the paperwork and disbursing funds needed to transfer the property.

Escrow Account (279) See *Impound Account*.

Extended Term (281) Recasting of a loan by extending the remaining term, thereby lowering monthly payments.

___

F

___

Fair Credit Reporting Act (250) Federal law that gives a rejected

borrower the right to inspect and correct his or her credit agency file.

Fair Market Value (FMV) (179) The price in terms of money that a parcel of property will bring on the open market when neither buyer nor seller is under any compulsion to act.

Federal Deposit Insurance Corporation (FDIC) (44) Insures accounts at member banks up to $100,000.

Federal Funds Rate (12) The rate one bank charges another bank for overnight use of excess reserves.

Federal Home Loan Bank (FHLB) Provides credit reserves systems for member state and federal savings banks.

Federal Home Loan Mortgage Corporation (FHLMC) (45, 108, 164) An agency known as Freddie Mac, which provides a secondary market for savings banks and other institutions.

Federal Housing Administration (FHA) Division of the US Department of Housing and Urban Development that insures residential mortgage loans made by approved lenders against loss through foreclosure.

Federal Housing Finance Board (FHFB) (33) Federal agency that regulates the 12 Federal Home Loan Banks.

Federal National Mortgage Association (FNMA) (106, 164) Popularly known as Fannie Mae, a private corporation whose primary function is to buy and sell mortgages in the secondary mortgage market.

Federal Reserve Bank Board (FRBB) (45) An agency that oversees the Federal Reserve System, regulates commercial banks, and regulates the flow of money and credit.

Federal Reserve System (4) Central banking system of the United States consisting of 12 Federal Reserve Banks and the Federal Reserve Board, which sets monetary policy.

FHA-Insured Loan (129) A loan made by a bank or mortgage company with insurance from the FHA against loss to the lender in the event the loan must be foreclosed.

FHA 203(b) Program (134) Loans insured by the FHA for one- to four dwelling units

FHA 245 Program (134) An adjustable rate loan program available under FHA.

FICO Score See *Credit Scoring*.

Fifteen-Year Mortgage (96) A loan with a 15-year term, designed to build up equity faster and obtain a lower interest rate.

Finance Charge (255) Charges paid separately or withheld from the proceeds of the loan, such as loan origination fees or mortgage insurance premiums.

Finance Company (68) A firm involved in lending usually to high-risk borrowers at high interest rates. Identified as an industrial bank.

Financial Calculator (331) An electronic calculator that is designed to compute loan payments, interest rates, and other calculations used in real estate financing.

Financial Institutions Reform, Recovery, and Enforcement Act (FIRREA) (44) Federal law that restructured deposit insurance funds and regulatory system for thrifts.

Financial Intermediary (33) A depository that pools funds of clients and depositors and invests them into real estate loans.

Finder's Fee A fee paid by a lender or broker for referring a borrower to a certain lending institution or real estate office, often paid to a nonlicensee.

First Deed of Trust or Mortgage The first recorded loan; it takes precedence over junior loans and encumbrances. Also called senior or primary lien.

Fiscal Policy (13) Programs by the federal government that are intended to influence economic activity by making changes in government expenditures and taxation, implemented by the U.S. Treasury.

Five-Step Financing Process (23) The process of borrowing money that includes making application, qualifying the borrower and property, processing documents, closing, and servicing the loan.

Fixed Rate Loans (82) Loans with constant fixed rates that will not change over the life of the loan.

Flipping Usually a predatory practice involving appraisal of run-down houses, much higher than FMV, and resold at inflated prices, usually to low-income buyers who end up in foreclosure.

Floor Loan (313) A minimum amount that a permanent lender will provide for construction until the developer can secure all the planned tenants for the project.

Forbearance (279) An arrangement that delays foreclosure action.

Foreclosure (271) Process whereby property pledged as security for a real estate loan is sold to satisfy the debt if the borrower defaults.

Fractional Reserve Banking (4) Money "created" by the banking system through monetary policy.

Front Money The money required to get a real estate project started.

Front-End Ratio (Top Ratio) (218) A ratio representing the borrower's mortgage payment divided by gross income.

Functional Obsolescence (189) Poor structural design or unusual floor plans that could affect marketability and value of a property.

G

Gap Commitment (313) A lender's commitment to provide the difference between the floor amount that a developer will receive for a project and the full amount to be received when all rentals are achieved.

GI Loans Common term for loans guaranteed by the Department of Veterans Affairs for qualified veterans. Also known as DVA loans.

Gift Deed Deed for which no consideration is given except love and affection.

Gift Letter (227) Verification that a gift to a borrower for a down payment is not really a loan.

Government Mortgage Insurance (293) Government programs that eliminate risk of loss to lenders from default on loans, thereby making the loans more attractive.

Government National Mortgage Association (GNMA) (164) A federal corporation popularly known as Ginnie Mae. It is mainly involved in the administration of the mortgage-backed securities program and other federal programs.

Government-Backed Loans (106) Loans obtained with the help of government agencies such as FHA, Department of Veterans Affairs, Cal-Vet, or other programs.

Government-Sponsored Enterprise (GSE) (164) Collective title for the secondary market consisting of the FNMA, FHLMC, GNMA.

Graduated-Payment Mortgage (GPM) Fixed interest rate loan on which the scheduled monthly payments start low, but rise later, then level off. Produces negative amortization.

Gross Income (218) Total stable income before deductions.

Gross Rent Multiplier (GRM) (194) A rule of thumb method of appraising income property that provides a "ballpark" figure only. It is an appropriate factor, usu-

ally determined by an appraiser, which, when multiplied by monthly or annual rents, indicates property value.

Gross Scheduled Income Total income from property before deducting any expenses.

Growth Equity Mortgage (GEM) Loan with fixed interest rate and scheduled annual increases in monthly payments, resulting in shorter maturity.

H

Hard Costs (305) Costs for which the builder must pay out money.

Hard Money Loan Loan usually from a private lender. Actual money loaned and secured by a deed of trust as opposed to a loan carried back by a seller, in which no money passes.

Hazard Insurance Covers dwelling and contents for fire, wind, and water damage, theft, and other specified losses.

Holdback (309) Final percentage of construction loan amount released after the filing period for mechanic's liens has expired.

HUD An abbreviation for the U.S. Department of Housing and Urban Development.

Hypothecate To give a thing as security without the necessity of giving up possession; for example, when real estate is used as security for a loan.

I

Impound Account (278) Funds retained in a special account by

a lender to cover property taxes and hazard insurance. Also called a trust fund account or loan trust fund.

Improvement Bond Act of 1915 (320) California law that provides for issuance of bonds for subdivision street improvements, to be paid from proportional assessments against affected property owners.

Imputed Interest (406) A minimum interest rate that is applied to all seller-financed transactions to prevent sellers from treating interest income as capital gains in order to pay less in federal tax.

Income Approach (193) One of three methods in the appraisal process, which analyzes income and expenses, then uses a capitalization rate to arrive at value.

Income Ratio (214) The monthly payment on a loan (including principal and interest, taxes, and insurance) divided by the borrower's monthly gross income.

Index (82) Base for interest rate changes on adjustable rate loans; must be beyond lender's control.

Indirect Lender (60) Individual who invests in loans through a mortgage broker in order to benefit from the broker's expertise.

Inflation Sharp increase in prices for goods and services resulting from too much money in circulation and/or rising costs of materials and labor.

Installment Note (19) A loan providing for payment of the principal in two or more installments.

Installment Sales Contract (22, 394) A sale in which legal title to the property remains with the seller until terms agreed upon have been satisfied.

Institutional Lender (40) A savings bank, commercial bank, or insurance company that deals in real estate loans.

Interest Change Clause Provision in an adjustable rate mortgage that the interest rate can change at specified intervals according to changes in a specified index.

Interest Rate The charge made for a loan of money expressed as a percentage of the principal.

Interest-Only Note A straight non-amortizing loan, in which only interest is paid. Interest can be paid periodically or at maturity, when principal is paid in a lump sum. Also called a "straight note."

Interim Loan (36) Any short-term financing, such as a *Swing Loan*, or a loan used to finance construction, due at the completion of the construction, which is usually paid off with the proceeds of a *Take-Out Loan*.

Intermediate-Term Loans Temporary short-term loans—ordinarily 3 to 10 years—that include home improvement loans, consumer loans, or loans for the purpose of permitting a developer to delay longer-term financing until more favorable loan terms become available.

Intermediation (7) When a financial institution acts as go-between for saver-depositors and borrowers.

J

Joint Note A note signed by two or more persons who have equal liability for payment. Usually expressed as "joint and several," which includes individual liability.

Judicial Sale (275) A sale of property by court proceedings to satisfy a lien.

Jumbo Loan (109, 168) Loan exceeding the maximum amount purchased by FNMA and FHLMC. Also called nonconforming loan.

Junior Mortgage (159) A subordinate or inferior lien.

L

Land Contract of Sale (146) See *Conditional Sale Contract*.

Late Charge An additional charge a borrower is required to pay as a penalty for failure to pay a regular installment when due, after the grace period expires.

Lease A contract between an owner and tenant, setting forth conditions upon which tenant may occupy and use the property.

Lender Appraisal Processing Program (LAPP) (143) A DVA program that allows applications to be processed through the Internet.

Letter of Credit Letter from a bank asking that the holder be allowed to withdraw money from the recipient bank or agency that will be charged back to the first bank.

Leverage (422) The relationship between an owner's equity and total debt on a property. The higher the leverage, the higher the debt in relation to the value of the property.

Lien A form of encumbrance that makes the property security for the payment of a debt. Examples include deeds of trust, mortgages, judgments, and mechanic's liens.

Life Insurance Company (39) A business that collects a person's savings by selling contracts (policies) paid for through periodic premiums and providing cash payment upon death.

Lifetime Cap Ceiling for rate increases over the life of an ARM, expressed either as a particular percentage rate or as so many points over or under the initial rate.

Liquidity of Investment The ease with which investments can be readily converted into cash.

Loan Application (240) The written form submitted by the borrower, usually the standard form of FNMA/FHLMC.

Loan Assumption (259) The lender's approval of a new borrower who takes over an existing loan.

Loan Closing When all conditions of the loan have been met, the lender authorizes the recording of documents.

Loan Commitment Agreement by a lender to make a loan subject to certain conditions being met, covering a specific period of time.

Loan Committee (248) A committee or one individual in a

lending institution that reviews loan packages and either approves or disapproves.

Loan Correspondent See *Correspondent*.

Loan Origination Steps involved in the loan application process prior to close of escrow.

Loan Origination Fee (257) A charge, usually measured by points, made by a lender for originating the loan. Included in nonrecurring closing costs.

Loan Package (248) Documentation consisting of all the forms, documents, and reports the lender needs in order to make a decision on the loan.

Loan Underwriting The process of approving or disapproving loan applications.

Loan-to-Value Ratio (35) The amount of loan, expressed as a percentage of a property's value or sales price, whichever is lower.

Lock-in Clause (40) A provision that prohibits paying off a loan before a specified date.

Lock-in Loan Lender's written guarantee that the rate quoted will be good for a specific period of time.

Long-Term Debt (216) How long a term outstanding debt is to last, the precise term varying by lenders and agencies.

Lot Release Provision (311) The release of an individual lot from the blanket trust deed covering a subdivision. Provides for a deed of partial reconveyance.

Low Down Payment Conventional Loans (114) Loans offered through programs of FNMA and FHLMC that relax the usual down payment requirements for purchasers with lower incomes and excellent credit.

Lump Sum Payment of the entire principal amount due at maturity on a straight note.

M

Margin (82) The amount added to the index rate to determine a borrower's adjusted interest rate on an adjustable loan.

Market Data Approach (191) An appraisal method in which the value of a property is estimated by means of comparing it with similar properties recently sold.

Market Price Amount paid for property, regardless of motives, knowledge, and so on.

Market Value See *Fair Market Value*.

Maturity Date The date upon which a real estate note or other negotiable instrument becomes due and payable.

Mechanic's Lien (314) A claim against the property by contractors, laborers, or material suppliers who have not been paid for their contributions to a building project. A summary right.

Mello-Ross Community Facilities Act (321) California law that authorizes setting up a taxing district that can issue bonds to pay for a housing development's improvements, such as roads, sewers, and community center.

MIS Mortgage Information System.

Monetary Policy (9) Policies of the Federal Reserve System that increase or decrease the supply of money in an effort to achieve designated economic goals.

Monthly Payments (211) These always include principal and interest, and may also, depending upon lender or loan, include taxes and insurance.

Moratorium (279) A temporary waiver or suspension of payments on a loan.

Mortgage A two-party instrument in which the borrower-mortgagor retains legal title during loan term while the real estate acts as collateral for the loan.

Mortgage Banker (58) The packaging of real estate loans to be sold to a permanent investor often with servicing retained for a fee. Mortgage bankers act as correspondents for investors.

Mortgage Brokers (55) Differ from mortgage bankers in that they invest no capital; their prime function is to bring together borrowers and lenders, and for this they are paid a fee.

Mortgage Company (57) A firm that may represent other investors in arranging and servicing real estate loans. May also invest its own funds.

Mortgage Correspondent (58) See *Correspondent*.

Mortgage Insurance Premium (MIP) (130) FHA insures lenders against loss from foreclosure on FHA loans. The premium can be paid up front or financed as part of the loan.

Mortgage Loan Disclosure Statement (60) A legally

required written statement to the borrower concerning estimated costs of a loan and the net amount to be received.

Mortgage Revenue Bonds (169) Taxexempt bonds issued by units of government to finance mortgages at rates below market rate.

Mortgage-Backed Securities (164) Investment securities similar to bonds, representing an interest in a pool of mortgages.

Mutual Mortgage Insurance (MMI) (131) A mortgage insurance premium paid monthly by purchasers under an FHA loan; it may be dropped when the remaining loan balance reaches 78 percent or less.

Mutual Savings Bank (42) A savings bank originated in the New England states in which the depositors place their savings with the right to borrow money for home loans. There are no mutual savings banks in California.

___

N

___

Negative Amortization (370) Loan payment schedule in which the outstanding principal balance goes up rather than down, because the payments do not cover the full amount of interest due. The shortfall is added to the principal.

Negative Cash Flow (420) The situation where income from investment property is less than outgo, so that money must be added to make the venture solvent.

Negotiable Instrument A promissory note or other instrument

that meets certain legal requirements, allowing it to circulate freely in commerce.

Neighborhood Data (188) Factors in the neighborhood that influence a property's value, such as attractiveness, adverse influences, and trends.

Net Operating Income (NOI) (194, 436) Gross annual income less vacancies, uncollectible rents, and other operating expenses.

Net Spendable Income Net operating income less debt service and income taxes on the property's taxable income.

Nominal Interest Rate The interest rate that appears on the real estate promissory note. Also called the note rate.

Nonconforming Loan (168) See *Jumbo Loan.*

Noninstitutional Lender Lenders on real estate loans other than commercial banks, insurance companies, and savings banks.

Nonrecurring Closing Costs (132, 256) Costs that are one-time charges paid at the close of escrow.

Nonsupervised Lender (249) Mortgage company that must be approved in advance by DVA to make automatic approvals of borrowers.

Note A signed instrument acknowledging a debt and a promise to repay per the terms outlined.

Notice of Abandonment (314) A notice filed in case a construction project is abandoned before completion.

Notice of Cessation of Labor (314) A notice filed in case construction is not completed due to various reasons.

Notice of Completion (314) A notice filed by the owner of a new construction project within 10 days after the job is completed, starting a period during which liens may be filed by contractors and other parties.

Notice of Default (272) Recorded notice that a default has occurred under a deed of trust and that the beneficiary intends to proceed with a trustee's sale.

Notice of Sale (272) Notice that property in default will be sold to pay off the loan. It must be advertised in a newspaper and posted at the property and in a public place.

NOW Accounts Standing for Negotiable Order of Withdrawal, a checking account permitted for savings banks.

___

O

___

Obligatory Advances Disbursements of money that the lender is required to make under the terms of a construction loan.

Office of Thrift Supervision (OTS) (44) A branch of the U.S. Treasury that regulates all federally insured savings banks.

Office Parks (434) Planned developments for office buildings and related services.

On-Line Loans (69) Refers to ability to apply for real estate loans through the Internet.

Open-End Deed of Trust (416) A deed of trust containing a clause that permits the borrower to obtain additional advances of money secured by the same deed of trust, if the lender permits, but not necessarily under the same terms.

Open-Market Operations (9) Federal Reserve actions to influence the money supply by selling or buying government securities.

Operating Costs The owner's expenses in operating investment property, such as utilities, repairs, and replacement of furnishings.

"Or More" Clause A clause in a note that permits extra payments on principal of the loan without penalty.

Origination Fee A charge for arranging and processing a real estate loan. See *Loan Origination Fee*.

P

Package Loan Loan secured by both real and personal property, often appliances and other fixtures.

Paper Term used by real estate agents, investors, and others to designate promissory notes, usually secured by deeds of trust.

Par (158) The face amount of a loan with no premium or discount.

Partial Amortization (329) A repayment schedule that does not pay back enough principal to completely pay off a loan by the due date, leaving a balloon payment.

Partial Entitlement (139) The amount of additional entitlement allowed to a veteran who had previously used an entitlement when maximum amounts were lower.

Partial Reconveyance Deed (311) A deed used to reconvey a portion of the land encumbered by a deed of trust.

Partial Release Clause (311) A clause in a deed of trust that provides for release of part of the property from the deed of trust upon payment of a specific portion of the debt.

Participation (163, 396) When a lending institution sells a part interest in a block of loans to another institution or agency. Also, when a lender receives part of the income from a property to increase its return on the loan. Also see *Equity Participation*.

Pass-Through Securities (164) Securities backed by a pool of FHA and DVA mortgages, issued by the Government National Mortgage Association.

Payout Schedule (307) The predetermined system of releasing money to the builder as construction progresses.

Pension Funds (43) Public and private retirement savings funds held in trust, which can be invested in real estate loans, stocks, or government securities.

Percentage Lease (435) A commercial lease in which the owner gets a percentage of the tenant's gross receipts.

Performance Bond A bond furnished to guarantee that a builder will perform in accordance with the contract terms and that the property at completion will be free of mechanic's liens.

Permanent Financing See *Take-Out Loan*.

Physical Depreciation (190) Deterioration of property caused by wear and structural problems.

PITI (214) An abbreviation for principal, interest, taxes, and insurance, commonly used when referring to the monthly loan obligation.

Planned Unit Development (PUD) (197) A land-use design that combines private fee ownership of a parcel and joint undivided ownership of common facilities such as grounds, parking, and recreational facilities.

Plans and Specifications Architectural and engineering drawings and specifications for construction of a building, including description of materials and manner in which they are to be applied.

Points (156) Amount paid by the borrower or the seller, which increases the effective yield for a lender. Each point equals 1 percent of the loan.

Portfolio Loan (107) Any loan retained by the lender, as contrasted with selling it in the secondary market.

Positive Cash Flow (428) The situation where income from investment property is greater than outgo, so that a profit is made.

Premium (156) An amount, usually measured in points, in

excess of the loan balance owing, paid for the purchase of a note and deed of trust.

Prepaid Finance Charge (255) Charges paid separately or withheld from the proceeds of the loan, such as loan origination fees or mortgage insurance premiums.

Prepaid Items Expenses paid by buyer-borrower at closing, such as taxes, insurance, and interest. Used by FHA. See *Recurring Closing Costs*.

Prepayment Penalty (260) A charge for the payment of a mortgage or deed of trust note before maturity.

Prepayment Privilege (260) Allows borrowers to make certain extra payments on the principal balance without penalty.

Price (158) The amount for which a lender will sell a loan to an investor, equal to the face value of the loan minus the discount or plus a premium.

Primary Mortgage Market (161) The market in which loans are made directly to the borrowers.

Prime Rate (11) Interest rate individual banks charge their most creditworthy preferred corporate customers.

Principal The face amount on a real estate loan, the amount upon which interest is calculated.

Private Lenders Individuals who invest their own funds into real estate loans, directly or through mortgage brokers.

Private Mortgage Insurance (PMI) (119) Insurance written by a private company, protect-ing the mortgage lender against specified loss in case of foreclosure.

Processing Preparation of loan application and supporting documents for consideration by a lender or insurer; all procedures up to close of escrow.

Progress Payments (308) Periodic payments to the builders as construction proceeds.

Promissory Note See *Note*.

Purchase Money Deed of Trust A trust deed securing a note given as part or all of the purchase price. Examples: carryback by a seller or a new loan from a lender.

Q

Qualified Mortgage Bond Program Use of low interest rate revenue bonds for targeted first-time home buyers under the Cal-Vet program.

Qualifying Ratio (214) A lender's policy on how much income a borrower should have in order to make the payments of principal, interest, taxes, and insurance on the desired loan; for example, payments not exceeding 28 percent of gross income.

Quitclaim Deed (278) A simple conveyance of rights in property without warranty.

R

Rate lock See *Lock-in Loan*.

Real Estate Investment Trust (REIT) (65) A corporation, trust, or association in which investors pool funds for investments in real estate but avoid double taxation as a corporation.

Real Estate Settlement Procedures Act (RESPA) (247) A federal law that requires lenders to provide borrowers with certain information on settlement (closing) costs.

Real Property Land and buildings as opposed to personal property.

Real Property (Mortgage) Loan Law (60) A California statute that governs real estate loan brokers, limiting commissions, requiring disclosure to the borrower, and regulating balloon payments and insurance requirements.

Recasting (280) A change in loan terms to assist the borrower, such as by extending the term or reducing the interest rate.

Reconveyance See *Deed of Reconveyance*.

Recurring Closing Costs (132, 257) Repeating expenses paid by the borrower at close of escrow, such as tax reserves, hazard insurance, and prepaid interest. See *Prepaid Items*.

Redlining (179, 287) The illegal practice of refusing to lend mortgage money in certain areas without regard to the creditworthiness of the individual borrower.

Refinance To renew or replace the existing loan with additional financing, or to secure a loan on a free and clear property already owned by the borrower.

Regulation Z See *Truth-in-Lending Law/Regulation Z*.

Reinstate To cure a default under a note secured by a deed of trust.

Reintermediation (8) Return of savings to thrift institutions from previously higher-paying investment outlets.

Release of Liability An agreement by the lender to terminate the personal obligation of the borrower.

Release of Mechanic's Lien (317) The lifting of a mechanic's lien, for example by written release, issuance of a bond, or satisfaction of a judgment.

Rent Control (426) Local laws that limit the amount of increase in residential rents.

Rental Achievement Clause (311) The provision in a loan agreement that the developer will secure tenants in advance for a new commercial or industrial project.

Replacement Cost Amount required to replace improvements of comparable quality, at today's prices. An appraiser's estimate of amount needed to rebuild an existing property at today's prices using cost approach.

Request for Notice of Default and Notice of Sale (272) A recorded notice made by anyone requesting that he or she be notified in the event that foreclosure proceedings are instituted or that time and place for the sale has been set.

Reserve Requirement (9) The amount of reserve funds that banks and thrift institutions must set aside in order to protect depositors; it may be raised or lowered by the Federal Reserve.

Residual Income (218) DVA's calculation that from gross income subtracts taxes, housing payment, and fixed expenses such as child support and long-term debts. Also used by Cal-Vet.

Reverse Annuity Mortgage (93) Stream of monthly payments provided to homeowners through an annuity purchased by a loan against the owners' accumulated equity in their home.

Right of Reinstatement (272) The trustor's right to reinstate a loan by paying all delinquent payments, late charges, and foreclosure fees. Starts with recording of notice of default and lasts up to five business days before scheduled sale.

Risk Rating A process used by lenders to determine the soundness of offering a loan.

Rollover Loan that may extend beyond certain intermediate maturities.

S

Sale-Leaseback (377) Land and/or buildings may be sold at 100 percent of value and then leased back by the seller. This is an alternative form of financing.

Sales Comparison Approach (191) See *Market Data Approach to Value.*

Savings and Loan Associations Deposit-type savings institutions that lend in the residential field. The name/title has been virtually replaced by "Savings Banks."

Savings Association Insurance Fund (SAIF) (44) Administered by the FDIC to insure deposits at savings banks and federal savings banks.

Savings Banks (33) Savings and loan associations using newly permitted designations.

Secondary Financing (161) A loan secured by a junior trust deed.

Secondary Mortgage Market (161) The purchasing and selling of existing notes secured by deeds of trust.

Securitization Debt issuance backed by mortgage portfolios or other types of assets.

Seller Carryback (376) The seller's agreement to take payments on a note secured by a trust deed to help the buyer finance all or a portion of the purchase price.

Servicing Supervising and administering a loan after it has been made. This involves such things as: collecting payments, keeping records, property inspections, and foreclosing on defaulted loans; any process after close of escrow.

Short Sale (290) Lender agreement to compromise a debt when the value of the security property is less than the debt owed.

Short-Term Construction Loan (304) An interim loan that covers the construction of a building and can be paid off by a take-out loan.

Sight Deposit See *Demand Deposit.*

Soft Costs (305) Costs to a builder for such noncash items as profit, overhead, and supervision.

Split Junior Loan (or Lien) (383) Seller financing divided into second and third trust deeds, which may be easier to resell than one larger second lien.

Stability of Income (225) The stability of the borrower's income, based on such things as length of time on the job and type of job.

Standby Commitment A contract—usually between FNMA/FHLMC and a lender—to buy a pool of loans in the future from a lender at a specified yield.

Stock Equity (403) Pledge of stock as collateral for the purchase of real estate, usually non-residential.

Straight Note (19, 340) See *Interest-Only Note.*

Street Improvement Act of 1911 (320) California law that allows assessments for street improvements to be paid off during the term of the bonds that are issued for them.

"Subject To" (261) The taking of real property "subject to" an existing loan is done without being personally liable to the existing lender. This is in contrast to assuming a loan, when the buyer assumes responsibility and liability for the loan.

Subordination Clause (310) An agreement under which a senior trust deed is made subordinate to an otherwise junior lien. Often used when a land loan subordinates to a new construction loan.

Subrogation (283) Assignment of rights.

Substantial Completion (314) The point from which a period for filing liens on a completed construction project is counted if a proper Notice of Completion is filed or not filed.

Supervised Lender (249) Institution such as a commercial bank or savings bank that is supervised by an agency of the state or federal government and can approve DVA borrowers automatically, if qualified.

Swing Loan (36) Used to assist in purchase of replacement house before sale of original house is completed. See *Bridge Loan.*

Syndication (64) Investors pooling their resources to purchase real estate, usually through a limited partnership.

——
T
——

Take-out Commitment (305) The terms involved when lenders agree to lend on a specified property to a specified borrower for a certain length of time at a certain interest rate.

Take-out Loan (35, 302) A permanent loan that pays off the existing construction loan.

Tax Service A fee paid to a tax service agency that each year reviews the records of taxing bodies and reports any delinquencies to the lender and borrower. The fee is usually paid by the borrower.

Tax Shelter (432) A strategy for investment that should result in reduced tax liability.

Tax-Deferred Exchange A method of deferring capital gains taxes by exchanging one or more properties for other like property.

Terms Refers to all conditions involved in a loan. The word *term* often also refers to the number of years over which the loan is repaid.

Thrift Institutions (38) Savings banks and other institutions that invest principally in real estate trust deeds.

Tight Money (17) A situation in which the demand for money exceeds the supply, causing interest rates to increase and borrower qualifications to be tightened.

Time Deposit (35) Savings account with a fixed maturity, as opposed to demand deposit.

Title Insurance Insurance written by a legal reserve title insurance company to protect property owners and lenders against loss due to certain title defects.

Total Monthly Expense (216) In qualifying for a loan, this is the addition of mortgage payments plus non-mortgage long-term debts. Used by FHA, DVA, and Cal-Vet.

Townhouse A residential unit connected to other similar units. Often a two-story structure. A style of architecture.

Trade Associations (37) Groups that promote the interests of the firms in their memberships and provide them with research and information.

Transaction Accounts Accounts used to make payments or

transfers to others, such as checking accounts.

Triple Net Lease (399) A lease arrangement in which the lessee pays for all repairs, maintenance, taxes, and operating expenses.

Trust Deed Deed from a borrower to a trustee who holds title for security purposes until loan terms are satisfied. Also called a *Deed of Trust*.

Trustee's Deed A deed given to the successful bidder at a trustee's sale (foreclosure).

Trustee's Sale (271) Sale of property in foreclosure by the trustee, rather than through a judicial sale.

Trustor (21) A borrower under a trust deed, who deeds property to trustee as security for the repayment of the debt.

Truth-in-Lending Law (Regulation Z) (251) A federal law designed to show a borrower the total cost of a loan. The annual percentage rate (APR) is the term used to disclose the effective rate of interest.

Two-Step Mortgage (95) Loan with low initial fixed interest rate, increasing after conversion period.

U

Underwriting Evaluation by lenders of loan applicant's ability to repay a real estate loan.

Unrestricted Funds (144) A Cal-Vet program for qualified veterans with wartime service.

Unsecured A loan that is not secured by a deed of trust, mortgage, or other property.

U.S. Treasury Cabinet-level agency that manages the federal government's spending and taxing policy.

Usury (286) The charging of interest in excess interest of that permitted by law.

Usury Law (57, 286) Unlawful rate of interest. In California, the greater of 10 percent or 5 percent over the Federal Reserve Board's discount rate at any given time; however, regulated lenders, such as banks, savings banks, and life insurance companies, are exempt from the usury law. Also exempt are loans arranged by licensed real estate brokers and sellers who carry back.

V

VA (Veterans' Administration) See *Department of Veterans Affairs (DVA)*.

Variable Interest Rate An interest rate that can go up or down according to an independent index, as contrasted with a fixed interest rate that stays the same over the life of the loan.

Verification of Deposit (VOD) Form sent to a loan applicant bank to verify funds for down payment and closing costs.

Verification of Employment (VOE) (248) Checking on the accuracy of the applicant's information, usually by mailing forms directly to the employer, or by original pay stubs and W-2s.

Vesting The names of owners of real estate and the method or manner in which title is held.

Voucher System (308) A plan to pay for construction costs upon presentation of receipted bills and lien waivers by licensed building contractors, subcontractors, and material suppliers.

VRM Variable Rate Mortgage. See *Adjustable Rate Mortgage (ARM)*.

Vrooman Street Act (320) California law that authorizes city councils to issue bonds secured by tax levies for street construction.

W

Waiver (279) Suspension of principal payments on a loan in order to help debtors.

Warehousing Temporary storage of loans pending sale to investors.

Warranties (285) Protection of the buyer in case of defects in major components of a house.

Wrap-Around Trust Deed (391) See *All-Inclusive Trust Deed (AITD)*.

Y

Yield (157, 339) The actual interest earned by the lender on the money loaned. Also called rate of return, it is usually expressed as a percentage.

INDEX